BENJAMIN FRANKLIN
His Wit, Wisdom, and Women

Some books we read, tho' few there are that hit
The happy point where wisdom joins with wit.

Poor Richard, 1746

BENJAMIN FRANKLIN

His Wit, Wisdom, and Women

by

Seymour Stanton Block

HASTINGS HOUSE · PUBLISHERS

New York

To G., whom I can never thank enough.

LIBRARY OF CONGRESS CATALOGING IN PUBLICATION DATA

Block, Seymour Stanton, 1918–
  Benjamin Franklin: his wit, wisdom, and women.

  Bibliography: p.
  1. Franklin, Benjamin, 1706–1790—Humor, satire, etc.
PS751.B56   973.3'2'0924 [B]   75-6561
ISBN 0-8038-0767-8

Published simultaneously in Canada by
Saunders of Toronto, Ltd., Don Mills, Ontario

Designed by Al Lichtenberg
Printed in the United States of America

CONTENTS

Introduction vii

PROLOGUE: BENJAMIN FRANKLIN IN FRANCE 1

PART ONE: FRANKLIN IN PRINT 25

1 A Youth with Promise 26
2 Adventures in Old Philadelphia 31
3 A Printer Versus His Competitors 40
4 *Poor Richard's Almanack* 45
5 Richard Saunders and His Wife Bridget 60
6 The Leeds Affair 72
7 Is This the Way to Run a Newspaper? 81
8 The Dogood Papers and The Busy Body 101

PART TWO: FRANKLIN IN PUBLIC LIFE 119

9 Franklin Becomes a Public Man 120
10 The Sage and the Savages 134
11 The Colonial Agent in London 147
12 A Patriot with Humor 164

13 With My Vizard On   177
14 To Tell a Whopper   196

PART THREE: THE WOMEN AND THE MAN   203

15 An American in Passy   204
16 The Romantic Impulse   219
17 A Man of Letters   245

PART FOUR: PEREGRINATIONS
            OF AN AGILE MIND   261

18 Everything Makes Me Recollect Some Story   262
19 On Getting Along with People   269
20 Science Can Be Fun   280
21 The Doctor's Merry Medicine   297

PART FIVE: FOUR SCORE AND MORE   313

22 Franklin and God   314
23 The Unmelancholy Philosopher   329
24 An American at Home   341
25 Without Vanity   365
26 Let the Experiment Be Made   378

    Acknowledgements   388
    Bibliography   392
    Index   395

INTRODUCTION

George Washington was first in war, first in peace, and first in the hearts of his countrymen. Benjamin Franklin was first in almost everything else. He was the first American diplomat, the first scientist, the first postmaster general, the first inventor, the first ambassador, the first economist. He was responsible for the first fire department, the first lending library, the first hospital, the first scientific society. He was the first internationally recognized American and he was his country's first humorist.

Franklin sparkled with wit and humor: it appears throughout his writings, in his newspaper and almanac, in his personal letters, even intruding in his scientific works and formal speeches. It has been said that Jefferson was selected to write the Declaration of Independence instead of Franklin because the founding fathers were afraid that Franklin would put a joke in it. The story is apocryphal but it illustrates Franklin's reputation as a funster. Franklin's entertaining almanac was a best seller of its time. His newspaper, with comic news items improvised out of the whole cloth, was like none other, then or now. Franklin was a master hoaxster, a skill he employed not only for fun but for political propagandizing. These jests sometimes had an uncharacteristic bitter taste. Franklin was a prolific letter writer and his letters were warm and familiar, amply fortified with witticisms, wisdom, and homely humor. With the ladies he could be a gay, charming tease, his mood varying from flippant to serious. Among Franklin's famous electrical experiments we find a number designed not to draw lightning but to draw laughter. From youth to old age, humor was Franklin's constant companion.

It is curious then that in the nearly 200 years since Franklin's death no book dealing with Franklin's humor has appeared. There are books dealing with many aspects of the life of this greatly talented American. The reader can find books on Franklin's military career, his ideas on education, his religion, his printing, his life in France, his activities in England, his influence on Italy, his politics, his science, even the mathematical puzzles he devised. But when it comes to Franklin's trademark, his ever-present wit and humor, there has been a void which this work now makes an attempt to fill.

Humor was to be found not only in Franklin's writing but in his conversation, which was characterized by his fund of anecdotes. In the memoirs of Thomas Jefferson, John Adams, John Jay, Benjamin Rush and many of Franklin's French friends are found delightful homespun stories that he told them to illustrate some point. He became the first in a line of native American story tellers in the oral tradition, called cracker barrel philosophers, which has claimed such notables as Mark Twain and Will Rogers. These anecdotes, like the rest of Franklin's humor, have never appeared in a collected form before. Why?

One can only speculate on the reasons. The 19th century public appeared to be interested in Franklin mainly as a success symbol and the 20th century public as a sex symbol. In the Victorian age Franklin's wonderfully entertaining pieces that were a bit risque or vulgar were rigidly suppressed and not even mentioned in his printed works. Many of Franklin's papers and letters were scattered in different places, difficult to find even by diligent scholarship. This deficiency is being remedied by the fine collection of Franklin's papers now being made by a group of editors at Yale University. At this writing the Yale series runs to 18 volumes and will have at least as many more when it is eventually completed. Until recently the charming pieces of correspondence comprising Franklin's romantic duels with ladies in France lay buried in the vaults of the American Philosophical Society until they were unearthed and translated by Claude A. Lopez for the Yale papers, and published in her delightful book, *Mon Cher Papa*. The modern scholarship in Frankliniana has been impressive, with the valuable contributions of Carl Van Doren, Alfred Owen Aldridge, I. Bernard Cohen, Verner W. Crane, Richard E. Amacher, William G. Roelker, J. M. Stifler, Bruce I. Granger, the editors and staff of the Franklin Papers, and others, to whom we are gratefully indebted.

The writer has been at this pursuit for many years, collecting items and eventually searching for what seemed like needles in a haystack. But what needles! The reward made the effort worthwhile. It is hoped that by bringing the sparkling bits and pieces from the newspapers, almanacs, letters, and documents and organizing them, as we have done, Franklin's contribution to the world of humor will be more widely appreciated and enjoyed. Actors sometimes object to a long run in a play when they have a morose role because they have trouble shaking off the atmosphere of the play. In my case, this occupation has been a joyful labor, and it is hoped that this book will bring to others some of the pleasure the author has derived through his literary association with that extraordinary man who has been described as a harmonious human multitude. Franklin was a marvelously complex individual, a Renaissance man whose accomplishments won him world acclaim. But from beginning to end, through war and tragedy, he was a jovial, fun-loving fellow whose greatest personal triumph was winning a smile.

PROLOGUE

Benjamin Franklin in France

Benjamin Franklin in France

"DO YOU KNOW, MY DEAR PAPA, that people have criticized the sweet habit I have taken of sitting on your lap, and your habit of soliciting from me what I always refuse?"

The speaker was a sensitive, artistic, intelligent and witty Frenchwoman, Anne-Louise d'Hardancourt Brillon de Jouy; the man addressed was none other than that robust old fellow, the affable minister plenipotentiary from the United States in Paris, Benjamin Franklin. The setting was the house in Passy of M. Brillon de Jouy, a wealthy nobleman, Treasurer of the Parliament of Paris, where Franklin was an intimate guest. Easily the most popular foreigner in France esteemed by the brilliant and witty women to whom he paid court, Franklin was no less approved by the husbands. "I am certain that you have just been kissing my wife, my dear Doctor," said M. Brillon de Jouy, "allow me to kiss you back."

The witness who lifts the veil from this remarkable household is none other than John Adams, destined to be the second President of the United States. "We were invited to dine at Monsieur Brillon's," wrote Adams, "a family in which Mr. Franklin was very intimate. Madame Brillon was one of the most beautiful women in France, a great mistress of music . . . M. Brillon was a rough kind of country squire. His lady was all softness, sweetness and politeness."

All was amity with this trio. Twice every week, usually on Wednesday and Saturday, Franklin and his grandson, Temple, would visit the Brillons, play chess, drink tea, and listen to Madam Brillon and her daughters play music. Sometimes Franklin played on the armonica, the instrument he invented. He attempted to make a match for Temple with one of the Brillon daughters, as he had previously attempted with Temple's father and Polly Stevenson, but for religious and economic reasons the Brillons refused the offer. Madam Brillon had lost her father, whom she had loved, and wanted Franklin to be her papa, to comfort and counsel her. He agreed but reached out for more. They exchanged frequent letters which, with their gallantry and coquettery and delectable display of wit, describe their special relationship:

Brillon: I had a father once, the best of men . . . I lost him too soon! . . . And you have told me about the humane custom of certain savages who adopt their prisoners of war and put them in the place of their own dead relatives. You have taken in my heart the place of that father whom I love and respected so much.

Franklin: I accept with infinite pleasure, my dear friend, the proposal you make with such kindness of adopting me as your father . . . Yes, my dear child, I love you as a father, with all my heart . . . It is true that I sometimes suspect that heart of wanting to go further but . . . if at my age it is not fitting to say that I am in love with a young woman, there is nothing to prevent me from confessing that I admire and love an assemblage of all female virtues.

Brillon: Do you know, my dear papa, that people have criticized the sweet habit I have taken of sitting on your lap, and your habit of soliciting from me what I always refuse? I despise slanderers and am at peace with myself, but that is not enough, one must submit to what is called propriety, to sit less often on your knees.

Franklin: A beggar asked an archbishop for charity, demanding a guinea—"A guinea to a beggar! That would be extravagant"—"A shilling then!"—"Oh, its still too much!"—"A penny then or your blessing."—"My blessing, of course, I will give you my blessing."—"I don't want it, for if it were worth a penny you wouldn't give it to me."

That is how the bishop loved his neighbor. Such was his charity. If I examine yours, I find it no greater . . . You were as rich as an archbishop in all Christian and moral virtues, yet you couldn't sacrifice even a small portion of them without telling me it is too much. Such is your charity toward an unfortunate one who used to enjoy plenty and is now reduced to begging.

Brillon: My dear papa, your bishop was a miser and your beggar a rascal. You are a very . . . skillful sophist . . . What would you say of your beggar if, after the bishop had given him his guinea, he had protested at not receiving two? Yet such is your case . . . You adopted me as a daughter . . . I love you as a daughter should love her father . . . You asked for a guinea, I gave it to you; and now you grumble about the second guinea, which is not in my power to grant.

Madam Brillon offered herself as Franklin's spiritual counselor. She announced that of all of the seven capital sins except one his soul was clear. The exception, "I shall not name it," she said, "all great men are tainted with it: it is called their weakness . . . Go on doing great things and loving pretty women . . ." Franklin was charmed, he stated, by the goodness of his spiritual guide, and, further, to be led to heaven on so delicious a road he announced he would travel there through the roughest of ways for the pleasure of her company. How kindly partial she was to her penitent, he concluded, in finding him guilty of only one capital sin and then only calling that by the gentle name of "foible." Then he expressed a doctrine all his own.

Franklin: People commonly speak of the Ten Commandments.—I have been taught that there are twelve. The first was increase and multiply and replenish the earth. The twelfth is, that you love one another. It seems to me that they are a little misplaced and the last should have been the first. However I never made any difficulty about that, but was always willing to obey them both whenever I had an opportunity. Pray tell me . . . whether my keeping religiously these two commandments . . . may not be accepted in compensation for my breaking so often one of the ten which forbids coveting my neighbor's wife, and which I confess I break constantly, God forgive me, as often as I see or think of my lovely confessor . . .

And now I am consulting you upon a case of conscience I will mention the opinion of a certain father of the church which I find myself willing to adopt though I am not sure it is orthodox. It is that the most effectual way to get rid of a certain temptation is, as often as it returns, to comply with and satisfy it. Pray instruct me how far I may venture to practice upon this principle?

Brillon: You are a man and I am a woman, and while we might think along the same lines, we must speak and act differently. Perhaps there is no great harm in a man having desires and yielding to them; a woman may have desires, but she must not yield . . . I want to confess . . . that in the matter of desire, I am as great a sinner as yourself. I have desired to see you, desired to know you, desired your esteem, desired your friendship . . . And now, I desire that you may love me forever . . . I have not the slightest doubt that all our desires will eventually lead us to Paradise!

Franklin: Since you have assured me that we shall meet and know each other in Paradise, I have been constantly thinking about how we shall arrange our affairs in that country . . . Probably more than forty years will elapse after my arrival there before you follow me. I am a little afraid that in the course of such a long period you may forget me. I have therefore thought of proposing that you give me your word of honor not to renew there your contract with Monsieur Brillon. I shall at the same time give you mine that I shall wait for you. But that gentleman is so good, so generous toward us . . . that I cannot think of this proposal without some scruples of conscience. And yet the idea of an eternity in which I shall be favored with no more than permission to kiss your hands, or sometimes your cheeks, and to pass two or three hours in your sweet society on Wednesdays and Saturdays is frightful. So I cannot make this proposal . . . Decide it as you will, I feel that I shall love you for all eternity.

If you reject me, perhaps I shall address myself to Madam d'Hardancourt [Madam Brillon's mother], and she may be willing to live with me; then I shall spend my hours at home agreeably with her, and shall be nearer at hand to see you. I shall have time during those forty years to practice on the armonica, and perhaps I shall play well enough to accompany you on your pianoforte. From time to time we shall have little concerts . . . chosen friends will make up our audience; and the dear good girls [Madam Brillon's daughters] accompanied by certain other young angels . . . will sing the hallelujah with us. We shall eat apples of Paradise roasted with butter and nutmeg. And we shall pity those who are not dead.

Brillon: I give you my word of honor to become your wife in Paradise, on condition, however, that you will not ogle the virgins too much while waiting for me. When I choose one for eternity I want a husband who is faithful . . .

I shall tell Mama tonight about your good intentions toward her. I fear, though, that if she plans to oppose my claims on you it will arouse a kind of jealousy between us. I am willing to yield anything to my mother except you . . .

Madam Brillon may have wanted a faithful husband but her own was something else. Monsieur Brillon was a man of simple tastes and urges. He was kind to his sensitive, emotional wife but he was not much interested in her intellect or artistry. He spent considerable time away from home, seeking his interests elsewhere. No doubt this encouraged Franklin's attentions toward his wife. But Brillon did have an interest at home and, again, we look to John Adams to tell us about it. When Adams was at the Brillon's he reported, ''I saw a woman in company, as a companion of Madam Brillon who dined with her at table and was considered one of the family. She was very plain and clumsy. When I afterward learned both from Dr. Franklin and his grandson, and from many other persons, that this woman was the *amie* of Mr. Brillon and that Madam Brillon consoled herself by the *amitie* of Mr. Le Vaillant, I was astonished that these people could live together in such apparent friendship and indeed without cutting each others throats. But I do not know the world. I soon saw and heard so much of these things in other families and among almost all the great people of the kingdom that I found it was a thing of course. It was universally understood and nobody lost any reputation by it.''

Adams was right, he did not know the world. He was wrong, however, about his hostess, Madam Brillon. His conclusion that she was the mistress of Le Vaillant [he meant Le Veillard, Franklin's friend and mayor of Passy] had no basis in fact. The lady was a redoubtable fortress of virtue whose morality did not correspond to the Paris that so shocked Adams. On the matter of the *amie* of Brillon, he was on firm ground. She was Mademoiselle Jupin, the governess of the Brillon children. Everyone knew of Brillon's affair with her, as Adams had discovered, except the scrupulous Madam Brillon. She was busy playing hide and seek with the ambassador from America.

> *Brillon:* You ask me for the list of your sins, my dear papa, it would be so long that I dare not undertake such a great work. And yet, you commit only one, but it has so many branches . . . And after all that, you would like me to forgive you—me, the director of your soul! . . . The dangerous system you are forever trying to demonstrate, my dear papa—that the friendship a man has for a woman can be divided ad infinitum—this is something I shall never put up with . . . from now on I shall try to be somewhat sterner toward your faults.

Franklin: What a difference, my dear friend, between you and me! You find innumerable faults in me, whereas I see only one fault in you, and perhaps that is the fault of my spectacles. The fault I mean is a kind of avarice which leads you to seek a monopoly on all my affections, and not to allow me any for the agreeable ladies of your country. Do you imagine that it is impossible for my affection to be divided without being diminished? You deceive yourself. You renounce and totally exclude all that might be of the flesh in our love, allowing me now and then only some kisses such as you might permit your little cousins. What is then remaining that I may not share with others, without diminishing that which belongs to you? . . . The sweet sounds brought forth from the pianoforte by your clever hands can be enjoyed by twenty people simultaneously without diminishing at all the pleasure you so obligingly mean for me, and I could, with as little reason, demand that no other ears but mine be allowed to be charmed by those sweet sounds.

You see by this time how unjust you are in your demands, and in the open war you declare against me if I do not comply . . . My poor little boy [Cupid], whom you should have cherished, instead of being fat and jolly, like those in your elegant paintings, is thin and almost starved to death for want of the substantial nourishment which you, his mother, inhumanly deny him! And yet you would now clip his little wings to prevent his seeking it elsewhere.

When the American forces won a brilliant victory at the battle of Saratoga, the talented Madam Brillon made festive the occasion by composing a musical score which she called, ''March of the Insurgents.'' How should the American representative respond to such loyalty? As a diplomat he knew what he must do. He offered Madam a peace treaty to settle their private war.

Franklin: I imagine that neither of us gain anything by this war. Therefore, feeling myself to be the weaker, I will do what indeed ought always to be done by the wiser—make proposals for peace. That a peace may be lasting, the articles of the treaty should be regulated upon the principles of the most perfect equity and reciprocity. In this view I have drawn up and offer the following.

1. There must be peace, friendship, and eternal love between Madam B. and Mr. F.
2. In order to maintain this inviolable peace, Madam B. on her part stipulates and agrees that Mr. F. shall come to her whenever she sends for him.

3. That he shall stay with her as long as it shall please her.
4. That when he is with her, he shall be obliged to drink tea, play chess, listen to music, or do any other thing that she may require of him.
5. And that he shall love no other woman than her.
6. And the said Mr. F. on his part stipulates and agrees that he shall go to Madam B's whenever he pleases.
7. That he shall stay there as long as he pleases.
8. That when he is with her he shall do anything he pleases.
9. And that he shall love no other woman as long as he finds her agreeable.

Let me know what you think of these preliminaries. To me they seem to express the true meaning and intention of each party more plainly than most treaties. I shall insist pretty strongly on the eighth article though without much hope of your consent to it, and also on the ninth, though I despair of ever finding any other woman that I could love with equal tenderness.

This treaty like so many other treaties was just a piece of paper. The participants to it and their motivations had not changed, and the battle continued on as before.

Brillon: Do you mean I shall see you only Saturday? Are you giving up so easily a Wednesday with me? Then, after that, you will say, as usual, "I love you furiously. I love you too much . . ." Now which of us two loves more and better?

Franklin: It is true I have often said I love you too much, and I have told the truth. Judge, by a comparison I am going to make, which of us two loves the most. If I say to a friend: "I need your horses to take a journey, lend them to me," and he replies: "I should be very glad to oblige you but I fear that they will be ruined by this voyage and cannot bring myself to lend them to anyone." Must I not conclude that the man loves his horses more than he loves me? And if, in the same case, I should willingly risk my horses by lending them to him, is it not clear that I love him more than my horses, and also more than he loves me? You know that I am ready to sacrifice my beautiful, big horses.

Brillon: You played a mean trick on me. You order your carriage for 8 o'clock and at 7:30 you run away, to punish me for having endured the boredom of walking around with ladies, while I could have had fun staying with you.

Franklin: Half an hour spent with an old man, who is not allowed to put it to its best use, is a mighty small matter, and you should not get angry over small things. Saturday evening I shall stay with you until you long for my departure, and in spite of the usual courtesy of your spoken words, I shall know that the time to leave has arrived when you will refuse me a little kiss.

Eventually Madam Brillon discovered the affair between her husband and the governess. In an age when faithfulness on the part of a man in Brillon's position would have been the rare exception rather than the rule, she nevertheless was deeply wounded. She wailed with mortification and her too-sensitive soul was tortured with anguish. She became ill with no other symptoms than nerves. When this condition remained over a long period of time, her physician prescribed an extended stay in the Mediterranean resort of Nice where she might escape from herself. She made her departure from Passy with her husband, children, and servants, leaving Franklin with a piece of her soul, as she said, to flit around him. Her trip was tiring, she wrote Franklin, she would like to be in Nice already, but her heart did not want to go any further.

Franklin: I keep thinking of the weariness you must be suffering on such a long trip; of the poor inns, the poor beds, the poor food, etc., and I fear for the delicate stuff you are made of. Such thoughts sadden me. I am annoyed not to be Angel Gabriel with his big wings. For if I were, I could spare you all the trouble by carrying you in my arms . . . and depositing you gently within half an hour in your apartment in Nice.

Brillon: I could not possibly accept your offer of carrying me in your arms, even though I am no longer very young or a virgin. That angel was a clever fellow, and your nature joined with his would become too dangerous. I would fear some miracle, and miracles between women and angels might not always bring a redeemer.

Franklin: I often pass your house. It appears desolate to me. Formerly I broke a commandment by coveting it, together with my neighbor's wife. Now, I don't covet it anymore, so that I am less of a sinner. But as far as the wife is concerned, I still think those commandments very bothersome and I am very sorry they were ever devised. If, in your travels, you ever come across the Holy Father, ask him to repeal them, as given only to the Jews and too much trouble for good Christians.

> Long ago, when I was young, I sometimes loved powerfully at a distance of a thousand leagues. But a few years ago . . . I did not believe myself capable of loving further than a league away. Now, I discover I was wrong, for you go every day further and further away from me and I don't see that my feeling diminishes.

In the provinces she was traveling through, Franklin said he had heard that the ladies were somewhat more libertine than in Paris. He hoped she might thereby acquire some of their attitude and return from her trip with "more vigor and less rigor." She would then perhaps be "less estimable, but much more amiable." She was determined, she assured him, to be even more estimable than before, but she was willing to make a concession. During her absence she would permit Franklin to kiss all the pretty women of their acquaintance in Passy. He responded that such bills of exchange were already pledged to cash but he would repay her the full amount with interest on her return. Considering his youth, Temple might be a more fitting collector, he supposed, but then observed that "love of cash does not diminish with age." He was fine, he told her, his health was good, and America had won a great victory (the surrender of Cornwallis at Yorktown). "Yet," he added, "I am not happy because Madam B. is no longer in Passy. Tonight I shall go to Madam Veillard's and find there some other friends of yours who suffer from the same disease . . . Only your return can cure us." When she felt better, Madam Brillon went for a little outing in a boat and became seasick. Franklin thought that if she would gradually take longer boat trips, she would get over her problem, and thus permit him to steal her away from Monsieur Brillon, and sail off to America.

Her health and her relations with Monsieur Brillon now improved, she returned to Passy. Franklin's visits continued, although they became less frequent as time went on. However, when he missed a regular evening, he always managed to find an excuse. "I did not have the pleasure of seeing you Wednesday evening, my dear friend," he explained, "because my horses were in Paris [with Temple] . . . and at the moment I have neither feet [due to the gout] nor wings. Had I wings, I would have come to you, and I fancy I would sometimes scratch on your bedroom window. It is a very mean trick of Nature to refuse us what she has granted so lavishly to so many little good-for-nothings, birds and flies." When Franklin was laid up with the gout, Monsieur Brillon, who had always been very friendly with him, and who had attacks of the gout himself, visited Franklin and told him funny stories that cheered him up. Madam Brillon complained, "My plump husband often goes to visit and tell you jokes. I am worried to death he has stolen some I have been keeping for the day of our re-union." Franklin responded, "If he stole some of your stories you can repeat them, for coming from your lips they will always please me." When he had suffered an earlier attack of gout, she had written him a poem, "The Sage and the Gout," which inspired his popular bagatelle "Dialogue between Dr. Franklin and the Gout." Later, when he compiled all his bagatelles in a bound volume, he included her poem and said, "I beg your pardon for having put among those of my own, one of your creation, which is certainly too charming to be placed in such company."

With the military victory accomplished, Franklin began to think ahead to his return to America and the painful separation from his dear friends in France. He wrote plaintively to Madam Brillon: "Since some day, my dear friend, it will be necessary for me to go away to America, without any hope of seeing you again, I have sometimes come to think that it would be a good idea to wean myself from you by degrees, seeing you only once a week at first, then every second week, once a month, etc., etc., so as to diminish gradually my inordinate desire for your enchanting society and to spare myself the great pain I would otherwise suffer upon our final separation. But trying out this experiment on a small scale, I find that absence, instead of diminishing such desire, increases it. Hence, there is no remedy for the pain I fear, and I shall come to see you tonight."

Finally, the time arrived for Franklin's departure from France. Madam Brillon found triumph in her sorrow: "Every day of my life I shall remember that a great man, a sage, has wanted to be my friend . . . My heart was so heavy yesterday when I left you . . . If it ever pleases you to remember the woman who loved you the most, think of me. Farewell, my heart was not meant to be separated from yours, but it shall not be; you shall find it near yours, speak to it and it shall answer you." Monsieur Brillon was less dramatic. He merely stated that he had nothing to add to what his wife had already written, but even if he had, he could not write it for his tears would not let him see.

But that was not the end. As they had corresponded when they were so close, they continued to correspond when they were far apart. Madam Brillon reminisced: "We were happy! To have been, to still be, forever, the friends of this amiable sage who knew how to be a great man without pomp, a learned man without ostentation, a philosopher without austerity, a sensitive human being without weakness, yes, my good papa, your name will be engraved in the temple of memory but each of our hearts is, for you, a temple of love.'' Monsieur Brillon's comments were nothing so ethereal. He observed: "Everybody wants to take up a lot of space, nowadays. The men wear hats that are just tremendous in height and width. The women's hairdos are like thick bushes; and they provide themselves with enormous bosoms, monstrous derrieres. If you think you saw some samples when you were here, I can tell you that you saw nothing at all.'' And then, in their last exchange, Madam Brillon referred to the portrait of him in a light blue coat that she had painted before he left. "How often have I looked at your portrait with a great melting tenderness, my sorrow made worse by the distance between us! How much have I thought of Passy, of the short way I had to go to find the best of friends and the wisest of men!'' In his response, Franklin also remembered the old days and assured her these were memories he would never forget. "Being now in my 83rd year, I do not expect to continue much longer a sojourner in this world, and begin to promise myself much gratification of my curiosity in soon visiting some other. Wherever I may hereafter travel, be assured, my dear friend, that if I shall be capable of remembering anything, the rememberance of your friendship will be retained, as having made too deep an impression to be obliterated, and will ever, as it always has done, afford me infinite pleasure. Adieu. Adieu.''

It may come as a surprise that Madam Brillon had a rival for Franklin's affection. She was more than twenty years older than Madam Brillon, yet Franklin was enamored of her, proposed marriage to her, and she refused him. And what may seem wholly out of character, Madam Brillon criticized her for it. The lady was Anne-Catherine de Ligniville Helvétius, the widow of a wealthy philosopher, who lived in Auteuil, a village neighboring Passy. To Franklin and the other distinguished men like Condorcet, Diderot (and even Voltaire) who frequented her salon she was a queen among women, a person of infinite grace, charm, and wit. She had once been a beauty and still maintained a striking appearance. In temperament she was totally different from Madam Brillon. Brillon was self-centered, moody, and utterly conventional in life style, whereas Helvétius was outgoing, vigorous, with a touch of the Bohemian in her manner. Abigail Adams vociferously attested to these characteristics when Franklin first invited the Adamses to meet Madam Helvétius. The prim, Puritan lady from Boston was not expecting what she saw when Madam Helvétius made her entry:

> She entered the room with a careless, jaunty air; upon seeing the ladies who were strangers to her, she bawled out, "Ah! mon Dieu, where is Franklin? Why did you not tell me there were ladies here?" You must suppose her speaking all this in French. "How I look!" said she, taking hold of a chemise of tiffany, which she had on over a blue lutestring, and which looked as much upon the decay as her beauty, for she was once a handsome woman.
>
> Her hair was frizzled; over it she had a small straw hat, with a dirty gauze half-handkerchief behind. She had a black gauze scarf thrown over her shoulders.
>
> She ran out of the room; when she returned, the Doctor entered at one door, she at the other; upon which she ran forward to him, caught him by the hand, "Helas, Franklin!" then gave him a double kiss, one upon each cheek, and another upon his forehead. When we went into the room to dine, she was placed between the Doctor and Mr. Adams. She carried on the chief of the conversation at dinner, frequently locking her hand into the Doctor's, and sometimes spreading her arms upon the backs of both the gentlemen's chairs, then throwing her arm carelessly upon the Doctor's neck.
>
> I should have been greatly astonished at this conduct, if the good Doctor had not told me that in this lady I should see a genuine Frenchwoman, wholly free from affectation or stiffness of behavior, and one of the best women in the world. I own I was highly disgusted, and never wish for an acquaintance with ladies of this cast.
>
> After dinner, she threw herself on a settee, where she showed more than her feet. She had a little lap-dog, who was, next to the Doctor, her favorite. This she kissed, and when he wet the floor she wiped it up with her chemise. This is one of the Doctor's most intimate friends, with whom he dines once every week, and she with him.

Abigail Adams was not only appalled at the boldness and freedom of the woman, she could not comprehend what attraction such a woman could hold for a man of such age and eminence as Franklin.

He, too, wondered what it was about her that charméd so many men of learning and wisdom. As a philosopher, Franklin philosophized upon it in a letter to Madam Helvétius.

> I have in my way been trying to form some hypothesis to account for your having so many friends and of such various kinds. I see that statesmen, philosophers, historians, poets, and men of learning attach themselves to you as straws to a fine piece of amber.
>
> It is not that you make pretension to any of their sciences, and if you did, similarity of studies does not always make people love one another. It is not that you take pains to engage them: artless simplicity is a striking part of your character. I would not attempt to explain it by the story of the ancient, who, being asked why philosophers sought the acquaintance of kings, and kings not that of philosophers, replied that philosophers knew what they wanted, which was not always the case with kings.
>
> Yet, thus far the comparison may go that we find in your sweet society that charming benevolence, that amiable attention to oblige, that disposition to please and be pleased, which we do not always find in the society of one another. It springs from you; it has its influence on us all; and in your company we are not only pleased with you, but better pleased with one another and with ourselves.

Madam Helvétius lived on a three acre estate crammed with all kinds of flowering plants which her friends brought her from everywhere. In this flowering forest she kept cats and dogs, deer, ducks, pigeons, chickens, and many kinds of birds. When someone, supposedly Napoleon Bonaparte, commented disparagingly on the small size of her grounds, she was reported to have replied, "General, you cannot imagine how much happiness can be squeezed into three acres of land." But Madam Helvétius, though she loved and cared for her birds, beasts, and flowers, needed human companionship. With her and her two daughters there resided two middle-aged monks and a young physician. The young man, Cabanis, a disciple of Turgot, was like an adopted son to Madam. The Abbé de la Roche (who loved books) and Morellet (who loved cream), had been friends of her husband who came to live with her after his death. With these friends, her daughters, her menagerie, and her salon, Madam Helvétius had a full life. With Franklin, it became even fuller. Turgot, the former Minister of Economics, brought Franklin to Madam Helvétius' party and soon Franklin, already a friend of Morellet, became one of the inner family.

They were all good friends enjoying a common interest in politics, philosophy, and books and a common bond in Madam Helvetius, whom Franklin named "Notre Dame d' Auteuil." Her daughters he called the "Etoiles," or stars. One day a week Franklin and Temple had dinner at Madam Helvétius' house, and another day Madam with Cabanis and the Abbés came to dinner with Franklin. Breakfasts were less formally arranged and were randomly exchanged. Into the atmosphere of jovial cameraderie that prevailed Franklin injected his friendly teasing and pretended to make himself the suffering victim of their neglect. In one such instance, Madam Helvétius, who was known to be absent-minded, had invited Franklin and his grandson to a breakfast at which Madam de la Freté was to be a guest. It was then cancelled but Madam Helvétius had forgotten to inform Franklin, as he reported in a letter addressed to Madam de la Freté, but intended more for the enjoyment of Madam Helvétius and her group.

As the invitation was for 11 o'clock and you were the guest, I expected to find a breakfast in the manner of a dinner; that there would be many guests; that we should have not only tea, but also coffee, chocolate, perhaps a ham and several other good things. I decided to go on foot; my shoes were a little too tight; and I got there almost crippled. Entering the courtyard, I was somewhat surprised to find it so empty of carriages and to see that we were the first to arrive. We went up the stairs. Not a sound. We went into the breakfast room. Nobody but the Abbé [de la Roche] and M. C— [Cabanis]. The breakfast ended, and eaten! Nothing on the table but some bits of bread and a little butter. They call: they run to tell Madam Helvétius that we have come for breakfast. She quits her dressing table and comes with her hair in disorder. They are surprised that I have come to breakfast . . . Finally, a new breakfast is ordered. One person runs for fresh water, another for charcoal. They bustle about vigorously. I am very hungry; it is late. Madam departs for Paris, leaving us. We begin to eat. The butter is soon gone. The Abbé asks if we want more? Yes, certainly. He rings. No one comes. We chat and he forgets the butter. I scrape the plate; then he snatches it up and runs to the kitchen to look for more. After a while he returns slowly, saying sadly, there is none in the house. To amuse me the Abbé suggests a walk. My feet will not permit it. Consequently, we leave the table and go up to his room in order to find something with which to finish our repast—his good books.

Franklin must have delighted Madam de la Freté and Madam Helvétius as well by the comparison drawn in his closing sentence: "There I was, completely desolate, having received instead of a half-dozen of your sweet kisses, affectionate and substantial, and strongly imprinted, that I expected of your charity, only the facsimile of a single one by Madam H———, with good grace, it is true, but the lightest and most superficial that one can imagine."

Franklin always needed a group to be with and he found himself right at home with Madam Helvétius and her entourage. If the thought ever crossed his mind that it might be unusual for the lady to live together with three men it did not remain there long. He accepted happily what he found without questioning. Not so, however, John Adams. He viewed this menage with dismay and alarm. Speaking of Madam Helvétius, he observed, "That she might not be, however, entirely without the society of gentlemen, there were four handsome abbés who daily visited the house and one at least resided there. These ecclesiastics, one or more of whom reside in almost every family of distinction, I suppose have as much power to pardon a sin as they have to commit one, or to assist in committing one. Oh mores! said I to myself. What absurdities, inconsistencies, distractions and horrors would these manners introduce into our republican governments in America . . ."

In corresponding with Madam Helvétius, Franklin used the literary ploy of writing his letters not directly to her but to someone close to her, usually one of her three satellites. This made the message a community affair within the group and added a delightful element of conspiracy to even the most mundane matter. Such was the case in a letter he sent to Cabanis in which he indulges a whimsical vision of four Helvétius ladies: "Mr. Franklin being up, bathed, shaved, combed, beautified as best he can, all dressed, and on the point of going out, his head full of the four Helvétius ladies, and the sweet kisses he intends to steal from them, is much mortified to find the possibility of this happiness put off to next Sunday. He will be as patient as he can, hoping to see one of those ladies at M. de Chaumont's on Wednesday. He will be there early, to watch her enter with that grace and dignity which have charmed him for seven weeks at the same place. He even plans to capture her and keep her with him for life. The three others, left at Auteuil, ought to be enough for the canaries and the abbés."

One of Franklin's saucy comments to Madam Helvétius was blunted, preserving only the humor, by using the device of sending it to Cabanis. In it he is, as usual, complaining of his mistreatment: "If Notre Dame is pleased to spend her days with Franklin, he would be just as pleased to spend his nights with her; and since he has already given her so many of his days, although he has so few left to give, she seems very ungrateful in never giving him one of her nights, which keep passing as pure loss, without making anyone happy except Poupon [the cat]."

They were all so happy together sitting around discussing ethics, politics and philosophy, Madam Helvétius leading Franklin on to flirt, the Abbé de la Roche recalled, that in his words, "we would gladly have renounced that other paradise to keep the one we had, and live just as we were for all eternity." Whether it was the result of her flirtation or his natural instincts, Franklin became closer to Madam Helvétius as time went on. He once sent her a note saying that if he were called to Paradise that morning he would ask for a delay until one o'clock to receive the kiss she had promised him earlier. In a charming bagatelle which he sent through the Abbé de la Roche, he had the flies in his rooms make the proposal that was in his heart, that his household and hers be joined into one. The flies, of course, have their own interests to look after, and although they admit he treats them well, she rather than he can be depended upon to sweep out their mortal enemies, the spiders.

The flies of the apartments of M. F————n request permission to present their respects to Madam H—————s, and to express in their best language their gratitude for the protection she has been kind enough to give them,

Bizz, izzz ouizz a ouizzz izzzzzzzz.

We have lived a long time under the hospitable roof of the said good man F————n. He has given us free lodging; we have also eaten and drunk the whole year at his expense without it having cost us anything. Often, when his friends and himself have used up a bowl of punch, he has left a sufficient quantity to intoxicate a hundred of us flies. We have drunk freely from it, and after we have made our sallies, our circles and our cotillions very prettily in the air of his chamber, and have gaily consummated our little amours under his nose.

Finally, we would have been the happiest people in the world, if he had not permitted to remain over the top of his wainscoating a number of our declared enemies who stretched their webbed nets to capture us, and who would destroy us without pity. People of a temperament subtle and fierce, abominable combination!

You, very excellent lady, had the goodness to order that all these assassins with their habitations and their snares be swept; and your orders, as they always should be, have been carried out immediately. Since that time we have lived happily and have enjoyed the beneficence of the said good man F————n without fear.

There only remains one thing for us to wish in order to assure the permanence of our good fortune; permit us to say it,

Bizz izzz ouizz a ouizzzz izzzzzzzz.

It is to see yours and his formed at last into single household.

While such an arrangement might be perfect for Mr. Franklin and his flies, how about the three recipients of Madam Helvétius' hospitality who enjoyed a paradise they would not exchange for the promised one? If Franklin's proposal was serious, they might have to bank more heavily on heavenly bliss for the future. Speaking of Notre Dame d'Auteuil and Franklin, Abbé Morellet said, "If I were the master of my life . . . I should always want to be between her and him. This, perhaps, would not suit Mr. Franklin who loves to be very close to the lady. Well, I should consent to place her between him and me. I think this arrangement is fitting for two philosophers who believe in the principle of freedom of trade and who do not like exclusive privileges."

There was another actor in this drama of love and marriage who was yet to be heard from. This was Turgot, who had brought Franklin and Madam Helvétius together, and now wished he hadn't. Turgot, a bachelor, was himself in love with Madam Helvétius and had been for years. He had proposed to her but she chose Helvétius instead. When Helvétius died, Turgot proposed again but she decided to remain faithful to the memory of her philosopher husband. They nevertheless remained close friends and Turgot more than anyone else was upset when Franklin made his formal proposal of marriage. Madam Helvétius gave the proposal serious consideration but after discussing it with Turgot she refused Franklin, giving the same reason she had given Turgot, to remain true to her former husband (to whom she had erected a monument depicting herself weeping over his tomb). Franklin was used to disappointments and he took the rebuff with good grace. But he did not retire without having his say. He had his triumph in the form of a bagatelle: "The Elysian Fields."

Chagrined by your barbarous resolution, stated so positively last night, to remain single the rest of your life in respect to your dear husband, I went home, fell on my bed, and, believing myself dead, found myself in the Elysian Fields.

I was asked if I desired to see some important persons.—Take me to the philosophers.—There are two who live nearby in the garden: they are very good neighbors and close friends of each other.—Who are they?—Socrates and H————.—I esteem them both prodigiously; but let me see H———— first, for I understand a little French but not a word of Greek.

He received me with great courtesy, having known me by reputation for some time, he said. He asked me a thousand things about war, and about the present state of religion, liberty, and the government in France.—But you are not asking at all of your dear friend Madam H————; still she loves you excessively, and I was with her but an hour ago.

Ah! said he, you make me remember my former happiness. But one must forget in order to be happy here. For several of the early years I thought only of her. Now I am consoled. I have taken another wife. One as similar to her as I could find. She is not, it is true, quite so beautiful, but she has just as much good sense, a little more wisdom, and she loves me infinitely. Her continual effort is to please me; and she has gone out right now to search for the best nectar and ambrosia to regale me with tonight. Stay with me and you will see her.—I notice, said I, that your former friend is more faithful than you: for several good matches have been offered her, all of which she has refused. I confess that I, myself, loved her madly; but she was hard-hearted toward me and has absolutely rejected me for the love of you.

I pity you, said he, for your bad fortune; for truly she is a good and beautiful woman and very lovable. But Abbé de la R————, and the Abbé M————, are they not still sometimes at her home?

Yes, assuredly, for she not lost a single one of your friends.

Now, if you had won over the Abbé M———— (with coffee and cream) to speak for you, perhaps you would have succeeded; for he is as subtle a debator as Duns Scotus or St. Thomas; he puts his arguments in such good order that they become almost irresistible. Or, better yet, if the Abbé de la R———— has been persuaded (by some beautiful edition of an old classic) to argue against you, that would have been better: for I have always observed that when he advises something she has a strong tendency to do the exact opposite.

As he was saying this, the new Madam H——————— entered with the nectar. I recognized her instantly as Madam F—————, my former American friend. I claimed her. But she told me coldly, I have been your good wife forty-nine years and four months, nearly half a century; be content with that. I have formed a new connection here, which will endure for eternity.

Indignant at this refusal by my Eurydice, I decided right then to leave these ungrateful spirits, and to return to this good earth, to see again the sun and you. Here I am! Let us revenge ourselves!

Franklin had once commented to the Abbé de la Roche on the remarkable similarity between himself and the late philosopher Helvétius. Though they were brought up in opposite parts of the world, he observed that they "loved the same studies, the same friends, and the same woman." Although Helvétius and Franklin were, in fact, quite different men in personality and philosophy, this notion may have inspired Franklin in generating his bagatelle. The subject of Paradise and the affairs he might conveniently arrange there, a favorite theme with Franklin, was on his mind at this time for he was busy sketching a paradise, a more conventional one with angels and music, for Madam Brillon. While he reluctantly gave up the hope of marriage to Madam Helvétius, and accepted his special, honored place in the little circle of dear friends, he nevertheless could not resist the temptation to make an occasional thrust in that direction. He said "I now and then offend our good lady, who cannot long retain her displeasure, but, sitting in state on her sofa, extends graciously her long, handsome arm, and says: 'there; take my hand; I pardon you,' with all the dignity of a sultaness." He noted her effort to make every creature about her happy, "from the abbés down through all the ranks of the family to the birds and Poupon." He told her, "Here is a problem a mathematician would be hard put to solve. Usually, when we share things, each person gets only a part; but when I share my pleasure with you, my part is doubled. The part is more than the whole."

After years of happiness the day of parting arrived. It was painful. According to Cabanis, "many honorable tears were shed on both sides." As he left, she wrote, "Come back, my dear friend, come back to us. My little retreat will be the better for your presence; you will like it because of the friendship you will find here and the care we will take of you. You will make our life happier, we shall contribute to your happiness, such are the things that you must know for sure, that you have read in my heart . . ." While waiting at dockside he answered his "dear Helvétia." "I am not sure that I shall be happy in America, but I must go back. I feel sometimes that things are badly arranged in this world when I consider that people so well matched to be happy together are forced to separate. I will not tell you of my love. For one would say that there is nothing remarkable or praiseworthy about it, since everybody loves you. I only hope that you will always love me some." And as the ship sailed, he made his last goodbye, "Farewell, my very, very, very dear friend."

In America again Franklin was literally immersed in a new world, but from time to time he would hear from his old friends and reminisce with them through correspondence. To Madam Helvétius he wrote, "I extend my arms toward you despite the immensity of the seas which separate us, in awaiting the celestial kiss which I firmly hope to give you one day." She, too, spoke of meeting again in the hereafter, she with a husband, he with a wife, commenting, however, "I believe you have been a rogue and will find more than one wife up there!" When people spoke of him, she wailed, "Ah, that great man, that poor dear man, we shall not see him anymore!" "Certainly through your fault," was Madam Brillon's response, blaming his departure on Madam Helvétius' refusal of his marriage offer. When Madam Helvétius wanted an American bird for her aviary, a cardinal, Franklin sent several but the trip was too much for them and they did not arrive alive. He knew they would be very happy once they were under her protection, he told her, but "they cannot come to her and she will not come to them." He reminded her of the offer he made her of 1,000 acres of woodland where she might carve out a great garden if she wished and have 1,000 aviaries. Cardinals, he stated, were plentiful in his large tract on the Ohio. "If I had been a cardinal myself," he mused, "perhaps I might have prevailed with her." Of course, he was just making a flamboyant gesture, for they both knew they would never see each other again. As his life glowed in its sunset he fondly recalled his friends dining at Notre Dame d'Auteuil's table while Madam served the whole company "with as much ease as pleasure." "But, alas, I was not there to take my share in that lovely, sensible talk, the wit and the friendship with which her meals are always seasoned!" The glow of past memories comforted her too. "What happiness you have spread in my little retreat, my dear Franklin. We all gathered to read and reread your sweet letter, to remember once more the days you spent with us and the light you poured into my soul. I never left you that I did not feel a little worthier the next day.'' And finally, his last words to her, ''I cannot let this chance go by, my dear friend, without telling you that I love you always . . . I think endlessly of the pleasures I enjoyed in the sweet society of Auteuil. And often, in my dreams, I dine with you, I sit beside you on one of your thousand sofas, or I walk with you in your beautiful garden.''

How does this picture of the romantic, witty Franklin in his association with women jibe with the portrait of the lustful, lecherous Franklin that is so frequently painted nowadays? Was he as we have seen him portrayed here by his own words or was he really an 18th Century swinger? If we hold with John Adams we would have to choose the latter position. Quoting Adams, on Franklin, ''You may depend on this, the moment an American minister gives a loose to his passion for women, that moment he is undone.'' Franklin certainly shocked Adams but as we have seen, it didn't take much to shock Adams. Was Madam Brillon Franklin's mistress? That is not very likely. No one has made a point of suggesting it and her conduct indicated strongly the contrary. Madam Helvétius? A. O. Aldridge, Franklin biographer, thinks so. He had based this deduction upon no further information than that presented here. Certainly the odds for it are greater than for that of Madam Brillon. But what of Turgot, the abbés and Cabanis? Would we not have heard from them if this were the case? Would Franklin have joked about Madam Helvétius spending one of her wasted nights with him and broadcast the joke through Cabanis if indeed she were already doing so?

Must we believe, then, that Franklin had no active sex life in that gay, free city of Paris during the reign of Louis XVI? This may be too somber a consideration even to be entertained. It is true, however, that he was 70 years old when he came to France, and a popular anecdote about Franklin in Paris tells of his proposition to one of the fair ladies to spend the night with him. When to his surprise, she accepted, he expressed his joy, but reflected, ''Perhaps we should wait until winter when the nights are longer.''

If Franklin's reputation for amour in Paris may have been ''sex-aggerated,'' we cannot suppose conversely that a man of his healthy appetites lived as celibate as a monk from 1757, when he left his wife to go to London, to see her again only for about a year, until his death in 1790. Most likely he followed the pattern of his youth prior to his marriage, which he mentioned in his autobiography: "that hard-to-be-governed passion of youth had hurried me frequently into intrigues with low women that fell in my way." His associations for physical satisfaction may have been of this type—furtive, clandestine, fleeting, with anonymous partners. If anything, Franklin was a prudent man and it would not have been like him to have advertised activities that would not have been acceptable at home. "Let all men know thee, but no man know thee thoroughly," was *Poor Richard's* counsel.

The only relationship we know about that could, if demonstrated, earn for Franklin his modern reputation, was his contact with Sir Francis Dashwood, Lord Le Despencer. Le Despencer was Franklin's superior in the post of Postmaster General and out of this relationship developed a friendship in which Franklin was occasionally an invited guest at the baron's grand estate at West Wycombe. Together they worked on and published a revised and abridged edition of the *Book of Common Prayer*. But Le Despencer was known better for other things, particularly his colorful past. He was one of the foremost libertines of his time and the founder of the notorious society of Medmenham Monks, sometimes called the Hell Fire Club. This secret society at West Wycombe was devoted to sacrilegious ceremonies and sexual excesses, and some of the most illustrious men in England were members. Franklin was socially accepted in the company at West Wycombe and although it is possible he could have been a member of the infamous club, there is no evidence to show that he was.

From what we know about Franklin, the current view of him as a super lover appears to be mistaken. Although he was a hearty man who thoroughly enjoyed the pleasures of life, he was no Casanova. Actually, the unwarranted emphasis on the physical side of Franklin's association with women does injury to the beautiful, enduring relationship he had with so many women of different backgrounds. Madam Brillon, analyzing his special charm with women, said to him, "You combine with the kindest heart, the soundest moral teaching, a lively imagination, and that droll roguishness which shows that the wisest of men allows his wisdom to be perpetually broken against the rocks of femininity."

Perhaps the most perceptive comment on Franklin's friendships with women has been made by Carl Van Doren: "Without the brevity of ordinary lust, or the perseverance of obsession, they had a general warmth which, while no doubt sexual in origin, made them strong, tender, imaginative, and humorous beyond the reach of mere desire, with its hard, impersonal appetite. Always a person himself, Franklin treated every woman as if she were a person too, and made her feel more truly one than ever before. Because he loved, valued, and studied women, they were no mystery to him, and he had no instinctive fear of them. Statesman and scientist, profoundly masculine, he took women into account as well as any other force of nature.''

PART ONE

Franklin in Print

1

A YOUTH WITH PROMISE

Oh! George, This wild November
We must not pass with you
For Ruth, our fragile daughter,
Its chilly gales will rue.

THESE MELODRAMATIC LINES COME FROM "The Lighthouse Tragedy,"
a ballad which depicted the drowning of a Boston lighthouse keeper
and his family in 1718. They launched the literary career of one of the
world's famous men, whose accomplishments encompassed many
fields but whose life and work were characterized by wisdom, wit, and
humor. "The Lighthouse Tragedy" sold wonderfully, according to the
author, and encouraged him to try his hand at another similar poem.
An event worthy of his dramatic ballad style fortunately had just occurred. The famous pirate, Captain Edward Teach, better known as
Blackbeard, had been killed in a sea battle:

Will you hear of a bloody battle,
Lately fought upon the seas,
It will make your ears to rattle,
And your admiration cease:
Have you heard of Teach the Rover,
And his knavery on the Main;
How of gold he was a lover,
How he loved ill got gain.

If you are not impressed with the quality of this poetry, you find
yourself in company with the author, who in his autobiography called
it "wretched stuff." But we cannot be too critical of his work, con-

sidering that he was only 12 years old at the time. The author, Benjamin Franklin, the youngest son in a candlemaker's family of 17 children, was born in Boston in the English Colony of Massachusetts on January 17, 1706. At the age of 8 his father entered him in grammar school where, by the end of the year, he had advanced to the head of the class. Here was a youth with promise. But his father's finances provided him with only one more year of schooling, after which he apprenticed at different trades, finally as a printer under his elder brother, James. Noting that the boy took a fancy to poetry, his brother encouraged him in that exercise. James printed the ballads and sent young Benjamin about the town to sell them. But their father stepped in, ridiculing the boy's performance, and assuring him that verse makers generally became beggars. Thus ended young Franklin's career as a swashbuckling poet.

As an apprentice, the boy used all his spare time for reading. He was always fond of reading and filled his insatiable curiosity for new knowledge by buying books with the money he could save. He suggested that his brother give him half the money James paid to board him out and he would provide his own food. His brother instantly agreed, and by living frugally on a vegetable diet Benjamin was able to save half of his food allowance, as an additional fund for buying books. In his papers, Thomas Jefferson quotes Franklin as saying "that when he was young, and had time to read he had not books, and now when he had become old, and had books, he had no time."

When Ben came upon a volume of Addison's *Spectator,* he was so delighted with it that he read it over and over and imitated it in developing his own writing ability. His efforts made him think that he might, in time, become a tolerable writer. He got his first chance at writing in the publication of *The New England Courant*.

The *Courant* was a newspaper printed and published by James Franklin, Benjamin's brother. In 1771 Benjamin was amused as he recalled the founding of the *Courant* in 1721. Some of James Franklin's friends tried to dissuade him from the venture as not likely to succeed: "one newspaper being in their judgment enough for America." [1] The writers for the *Courant* were a group of young men

[1] Actually, the *Courant* was the fourth newspaper. The *Boston News-Letter* was founded in 1704, the *Boston Gazette* in 1719, and the *American Weekly Mercury* in 1719. In 1771, according to Franklin, there were no less than 25 newspapers in America.

who protested the authority of the theocratic Puritan government of Boston, controlled by the preachers Increase Mather and Cotton Mather, and their followers. Not daring to be bluntly critical of the established regime, the Couranteers expressed themselves obliquely by writing satirical but entertaining essays, poetry, and letters in the manner of the *Spectator* and other popular English periodicals. The apprentice was inspired and challenged by their material, which was fresh and vigorous and different from anything staid Boston had ever produced.

One morning James Franklin found a letter under the door. It was signed, Silence Dogood. Was that a real name? Not likely; the *Courant* writers were careful to use fictitious names like Ichabod Henroost, Fanny Mournful, and Tabitha Talkative. James Franklin and his friends were delighted with the letter and decided that it should be published. The apprentice author, innocently standing nearby, had "the exquisite pleasure" of hearing his work praised. He was even more pleased to hear the men guessing who the author might be, mentioning none but people of standing and learning.

Later in his life, Benjamin Franklin was to create many fictitious literary characters, or *personae,* but his first, Silence Dogood, was the most completely developed and realistic of them all. In this charming hoax on the Couranteers, the 16-year-old boy conjured himself up to be a widow with three children, who proclaimed herself an "enemy of vice, and a friend to vertue." In this first letter, and those that followed, Ben gave Silence an identity.

Silence told her story, which was full of hokum, about being orphaned and reared by a young minister who later took her as his wife, only to leave her a widow. She was a personality in her own right, having opinions on all sorts of subjects, which she expressed in a series of letters that James Franklin published without realizing the identity of the real author. *See Chapter 8.*

During the time the younger Franklin was anonymously issuing his Dogood letters to the *Courant,* the elder brother was continuing to be freely critical of the authoritarian ministerial government, and finally his audacity landed him in jail. During James' confinement in jail, Benjamin managed the paper and Silence submitted letters staunchly defending freedom of speech and rebuking political and religious hypocrites. When the true identity of Mrs. Dogood became known, James Franklin felt very kindly toward his brother.

The Dogood papers finally came to an end and two months later a disappointed correspondent wrote to the Courant to ask Mrs. Dogood why she had become silent. Had she married or died, or was her homespun wit and stock of matter all spent? In his autobiography Franklin was later to confirm the latter possibility: "My small fund of sense for such performances was pretty well exhausted."

Benjamin did write other pieces for the *Courant* but, unfortunately, the authorship of most of the pieces is uncertain. One which scholars agree can be attributed to Franklin is "Titles of Honor." Like so many of Franklin's writings, it reflects his native democratic bias. He was purely American in feeling that people should earn respect by their deeds and not through titles of rank or honor. Knowing that the Bible could not be refuted, he ridiculed such titles by applying them to biblical personalities.

> In old time it was no disrespect for men and women to be called by their own names: Adam, was never called *Master* Adam; we never read of Noah *Esquire,* Lot *Knight* and *Baronet,* nor the *Right Honourable* Abraham, *Viscount Mesopotamia, Baron of Carran;* no, no, they were plain men, honest country grasiers, that took care of their families and their flocks. Moses was a great prophet, and Aaron a priest of the Lord; but we never read of the *Reverend* Moses, nor the *Right Reverend Father in God,* Aaron, by divine providence, *Lord Arch-Bishop of Israel:* Thou never sawest *Madam* Rebecca in the Bible, my *Lady* Rachel, nor Mary, tho' a princess of the blood after the death of Joseph, called the *Princess Dowager of Nazareth;* no, plain Rebecca, Rachel, Mary, or the *Widow* Mary, or the like: It was no incivility then to mention their naked names as they were expressed.

In 1784, an aged Franklin would again take up his pen in battle against the use of titles. The Society of the Cincinnati, an honorary organization of American officers, with General George Washington at its head, had been formed after the Revolution. Memebership was to be hereditary as in the case of titles of nobility, passing through the line of the eldest son. Franklin noted the absurdity of this hereditary honor by calculating that in nine generations the family line would have been so diluted biologically that the then titled gentleman would have in him only one part in 1022 of the honor received from his ancestor in 1784.

During the months following James Franklin's release from jail, the relations between the two brothers became strained. Benjamin later admitted that he might have been saucy and provoking, feeling the independence he had enjoyed while his brother was away. Nevertheless he resented his brother's anger and beatings. The actual fact was that Ben had outgrown his apprenticeship; he was already more able than his teacher and both of them realized it. Benjamin solved his problem by running away to Philadelphia. Two weeks later James Franklin ran an advertisement in the *Courant* seeking "a likely lad for an apprentice." He was not to get the likes of what he had lost. In three years the *Courant* was out of business, but in Philadelphia the newspaper business was to become very lively.

2

ADVENTURES IN OLD PHILADELPHIA

WHEN THE YOUNG APPRENTICE MADE HIS ESCAPE from Puritan Massachusetts to Quaker Pennsylvania he did not fail to display the fertile imagination that had marked his early career. He concocted a melodramatic tale that he "had got a naughty girl with child" and since her friends would catch him and compel him to marry her, he had to make his escape. Through his friend Collins he sold some of his books and obtained money to purchase passage on a sloop bound for New York. The Captain, whether sympathetic to his plight or merely interested in the fare, took him aboard secretly and Benjamin was on his way to seek his fame and fortune.

On the voyage from Boston, the ship was becalmed off Block Island and the hands started fishing, catching a great many cod. Benjamin, a self convert to vegetarianism, looked upon fishing as unprovoked murder. None of the fish, his reason told him, had done any injury to the men to deserve this slaughter. But when he caught the smell of the cod in the frying pan he was torn between principle and inclination. Then he recollected that when the fish were cut open he saw smaller fish taken out of their stomachs, and said to himself. "If you eat one another, I don't see why we mayn't eat you." So he dined very heartily upon cod and philosophized how convenient it was to be a reasonable creature, since it enabled one to find a reason for everything one had a mind to do.

With a fair wind, the ship arrived in New York in three days. New York, a small city, did not have a newspaper but it did have a printer, one William Bradford, to whom Ben applied for a job. Bradford had no job for the boy but recommended that he go to Philadelphia where his son Andrew, also a printer, had just lost his principal assistant. After some misadventures along the way, Ben arrived in Philadelphia, hungry and dirty in his work clothes, his pockets stuffed out with shirts and stockings. He went immediately to the bakery shop, where not being familiar with the local products, he asked the baker for three pennies worth of bread of any sort. To his surprise he got three great, puffy rolls. Having no more room in his pockets, he put a roll under each arm and walked off eating the third. Thus occurred that famous scene where Benjamin Franklin, awkward and ridiculous in appearance, was first witnessed by the young lady who was later to be his wife. Continuing down the street he saw many neatly dressed people going in the same direction and joining them, found himself in the Quaker Meeting House. Sitting down and hearing nothing said, his exhaustion caught up with him and he fell sound asleep not waking until the meeting broke up, when someone was kind enough to rouse him. This was his first taste of Philadelphia's hospitality and it was a good beginning for him in this city of brotherly love.

The next day, seeking employment, he called on Andrew Bradford. Bradford had just hired a hand but referred him to Samuel Keimer, a new printer in town, who was able to give him work. Franklin did not develop a high opinion of Keimer, whom he found to have a good deal of the knave in his personal makeup. Keimer loved argumentation and so did his new assistant. Franklin had studied the Socratic method of argument and constantly used it to trap his opponent. In their contests, Ben would lead Keimer into answering seemingly innocent questions which later would bring him into difficulties, finally causing him the embarrassment of contradicting himself. This eventually led Keimer to be so absurdly cautious that he would not answer even the simplest question without first asking, "What do you intend to infer from that?"

Keimer didn't like to be bested, but being a schemer he decided to put the boy's talent to use. He conceived of setting up a new sect in which he would preach the doctrine and Benjamin would confound the opponents with his infallible technique. Ben didn't like some of the practices, like wearing a full beard, as Keimer did, but he agreed to cooperate providing Keimer would adopt his practice of taking no animal food. The boy knew Keimer was a glutton and in this proposal he was making sport of him, but Keimer was not aware of it. Very seriously, Keimer asserted that his constitution would not bear such a diet. Benjamin fully assured him that the vegetable diet would not ruin his constitution, but would even improve it. Keimer finally gave in, provided Franklin would keep him company at these meals. Ben consented and gave a neighbor woman a list of 40 dishes lacking meat, fish or fowl that she would prepare for them. Franklin enjoyed the meals and saved money in the bargain, but Keimer suffered grievously. After three months of longing for "the fleshpots of Egypt," he broke down and ordered a roast pig for dinner. Generously he invited his assistant and two woman friends to join him in the celebration, but as the guests sadly discovered, the feast was so tempting that he ate the whole pig himself before they even arrived.

Franklin gradually acquired young friends of his own tastes, all lovers of reading. Among them were Charles Osborne, a clerk, whom Franklin described as sensible and sincere but in literary matters too fond of criticizing; and James Ralph, a budding poet, genteel and eloquent. The friends liked to compose literary pieces for their own entertainment and improvement. Ralph hoped eventually to earn his living as a poet but Osborne dissuaded him, saying he had no genius for poetry and had better stick to the mercantile world where by diligence and punctuality he might with luck become a success. On one occasion the young friends decided that each of them would try his hand at paraphrasing the 18th Psalm using whatever literary style he wished. When the time came to compare the result, Ralph paid a call on Franklin to show him his version. Franklin found it excellent and gave it wholehearted praise. He, himself, had been too busy to write anything but it occurred to Ralph that they might pretend that he had written Ralph's piece and submit it as his own. Ralph was sure that Osborne would be so jealous of him that he would not acknowledge merit in anything he produced. Since Osborne did not have this antagonism toward Franklin, the work had a better chance coming from him.

It was agreed and the companions met to listen to each other's efforts. When Osborne's piece was read, Ralph did it justice; he commented on the flaws but applauded the beauties. He offered no work of his own. Franklin was next. He was modest, desirous of being excused, explaining that he did not have enough time to go over his work and correct it. No excuses were allowed, however, and he had to submit "his contribution" for criticism. Upon hearing it, Osborne gave up the contest and applauded enthusiastically. Ralph did not praise it but made only criticisms of it and proposed amendments. Osborne was scornful of Ralph, saying that he was no better a critic than a poet. Osborne and Ralph walked home together and, referring to the piece again, Osborne divested himself of restraint in his acclaim. "But who would have imagined," he said "that Franklin had been capable of such a performance; such painting, such force, such fire! He has even improved the original! In his common conversation, he seems to have no choice of words; he hesitates and blunders; and yet, good God, how he writes!"

Osborne later went to the West Indies where he became an eminent lawyer and made money but died young. His fame will rest, however, in his joining with Franklin in the latter's first scientific experiment. The two devised a plan to test communication with the world of the hereafter. They agreed that the one who happened to die first, should if possible, make a friendly visit to the other and acquaint him how he found things in that separate state. Osborne was the first to die, "But" said Franklin, "he never fulfilled his promise." The same experiment was tried again some 200 years later by the magician Houdini. Despite his reputation as an escape artist, he was no more successful than Osborne.

After a year in Philadelphia, the runaway returned to Boston for a visit. He was happily welcomed by his family, except for his brother James, who was humiliated and furious at the boy for first having broken his indenture as an apprentice and having returned with a new suit, a watch, and pockets lined with silver coins, which he had the effrontery to spread out before the pop-eyed journeymen in James' printing shop.

Collins, the young friend who had conspired in Ben's escape a year before, was excited by the stories Franklin told of the new country and decided he would go there too. Ben was delighted with Collins' decision, since the two had been friends from childhood. Unfortunately Franklin didn't know that during the year he was absent Collins had taken to sotting with brandy and gambling his money away. This was to put him constantly in debt to Franklin. When Collins was intoxicated he became very fractious and the two friends frequently quarreled. On one such occasion they were on a boat on the Delaware river with some other young men and Collins refused to row in his turn: "I will be rowed home, says he. We will not row you, says I. You must or stay all night on the water, says he." The others wanted to concede but Franklin adamantly refused. Collins swore he would make Franklin row or throw him overboard. To make good his threat, Collins stepped toward Franklin and struck at him. Franklin ducked and grabbing Collins under the crotch pitched him headfirst into the river. Collins was a good swimmer and made for the boat, but as he got a few strokes from the boat the oarsmen pulled it out of his reach. Each time he drew near they asked him if he would row and in the absence of his assent they slid the boat away from him. He was ready to die of vexation but obstinately refused to give in and row. Finally seeing him tire, they lifted him into the boat and brought him home dripping wet. The two friends hardly exchanged a civil word afterwards. Collins got a position as tutor for the sons of a gentleman in Barbados and Franklin never saw him again, nor the money he had promised to repay.

A sea captain from Boston who was related to the Franklins traded between Boston and Delaware, and when he docked near Philadelphia he contacted Ben. Ben replied with a letter which the captain showed to the man who happened to be with him. The man was the Governor of Pennsylvania and he was impressed with the letter, especially when he learned the writer's age. He thought he might like to meet this young constituent of his and take an interest in him. Shortly thereafter, the Governor and a friend appeared at Keimer's shop. Keimer ran down immediately, thinking the visitors had come to see him. Instead they made their way upstairs where Ben was working, and the Governor spoke to him with great politeness, paying him many compliments and inviting him to go with them to a tavern where excellent wine was served. Franklin admitted he was not a little surprised by this incident but Keimer, as Franklin unflatteringly described him, "stared like a pig poisoned."

The Governor stated that the province did not have a good printer but needed one. He liked the boy and offered to help him get set up in his own business. It sounded too good to be true. But why should he not believe it? It was the Governor himself who made the offer. The Governor frequently invited the boy to his house and they talked of their plans as already fixed. The Governor further proposed that Ben go to London to pick out the best printing presses and types for his shop. He said he would provide Ben with letters of credit for purchasing the equipment, and Franklin boarded the ship ready for his first trip across the Atlantic. The letters of credit never arrived; they had never even been written. The Governor was long on promises, short on fulfillment. He had just been leading the boy on, enjoying his company and his good will, but never intending to make good on his promises. As Franklin charitably explained, "he wished to please everybody; and, having little to give, he gave expectations."

Now young Franklin found himself stranded in London, thrown on his own resources, as he was when he landed in Philadelphia. But this time he was not alone; his friend James Ralph had joined him on his trip to London. Wanting desperately to become a poet, Ralph felt that opportunity would not be found in Philadelphia but rather in London. In London he tried to get work as an actor and as a writer but all attempts failed. He lived by borrowing from Ben, who had the good fortune to get a job at a famous printing house where he was to further develop his skill as a printer. The two boys took lodgings together, went to plays, and entertained themselves splendidly in the big city. Ralph had a wife and child in Philadelphia but he quickly forgot about them and became friendly with a young milliner who lodged in the same house. She was genteelly bred, lively and sensible. Ralph read plays to her, they became intimate, and when she took another lodging, he followed her. As her income was insufficient for the two of them and her child, he was forced to leave London to become schoolmaster at a country school. Considering the great future he envisioned for himself, he felt this employment beneath him and took the position under an assumed name. Ralph wrote to Ben recommending the milliner to his care, asking him when he replied to direct his correspondence in the name of Benjamin Franklin, Schoolmaster.

Meanwhile the young woman had lost her friends and business due to her affair with Ralph, and being in distress, she sent for the real Benjamin Franklin to assist her with funds. He reports that he grew fond of her company and feeling justified by her dependence on him in Ralph's absence, followed the simple course of his instincts. He attempted familiarities with her, only to be angrily repulsed, with the injured lady indignantly reporting the incident forthwith to the schoolmaster. This caused a breach between the two Benjamin Franklins, whereby Ralph felt compelled to cancel all his financial obligations to his friend. Franklin was not greatly disturbed since Ralph was not able to pay anyway, and by losing this friendship he was also relieved of the burden of Ralph's continual borrowing.

In London, Franklin made an agreement with a bookseller, who had an immense collection of second-hand books, to read and return any of his books for a small sum, there being no leading libraries in those days. He wrote and printed a short book on religion, which he later regretted and destroyed. Through the reputation he gained by it, however, he was taken into the company of learned people like the physician-philosopher, Bernard Mandeville, who had a club of followers who met at a tavern and listened to his entertaining, facetious remarks. Franklin was also promised an opportunity to meet Sir Isaac Newton and was very disappointed that it never came about. He demonstrated his prowess as a swimmer, and his demand as a swimming teacher led him to consider opening a swimming school. Instead he took an offer to go back to America and work for a Quaker merchant from Philadelphia with whom he had become acquainted on the ocean voyage to London.

On the trip back to Philadelphia, Franklin kept a journal of events and observations. He recorded in it the porpoises he saw, the sharks and their retinue of pilot fish, the strange flying fish, and the beautifully colored dolphin that the passengers caught and ate. The dolphin, whose well-shaped body he described as colored bright green mixed with silver and having a shining golden-yellow tail, was shown in paintings of the time as a crooked monster with head and eyes like a bull, a hog's snout, and a tail like a blown tulip. He thought that this representation might be due to the painters' poor attempt to imitate the fish in the posture of leaping. But he found that the sailors had another explanation, though a whimsical one. "As this most beautiful fish is only to be caught at sea and far to the Southward, they say, the painters willfully deform it lest pregnant women should long for what is impossible to procure for them."

Part of the reason for Franklin's keeping his journal may have been to fight boredom. He remarked about the oppressive boredom of confinement on the small ship for nearly three months. It made the passengers ill tempered and poor company. Franklin noted a common opinion among the women that if a man has a bad disposition it will come out when he has been drinking. But Franklin knew too many exceptions to this rule and suggested instead a long sea voyage for this disclosure. To pass the time Franklin read, talked, played checkers and cards. He thought playing cards to be trifling and childish, but being so bored, "we fly to it for entertainment." One incident, however, served to break the monotony. One of the passengers was accused of having marked the playing cards and a trial was called where evidence was presented. A Dutchman who spoke no English reported through an interpreter that he had plainly seen the accused mark all the cards on the back with a pen. Franklin commented in his journal that in speaking to foreigners we often speak louder than necessary as if to make up in sound for what is lacking in understanding. He thought that something of the same phenomenon took place in the case of the accused, who fancied that since the Dutchman could not understand what he heard that he would not understand what he saw, and, therefore, boldly performed his nefarious deed in plain view of the other. The jury found the man guilty and he was condemned to pay a fine of two bottles of brandy and to be carried up to the round top, where the crime was comitted, and there made fast for three hours in view of the ship's company. The prisoner, however, refused to submit to punishment and as Franklin related, "one of the sailors stepped up aloft and let down a rope to us, which we with much struggling made fast about his middle and hoisted him up into the air, sprawling, by main force. We let him hang, cursing and swearing, for near a quarter of an hour; but at length he crying out murder! and looking black in the face, the rope being overtight about his middle, we thought proper to let him down again; and our mess have excommunicated him till he pays his fine, refusing either to play, eat, drink, or converse with him."

After nearly two years absence, the youth landed again in Philadelphia. The passengers thanked God and congratulated each other on having completed such a tedious and dangerous voyage. Ben began working for the Quaker merchant, who treated him like a son, and his prospects were never brighter. But the merchant was taken ill and suddenly died, leaving Ben with no better alternative than to return to his former employer, Samuel Keimer.

On his earlier trip to Boston to see his parents, the young man also paid his respects at another door. He called on Cotton Mather in a gesture of reconciliation which the old man appreciated. This young fellow was no longer a thorn in his side and the old man could afford to forgive and forget. As for Franklin, he respected Mather and was pleased to display his success before him. Though neither of the men realized it, it was indeed a memorable meeting. Each of the participants was later to be regarded as the most celebrated American of his own time. Cotton Mather was the first man of letters that America produced and Franklin was the next. Cotton Mather was a distinguished scholar, having written some 450 articles and books in the fields of religion, history, biography, and science. The ideas and attitudes of the two men were as different as day and night, yet Cotton had some influence on Benjamin. Mather's moralistic "Essays To Do Good" affected the young Franklin, and their essence was incorporated in his own Dogood essays and later writings.

When their pleasant conference in the library of the Mather home was over, Cotton showed Ben a shorter way out of the house, through a narrow passage which was crossed by an overhead beam. The two were busily talking as they made their way out, with the guest ahead and the host behind. Turning partly toward his host as they proceeded and conversed, Franklin heard Mather say hastily, *"Stoop, stoop!"* Ben did not understand the purpose of these words until he felt his head crash against the beam. As a lifelong preacher Cotton Mather never missed an occasion to give moral instruction, and while Ben was convulsed in agony holding his aching head, Cotton said to him: "You are young, and have the world before you; *stoop* as you go through it, and you will miss many hard thumps." This advice, thus beat into his head, was a lesson that Franklin was never to forget. He thought of it throughout his life when he saw proud people, who carried their heads too high, become humbled and suffer misfortune and mortification. He may have thought of it as he began again to pick up the threads of his life in the bustling city of Philadelphia.

3

A PRINTER VERSUS HIS
COMPETITORS

ALTHOUGH FRANKLIN WAS KNOWN FOR HIS GENIAL disposition he also had a strongly competitive nature. He seemed to need an adversary to battle, whether it was the Puritan clergy of Boston in his youth, the proprietary governors of Pennsylvania in his middle age, or the British rulers in his later years. His weapon was his pen, supported by his keen mind and neverfailing sense of humor.

When young Franklin entered the printing business in Philadelphia he had to compete with men already established in the trade. Not only did he ply his trade with diligence, but he took on his competitors as adversaries, lampooning them in print and making them appear ridiculous. The public was entertained and the young printer prospered. The first competitor to feel the bite of Franklin's wit was his former employer Samuel Keimer.

Keimer had treated Franklin badly, having exploited him and publicly humiliated him, so as soon as Ben was financially able he left Keimer and set up shop for himself. He conceived as his main project putting out a newspaper to rival the *American Weekly Mercury,* published by the other Philadelphia printer, Andrew Bradford. Unfortunately Franklin made the mistake of confiding his plans to a former associate at Keimer's, who reported them to Keimer. As a result Keimer rushed in to print with his own newspaper, dashing Franklin's plans, since Philadelphia in 1728 could not support three newspapers. Franklin retaliated with his pen, as he commented in his *Autobiography:* "I resented this; and, to counteract them, as I could not yet begin our paper, I wrote several pieces of entertainment for Bradford's paper under the title of 'The Busy Body'. By this means the attention of the publick was fixed on that paper, and Keimer's proposals, which we burlesqued and ridiculed, were disregarded." Bradford must have appreciated Franklin's contributions, for Keimer had attacked the *Mercury* in the advertisement for his new paper, saying it was wretchedly performed, a reproach to the province, and a scandal to the very name of printing. In contrast, Keimer had promised his paper would "please all and offend none."

Just before he began the Busy Body series, Franklin impersonated a woman, as he had previously done in the Dogood Papers and took a couple of written blasts at Keimer. Being no newspaperman, Keimer had tried to keep his columns filled by reprinting material from an encyclopedia, and beginning alphabetically, he had unwittingly printed an article on abortion. This article produced letters from two indignant women of Franklin's invention, Martha Careful and Caelia Shortface, who were outraged at Keimer's immodesty. In a letter dated January 24, 1729, Martha warned the blundering editor of the *Gazette* that "if he proceed further to expose the secrets of our sex in that audacious manner . . . I say if he publish any more of that kind . . . my sister Molly and myself, with some others, are resolved to run the hazard of taking him by the beard . . . and making an example of him for his immodesty." The letter by Miss Shortface promised Keimer; "If thou proceed any further in that scandalous manner, we intend very soon to have thy right ear for it."

If the Busy Body essays were intended to provoke Keimer they were successful. He published several pieces in his paper attacking and ridiculing the Busy Body:

> "You think there's no one can be smarter,
> But now you'll find, you've caught a Tartar.
> What a confounded noise and racket
> There is about your weekly pacquet?
> You hinted at me in your paper,
> Which now has made me draw my rapier.
> With scornful eye, I see your hate,
> And pity your unhappy fate:"

Contrary to Keimer's forecast, the unhappy fate was his own. Whether the Busy Body papers had the punishing effect on Keimer's papers that Franklin thought, or whether Keimer's own inept management was responsible, the result was the same. Before the year was out Keimer's *Gazette* failed and Franklin bought it for a small sum.

Under Keimer, the *Gazette* never had more than 90 subscribers. To succeed, the readership had to be greatly increased. Toward that end Franklin gave the newspaper good business management, improved editing, and a new element that was to become his trademark, wit and humor. Now that Keimer was gone, Franklin's competitive spirit sought a new target for his barbs. The publisher of the *Mercury* was the natural assailant, thus Bradford and his paper were sighted in the *Gazette's* humor-loaded cannons.

After Franklin bought the *Gazette* from Keimer he began his effort to build its circulation to compete with Bradford's *Mercury*. He prominently displayed his slogan, "the freshest advices [news] foreign and domestick," but this boast was soon challenged by a pretended correspondent named Memory. "As you sometimes . . . correct the Publick, you ought . . . patiently to receive of public correction," he wrote.

Memory complained that Franklin was not living up to his promise to print only fresh news in his paper:

> My quarrel against you is, your practice of publishing under the notion of news, old transactions which I suppose you hope we have forgot. For Instance, in your Numb. 699, you tell us from London of July 20, that the losses of our merchants are laid before the Congress of Soissons, by Mr. Stanhope, etc., and that Admiral Hopson died the 8th of May last. Whereas 'tis certain, there has been no Congress at Soissons nor any where else these three years at least; nor could Admiral Hopson possibly die in May last, unless he has made a resurrection since his death in 1728. And in your Numb. 670., among other articles of equal antiquity, you tell us a long story of a murder and robbery perpetrated on the person of Mr. Nath. Bostock, which I have read word for word not less than four years since in your own paper. Are these your freshest Advices foreign and domestick? I insist that you insert this in your next, and let us see how you justify yourself.

Franklin, the publisher, then defended himself against Memory's charges:

I need not say more in vindication of my self against this charge, than that the letter is evidently wrong directed, and should have been To the Publisher of the Mercury: Inasmuch as the Numb. of my paper is not yet amounted to 669, nor are those old articles any where to be found in the *Gazette,* but in the *Mercury* of the two last weeks. I may however say something in his excuse, *viz.,* that 'tis not to be always expected there should happen just a full Sheet of New occurrences for each week; and that the oftener you are told a good thing, the more likely you will be to remember it.

At another time Franklin told the readers of the *Gazette:*

When Mr. Bradford publishes after us, and, has occasion to take an article or two out of the *Gazette,* which he is always welcome to do, he is desired not to date his paper a day before ours, (as last week in the case of the letter containing Kelsey's speech, etc.) lest distant readers should imagine we take from him, which we always carefully avoid.

In another letter to his paper, Franklin assumed the role of a correspondent who decided to reveal his name to the public.

"Mr. Franklin, I am the author of a copy of verses in the last *Mercury.* It was my real intention [to] appear open, and not basely with my vizard on, attack a man who had fairly [been] unmasked. Accordingly I subscribed my name at full length, in my manuscript sent to my Brother B——d [Bradford] but he, for some incomprehensible reason, inserted the two initial letters only, *viz.* B. L. 'Tis true, every syllable of the performance discovers me to be the author, but as I meet with much censure on the occasion, I request you to inform the publick, that I did not desire my Name should be concealed: and that the remaining Letters are, O, C, K, H, E, A, D."

The competition between Franklin and Bradford extended beyond the newspaper business. As printers they sought additional outlets for their work and within the same week both started magazines, the first magazines to be published in America. Once again, as with Keimer, Franklin's intention to begin a new venture was revealed to his competitor, Bradford, who then beat him into print by three days. The controversy raged between Franklin and John Webbe, editor of Bradford's magazine, whom Franklin accused of violating his confidence to Bradford in order to get a lucrative job writing for Bradford's magazine. Determined to win this new competition for what was only a limited market, Franklin priced his *General Magazine* lower than Bradford's *American Magazine*. Bradford retaliated by claiming that his price was higher because he was printing original articles, not reprinting "rubbish and sweepings." Franklin apparently was stung by this criticism and returned to the battle with vigor, employing his old weapon of ridicule. With doggerel verse, Franklin painted Bradford as a bungling, comic Irishman speaking in a thick brogue. Bradford was neither Irish nor an immigrant, and Franklin had nothing against Irishmen. But Franklin was trying to create a figure to be laughed at and the dim-witted, tipsy Irishman was a convenient stock character of the period to provide the needed image. The poem, which is in direct response to Bradford's asking his readers to try the more economical yearly rate, contains lines such as these mocking a thick brogue:

> Prishe shingle one shilling: but shubscribe for a year
> You shall have it sheaper, at the shame prishe, Honey dear.

If the poetry had its shortcomings, it should be mentioned that Franklin had apologized in advance. In his preface he stated: "The Reader, I hope will excuse the want of smoothness in my verses, the Pegasus I ride being a hobbling jade and a trotter." Heeding his father's stern advice following the youthful hawking of his blood-tingling poetry on pirates, Franklin rarely returned to that medium. There were some exceptions, as in the several cases of doggerel in *Poor Richard's Almanack*.

This almanac was another of Franklin's ventures to expand his business. Almanacs were popular in colonial America, often being the only reading matter in the homes other than the Bible. Bradford printed four almanacs, including Titan Leed's *American Almanac*, which was the most popular in Pennsylvania. Until 1732, Franklin printed two almanacs, those of Godfrey and Jerman, when these philomaths (almanac writers) gave their printing to Bradford. Franklin had given some thought to publishing an almanac of his own and this action by Godfrey and Jerman triggered his plans. Through his impersonation of Richard Saunders Franklin was able to continue his entertaining and profitable duel with his competitors.

4

POOR RICHARD'S ALMANACK

FEW PEOPLE HAVE SEEN OR READ *Poor Richard's Almanack,* yet many know sayings that it made famous. The first almanac was announced in December, 1732, as having been written by Richard Saunders, astrologer, and printed by B. Franklin. Poor Richard Saunders was a fictitious character, a secret Franklin kept from the public for a number of years. This almanac was different from its competitors. Some almanacs had a religious or political bias, something Franklin strictly avoided. Some almanacs contained literary material, others humor. The *Poor Robin Almanac,* which influenced Franklin, contained droll nonsense such as events of the fantastic year 1057, when "there were no cockolds" and "young maids were as cold as cow-cumbers." It told of an invention for detecting a Leicestershire man, namely, "taking him by the shoulder and shaking him as you would shake a pear tree, and if the beans rattle in his belly; then he is a Leicestershire man, else not."

Poor Richard became known for its proverbs, its wise and witty sayings and poems which Franklin stuffed in between the lines concerning eclipses, weather, etc. Franklin told his readers: "Besides the astronomical calculations, and other things usually contained in Almanacks, I have constantly interspersed moral sentences, prudent maxims, and wise sayings . . . to leave strong and lasting impressions . . . on young persons, whereby they may receive benefit as long as they live, when both Almanack and Almanack-maker have been long forgotten.'' And he explains that the purpose of his humor is also to serve the young: ''If I now and then insert a joke or two . . . my apology is, that . . . their . . . light airy minds may peruse the rest, and so are struck by . . . more weight and momentum.'' In this apology Franklin is paying lip service to the prevailing Puritan principle that humor for mere entertainment is not acceptable; but in actual fact, humor was enjoyed for its own sake by the adults who paid for the almanac as well as their children, and Franklin capitalized on that. In another edition he apologized in a different manner: ''And be not thou disturbed, O grave and sober reader, if among the many serious sentences in my book, thou findest me trifling now and then, and talking idly. In all the dishes I have hitherto cooked for thee, there is solid meat enough for thy money. There are scraps from the table of wisdom, that will if well digested, yield strong nourishment to thy mind. But sqeamish stomachs cannot eat without pickles; which 'tis true are good for nothing else, but they provoke an appetite.'' Franklin was generous in his servings of pickles and they helped to provoke a keen appetite for his almanac.

The almanac was an instant success. It captured the reader's imagination with its engaging characters, Richard and Bridget Saunders, and its hoax on Franklin's competitor in almanacs, Titan Leeds. But before they saw the almanac, the readers of the *Pennsylvania Gazette* had their curiosity piqued by this startling advertisement:

> JUST PUBLISHED, FOR 1733: POOR RICHARD: AN ALMANACK containing the Lunations, Eclipses, Planets Motions and Aspects, Weather, Sun and Moon's rising and setting, Highwater, &c. besides many pleasant and witty Verses, Jests and Sayings, Author's Motive of Writing, Prediction of the Death of his friend Mr. Titan Leeds, Moon no Cuckold, Batchelor's Folly, Parson's Wine and Baker's Pudding, Short Visits, Kings and Bears, New Fashions, Game for Kisses, Katherin's Love, Different Sentiments, Signs of a Tempest, Death a Fisherman, Conjugal Debate, Men and Melons, H. the Prodigal, Breakfast in Bed, Oyster Lawsuit, &c. by RICHARD SAUNDERS, Philomat. Printed and sold by B. Franklin, Price 3s. 6d. per Dozen. Of whom also may be had Sheet Almanacks at 2s.

How could a little pamphlet that fit in the pocket promise so much? The answer was that it gave in quality what it lacked in quantity. *Men and Melons* turned out to be a proverb, "Men and Melons are hard to know." *Kings and Bears* was "Kings and Bears often worry their keepers." And there were many more that were not advertised like, "A rich rogue, is like a fat hog, who never does good til as dead as a log"; "Ne'er take a wife till thou hast a house (and a fire) to put her in"; "The poor have a little, beggars none, the rich too much, enough not one"; "There is no little enemy" or "Cheese and salt meat, should be sparingly eat"; "Keep your mouth wet, feet dry." "Breakfast in Bed" was a poem that generated a response from Bridget Saunders, the peppery wife of the philomat. The intriguing Oyster lawsuit was a bit of satirical wit set to rhyme.

> Two beggars travelling along,
>   One blind, the other lame,
> Picked up an oyster on the way
>   To which they both laid claim:
> The matter rose so high, that they
>   Resolved to go to law,
> As often richer fools have done,
>   Who quarrel for a straw.
> A lawyer took it strait in hand,
>   Who knew his business was,
> To mind nor one nor t'other side,
>   But make the best o' th' cause;
> As always in the law's the case:
>   So he his judgment gave,
> And lawyer-like he thus resolved
>   What each of them should have:
>   Blind Plaintiff, lame Defendant, share
>   The friendly laws impartial care,
>   A shell for him, a shell for thee,
>   The middle is the lawyer's fee.

Franklin's almanac was useful, instructive, and entertaining. It was wise, clever, coy, comic, spicy, and vulgar. But it was never dull. It encouraged the poor colonists to work and save, but it also brought them much needed relaxation and laughter. It contained riddles, planting days, and holidays; it was a potpourri of what was utilitarian, inspirational, and amusing. And behind it, in the guise of the humble Poor Richard Saunders, was the skillful journalist Ben Franklin. Above a sketch in the almanac representing the zodiac the following lines appeared, giving a quaint self-portrait of the disguised author:

Here I sit naked, like some fairy elf,
My seat a pumpkin; I grudge no man's pelf;
Though I've no bread, nor cheese upon my shelf;
    I'll tell thee gratis, when it safe is,
To purge, to bleed, or cut, thy Cattle, or—thyself.

Most of the literary material in the almanac was not original. Franklin carefully collected his poems and aphorisms from anthologies and the published works of famous writers. From Montaigne he extracted, "The greatest monarch on the proudest throne, is obliged to sit on his own arse," and from La Rochefoucald, "There are no fools troublesome as those that have wit." No wonder the people liked *Poor Richard;* Franklin had distilled into it the world's wit and wisdom and added some of his own. He did not claim originality; he was satisfied to be a successful journalist and publisher. Referring to the verses which he put at the head of the page for each month Franklin says, "I need not tell that many of them are not of my own making . . . I know as well as thee, that I am no poet born; and it is a trade I never learnt, nor indeed could learn. If I make verses, 'Tis in spite—Of nature and my stars, I write. Why then should I give my readers bad Lines of my own. when good Ones of other people's are so plenty."

But Franklin did more than just borrow his material. He clipped it, expanded it, revised it, and adapted it for his clientele. Regarding the old proverbs, he usually refined the syntax and improved the cadence: He changed "A man in passion rides a horse that runs away with him" to "A man in a passion rides a mad horse." He modified "As soon as men have understanding enough to find a fault, they have enough to see the danger of mending it" to "Men take more pains to mask than mend." He sharpened "Nor wife nor wine, nor horse ought to be praised" to "Never praise your Cyder, Horse, or bedfellow." He simplified "The woman who hearkens, and the town which treats, the one will yield, and the other will do," to "Neither a fortress or a maidenhead will hold out long after they begin to parley." He improved the image and rhythm of "A gloved cat was never a good hunter" in "The cat in gloves catches no mice." He personalized "He had a mouth for every matter" with "Henry Smatter has a mouth for every matter." He dramatized "The tongue talks at the head's cost" in "The tongue offends, and the ears get the cuffing." He expanded "A good friend is my nearest relation" to "Relation without friendship, friendship without power, power without will, will without virtue, are not worth a farto." He contracted "The greatest talkers are the least doers" to "Great talkers, little doers." He gave substance to "Slander would not stick, if it had not always something to lay hold of" in "Act uprightly, and despise calumny; dirt may stick to a mud wall, but not to polished marble." He made famous "Help thyself and God will help thee" by converting it to "God helps them that help themselves."

Sometimes he introduced rhyme in changing "Pride is scarce ever cured" to "Pride and the gout, are seldom cured throughout," and "A quiet conscience sleeps in thunder" to "A quiet conscience sleeps in thunder, but rest and guilt live far asunder." As in "Kings and Bears," we get a preview of Franklin's democratic leanings when he modified a saying relating to the wastefulness of royal courts, to "The King's cheese is half wasted in parings; but no matter, 'tis made of the people's milk."

One proverb, thought to be of Franklin's own making, appeared three times in different forms. In the 1740 almanac it appeared as "An empty bag cannot stand upright." In 1750, in hope of clarifying the meaning, he changed it to "Tis hard (but glorious) to be poor and honest. An empty sack can hardly stand upright; but if it does, 'tis a stout one." Finally in 1758 he reverted to a briefer version, "Tis hard for an empty Bag to stand upright."

Franklin did so well in improving maxims that it might be wished he had worked a little harder on this one that appeared in the 1736 Almanac: "Don't throw stones at your neighbor's, if your own windows are glass." Abraham Lincoln did improve on *Poor Richard's* "You may be too cunning for one, but not for all" with "You may fool all the people some of the time; you can even fool some of the people all the time; but you can't fool all of the people all of the time."

The almanac for 1739 contained an article headed "A True Prognostication," which Franklin modified from Rabelais. The latter's "Pantagruelian Prognostication" was a nonsense piece satirizing astrology, the Church, and life in France 200 years before *Poor Richard*. Franklin trimmed it and added some of his own predictions to make it suitable for his Pennsylvania audience. The predictions are divided into subjects, one being on eclipses and their unusual effect on life on earth. Franklin substituted for the Catholic religious references in Rabelais the strange effect on the speech of people in the American Colonies.

During the first visible Eclipse Saturn is retrograde: For which reason the crabs will go sidelong, and the ropemakers backward. The belly will wag before, and the a--- shall sit down first. Mercury will have his share in these affairs, and so confound the speech of people, that when a Pennsilvanian would say panther, he shall say painter. When a New Yorker thinks to say (this) he shall say (diss) and the People in New England and Cape May will not be able to say (cow) for their lives, but will be forced to say (keow) by a certain involuntary twist in the root of their tongues. No Connecticut man nor Marylander will be able to open his mouth this year, but (Sir) shall be the first or last syllable he pronounces, and sometimes both.

Of course, like the crabs that normally move sidelong and the rope makers who move backward in braiding their rope, Franklin has imitated the normal speech of the Pennsylvania Germans, the New York Dutch, and the New England Yankees. Under "Of the Diseases of the Year," Franklin agrees with the physician Rabelais that old age " 'twill be incurable this year, because of the years past," that whole flocks of sheep will go to pot, and the worst disease of all will be "a certain most horrid, dreadful, malignant, catching, perverse and odious malady . . . lacko'mony." But in America, where farmers grow corn, Franklin forsees pathological behavior, "and towards fall some people will be seized with an unaccountable inclination to roast and eat their own ears." On the topic, "the conditions in some countries," Rabelais gives occurrences expected in many places from Saxony to Sicily, but Franklin substitutes a weather report for America:

I foresee an universal drougth this year thro' all the Northern Colonies. Hence there will be dry rice in Carolina, dry tobacco in Virginia and Maryland, dry bread in Pennsylvania and New York; and, in New England, dry fish and dry doctrine. Dry throats there will be every-where; but then how pleasant it will be to drink cool cyder!

The maxims of *Poor Richard* and the life of Franklin as told in his autobiography had a tremendous influence on the lives of aspiring Americans in the first century of the republic that was to come. It was a century of great development and great opportunity for the economically repressed of many lands. The people sought in Franklin's example and in his proverbs the formula for the success that he had achieved. They embraced and emphasized those maxims dealing with diligence, perseverance, frugality, and thrift. But in the 20th Century, with the achievement of greater national affluence, Franklin has been vigorously attacked for epitomizing these same bourgeois qualities. He has been disparagingly called "the patron saint of bank accounts," and the novelist D. H. Lawrence referred to him as a "snuff-colored little man," without soul or spirit. These characterizations are grossly inaccurate and unfair. They represent a narrow view of a very broad man, based upon a limited selection of the Almanac like "The Way to Wealth," or "Father Abraham's Speech," as it was sometimes called. This appeared in the 1758 Almanac and is a story that incorporates most of the maxims on prudence and industry used in earlier almanacs. It was a tremendous success and was reprinted many times, whereas the almanacs themselves were not reproduced and became worn out, lost, and obscure, thus giving the impression that "The Way to Wealth" was representative of *Poor Richard* and Franklin. In a jocular sketch on Franklin, Mark Twain complained that through his aphorisms and maxims Franklin became the enemy of all boys, whose fathers wanted them to strictly live up to the rules in them. If a boy wanted to spin his top after his work was done, Twain joshed, his father quotes "Procrastination is the thief of time." If the boy does a virtuous action, he never gets anything for it, because *Poor Richard* said "Virtue is its own reward."

Poor Richard's maxims dealt with a great many aspects of life and were not employed by Franklin to propagate any narrow philosophy. In fact, many proverbs are even contradictory. Compare "Avarice and Happiness never saw each other, how then should they become acquainted" (1734), with "Nothing but money, is sweeter than honey" (1735); "Never spare the parson's wine or the baker's pudding" (1733), with "Deny self for self's sake" (1735); "Do good to thy friend to keep him, to thy enemy to gain him" (1734), with "Many foxes grow grey, but few grow good" (1749); "Sloth and silence are a fool's virtues" (1735), with "None preaches better than the ant, and she says nothing" (1736); "He that can take rest is greater than he that can take cities" (1737), with "Lost time is never found again" (1748); A house without a woman and firelight is like a body without soul or sprite (1733), with "He that takes a wife takes care" (1736); "He does not possess wealth; it possesses him" (1734), with "An empty bag cannot stand upright" (1740); "An egg today is better than a hen tomorrow" (1734), with "He that can have patience, can have what he will" (1736).

It is true that in *Poor Richard* Franklin did encourage his readers to strive for success in their occupations by early rising—"The sleeping fox catches no poultry. Up! Up!," and steady work; "Little strokes fell great oaks," but he did not forget that there was another side to life, "The Muses love the Morning." Certain occupations received special attention. Doctors and lawyers got a goodnatured drubbing from *Poor Richard*. Franklin had great respect for these learned professionals and many were to become his closest friends, but no matter, they were fair game for his shots: "God heals, and the doctor takes the fees"; "He's a fool that makes his doctor his heir"; "Beware of the young doctor and the old barber".

> Whimsical Will once fancy'd he was ill,
> The doctors called, who thus examined Will;
> *How is your appetite?* O, as to that
> I eat right heartily, you see I'm fat.
> *How is your sleep anights?* 'Tis sound and good;
> I eat, drink, sleep as well as e'er I could.
> *Well,* says the doctor, clapping on his hat;
> *I'll give you something shall remove all that.*

"There's more old drunkards than old doctors." (1736) "He's the best physician that knows the worthlessness of the most medicines" (1733).

> Honest men often go to law for their right; when wise men would sit down with the wrong, supposing the first loss least. In some countries the course of the courts is so tedious, and the Expense so high, that the Remedy, Justice, is worse than, Injustice, the Disease. In my Travels I once saw a sign call'd The Two Men at Law; One of them was painted on one side, in a melancholy posture, all in rags, with this scroll, I have lost my cause. The other was drawn capering for Joy, on the other side, with these words, I have gain'd my suit; but he was stark naked.

"A countryman between two lawyers, is like a fish between two cats" (1737). "God works wonders now and then; Behold! a lawyer an honest man!" (1733). "A good lawyer, a bad neighbor" (1737). Judges and ministers got some buffeting as well.

> Certainlie these things agree,
> The priest, the lawyer, and death all three:
> Death takes both the weak and the strong.
> The lawyer takes from both right and wrong,
> And the priest from living and dead has his fee.

"Lawyers, preachers, and tomtits eggs, there are more of them hatched than come to perfection" (1734).

A Farmer once made a complaint to a judge,
My bull, if it please you, Sir, owing a grudge,
Belike to one of your good worship's cattle,
Has slain him out-right in a mortal battle:
I'm sorry at heart because of the action,
And want to know how must be made satisfaction.
Why, you must give me your bull, that's plain
Says the judge, or pay me the price of the slain.
But I have mistaken the case, Sir, says John,
The dead bull I talk of, and please you, 's my own:
And yours is the beast that the mischief has done.
The judge soon replies with a serious face:
Say you so; then this accident alters the case.

But *Poor Richard* has some serious advice too, like "Don't misinform your doctor nor your lawyer" (1737).

Franklin was especially sensitive to visitors who overstayed their leave. He observed, "Fish and visitors stink in 3 days" (1736); "After three days men grow weary, of a wench, a guest, and weather rainy," and "Visit your Aunt, but not every Day; and call at your Brother's, but not every night." He had a similar distaste for garrulousness. "He that speaks much, is much mistaken." "Here comes the orator! With his flood of words and his drop of reason." "Speak and speed: the close mouth catches no flies." "Here comes glib-tongue: who can outflatter a dedication; and lie, like ten epitaphs."

He spoke of hope: "Hope and a Red-Rag, are Baits for Men and Mackerel" (1742). "He that lives upon Hope, dies farting" (1736). A less breezy version of the latter appeared in 1758 in Father Abraham's Speech in which the last word is changed to "fasting".

He spoke of youth and old age and death:

Youth is pert and positive, Age modest and doubting: So ears of corn when young and light, stand bolt upright, but hang their heads when weighty, full, and ripe.

"Old boys have their playthings as well as young ones, the difference is only in the price" (1752).

What death is, dost thou ask of me;
Till dead I do not know;

> Come to me when thou hear'st I'm dead;
>   Then what 'tis I shall show.
> To die's to cease to be, it seems,
>   So Learned Seneca did think;
> But we've philosophers of modern date,
>   Who say 'tis death to cease to drink.

"If the wind blows on you thro' a hole, make your will and take care of your soul" (1736), and in 1738, one that Franklin quoted throughout his life and tried to live up to:

> "If you would not be forgotten
> As soon as you are dead and rotten,
> Either write things worth reading,
> Or do things worth the writing."

He even spoke of teeth and toothache: "Love and toothache have many cures, but none infallible, except possession and dispossession" (1751). "Sal laughs at everything you say. Why? Because she has fine teeth" (1735). "Maids of America, who gave you bad teeth? Hot Soupings and frozen apples" (1736). "Hot things, sharp things, sweet things, cold things all rot the teeth, and make them look like old things" (1734). But as in the example of his two characters, Poor Richard and Bridget, the theme that received the most attention and provided the most entertainment was the battle of the sexes. Franklin neither favored nor spared either sex in this eternal contest.

> On his death-bed poor Lubin lies;
>   His spouse is in despair;
> With frequent sobs, and mutual cries,
>   They both express their care.
> A diff'rent cause, says Parson Sly,
>   The same effect may give;
> Poor Lubin fears that he shall die;
>   His wife, that he may live.

"Keep your eyes wide open before marriage, half shut afterwards" (1738).

> Dick told his spouse, he durst be bold to swear,
> Whate'er she prayed for, heaven would thwart her prayer:
> Indeed! says Nell, 'tis what I'm pleased to hear;
> For now I'll pray for your long life, my dear.

"Are Women Books? says Hodge, then would mine were an Almanack, to change her every year" (1737).

> Good Death, said a woman, for once be so kind
> To take me, and leave my dear husband behind,
> But when Death appear'd with a sour grimace,
> The woman was dashed at his thin hatchet face;
> So she made him a courtsey, and modestly sed,
> If you come for my husband, he lies there in bed.

"Let thy maidservant be faithful, strong, and homely" (1736).

> Luke, on his dying bed, embraced his Wife,
> And begged one favour: Swear, my dearest life,
> Swear, if you love me, never more to wed,
> Nor take a second husband to your bed.
> Anne dropt a tear. You know, my dear, says she,
> Your least desires have still been laws to me;
> But from this oath, I beg you'd me excuse;
> For I'm already promis'd to J——n H——s. [John Hughes (?)]

"One good husband is worth two good wives; for the scarcer things are the more they're valued" (1742).

> Sam had the worst wife that a man could have,
> Proud, lazy, sot, could neither get nor save,
> Eternal scold she was, and what is worse,
> The D——l burn thee, was her common curse.
> Forbear, quoth Sam, that fruitless curse so common,
> He'll not hurt me who've married his kinswoman.

"He that whines for Glass without G, Take away L and that's he" (1746).

> Sam's Wife provoked him once; he broke her crown,
> The surgeon's bill amounted to five pound;
> This blow (she brags) has cost my husband dear,
> He'll ne'er strike more. Sam chanced to over-hear.
> Therefore before his wife the bill he pays,
> And to the surgeon in her hearing says:
> Doctor, you charge five pound, here e'en take ten;
> My wife may chance to want your help again.

But *Poor Richard* also said "A good wife and health, is a man's best wealth" (1746), and:

Good women are like stars in darkest night,
Their virtuous actions shining as a light
To guide their ignorant sex, which oft times fall,
And falling oft, turns diabolical.
Good women sure are angels on the earth,
Of those good angels we have had a dearth;
And therefore all you men that have good wives,
Respect their virtues equal with your lives.

If you prefer perplexing puzzles to pithy platitudes, the pleasing pauper does his best for you. Under the title, Enigmatical Prophesies, *Poor Richard* in 1736 tries to test you with these three riddles:

1. Before the middle of this year, a wind at N. East will arise, during which the water of the sea and rivers will be in such a manner raised, that great part of the towns of Boston, Newport, New York, Philadelphia, the low lands of Maryland and Virginia, and the Town of Charlstown in South Carolina, will be under water. Happy will it be for the sugar and salt, standing in the cellars of those places, if there be tight roofs and ceilings overhead; otherwise, without being a conjurer, a Man may easily foretell that such commodities will receive damage.

2. About the middle of the year, great numbers of vessels fully laden will be taken out of the ports aforesaid, by a power with which we are not now at war, and whose forces shall not be descried or seen either coming or going. But in the end this may not be disadvantageous to those places.

3. However, not long after, a visible army of 20000 Musketers will land, some in Virginia and Maryland, and some in the lower counties on both sides of Delaware, who will overrun the country, and sorely annoy the inhabitants: But the air in this climate will agree with them so ill towards winter, that they will die in the beginning of cold weather like rotten sheep, and by Christmas the inhabitants will get the better of them.

After waiting a year with baited breath, you are not to be disappointed for, as promised, the Almanac for 1737 brings you the solutions, to wit:

1. The water of the sea and rivers is raised in vapors by the sun, is formed into clouds in the air, and thence descends in rain. Now when there is rain overhead, (which frequently happens when the wind is at N.E.) the cities and places on the earth below, are certainly under water.

2. The power with which we were not then at war, but which, it was said, would take many full laden vessels out of our ports before the end of the year, is the wind, whose forces also are not descried either coming or going.

3. The army which it was said would land in Virginia, Maryland, and the Lower Counties on Delaware, were not musketeers with guns on their shoulders as some expected; but their namesakes, in pronunciation, tho' truly spelt moschitos, armed only with a sharp sting. Every one knows they are fish before they fly, being bred in the water; and therefore may properly be said to land before they become generally troublesome.

Franklin's fame for his *Poor Richard* spread beyond America's shores. Years later when he arrived in France as an American emissary during the Revolutionary War, Franklin discovered that his fame had preceded him. The French honored him both for his discoveries in electricity and his wisdom in *Poor Richard*. They compared him to Socrates and publicly applauded him with their own beloved Voltaire. The warship the French gave Admiral John Paul Jones they called "Le Bonhomme Richard" which was their non-literal translation of *Poor Richard*. The nuggets of wisdom and humor from the almanacs endeared Franklin to all ranks of Frenchmen from peasant to aristocrat.

Here is a sampler of Poor Richard's maxims, published in the course of 25 years, from 1738 to 1758:

A fat kitchen, a lean will.
He that drinks fast, pays slow.
He that lies down with dogs, shall rise up with fleas.
To lengthen thy life, lessen thy meals.
You cannot pluck roses without fear of thorns, nor enjoy a fair wife
    without danger of horns.
As charms are nonsense, nonsense is a charm.
A learned blockhead is a greater blockhead than an ignorant one.
Marry your son when you will, but your daughter when you can.
Where there's marriage without love, there will be love without mar-
    riage.
What one relishes, nourishes.
Sam's religion is like a Cheddar cheese, 'tis made of the milk of one
    and twenty parishes.
Onions can make even heirs and widows weep.
There's many witty men whose brains can't fill their bellies.
A ship under sail and a big-bellied woman, are the handsomest two
    things that can be seen common.

Three may keep a secret, if two of them are dead.

Keep thy shop, and thy shop will keep thee.

He that has neither fools, whores, nor beggars among his kindred, is the son of a thunder gust.

She that paints her face, thinks of her tail.

Three things are men most liable to be cheated in, a horse, a wig, and a wife.

Now I've a sheep and a cow, everybody bids me good morrow.

Lovers, travellers, and poets, will give money to be heard.

If you know how to spend less than you get, you have the philosopher's stone.

A traveller should have a hog's nose, deer's legs, and an ass's back.

There are no ugly loves, nor handsome prisons.

Love, cough, and smoke, can't well be hid.

Three good meals a day is bad living.

There are three faithful friends, an old wife, an old dog, and ready money.

He that would have a short Lent, let him borrow money to be repaid at Easter.

Eat to please thyself, but dress to please others.

He that falls in love with himself, will have no rivals.

When man and woman die, as poets sing, his heart's the last part moves, her last, the tongue.

A wolf eats sheep now and then, ten thousands are devoured by men.

Thou hadst better eat salt with philosophers of Greece, than sugar with the courtiers of Italy.

Quarrels could never last long, if on one side only lay the wrong.

He that speaks ill of the mare, will buy her.

Money and good manners make the gentlemen.

Ill company is like a dog who dirts those most that he loves best.

He that drinks his cider alone, let him catch his horse alone.

Light-heel'd mothers make leaden-heeled daughters.

Many complain of their memory, few of their judgment.

The tongue is ever turning to the aching tooth.

A life of leisure, and a life of laziness, are two things.

When the well's dry, we know the worth of water.

A mob's a monster: heads enough but no brains.

Lost time is never found again.

If Jack's in love, he's no judge of Jill's beauty.

Nine men in ten are suicides.

If your head is wax, don't walk in the sun.

Having been poor is no shame, but being ashamed of it is.

Many would live by their wits, but break for want of stock.

There are three things extremely hard, steel, a diamond and to know one's self.

Tim was so learned, that he could name a Horse in nine languages; so ignorant, that he bought a cow to ride on.

Discontented minds, and fevers of the Body are not cured by changing beds or businesses.

Pray don't burn my house to roast your eggs.

Many a man would have been worse, if his estate had been better.

Most people return small favours, acknowledge middling ones, and repay great ones with ingratitude.

'Tis easier to suppress the first desire, than to satisfy all that follow it.

For want of a nail the shoe is lost; for want of a horse the rider is lost.

Success has ruined many a man.

If you have no honey in your pot, have some in your mouth.

A pair of good ears will drain a hundred tongues.

If you'd know the value of money, go and borrow some.

The bell calls others to church, but itself never minds the sermon.

Love your neighbor, yet don't pull down your hedge.

If you would be loved, love, and be lovable.

Where there is hunger, law is not regarded; and where law is not regarded, there will be hunger.

Laws too gentle are seldom obeyed; too severe seldom executed.

Work as if you were to live 100 years, pray as if you were to die tomorrow.

The way to be safe, is never to be secure.

When you're an anvil, hold you still, when you're a hammer, strike your fill.

Half the truth is often a great lie.

"With the old Almanack and the old year, leave the old vices, tho' ever so dear," wrote *Poor Richard*. Franklin had a feeling of pride and satisfaction in his authorship of the almanacs. He told the reader, "I have constantly interspersed in every little vacancy, moral hints, wise sayings, and maxims of thrift, tending to impress the benefits arising from honesty, sobriety, industry, and frugality; which if thou hast duly observed, it is highly probable thou art wiser and richer many fold more than the pence my labours have cost thee." And as an extra benefit he adds: "Howbeit, I shall not therefore raise my price because thou art better able to pay."

5

RICHARD SAUNDERS AND
HIS WIFE BRIDGET

WHEN FRANKLIN BEGAN *Poor Richard's Almanack* he created not only an almanac but also its author. Franklin wanted a character to give the almanac a unique life and style and Poor Richard was to become the most famous of Franklin's string of *personae*. The name of the almanac was suggested by *Poor Robin's Almanac* and the name of Richard Saunders came from a 17th century astrologer and philomath. The character of "Poor" Richard was fashioned after that of the successful almanac publisher John Partridge, as described by Jonathan Swift in the Bickerstaff papers. According to the Bickerstaff account, Partridge on his death bed confesses his errors and pleads poverty as his excuse for hoodwinking the public via his almanac: He did it, he said, "to make my almanack sell, having a wife to maintain, and no other way to get my bread, for mending old shoes is a poor livelihood."

Each edition of *Poor Richard's Almanack* is introduced with a preface by the author. In the preface of the first edition, Franklin, writing as Richard Saunders, greets his readers and with unusual candor explains what prompted him into becoming a philomath.

Courteous Reader:
    I might in this place attempt to gain thy favour, by declaring that I write almanacks with no other view than that of the publick good; but in this I should not be sincere; and men are now a-days too wise

to be deceived by pretences how specious soever. The plain truth of the matter is, I am excessive poor, and my wife, good woman, is, I tell her, excessive proud; she cannot bear, she says, to sit spinning in her shift of tow [coarse linen], while I do nothing but gaze at the stars; and has threatned more than once to burn all my books and rattling-traps (as she calls my instruments) if I do not make some profitable use of them for the good of my Family. The printer has offered me some considerable share of the profits, and I have thus begun to comply with my dame's desire.

Indeed this motive would have had force enough to have made me publish an Almanack many years since, had it not been overpowered by my regard for my good friend and fellow student, Mr. Titan Leeds.

Saunders then predicts the death of his good friend and fellow student, Leeds, which frees him to go ahead with his plans for the almanac. He closes the preface with the statement: "The Buyer of my Almanack may consider himself, not only as purchasing an useful utensil, but as performing an act of charity, to his poor friend and servant, R. Saunders."

In this first preface (1733) Franklin gives us a glimpse of his two characters, the poor, henpecked astrologer and his stormy, domineering wife. Knowing these are fictitious characters we can be quietly amused, but imagine the effect of this preface on the unsuspecting colonists who believed Saunders was a real person. It is not surprising that the whole edition of *Poor Richard* sold out in one month and two extra editions had to be printed to meet the demand. Did success spoil Poor Richard Saunders? To find the answer we have to turn to the next year's almanac.

Your kind and charitable assistance last year, in purchasing so large an Impression of my *Almanacks*, has made my circumstances much more easy in the world, and requires my grateful acknowledgement. My wife has been enabled to get a pot of her own, and is no longer obliged to borrow one from a neighbour; not have we ever since been without something of our own to put in it. She has also got a pair of shoes, two new shifts, and a new warm petticoat; and for my part, I have bought a second-hand coat, so good that I am now not ashamed to go to town or be seen there. These things have rendered her temper so much more pacifick than it used to be, that I may say I have slept more, and more quietly within this last year than in the three foregoing years put together. Accept my hearty thanks therefore, and my sincere wishes for your health and prosperity.

I suppose in all honesty we would have to say that Saunders was not spoiled by his success. Who would deny him his second-hand coat or his wife a pot of her own? And Poor Richard is so grateful; he never forgets where his good fortune comes from.

> I must not omit here to thank the publick for the gracious and kind encouragement they have hitherto given me: But if the generous purchaser of my labours could see how often his Fi'-pence helps to light up the confortable fire, line the pot, fill the cup and make glad the heart of a poor man and an honest good old woman, he would not think his money ill laid out, tho' the Almanack of his friend and servant, R. SAUNDERS were one half blank paper.

One may notice how Franklin incorporates the complimentary close and signature of a letter into the text. He liked to do this as a change from the formality and monotony of the normal form.

Even after years of successful publication Saunders repeats the old script, and plays the same part of the humble, grateful servant of the public, but displaying the same disarming candor with regard to his self interest. Richard refers to his wife as the gracious, peaceful, silent Lady Bridget. None of these adjectives apply to the scrappy, outspoken Bridget Saunders. In the first almanac Richard featured a poem condemning the wife who takes her breakfast in bed, spends the morning dressing her head, and sits at dinner like a maiden bride. The poem ends with the lament:

> God in his mercy may do much to save her.
> But what a case is he that shall have her.

In the next almanac the philomath inserts verse from Mrs. Bridget Saunders, "my Dutchess," as he calls her, in answer to that above. This verse bemoans the man who for the sake of drink neglects his trade, spends each night in taverns till late, and disregards his starving family. It concludes with:

> God in his mercy may do much to save him,
> But, woe to the poor wife, whose lot it is to have him.

It is obvious Bridget is no quaking Nellie but a fighter for her rights and those of her sex. This observation is confirmed in the almanac for 1738 where Mistress Saunders substitutes her own preface for that of her husband.

Dear Readers:

My good man set out last week for Potowmack, to visit an old stargazer of his acquaintance, and see about a little place for us to settle and end our days on. He left the copy of his Almanack sealed up, and bid me send it to the press. I suspected something, and therefore as soon as he was gone, I opened it, to see if he had not been flinging some of his old skitts at me. Just as I thought, so it was. And truly he had put into his preface that his Wife Bridget— was this, and that, and t'other. What a peasecods! Cannot I have a little fault or two, but all the country must see it in print! They have already been told, at one time that I am proud, another time that I am loud, and that I have got a new petticoat, and abundance of such kind of stuff; and now, forsooth! all the world must know, that Poor Dick's wife has lately taken a fancy to drink a little tea now and then. A mighty matter, truly, to make a song of! 'Tis true, I had a little tea of a present from the printer last year; and what, must a body throw it away? In short, I thought the preface was not worth a printing, and so I fairly scratched it all out, and I believe you'll like our Almanack never the worse for it.

Upon looking over the months, I see he has put in abundance of foul weather this year; and therefore I have scattered here and there, where I could find room, some fair, pleasant, sunshiny, &c. for the good-women to dry their clothes in. If it does not come to pass according to my desire I have shown my good-will, however; and I hope they'll take it in good part.

I had a design to make some other corrections; and particularly to change some of the verses that I don't very well like; but I have just now unluckily broke my spectacles; which obliges me to give it to you as it is, and conclude, Your loving friend,

BRIDGET SAUNDERS

Some of those verses Bridget didn't like appear to have had her in mind.

> Dick's wife was sick, and posed the doctor's skill,
> Who differed how to cure the inveterate ill.
> Purging the one prescribed. No, quoth another,
> That will do neither good nor harm, my brother.
> Bleeding's the only Way; 'twas quick replyed,

> That's certain death;—But e'en let Dick decide.
> "Ise no great skill," quoth Richard, "by the rood [cross];
> "But I think bleeding's like to do most good."

Dick was certainly not ready for a direct confrontation with Bridget, but in the 1739 almanac he slyly counterattacks with more verses.

> *On his late Deafness.*
> Deaf, giddy, helpless, left alone,
> To all my friends a burthen grown,
> No more I hear a great church bell,
> Than if it rang out for my knell:
> At thunder now no more I start,
> Than at the whispering of a f——t.
> Nay, what's incredible, alack!
> I hardly hear my Bridget's clack.

In an ironic piece pretending to be true prognostications for the year 1739, Saunders lists under the title "Of the Diseases This Year", . . . "the stone-blind shall see but very little; the deaf shall hear but poorly; and the dumb shan't speak very plain. And it's much, my Dame Bridget talks at all this year."

And again the following year, the almanac contains reference to strained relations between Dick and his spouse.

> My sickly spouse, with many a sigh
> Once told me—Dicky I shall die:
> I grieved, but recollected strait,
> 'Twas bootless to contend with fate:
> So resignation to heaven's will
> Prepared me for succeeding ill;
> 'Twas well it did; for, on my life,
> 'Twas heaven's will to spare my wife.

By 1744 heaven's will may have changed, for Richard inserts in that almanac this brief epitaph:

> *Epitaph on a Scolding Wife by her Husband*
> Here my poor Bridget's corpse doth lie,
> She is at rest—and so am I.

Franklin's disguise as Richard Saunders could not last. Poor Richard had become so popular that people were curious about this clever man and his colorful wife. Where did they live? What did they look like? What church did they attend? The identity of Poor Richard was a mystery. There was even some speculation that he did not exist; that this almanac was really the work of the printer. Franklin never expected to win this game of tongue-in-cheek deception, but he played it for all the fun that was in it. Saunders attributed these rumors doubting his existence to his jealous competitors, maintaining earnestly that he did exist. In his preface for 1736 Saunders meets the issue head on.

> Loving Readers:
>
> Your kind acceptance of my former Labours, has encouraged me to continue writing, tho' the general approbation you have been so good as to favour me with, has excited the envy of some, and drawn upon me the malice of others. These ill-willers of mine, despited at the great reputation I gained by exactly predicting another man's death, have endeavoured to deprive me of it all at once in the most effectual manner, by reporting that I myself was never alive. They say in short, That there is no such a Man as I am; and have spread this notion so thoroughly in the country, that I have been frequently told it to my Face by those that don't know me. This is not civil treatment, to endeavour to deprive me of my very Being, and reduce me to a non-entity in the opinion of the publick. But so long as I know myself to walk about, eat, drink and sleep, I am satisfied that there is really such a man as I am, whatever they may say to the contrary: And the world may be satisfied likewise; for if there were no such man as I am, how is it possible I should appear publickly to hundreds of people, as I have done for several years past, in print? I need not, indeed, have taken any notice of so idle a report, if it had not been for the sake of my printer, to whom my enemies are pleased to ascribe my productions; and who it seems is as unwilling to father my offspring, as I am to lose the credit of it. Therefore to clear him entirely, as well as to vindicate my own honour, I make this publick and serious declaration, which I desire may be believed, to wit, That what I have written heretofore, and do now write, neither was nor is written by any other man or men, person or persons whatsoever. Those who are not satisfied with this must needs be very unreasonable.

It is of interest to observe that for this "sincere" appeal, Saunders has changed his salutation, Courteous Readers or Kind Readers, as in earlier and later almanacs, to Loving Readers. How could people doubt this poor man who so passionately asserted his being?

Six years later Poor Richard returned again to the same theme, this time arguing his right to privacy and explaining why he preferred to remain secluded from the rest of the people. Whether he still continued to convince or even confuse the public on this subject is very doubtful, but those who knew better enjoyed the pretense and elaborate masquerade that Franklin put on for their entertainment.

This is the ninth year of my endeavours to serve thee in the capacity of a calendar-writer. The encouragement I have met with must be ascribed, in a great measure, to your charity, excited by the open honest declaration I made of my poverty at my first appearance. This my Brother Philomaths could, without being conjurers, discover; and Poor Richard's success, has produced ye a Poor Will, and a Poor Robin; and no doubt Poor John, &c. will follow, and we shall all be in name what some folks say we are already in fact, A parcel of poor almanack makers. During the course of these nine years, what buffetings have I not sustained! The fraternity have been all in arms. Honest Titan, deceased, was raised, and made to abuse his old friend. Both authors and printers were angry. Hard names, and many, were bestowed on me. They denied me to be the author of my own works; declared there never was any such person; asserted that I was dead 60 Years ago; prognosticated my death to happen within a twelve month: with many other malicious inconsistences, the effects of blind passion, envy at my success; and a vain hope of depriving me (dear Reader) of thy wonted countenance and favour. *Who knows him?* they cry: *Where does he live?* But what is that to them? If I delight in a private life, have they any right to drag me out of my retirement? I have good reasons for concealing the place of my abode. 'Tis time for an old man, as I am, to think of preparing for his great remove. The perpetual teasing of both neighbours and strangers, to calculate nativities, give judgments on schemes, erect figures, discover thieves, detect horse-stealers, describe the route of run-aways and strayed cattle; the croud of visitors with a 1,000 trifling questions; Will my ship return safe? Will my mare win the race? Will her next colt be a pacer? When will my Wife die? Who shall be my husband, and how long first? When is the best time to cut hair, trim cocks, or sow sallad? These and the like impertinences I have now neither taste nor leisure for. I have had enough of 'em. All that these angry folks can say, will never provoke me to tell them where I live. I would eat my nails first.

In playing this game of identity, Saunders not only makes the case for his own existence, he takes care to keep himself and the printer, Mr. B. Franklin, separate and apart, as distinct personalities.

Some people observing the great yearly demand for my almanack, imagine I must by this time have become rich, and consequently ought to call myself Poor Dick no longer. But, the case is this, When I first begun to publish, the printer made a fair agreement with me for my copies, by virtue of which he runs away with the greatest part of the profit. However, much good may't do him; I do not grudge it him; he is a man I have a great regard for and I wish his profit ten times greater than it is. For I am dear Reader his, as well as thy affectionate friend,   R. SAUNDERS

When readers complain of errors in the almanac, Dick admits his own mistakes but makes no effort to cover up for the printer, who, after all, pockets most of the profit.

.   In my last, a few falts escaped; some belong to the author, but most to the printer: Let each take his share of the blame, confess, and amend for the future. In the second page of August, I mentioned 120 as the next perfect number to 28; it was wrong, 120 being no perfect number; the next to 28 we find to be 496. The first is 6; let the curious reader, fond of mathematical questions, find the fourth. In the 2d line of March, in some copies, the earth's circumference was said to be nigh 4,000, instead of 24,000 miles, the figure 2 being omitted at the beginning. This was Mr. Printer's fault; who being also somewhat niggardly of his vowels, as well as profuse of his consonants, put in one place, among the poetry, mad, instead of made, and in another wrapped, instead of warped; to the utter demolishing of all sense in those Lines, leaving nothing standing but the rhime. These, and some others, of the like kind, let the readers forgive, or rebuke him for, as to their wisdom and goodness shall seem meet: For in such cases the loss and damage is chiefly to the reader, who, if he does not take my sense at first reading, 'tis odds he never gets it; for ten to one he does not read my works a second time.

Printers indeed should be very careful how they omit a figure or a letter: For by such means sometimes a terrible alteration is made in the sense. I have heard that once, in a new edition of the *Common Prayer*, the following sentence, ''We shall all be changed in a moment, in the twinkling of an eye;'' by the omission of a single letter, became, ''We shall all be hanged in a moment, &c.'' to the no small surprise of the first congregation it was read to.

The playful Saunders even has the temerity to take a dig at the printer in a two-line witticism which he sneaks into the mix of aphorisms and verses in the body of the almanac.

> Ben beats his Pate, and fancies wit will come;
> But he may knock, there's nobody at home.

One of the most valued services provided by old almanacs was prediction of the weather. In the absence of modern scientific climatology, people depended on astrological signs as interpreted by the philomaths and reported for the year in their almanacs. The uncertainties of weather being what they are, even astrologers had difficulty in predicting it for a whole year in advance. Some couched their predictions in vagueness but Richard Saunders found a handy scapegoat in the printer.

> We modestly desire only the favourable allowance of a day or two before and a day or two after the precise day against which the weather is set; and if it does not come to pass accordingly, let the fault be laid upon the printer, who, 'tis very like, may have transposed or misplaced it, perhaps for the conveniency of putting in his holidays: And since, in spite of all I can say, people will give him great part of the credit of making my almanacks, 'tis but reasonable he should take some share of the blame.

While many of the educated people of the 18th century rejected astrology, it is likely that most of the almanac readers accepted it and considered the astrologer to be a highly skilled practitioner of a mysterious, ancient science. Although he makes his living practicing this occult profession in providing the expected weather predictions, it is evident that the puppeteer who pulls Saunders' strings is no true believer. While outwardly keeping a serious mien, he treats the subject of astrology with refreshing levity which, though apparent to his readers, is accepted by them with good humor. The canny Saunders discusses his weather prophecies and then unexpectedly reveals his secret methods and treats us to a peep through his telescope.

> Ignorant men wonder how we astrologers foretell the weather so exactly, unless we deal with the old black devil. Alas! 'tis as easy as pissing abed. For instance; The stargazer peeps at the heavens thro' a long glass: He sees perhaps Taurus or the great bull, in a mighty chase, stamping on the floor of his house, swinging his tail about, stretching out his neck, and opening wide his mouth. 'Tis natural from these appearances to judge that this furious bull is puffing, blowing, and roaring. Distance being considered, and time allowed for all this to come down, there you have wind and thunder. He

spies perhaps Virgo (or the Virgin); she turns her head round as it were to see if any body observed her; then crouching down gently, with her hands on her knees, she looks wistfully for a while right forward. He judges rightly what she's about: And having calculated the distance and allowed time for it's falling, finds that next spring we shall have a fine April shower. What can be more natural and easy than this?

Richard is particularly pleased to hear that his predictions of the weather give such general satisfaction. He claims that he takes such care in his calculations that not a single one of his predictions, whether it be snow, rain, hail, frost, fogs, wind or thunder but comes to pass punctually and precisely on the very day predicted. But he cautiously continues, "in some place or other on this little dimunitive globe of ours . . ." He takes care also in his calculations of astronomical events such as eclipses. In 1734 he announced two eclipses, the first April 22 at 5:18 a.m. and the second October 15 at 1:36 p.m. "Both of the sun and both, like Mrs. ——s's modesty, and old Neighbor Scrape-all's money, invisible. Or, like a certain storekeeper late of ——— County, Not to be seen in these parts." He pretends to bemoan the decline of astrology and blames this trend quite properly on the influence of the modern scientists like Newton, Halley, and Whiston. But Saunders gleefully reports that Whiston repented in his old age, and like the astrologers of old, interpreted remarkable astronomical signals to make great prophecies of wonders to come. Franklin spoons his satire with a large ladle. As a scientist, Franklin was careful in his own research not to mix his physics with metaphysics. *Poor Richard* comments on Whiston's predictions.

From these Astronomical Signs, he foretells those great events, that within 10 years from this Time, "the Millennium or 1000 years reign of Christ shall begin, there shall be a new heavens, and a new earth; there shall be no more an infidel in Christendom, . . . nor a gaming-table at Tunbridge!" When these predictions are accomplished, what glorious proofs they will be of the truth of our art? And if they happen to fail, there is no doubt but so profound an astronomer as Mr. Whiston, will be able to see other signs in the heavens, foreshowing that the conversion of infidels was to be postponed, and the Millennium adjourned. After these great things can any man doubt our being capable of predicting a little rain or sunshine? Reader, farewell, and make the best use of your years and

your almanacks, for you see, that according to Whiston, you may
have at most, but sixteen more of them.

As the years wear on, the prefaces contain fewer details of the
private lives of Mr. and Mrs. Richard Saunders. The preface of 1746
gives us our last glimpse of the now comfortable couple. In response
to the frequent questions, "Who is Poor Richard? Where does he live?
What is he?" Dick says, "Somewhat to ease your curiositie, take
these slight sketches of my Dame and me."

> Thanks to kind readers and a careful wife
> With plenty blessed, I lead an easy life;
> My business writing, hers to drain the mead
> Or crown the barren hill with useful shade;
> Press nectarous cyder from my loaded trees,
> Print the sweet butter, turn the drying cheese.
> Some books we read, tho' few there are that hit
> The happy point where wisdom joins with wit;

In reality the sketches more closely resemble the Franklins than
the Saunders. In later editions there is more practical information,
such as how to make wine from wild grapes and what timber to grow
for better fencing. There is an occasional travelogue to bring romance
to the routine lives of the hardworking provincials.

> We complain sometimes of hard winters in this country; but our
> winters will appear as summers, when compared with those that
> some of our countrymen undergo in the most northern British Co-
> lony on this continent. . . . Captain Middleton, a member of the
> Royal Society, who had made many voyages thither, and wintered
> there 1741–2, when he was in search of the North-West Passage to
> the South Sea, gives an account of it to that society, from which I
> have extracted these particulars.

Saunders then tells of the mysteries and unbelievable hardships of
life in the Hudson Bay territory where brandy and strong brine freeze
in 3 or 4 hours, fowl is preserved outdoors all winter with "feathers
on and guts in," and 4 or 5 hours after the fire in the house is out "the
inside walls and Bed-places will be 2 or 3 inches thick with ice, which
is every morning cut away with a hatchet," and innumerable hair-like
icicles form in the clothes and raise hard skin blisters. After pages of
ice and icicles, Dick snuggles up to his readers and says: "And now,
my tender reader, thou that shudderest when the wind blows a little at

N-West, and criest, 'Tis extrrrrream cohohold! 'Tis terrrrrible cohold! What dost thou think of removing to that delightful country? Or dost thou not rather chuse to stay in Pennsylvania, thanking God that He has caused thy Lines to fall in pleasant Places [see Psalms 16:6]."

It is easy to see why Poor Richard with his warmth and wit was such a welcome visitor in American homes. It really did not matter whether he was a phantom of the printer's versatile imagination or a real person jealously guarding his privacy. It has been said Franklin needed the comic, homely identity of Saunders in order to express himself. In spite of Franklin's intelligence and ability it was said "he never achieved that winning combination of peasant cunning, bourgeois prudence, and moral prestige that made Poor Richard so beloved of the people." That is like saying that the puppet, Charlie McCarthy, was much funnier than Edgar Bergen, the ventriloquist on whose lap he sat. Charlie should have been funnier—he was given all the lines. It is intimated that through the homespun Saunders, Franklin was able to give issue to his own philosophy without causing offense and opposition. In reality, Franklin was not so much selling a philosophy: he was trying to sell the almanac itself, and its sale extended from Pennsylvania to all the English colonies in America. If the people enjoyed the simple comedy of Richard Saunders, his troubles with his wife, the hijinks with his rivals, and his unorthodox methods of foretelling the weather, it can be certain that Franklin had as much pleasure bringing this entertainment to them.

There is an anecdote, not one of Franklin's, that purports to illustrate the reliance of the country people on the weather predictions. It is about a Philadelphia philomath, Somer, who had to face an irate customer when his prediction turned out to be inaccurate. A German farmer, his clothes soaked and dripping, came into Somer's shop furiously demanding compensation for damages. He had set out for the city with his produce early that morning. Having consulted the almanac he was assured the weather would be fair, so he did not cover the wagon nor wear a coat. When he was too far along to turn back it began to rain, then to pour without letup, and by the time the poor man reached the city he was nearly drowned and his produce was ruined. In his wrath he accused the philomath of selling him a false almanac. Somer was prepared for the challenge. He replied, "No, dear friend, be thou not angry with me, for although it was I that made the almanac, the Lord God made the weather."

6

THE LEEDS AFFAIR

IN FRANKLIN'S FIRST ALMANAC, *Poor Richard's Almanack* for 1733, he began by facetiously assailing his chief competitor in almanacs, Titan Leeds, and through him Leed's printer, Bradford. He did not actually attack Leeds; in fact, he pretended great friendship for his fellow philomath. He just predicted Leeds' death!

Franklin had found the idea for his prediction in an old copy of *The Spectator,* in which one Isaac Bickerstaff in his "Predictions for the Year 1708," had ridiculed astrologers and philomaths, terming them conjurers. Bickerstaff declared his own predictions would not be so purposely vague as to allow for any possible occurrence. His predictions would be clear and specific, as in the following case:

> My first prediction relates to Partridge, the Almanackmaker; I have consulted the Star of his Nativity by my own rules, and find he will infallibly die upon the 29th of March next, about eleven at night, of a raging fever; therefore I advise him to consider of it, and settle his affairs in time.

Just as Saunders was Franklin, so Bickerstaff was Jonathan Swift, the author of *Gulliver's Travels.* Partridge was a real philomath whose activities particularly annoyed Swift. According to Bickerstaff's next account, Partridge died of fever on the very day predicted, some four hours earlier than his prediction. Swift's practical joke was published in *The Spectator,* where years later young Franklin discovered it and thereafter kept it stored in his huge memory bank. Now, the temptation to try it on Titan Leeds was overwhelming. He succumbed to the temptation with obvious delight and anticipation.

Saunders explains that he would have published his almanac years before had it not been for this circumstance:

> my Regard for my good friend and fellow-student, Mr. Titan Leeds, whose interest I was extremely unwilling to hurt: But this obstacle (I am far from speaking it with pleasure) is soon to be removed, since inexorable death, who was never known to respect merit, has already prepared the mortal dart, the fatal sister has already extended her destroying shears, and that ingenious man must soon be taken from us. He dies, by my calculation made at his request, on Oct. 17. 1733. 3 ho. 29 m. p.m. at the very instant of the ♂ of ☉ and ☿: By his own calculation he will survive till the 26th of the same month. This small difference between us we have disputed whenever we have met these 9 years past; but at length he is inclinable to agree with my Judgment: Which of us is most exact, a little time will now determine. As therefore these Provinces may not longer expect to see any of his performances after this year, I think myself free to take up the task, and request a share of the publick encouragement . . .

Apparently Leeds had not read the Bickerstaff Papers, for he fell into the trap and like his predecessor Partridge, protested his death, hurling invectives at his "executioner". In the Bickerstaff hoax, Swift has Partridge admit on his deathbed that he is a fraud, whereas Franklin is much kinder to his victim. As is noted above, Saunders' obituary praises Leeds for being skillful at his profession and lauds him for his personal virtues and friendship. A man with such noble qualities would not abuse his dear friend Saunders, thus showing that the real Titan Leeds was dead as predicted and the protestor must be an imposter.

In *Poor Richard's Almanack* for 1734 Saunders discussed his earlier prediction and explained that he could not positively assure his readers whether Leeds had died, but he wove a circumstantial web of evidence to remove any doubt. He wrote:

> There is, however the strongest probability that my dear friend is no more; for there appears in his name, as I am assured, an Almanack for the year 1734, in which I am treated in a very gross and unhandsome manner; in which I am called a false predicter, an ignorant, a

conceited scribler, a fool, and a liar. Mr. Leeds was too well bred to use any man so indecently and so scurrilously, and moreover his esteem and affection for me was extraordinary: So that it is to be feared that pamphlet may be only a contrivance of somebody or other, who hopes perhaps to sell two or three year's Almanacks still, by the sole force and virtue of Mr. Leed's name; but certainly, to put words into the mouth of a gentleman and a man of letters, against his friend, which the meanest and most scandalous of the people might be ashamed to utter even in a drunken quarrel, is an unpardonable injury to his memory, and an imposition upon the publick.

Mr. Leeds was not only profoundly skillful in the useful science he professed, but he was a man of exemplary sobriety, a most sincere friend, and an exact performer of his word. These valuable qualifications, with many others so much endeared him to me, that although it should be so, that, contrary to all probability, contrary to my prediction and his own, he might possibly be yet alive, yet my loss of honour as a prognosticator, cannot afford me so much mortification, as his life, health and safety would give my joy and satisfaction.

In his almanac for 1734, Leeds is confused by the praise Saunders has lavished on him while at the same time insisting he is dead. Leeds writes "it may be expected by some that I shall say something concerning . . . Richard Saunders' Almanac, wherein he useth me with such manners, I can hardly find what to say to him."

Franklin's almanac was thriving on the controversy, sales were booming, and Leeds continued to add fuel to the fire by denying and accusing. Leeds advised his readers that Saunders should "not to be too proud because of his predicting my death," thus leading to the success of his almanac, and "never to take upon him to predict or ascribe any person's death till he has learned to do it better." Being a good businessman, Franklin returned to the fray again in his almanac for 1735, continuing with the same amusing sophistry. When Saunders credits Leeds with concurring with him on the prediction of his death, Leeds emphatically denies it and states it to be a great falsehood "that by my own calculation I shall survive until the 26th." Franklin is now able to argue that if it is untrue, as Leeds himself says, that he survived until the 26th, he must have died before that, and is presumably still dead. Saunders appeals to his readers:

> Whatever may be the musick of the spheres, how great soever the harmony of the stars, 'tis certain there is no harmony among the stargazers; but they are perpetually growling and snarling at one

another like strange curs, or like some men at their wives: I had resolved to keep the peace on my own part, and affront none of them; and I shall persist in that resolution: But having received much abuse from Titan Leeds deceased, (Titan Leeds when living would not have used me so!) I say, having received much abuse from the ghost of Titan Leeds, who pretends to be still living, and to write Almanacks in spite of me and my predictions, I cannot help saying, that tho' I take it patiently, I take it very unkindly.

And whatever he may pretend, 'tis undoubtedly true that he is really defunct and dead. First because the stars are seldom disappointed [wrong] . . . and they foreshowed his death at the time I predicted it. Secondly, 'Twas requisite and necessary he should die punctually at that time, for the honour of astrology, the art professed both by him and his father before him. Thirdly, 'Tis plain to every one that reads his two last almanacks (for 1734 and 35) that they are not written with that life his performances use to be written with. The wit is low and flat, the little hints dull and spiritless, nothing smart in them but Hudibras's verses against astrology . . . which no astrologer but a dead one would have inserted, and no man living would or could write such stuff as the rest.

But lastly, I shall convince him from his own words that he is dead . . . For in his preface to his Almanack for 1734, he says, "Saunders adds another gross falsehood in his almanack, viz. that by my own calculation I shall survive until the 26th of the said month October, 1733, which is as untrue as the former." Now if it be, as Leeds says, untrue and a gross Falsehood that he surviv'd till the 26th of October, 1733, then it is certainly true that he died before that time. And if he died before that time, he is dead now, to all intents and purposes, any thing he may say to the contrary notwithstanding. And at what time before the 26th is it so likely he should die, as at the time by me predicted, viz. the 17th of October aforesaid?

But if some people will walk and be troublesome after death, it may perhaps be borne with a little . . . However, they should not presume too much upon the liberty allowed them. I know confinement must needs be mighty irksome to the free spirit of an astronomer, and I am too compassionate to proceed suddenly to extremities with it. Nevertheless, tho' I resolve with reluctance, I shall not long defer, if it does not speedily learn to treat its living friends with better manners.

Again in 1737 Franklin returned to the Leeds affair, but this time he switched the attack from Poor Richard to the *Gazette*. In an essay entitled, ''Those, labors of the learned called almanacs'' he describes

Leeds' writing as a mixture of "dullness and nonsense." As Benjamin Franklin, printer and publisher of the *Pennsylvania Gazette* rather than as Richard Saunders, he is not officially a party to the hoax of Leeds' death, so he must content himself with such mild criticism. But in 1740 he returns to the hoax again in *Poor Richard's Almanack*. By this time Leeds had actually died, but the Bradfords claimed he left them his astrological calculations for seven years to come, so they could continue to print his almanac. Franklin responds to this with a highly imaginative report of a visit from Titan's ghost.

> On the 4th Instant, towards midnight, as I sat in my little study writing this preface, I fell fast asleep; and continued in that condition for some time, without dreaming any thing, to my knowledge. On awaking, I found lying before me the following letter:

> "Dear Friend Saunders;
> "My Respect for you continues even in this separate State, and I am grieved to see the aspersions thrown on you by the malevolence of avaricious publishers of almanacks, who envy your success. They say your prediction of my death in 1733 was false, and they pretend that I remained alive many years after. But I do hereby certify, that I did actually die at that time, precisely at the hour you mentioned, with a variation of 5 min. 53 sec. which must be allowed to be no great matter in such cases. And I do farther declare that I furnished them with no calculations of the planets' motions, etc., seven years after my death, as they are pleased to give out, so that the Stuff they publish as an almanack in my name is no more mine than 'tis yours.

> "You will wonder perhaps, how this paper comes written on your table. You must know that no separate spirits are under any confinement till after the final settlement of all accounts. In the mean time we wander where we please, visit our old friends, observe their actions, enter sometimes into their Imaginations, and give them hints waking or sleeping that may be of advantage to them. Finding you asleep, I entered your left nostril, ascended into your brain, found out where the ends of those nerves were fastened that move your right hand and fingers, by the help of which I am now writing unknown to you; but when you open your eyes, you will see that the hand written is mine, tho' wrote with yours.

This story may be a little extravagant even for *Poor Richard's* readers, but Titan's good-natured ghost obligingly provides some tests of its credibility and thereby permits Franklin to set up his new adversary, John Jerman.

"The people of this infidel age, perhaps, will hardly believe this story. But you may give them these three signs by which they shall be convinced of the truth of it. About the middle of June next J. J——n [1] Philomat, shall be openly reconciled to the Church of Rome, and give all his goods and chattels to the chappel. On the 7th of September following my old friend W. B——t [2] shall be sober 9 hours, to the astonishment of all his neighbours: And about the same time W.B. and A.B. [3] will publish another Almanack in my Name, in spight of truth and common-sense.

"As I can see much clearer into futurity, since I got from the dark prison of flesh, in which I was continually molested and almost blinded with fogs arising from tiff [4], and the smoke of burnt drams; I shall in kindness to you, frequently give you Informations of things to come, for the Improvements of your almanack: Being Dear Dick, your affectionate friend, T. LEEDS."

For my own part I am convinced that the above Letter is genuine. If the reader doubts of it, let him carefully observe the three signs; and if they do not actually come to pass, believe as he pleases.

Although Dean Swift had been definite about Partridge's death, Franklin was more circumspect about Leeds' demise, always intimating but never asserting it positively. Thus, the whole matter can be taken as comedy rather than satire, as in the tall tale above. While Franklin does here represent the strange letter as fact, he hardly expects anyone to take it seriously. The evidence to prove it genuine involves more predictions directed at his rivals, William and Andrew Bradford—who did, as he predicted, print an almanac for 1740 which they claimed was by Titan Leeds—William Birkett, of *Poor Will's Almanac,* and John Jerman, author of the *American Almanac,* who had earlier taken his printing from Franklin to Bradford. Franklin had already begun tendering Jerman his not-so-gentle ministrations in his almanacs for 1737 and 1739. In his 1737 edition he laughs at "my Brother Jerman's" weather predictions.

As to the weather, if I were to fall into the method my Brother J——n sometimes uses, and tell you, *Snow here or in New England,—Rain here or in South-Carolina,—Cold to the Northward,— Warm to the Southward,* and the like, whatever errors I might com-

[1] John Jerman.   [3] William Bradford and Andrew Bradford.
[2] Will Birkett.   [4] Liquor or beer.

mit, I should be something more secure of not being detected in
them: But I consider, it will be of no service to any body to know
what weather it is 1,000 miles off, and therefore I always set down
positively what weather my reader will have, be he where he will at
the time.

It was in 1737 that Jerman had again given his printing to Bradford, after having come back for two years with Franklin. In the 1739
edition Franklin again remembers "my Brother Jerman":

O the wonderful Knowledge to be found in the stars! Even the
smallest things are written there, if you had but skill to read. When
my Brother J———m———n erected a scheme to know which was best
for his sick horse, to sup a new-laid egg, or a little broth, he found
that the stars plainly gave their verdict for broth, and the horse having supped his broth; now, what do you think became of that horse?
You shall know in my next.

What happened to the horse? We can only hope for the best and
expect the worst. But we shall never know, for Franklin apparently
forgot about it in his enthusiasm for Jerman's new role. With Leeds
actually dead, Franklin needed a new foil, and his old competitor Jerman was selected. In making his prediction about Jerman being reconciled to the Church of Rome, Franklin took advantage of the strong
anti-Catholic sentiment in the Protestant colonies. Franklin, himself,
was not anti-Catholic; he was unusually tolerant of all faiths. He had,
in fact, delivered a message on tolerance toward Catholics when he reported in his newspaper the account of the hospitality shown by Catholic St. Augustine to Protestant seamen whose ship had foundered off
the Florida coast. But this matter with Jerman was different; it was a
prank, conceived in fun, and delivered with the subtlety of a hard
kick.

The kick hit its mark. Like philomaths Partridge and Leeds before
him, Jerman walked right into the trap. In his almanac for 1741, he
protested vehemently. He accused *Poor Richard's Almanac* of false
prophecy, denied the predictions, and labelled Saunders "one of
Baal's false prophets." Interestingly enough, not knowing Saunder's
identity he gave this issue of the almanac and the next to Franklin to
print.

In *Poor Richard's Almanack* for 1742, Franklin defends his prediction against Jerman's charges.

My last adversary is J. J——n, philomat. who declares and protests (in his preface, 1741) that the false prophecy put in my Almanack, concerning him, the year before, is altogether false and untrue: and that I am one of Baal's false prophets. This false, false
prophecy he speaks of, related to his reconciliation with the Church
of Rome; which, notwithstanding his declaring and protesting, is, I
fear, too true. Two things in his elegic verses confirm me in this suspicion. He calls the First of November by the name of All Hallows
Day. Reader, does not this smell of popery? Does it in the least
savor of the pure language of Friends? [1] But the plainest thing is his
adoration of saints, which he confesses to be his practice, in these
words:

> When any trouble did me befall,
> To my dear Mary then I would call.

Did he think the whole world were so stupid as not to take notice
of this? So ignorant as not to know, that all Catholicks pay the
highest regard to the Virgin Mary? Ah! Friend John, We must allow
you to be a poet, but you are certainly no Protestant. I could dearly
wish your religion were as good as your verses.

RICHARD SAUNDERS

Now aware that Richard Saunders and his printer were the same
the angered Jerman gave the 1743 issue of this almanac to Bradford
for printing. Jerman retorted:

> "The reader may expect a reply from me to R—— S——rs alias
> B—— F——ns facetious way of proving me no Protestant. I do
> hereby protest, that for that and such kind of Usage the Printer of
> that witty performance shall not have the benefit of my Almanack
> for this year. To avoid further contention, and judging it unnecessary
> to offer any proofs to those of my acquaintance that I am not a
> papist, I shall . . . conclude . . ."

In his almanac for 1744, Franklin disputes an eclipse predicted by
Jerman and turns the tables by contending that it is not he but his adversary who is really "Baal's false prophet."

> My adversary J——n J——n has indeed made an attempt to out-
> shine me, by pretending to penetrate deeper into futurity; and giving
> his reader gratis in his Almanack for 1743, an eclipse of the Year
> 1744, to be beforehand with me. His words are, "The first day of
> April next Year 1744, there will be a great eclipse of the sun; it

[1] Society of Friends, or Quakers.

begins about an hour before sunset. It being in the sign Aries, the house of Mars, and in the 7th, shows heat, different and animosities between persons of the highest rank and quality,'' etc. I am very glad, for the sake of these persons of rank and quality, that there is no manner of Truth in this Prediction: They may, if they please, live in love and peace. And I caution his readers (they are but few, indeed, and so that matter's the less) not to give themselves any trouble about observing this imaginary Great Eclipse; for they may stare till they're blind without seeing the least sign of it.

I might, on this occasion, return Mr. J———n the name of Baal's false Prophet he gave me some years ago in his wrath, on account of my predicting his reconciliation with the Church of Rome, (tho' he seems now to have given up that point) but I think such language between old men and scholars unbecoming; and I leave him to settle the affair with the buyers of his almanack as well as he can, who perhaps will not take it very kindly, that he has done what in him lay (by sending them out to gaze at an invisible eclipse on the first of April) to make April Fools, of them all. His old threadbare excuse he repeats year after year about the weather, ''That no man can be infallible therein, by reason of the many contrary causes happening at or near the same time, and the Unconstancy of the summer showers and gusts,'' etc. will hardly serve him in the affair of Eclipses; and I know not where he'll get another.

This was the last episode of Franklin's bout with Jerman or his other competitors. By this time Franklin had become a successful businessman whose interests in public service and science were demanding more of his time and attention, to the relief of his competitors. In *Poor Richard* and the *Gazette,* Franklin had made his mark and could now live on his reputation without the benefit of adversaries. In his 26th and last personal appearance as Richard Saunders, Franklin once again referred to his competitors, shedding mock tears that they did not praise him and quote his wise sayings. He takes consolation, however, in the fact that the people are the best judge of his merit and his almanacs have sold well bringing him generous remuneration or, as he put it, ''some solid pudding.'' Evidence that peace brings its rewards may be found in a printing job that the new, reformed Franklin was once again to receive: the almanac of fellow philomath, ''my Brother Jerman.''

7

IS THIS THE WAY TO RUN
A NEWSPAPER?

A SUBSCRIBER TO YOUNG BENJAMIN FRANKLIN'S NEWSPAPER, the *Pennsylvania Gazette* would have read in the October 2, 1729 issue under Foreign Affairs, London:

> They tell us from Holt in Wiltshire that a man aged 66, was married to a Maid of 26 . . . the match being made . . . on Wednesday . . . they were married on Thursday, and the man died . . . Friday: So that the bride was courted, married, became a wife, widow, and we presume was left a maid, all within 24 hours.

This news item appeared in the first issue of the newspaper Franklin published. The journals of this period usually contained long speeches by the Governor or articles of foreign news gleaned from the English press. Franklin's paper was not very different except for its superior writing and one of Franklin's jolliest innovations, the invented news item.

Franklin was a serious publisher, but in those days there were no comic strips or other diversions from the heavy news, so he filled the void with such items as this: "And sometime last week, we are informed, that one Piles a fiddler, with his wife, were overset in a canoe near Newtown Creek. The good man, 'tis said, prudently secured his fiddle, and let his wife go to the bottom." A suicide story, brief and lacking in detail may have surprised Franklin's readers who had not heard of the event: "A servant girl near Christine Bridge hanged herself lately with a design, as 'tis thought, to haunt a young fellow who refused to marry her." But not all "news" had to be so morbid. On February 10, 1730, you might have picked up your *Gazette* and read: "An unhappy man, one Sturgis, upon some difference with his wife determined to drown himself in the river, and she (kind wife) went with him, it seems to see it faithfully performed, and accordingly stood by silent and unconcerned during the whole transaction: he jumped near Carpenter's Wharf, but was timely taken out again before what he came about was thoroughly effected; so that they were both obliged to return home as they came and put up for that time with the disappointment."

The *Gazette's* slogan advertised "the freshest advices foreign and domestick." Some of the "advices," were indeed fresh—right out of the editor's head: "We are credibly informed, that the young woman who not long since petitioned the Governor, and the Assembly to be divorced from her Husband, and at times industriously solicited most of the magistrates on that account, has at last concluded to cohabit with him again. It is said the report of the physicians, who in form examined his abilities, and allowed him to be in every respect sufficient, gave her but small satisfaction; whether any experiments more satisfactory have been try'd, we cannot say; but it seems she now declares it as her opinion, that "George is as good as de best." In Franklin's day the law stipulated that a married couple's possessions were the property of the man, thus helping to explain this tidbit: "On Tuesday last a widow of this town was married in her shift without any other apparel, upon a supposition that such a procedure would secure her husband in the law from being sued for any debts of his predecessor."

The *Gazette* hired no reporters. The publisher served as reporter, editor, typesetter, printer, circulation man and business manager. To help in gathering the news, Franklin asked his country subscribers to acquaint him with every remarkable accident and occurrence fit for public notice. Could one of his country correspondents have sent him this choice morsel? "We hear from Chester County, that last week at a vendue held there, a man being unreasonably abusive to his Wife upon some trifling occasion, the women form'd themselves into a court, and ordered him to be apprehended by their officers and brought to trial: being found guilty he was condemned to be ducked 3 times in a neighbouring pond, and to have one half cut off, of his hair and beard (which it seems he wore at full length) and the sentence was accordingly executed, to the great diversion of the spectators.'' Some of the news was gathered from neighboring provinces, either reprinted directly from their newspapers, as was the custom, or brought by travelers and sea captains. From New York, Franklin reported, there had been terrible thunder and lightning but no great damage was done. ''The same day,'' the report continues, ''we had some very hard claps in these parts; and 'tis said, that in Bucks County, one flash came so near a lad, as, without hurting him, to melt the pewter button off the wasteband of his breeches. 'Tis well nothing else thereabouts was made of pewter.''

One of Franklin's public projects as a young Philadelphian was to reform the police. The city watch, as it was called, was in the hands of constables, who took their duty lightly, and instead of walking the rounds, spent the night in tippling or other unprofessional activities. Such an instance was reported in the *Gazette:*

> We hear, that on Tuesday last, a certain c——n——table having made an agreement with a neighbouring female, to watch with her that night; she promised to leave a window open for him to come in at; but he going his rounds in the dark, unluckily mistook the window, and got into a room where another woman was in bed, and her husband it seems lying on a couch not far distant. The good Woman perceiving presently by the extraordinary fondness of her bedfellow that it could not possibly be her husband, made so much disturbance as to wake the good man; who finding somebody had got into his place without his leave, began to lay about him unmercifully; and 'twas thought, that had not our poor mistaken galant, called out manfully for help (as if he were commanding assistance in the King's Name) and thereby raised the family, he would have stood no more chance for his Life between the wife and husband, than a captive L—— [Louse] between two thumb nails.

The theme of this account must have been a popular one, or so the writer thought, for he had used it previously with no complaints in the case of the unfortunate (or fortunate) stonecutter:

> Friday Night last, a certain st——n——c——tt——r was, it seems, in a fair way of dying the death of a nobleman; for being caught napping with another man's wife, the injured husband took the advantage of his being fast asleep, and with a knife began very di-

ligently to cut off his head. But the Instrument not being equal to the intended operation, much struggling prevented success; and he was obliged to content himself for the present with bestowing on the aggressor a sound drubbing. The gap made in the side of the st———n———c———tt———r's neck, tho' deep, it not thought dangerous; but some people admire, that when the person offended had so fair and suitable an opportunity, it did not enter into his head to turn st———n———c———tt———r himself.

It is said that a humorist must be able to laugh at himself, and in his creation of entertaining news the editor was not above making himself the object of his own ridicule, as in this pun-filled squib on a certain printer:

> Thursday last, a certain P———r ('tis not customary to give names at length on these occasions) walking carefully in clean clothes over some barrels of tar on Carpenter's Wharf, the head of one of them unluckily gave way, and let a Leg of him in above his knee. Whether he was upon the catch [ketch] at that time, we cannot say, but 'tis certain he caught a Tartar. 'Twas observed he sprung out again right briskly, verifying the common saying, As nimble as a bee in a tarbarrel. You must know there are several sorts of bees: 'tis true he was no honey bee, nor yet a humble bee, but a boo bee he may be allowed to be, namely B.F.
>
> N.B. We hope the gentleman will excuse this freedom.

It should be pointed out that these items of refreshing nonsense have been gathered from many issues of the *Gazette*. Franklin used them sparingly, for comic relief, sneaking one in now and then between a fire and a robbery. But even in his quest for real news he found "remarkable" events to titillate the reader's interest. In April, 1730, he reported some high jinks on the high seas. The pirate mentioned in the last issue, he explained, was not a pirate at all but one Captain Booth from the West Indies bound for Southold in Long Island. "Booth says they only fired at the ship *Whaleman* to make sport, but they did not consider the consequences of this mischievous folly, such as the sinking of the whaling sloop, the alarming of the whole coast, the embargo laid on all vessels in New York, and the expense of fitting out a man-of-war, his Majesty's ship *Shoreham,* to apprehend the pirate. It is comforting to know that Booth and his crew are now in custody and the Admiralty will take cognizance of their actions."

Alas, not all offenders were well-meaning pranksters; some practiced skullduggery for profit. In August, 1732, we hear that one James Hill traveled about the country on foot, pretending to be dumb, and making a great profit on people's charity and credulity. He carried with him a counterfeit brief describing his capture and seven years of slavery in Turkey. When he attempted to escape they barbarously cut out his tongue and burned him on each arm, leaving two grievous sores. At Goshen in Chester County, some people suspecting fraud found the sores to be artificial, and when they threatened him he was found to speak very well. Hill confessed his roguery and showed them his trick of shrinking his tongue into the back of his mouth so as to appear as if it were cut away. It being harvest time, they were too busy to take him to a magistrate so they gave him his liberty and he now continues the same practice, going from house to house.

In another account an enterprising man offered a woman employment. He took her to a deserted place in the country where he tried to employ her in a different manner. Quoting from the court record, Franklin considerately spared the sensibilities of his more sensitive readers: "Whereupon he took her in his arms and — (NB. We omit those expressions which though used in open court, we apprehend may be offensive to the ear of a modest reader)."

Although Franklin published a newspaper and an almanac, and was a merchant as well, he always thought of himself first as a printer. He was therefore sensitive to the errors that inevitably crept into his paper. He hoped, however, his judicious readers would distinguish accidental errors (his own) from blunders of ignorance (the errors of his competitors) and more readily excuse the former. He capitalized on these faults by humorously discussing printer's errors in a letter he composed and signed J. T. The letter referred to the article in the preceding paper concerning Governor Belcher, which stated: "After which his Excellency, with the gentlemen trading in New England, died elegantly at Pontack's." Since Pontack's was a noted tavern, the correspondent assumed the word "died" should have been "dined," but, he said, the omission of the one letter gave us as much entertainment as any part of your paper. One of their company took this occasion to tell about an edition of the Bible in which the printer caused David to say, instead of "I am fearfully and wonderfully made," "I am fearfully and wonderfully mad." This caused an ignorant preacher using this text to harangue his audience for half an hour on the subject of spiritual madness. In another Bible misprint, the word "not" was left out of the seventh commandment, to read, "Thou shalt commit adultery." Another of the company said he suspected that many of our modern gentlemen must have copies of this edition and are not aware of the mistake.

Franklin was a self-taught writer who continued to work at improving himself. There were few outstanding men who, to his knowledge, did not have the need to communicate well in writing. He thought good writing should be smooth, clear, and short, and amplification, which he called "the art of saying little in much" was to be avoided. It might perhaps, be tolerated in spoken language, for preachers and lawyers. For lawyers, amplification is so effective because the ignorant people in a jury can scarcely believe it possible that a man can talk so much and so long without being in the right. Let them repeat the same sentence in other words, let them use an adjective with every noun, and double every noun with a synonym, for this is more agreeable than posturing, spitting, taking snuff or any other means of concealing hesitation. Permit them in speaking to detail causes and effects, enumerate all the consequences, and express half by metaphor and circumlocution. But when a discourse is written down on paper, every needless thing gives offense and must be eliminated if it does not lead to the desired end. Had this always been done, many large tiresome volumes would have shrunk into pamphlets, and many a pamphlet into a single period.

Lawyers, unfortunately, not only use amplification in pleading cases but in writing deeds. In the reign of William the Conqueror the conveyance of a large estate might be made in about half a dozen short lines, but now they have grown to such a vast bulk they must be abridged to be understood. And when you discover how little information there is in this accumulation of writing, you are as surprised as a stranger in opening a pumpkin. Franklin relates that the lawyer in one of Steele's comedies instructs his pupil that tautology is the first, second, and third parts of his profession, that is to say, the whole of it. And he adds that he hopes to see the time when it will require as much parchment to convey a piece of land as will cover it. That time, Franklin predicts, will not be far off, and as a prime example he presents the petition of Dermond O'Folivey, an attorney of Ireland, with which none can compare for multiplicity, variety, particularity, and prodigious flow of expression. The petition to the judge begins as in the following illustration and keeps going for several pages:

Most humbly, and most submissively, and most obediently, and most dutifully, by shewing, and expressing, and declaring to your Lordship, that whereby, and whereas, and wherein, the most major, and most greater, and most bigger, and the most stronger part of the most best, and the most ablest, and the most mightiest sort of the people of the Barony of Torrough and County of Kerry, finding, and knowing, and certifying themselves, both hereafter, and the time past, and now, and then, and at the present time, to be very much oppressed, and distressed, and overcharged in all taxes, and quit-rents, and other levies, and accidental applotments, and collections, and gatherings-together in the Barony of Torrough and County of Kerry aforesaid.

In the early years, there was a personal and informal relationship between publisher and subscribers. When Franklin went to New Jersey to print paper money the *Gazette* announced: "The printer hopes the irregular publication of this paper will be excused." When he could not find his law book, a note appeared in the paper reading: "The person that borrowed B. Franklin's law book of this Province is hereby desired to return it, he having forgot to whom he lent it." And when his wife's prayer book disappeared, the *Gazette* carried this appeal: "Taken out of a pew in the church some months since, a *Common Prayer* book, bound in red, gilt, and lettered DF on each corner. The person who took it is desired to open it and read the Eighth Commandment, and afterwards return it into the same pew again; upon which no further notice will be taken."

As the business manager of the paper, Franklin found it necessary occasionally to nudge his subscribers for payment: "This present paper, No. 303, finishes the fifth year since the printer hereof undertook the *Gazette;* no more need be said to my generous subscribers to remind them that every one of those above a twelve-month in arrears has it in his power to contribute considerably toward the happiness of his most obliged humble servant, B. Franklin." In case some recalcitrant subscribers were not moved by this gentle reminder, stronger action was threatened: "This *Gazette* number 564, begins the 11th year since its first publication: And whereas some persons have taken it from the beginning, and others for 7 or 8 years, without paying in one farthing, I do hereby give notice to all who are upwards of one year in arrears, that if they do not make speedy payment, I shall discontinue the papers to them, and take some proper method of recovering my money."

Franklin despaired of collecting his bad debts; he called them "an estate in the clouds" and in his will he left them to charity, hoping that the deadbeats had a better nature to be reached in this way. It was a brilliant idea, allowing him to collect his debts and be charitable at the same time. Unfortunately, it was an experiment that failed, for the charities were hardly more successful in making good the debts than Franklin himself.

In his essay on writing, which Franklin wrote for the Junto and published in the *Gazette,* he stated, "I believe there is no better means of learning to write well than attempting to entertain the publick now and then in one of your papers." Humorous pieces, he said, are the hardest to succeed in. If they are not natural they are nothing, for there can be no real humor in an affectation of humor. That humorous pieces were difficult to write successfully did not discourage Franklin from writing them to entertain his public. One further ingredient was necessary for his recipe—anonymity. He wrote in his essay: "When the writer conceals himself, he has the advantage of hearing the censure both of friends and enemies expressed with more impartiality." As in the Dogood and Busy Body papers, Franklin wrote pieces for the *Gazette* in the form of letters unsigned or signed with fictitious names.

Such an unsigned letter, which appeared in the April 23, 1730, issue, might be titled, "The Devil of a Drummer." Although it is clearly in Franklin's style and mirrors his often-expressed sentiments, it has escaped inclusion in collections of Franklin's works. It is a satirical spoof on spookery with the accompaniment of a drumbeat and Scottish ceremonial music. Addressed, "To the publisher of the *Gazette,"* it begins:

> I know well that the age in which we live abounds in Spinozists, Hobbists, and most impious free-thinkers, who despise revelation, and treat the most sacred truths with ridicule and contempt: Nay, to such an height of iniquity are they arrived that they not only deny the existence of the Devil, and of spirits in general, but would also persuade the world, that the story of Saul and the Witch of Ender is an imposture; and which is still worse, that no credit is to be given to the so well-attested one of the Drummer of Tedsworth.[1]

[1] The Drummer of Tedworth (not Tedsworth) was a celebrated case of supernatural drumming, music and other unusual events reported to have occurred at Tedworth in Wiltshire, England, in the 17th century.

The correspondent confesses that the arguments of some of these unbelieving gentlemen on the subject of spirits, apparitions, witches, etc., were so reasonable that he was strongly inclined to think them correct. As a result, he lived for several years past without any fear or apprehension of demons or hobgoblins; but now all that is changed and, whereas he used to sleep without drawing the curtains, he is now so fearful that he pins them closed every night with corking pins and covers himself head over ears with the bedclothes.

"What has brought about this precipitous change? It is not, as you would imagine, due to any frightful apparition or uncommon noise, but to a most amazing account he received from a reverend gentleman of a certain house being haunted with the d---l of a drummer. This gentleman of unquestioned veracity had met four of his brethren at a town fifteen miles below Philadelphia to settle some church affairs and consider measures to prevent the growth of atheism. Since it was unprecedented to proceed with business at their first meeting, they spent the evening cheerfully, though soberly, and retired about 10 o'clock. Each pair lodged in a separate room, and no sooner were he and his companion warm in their bed than they heard a drum beating very loud, now on this side of their bed, then on the other, and later on the canopy, whereupon they distinctly heard the *Scots Traveller,* and at other times, the *Grenadiers March.* This noise continued all night, frightening them almost to death, and yet, which is the strangest and unaccountable part of the story, it disturbed no mortal in the house save themselves. Their friends had slept well, heard no drum, and upon hearing such a question, believed them to be out of their senses. To explain, the reverend gentleman related to them the adventures of the night, so full of horror, with all the particulars I have mentioned, and many more which I have omitted, that at first they seemed to give little credit to what he said; but upon his bedfellow's affirming it to be true, they appeared to be satisfied of the reality of the fact."

The next night the two went to bed in the same room in which they had been so terribly frightened. They had not taken their first nap when they heard an uncouth noise under them. Shortly afterwards, his companion was seized violently and forcibly by the big toe and was in great danger of being pulled out of bed. But at the same instant the beating of the drum began and his toe was released, and to prevent any future attacks they hoisted their knees up to their very noses.

"The noise still growing louder, they felt a most prodigious weight on them, heavier, as he said, than the nightmare. But by the voice they discovered it to be one of their brethren, who had come into their room to scare them, believing they had told him a fib or just had imagined they had heard a drum. But mark, said the story teller to me: According to the old proverb, 'Harm watch, harm catch;' he was so frightened himself that he would not have ventured back to his own room though he were sure to be made a bishop; so that we were obliged to share our bed with him, in which we lay sweating, and almost dead with fear, until morning.

Thus concluded this surprising story, which had so powerful an effect on the correspondent that he could no longer doubt the devil's having played them this prank. Of course he knows that some folks will say it is all a lie, a forgery, and raise an infinite number of objections. When he told it to a certain person, he swore it could not be true because the learned Greutzius reported that all the divines of Germany were clearly of the opinion that the devil never begins to play his pranks until after midnight, and this noise began between 10 and 11 both nights.

No, it couldn't have been the devil, but this gentleman had another explanation which he illustrated with this tale:

> . . . A certain curate lived in the island of Jamaica, who loved his bottle, no curate better; he chanced to be drinking in a tavern, when he was called upon to do the last offices to a brother departed; upon which with great reluctance he leaves his company, but told them he would return immediately. Away he hies to the place of burial, and, as is usual, reads over the service for the dead, until he came to the words: "I heard a voice from heaven, saying, blessed, etc." at which he was interrupted by one of his companions, who had followed him from the ale house with a "By G—— that's a d——d lie, for I have been drinking with you all day at Mother ——s, and if you had heard the voice, I could have heard it too, for my ears are as good as yours." The gentleman left me to apply the story.

This hocus pocus, entertaining as it was, was more than a hilarious romp. Many of Franklin's readers believed in demons and assorted supernatural phenomena and Franklin did well not to sign the letter which ridiculed their beliefs. In fact, a letter from Burlington in the April 30 issue took the publisher to task for the drummer piece: "I am puzzled to think what could induce you to insert that odd letter of the drum in your last *Gazette*." The author's design was apparent, he said; it was to bring the dispensers of religion into contempt. True wit and humor, he continued, cannot be employed in ridiculing things which are serious and sacred. After all, "we can't be certain there are no spirits existing; it is highly probable that they are." The writer signs himself *Philoclerus* (lover of the clergy), and although we have no absolute proof of the authorship of either letter, the evidence leaves no doubt they are one and the same Benjamin Franklin, who is having double the enjoyment by playing both prosecutor and defense. This was a favorite practice of the versatile publisher, who was his own best correspondent.

When a "correspondent" wrote, "I am about courting a girl I have but little acquaintance with. How shall I come to a knowledge of her faults?" The answer was simple and direct, "Commend her among her female acquaintance." Elsewhere he converted this joke into verse:

> Daphnis, says Clio, has a charming eye;
> What pity 't is her shoulder is awry!
> Aspasia's shape indeed—but then her air,
> 'T would task a conjurer to find beauty there.
> Without a but, Hortensia she commends,
> The first of women, and the best of friends;
> Owns her in person, Wit, fame, virtue, bright;
> But how comes this to pass? She died last night."

Another "correspondent" placed this notice in the *Gazette:* "Mr. Franklin, pray let the prettiest creature in this place know that if it were not for her affectation, she would be absolutely irresistible." Would you believe that this message produced no less than six replies in just a week? We have Franklin's word for it and also the replies, which he printed in the next issue, and of which this is a sampling:

> Sir: Since your last week's paper I have looked in my glass a thousand times, I believe, in one day, and if it was not for the charge of affectation I might, without partiality, believe myself the person meant.
> Sir: Your sex calls me pretty; my own affected. Is it from judgment in the one, or envy in the other?
> Mr. Franklin: They that call me affected are greatly mistaken, for I don't know that I ever refused a kiss to anybody but a fool.

Was this the way to run a newspaper? The answer must be yes, for the circulation boomed, to become the largest of any newspaper in America, the paper being distributed from New York to Virginia. The amount of advertising also increased and with it the profit to the publisher, which Franklin was happy to acknowledge. Having succeeded with humor, he tried other means of entertainment, like riddles and ethical problems. His predecessor had run a column called The Casuist, and Franklin adopted the title. A casuist is defined as one who determines what is correct in matters of conscience or conduct and Franklin, using a false name, would propse a question and then answer it as the Casuist. "The Case of the Trespassing Horse" was the first problem for the Casuist. A man preparing to shoot deer in his cornfield shot someone else's horse by mistake when it strayed into his field. Who ought to pay? In the second case, "The Case of the Missing Horse," a man put his horse out to board for six months when he went away. When he returned he was told his horse had been lost just a few days after he left. The man who boarded the horse must pay for it, but the question is whether he may properly deduct the full six month's board fee originally agreed upon.

The third case is different; it is "A Case of Conscience." The question itself signals the humor of the answer: "The Case is this: Suppose A discovers that his neighbour B has corrupted his wife and injured his bed: Now, if 'tis probable, that by A's acquainting B's wife with it, and using proper solicitations, he can prevail with her to consent, that her husband be used in the same manner, is he justifiable in doing it? P.S. If you are acquainted with Mr. Casuist, you may give him this privately, and I will cause one to call at your house sometime hence for his answer. But if you know him not, please to publish it, that he may read it in your paper."

The Casuist's reply does not condone wife swapping, as might be expected, considering the morality of colonial Pennsylvania. It mentions the commandment against adultery, it talks of returning good for evil, and it asks—if an ass kicks me, should I kick him back? There is another reply, however, which uses the author's expert skill at casuistry and makes a case for the other side. This one is signed by the Anti-Casuist, who employs the following lines of argument: "If my wife commits adultery, it being an accepted cause for divorce in every country, she thereby dissolves the bond of marriage and makes us separate and single people. The same applies to B's marriage, so we are now four single people. If I therefore enjoy his wife, I do not commit adultery.

"But now suppose the marriage is not dissolved and she is still his wife. If he has injured his wife by defrauding her of her due benevolence, bestowing it where it was not due, on my wife, my family is properly debtor and his wife is creditor. If I then bestow on his wife the benevolence which was formerly due to mine, my wife has no cause to complain. And with respect to his wife, it is not doing her an injury but righting the injured or paying a just debt. It is not revenge, as the Casuist asserts, for as he took my wife, I give myself for his wife's use; which is the same thing as if a man demanded my bed and I gave him the coverlid also.

"As to the matter of injury, no injury can be done where nobody is injured and I challenge the Casuist or anybody else to show who is injured in this case, provided the matter is never made public. How many in A's position would act so prudently and not murder their wives and perhaps the agressor as well? But if A does not respond in any way, as the Casuist recommends, and the books are not balanced, might not B fear A's revenge and possibly kill him first? When B knows that A is even with him, however, he has no further fear and the two may embrace with open hearts like brothers and be good friends ever after."

The Anti-Casuist concludes with a parting shot at the Casuist, observing that when the latter kept to the subject of horses he did all right, but when he meddles in the affairs of husband and wife, it plainly shows he is nothing but a Horse Casuist. This piece, along with the query and the answer by the Casuist, were found together in Franklin's handwriting in his Commonplace Book. He had written all three but his readers were spared the pleasure, or more likely the shock, of the Anti-Casuist's reply for he never dared to print it.

This was the last of the Casuist, but Franklin would occasionally propound a riddle for his readers, and a prize:

> Who in good verse explains me clear
> Shall have this *Gazette*, free one year.

The year 1732 was a busy one for the creative journalist. It was the year Franklin produced his first almanac, and for the *Gazette* he wrote original pieces like the Casuist and a series of three character sketches. The first sketch was of Anthony Afterwit, an honest tradesman with an extravagant wife. Anthony writes that his affairs went smoothly when he was a bachelor but now he has met with some difficulties which he wishes to explain. About the time he met his spouse, her father let it be known that if she married a man he liked he would give them 200 pounds on the day of their marriage. As a result,

Anthony formed several fine schemes on how he would use this money, only to have her father, the old curmudgeon, trick him out of it. As soon as her father saw that the match had gone too far to be easily broken off, he suddenly pretended to become very angry and said if his daughter married Anthony they would not get a farthing.

After the wedding, Anthony took his bride to his house where they lived in not quite so poor a condition as the couple described in the Scotch Song: "Neither pot nor pan, but four bare legs together." Anthony relates that his house was tolerably furnished for an ordinary man, "no thanks to Dad, who I understand was very much pleased with his politick management." It was evident that with care and industry the couple might live tolerably easy and be a credit to their neighbors. But there was a rub. His wife had a strong inclination to be a gentlewoman. In consequence, his old-fashioned looking-glass was unaccountably broken one day, and they could not be without a glass in the room. "My dear," says she, "we may as well buy a large fashionable one that Mr. Such-a-one has to sell; and it will cost but a little more than a common glass and will be much handsomer and more creditable." Accordingly the glass was bought. But in a weeks time he was made aware, little by little, "that the table was by no means suitable to such a glass." And having procured a proper table, Mrs. Afterwit, who is conceeded by her husband to be an excellent contriver, informed him that some very handsome chairs would be desirable. "And thus, by degrees, I found all my old furniture stowed up in the garret, and every thing below altered for the better."

Had it stopped there, bemoans poor Anthony, they might have done well enough. But his wife being entertained at tea by the good women she visited, could do no less in return, "and so we got a tea-table with all its appurtenances of china and silver. Then his wife overworked herself in doing housework so they could no longer do without a maid. Next, to get his dinner on time, she must buy a clock, which she observed, "was a great ornament to the room." And lastly to his grief, to relieve some ailment or other she must take up riding, so he bought her a very fine pacing mare, which cost 20 pounds.

He could see all along this way of living was beyond his means but he couldn't find the resolve to do something about it until he received a severe dun warning of court action. He tells us of his actions: "Last Monday my Dear went to see a relation, and stay a fortnight. In the interim, I have turned away the maid, bag and baggage; sold the fine pacing mare, and bought a good milch cow with 3 pounds of the money; disposed of the tea-table, and put a spinning wheel in its place, which looks very pretty."

He stuffed flax for the spinning wheel into nine empty cannisters and bought a set of knitting needles "for to tell you a truth, which I would have go no further, I begin to want stockings." This is one of B.F.'s favorite little jokes, the confidence meant not to be kept, which in this absurd case is a secret to be published in a newspaper. Anthony makes a great saving by exchanging the stately clock for an hour glass and remarks, "I am mightily pleased when I look at my hour glass, what an ornament it is to the room." One of the pieces of the old looking-glass is repaired and is substituted for the great one, which is stored away in a closet. His debts are paid and he has money in his pocket. Now all he must do is bravely prepare for his wife's reaction on returning home. He tells himself:

> If she can conform to this new scheme of living, we shall be the happiest couple perhaps in the Province, and by the blessing of God, may soon be in thriving circumstances. I have reserved the great glass, because I know her heart is set upon it. I will allow her when she comes in, to be taken suddenly ill with the headache, the Stomachache, fainting fits, or whatever other disorders she may think more proper; and she may retire to bed as soon as she pleases; But if I do not find her in perfect health both of body and mind the next morning, away goes the aforesaid great glass, with several other trinkets I have no occasion for that very day. Which is the irrevocable resolution of, Sir, her loving husband, and your very humble servant, Anthony Afterwit.

The last word is saved not for his wife but for her father. In a postscript Anthony forsees that they could return to their luxurious way of living if only Dad would be willing to bear the expense of it. However remote in its realization, it is an illusion common to all young husbands.

In 1742 Samuel Richardson wrote *Pamela,* the first modern English novel, and Franklin in 1744 was the first printer in America to publish it. Some people have wondered, could Franklin have become a successful novelist like Richardson or Fielding, who wrote *Tom Jones* in 1749? This is empty speculation, for Franklin never contemplated becoming a novelist, but the three character sketches show that he had talent along this line. In the second letter, by Celia Single, Franklin uses considerable dialogue, which he states in his autobiography he first saw used in *The Pilgrim's Progress.*

It was Franklin's custom to air both sides of a dispute, if only for fun; Celia writes criticizing the publisher for printing Anthony Afterwit's letter as doing more harm than good in the community. It has broken the peace of several families by causing differences between men and their wives, of which she gives an instance where she was both an eye and ear witness.

Last Wednesday morning Celia happened to be in Mrs. C——s's house when her husband came home with some balls of thread he had bought.

"My dear," says he, "I like mightily those stockings which I yesterday saw neighbor Afterwit knitting for her husband, of thread of her own spinning: I should be glad to have some such stockings myself: I understand that your maid Mary is a very good knitter, and seeing this thread in the market, I have bought it, that the girl may make a pair or two for me."

Mrs. Careless was at the mirror, dressing her hair, and turning around with the pins in her mouth, "Lord, child," says she, "are you crazy? What time has Mary to knit? Who must do the work, I wonder, if you set her to knitting?"

"Perhaps, my dear," says he, "you have a mind to knit 'em yourself; I remember, when I courted you I once heard you say you had learned to knit of [from] your mother."

"I knit stockings for you?" says she, "not I truly; there are poor women enough in town that can knit, if you please you may employ them."

"Well, but my dear," says he, "you know a penny saved is a penny got, a pin a day is a groat a year, every little makes a mickle, and there is neither sin nor shame in knitting a pair of stockings; Why should you express such an aversion to it? As to poor women, you know we are not people of quality, we have no income . . . but from my labour and industry."

"I wonder," says she, "how you can propose such a thing to me; did you not always tell me you would maintain me like a gentlewoman? If I had married Capt. ———, he would have scorned even to mention knitting of stockings."

"Prithee," says he, (a little nettled) "what do you tell me of your Captains? If you could have had him, I suppose you would. If I did promise to maintain you as a gentlewoman, I suppose 'tis time enough for that when you know how to behave like one."

"Pray," says she, (somewhat fiercely, and dashing the puff into the powder-box) don't use me after this manner, for I assure you I won't bear it. This is the fruit of your poison newspapers . . ."

"Bless us," says he. "Must a tradesman's daughter and the wife of a tradesman necessarily and instantly be a gentlewoman? I am forced to work for a living; if you are too great to do the like, there's the door, go and live on your estate, if you can find it. In short, I don't desire to be troubled w'ye."

Celia cannot tell us what answer was made to this, for knowing that a man and wife are apt to quarrel more violently in the presence of strangers than by themselves, she departed hastily. But she learned from Mary that evening that Mr. and Mrs. Careless dined peacefully, the balls of thread that had caused the trouble being thrown into the kitchen fire.

One of the early advocates of women's rights, Celia faults the *Gazette* for reflecting on women's idleness and extravagance but ignoring similar imperfections in men. If she were disposed to be censorious, she could furnish the paper with many examples of men's failings. She could mention Mr. Billiard, who spends more than he earns at the green table; Mr. Finikin, who has seven suits of fine clothes while his wife and children go half naked; Mr. Crownhim, who is always dreaming over the checker board and is oblivious of the real world; Mr. Bookish, Mr. Tweedledum, Mr. Toot-a-toot and others. But she hates to be thought a scandalizer of her neighbors and therefore forebears mentioning names. She has, however, some advice for the publisher; she tells him to entertain his readers with something other than peoples' reflections on one another, for remember, says she, "there are holes enough to be picked in your coat as well." And with unexpected sagacity she observes that those who are affronted by the satires he publishes will not consider so much who wrote them as who printed them.

The subject of scandal with which Celia finishes her remarks is the author's lead-in to the third letter in the series, that of Alice Addertongue, the gossip monger. This piece is a homely satire on the practice of scandalizing in which Franklin, as he had done as the anti-casuist, has fun making an argument for the unpopular side, and generates some laughs in the process. The week preceding the Addertongue letter, Franklin had placed a semi-serious article in the *Gazette* defending censure, or backbiting, and elaborating the many reasons why it should be considered a virtue instead of a vice.

Alice begins her letter noting her pleasure at last week's paper in its unusual attitude on scandal, a position like her own. She reproves a writer in Thursday's *Mercury,* the competitor that Franklin enjoys deriding, for his impertinence in claiming that "the fair sex are so peculiarly guilty of this enormous crime." Every blockhead who could ever handle a pen, she notes, has taken it upon himself to cant in this same senseless strain: "If to scandalize be really a crime, what do these puppies mean? They describe it, they dress it up in the most odious, frightful and detestable colours, they represent it as the worst of crimes, and then soundly and charitably charge the whole race of womankind with it. Are they not guilty of what they condemn, at the same time that they condemn it? If they accuse us of any other crime, they must necessarily scandalize while they do it. But to scandalize us with being guilty of scandal is in itself an egregious absurdity, and can proceed from nothing but the most consummate impudence in conjunction with the most profound stupidity." (Franklin, who was so careful not to offend in his own utterances, must have enjoyed this eloquently vituperative discharge as an outlet for his pent-up feeling). Now, crediting the *Gazette's* article for dispelling the absolutely erroneous opinion that scandalizing is a crime, Alice says: "Let us leave these idiot mock-moralists, while I entertain you with some account of my life."

The first thing Alice tells us about herself is that she is a young girl of about 35. Franklin has used this "side-splitter" in one of his Dogood papers, but that was long ago in Boston, so he tried it here as an opening gag. She has no care upon her head for earning a living and therefore feels it her duty to exercise her talent at censure for the good of the community. Yet, whatever good she may thereby do, she admits she did not begin the practice of this virtue simply from a principle of public spirit. As a child, she remembers having a violent inclination to be always praising herself, and being scolded and whipped for such poor manners. She then changed her tactics and instead of praising herself she began to dispraise others, which she found more agreeable to company and almost as satisfying to herself. She looks at it quite objectively: "For what great difference can there be, between putting yourself up, or putting your neighbor down? Scandal, like other virtues is in part its own reward, as it gives us the satisfaction of making ourselves appear better than others, or others no better than ourselves."

Alice lived with her mother, who held more traditional views than her daughter. Her mother believed that scandal spoiled all good conversation, while Alice insisted there would be no such thing without it. Once at tea this dispute rose to such a height that Alice left the table and entertained her acquaintances in the kitchen. When her mother's visitors arrived, they drank tea in the parlor. Her mother, good woman, would hear no ill of any one's character. She spoke like this:

"I am mightily pleased that the world is not as bad as people imagine it to be. There is some good quality in every body. Such a one is very dutiful to her father, and methinks has a fine set of teeth; such a one is very respectful to her husband; such a one is very kind to her poor neighbors, and besides has a very handsome shape; such a one is always ready to serve a friend . . ." This fine kind of talk lasted nearly half an hour when she said, "I do not doubt but every one of you have made like observations, and I should be glad to have the conversation continued upon this subject." Just at this juncture Alice peeped in at the door and never before in her life saw such a set of simple, vacant faces: "They looked somehow neither glad, nor sorry, nor angry, nor pleased, nor indifferent, nor attentive; but (excuse the simile) like so many blue wooden images of rye dough."

In the kitchen, on the other hand, things were more lively. Alice had begun a ridiculous story of Mr ———'s intrigue with his maid and his wife's behavior on discovering it. They laughed heartily and one of the gravest of mama's company got up to see what the girls were so merry about. She was followed by a second, then a third, till finally the old gentlewoman found herself quite alone and came to finish her tea in the kitchen with the rest.

With industry and application Alice had been able to make herself the center of all scandal in the Province. There was little stirring but she heard of it. Whenever she received a good story she generously gave two or more in return. Her punctuality plus diligence, with efficient business and accounting methods, brought a stock of defamation flowing into her. In addition, she developed the art of pumping scandal out of people who had the least inclination toward it. Would she reveal her secret? "Yes," she says, "to let it die with me would be inhuman." If she never hears ill of some person, she imputes it to defective intelligence, "for there are none without their faults, no not one." If the person is a woman, Alice tells her friends she has heard one of the handsomest men in town praise her beauty, which naturally turns the conversation to her failings, past, present, and future. Using the same method she causes every man of reputation to be praised in front of his competitors whether it be in regard to love, business or esteem. At election time, she commends every candidate to some of the opposite party, but of late she has found commendations are not at all necessary, she need only listen to what they freely say of one another.

Some thoughtless persons may condemn Alice in their hearts for her practice of embellishing stories to improve them, but she feels justified in doing so. She knows how hard people try to conceal their vices and follies, and taking all of mankind in a lump she doubts that even a fifth of these secrets are ever revealed. Therefore, when she hears of any person's misdeeds she tries to keep within bounds by making them only three times worse than they are. Besides that, she reserves for herself the privilege of charging them with only one fault in four of which, for all she knows, they may be entirely innocent. "You see," she proudly proclaims, "there are but few so careful of doing justice as myself; what reason then has mankind to complain of scandal? . . . the worst that is said of us is only half what might be said, if all our faults were seen."

But alas for poor Alice, she has lately developed a bad cold so she can scarcely speak, and a most terrible toothache that won't let her open her mouth. For some days past she has received ten stories for each she has returned and she cannot balance her accounts. She appeals to the publisher of the *Gazette:* "I have long thought that if you would make your paper a vehicle of scandal you would double the number of subscribers. I send you herewith account of 4 knavish tricks, 2 cracked m——n——ds [maidenheads], 5 cu——old——ms [cuckoldoms], 3 drubbed wives, and 4 henpecked husbands, all within this fortnight, which you may as articles of news deliver to the publick; and if my toothache continues, shall send you more."

Following the letter, the publisher gives his reply to Alice's invitation. "I thank my correspondent Mrs. Addertongue for her goodwill; but desire to be excused inserting the articles of news she has sent me; such things being in reality no news at all." The impeccable publisher appears as Dr. Jekyll to his readers, but in private he finds it more fun to play at being Mr. Hyde. The distinction should properly be made, however, between playing and being. While Franklin wrote facetiously about scandal, he scrupulously avoided making his newspaper a scandal sheet, as were some of the early papers.

8

THE DOGOOD PAPERS
AND THE BUSY BODY

FRANKLIN'S EARLY LITERARY PAPERS, USUALLY WRITTEN in letter form, give a preview of the man to come. They disclose his wide range of interests, his keen observation of the social and political scene, his deep-seated democratic convictions, his attraction to controversy, his fondness for satire, and his natural propensity to humor.

At the age of 16 Franklin, as noted in Chapter I, entered the Boston literary scene with a series of essays now known as *The Dogood Papers*. These were published in the *New England Courant* from April to October, 1722, under the name of Silence Dogood. In them the young Benjamin demonstrates his vivid imagination, his sense of the ridiculous, and the positive opinions he held on an unlikely assortment of subjects. In the first three letters he has the widow Dogood establish her credentials by relating her personal history.

At the time of my birth, my parents were on ship-board in their way from London to N. England. My entrance into this troublesome world was attended with the death of my father, a misfortune, which tho' I was not then capable of knowing, I shall never be able to forget; for as he, poor man, stood upon the deck rejoicing at my birth, a merciless wave entered the ship, and in one moment carried him beyond reprieve. Thus, was the first day which I saw, the last that was seen by my father; and thus was my disconsolate mother at once made both a parent and a widow.

Except for the absence of rhyme, Silence seems to begin where "The Lighthouse Tragedy" left off. The infant was brought up near Boston and when old enough was put in the charge of a young, country minister. Her guardian was a good man who "labored with all his might to instill virtuous and godly principles into my tender soul." He saw to it that she became accomplished in needlework, writing, and arithmetic. When he observed that she, like the true author of the letter, took more than an ordinary delight in reading books, he gave her free use of his library to enable her mind "to frame great and noble Ideas."

Tragedy again struck Silence with the departure from this life of her indulgent mother, leaving her an orphan with no known relatives. But the minister continued to take care of her, and she grew up living a cheerful country life in the company of neighboring females and books.

Now the plot thickens. The young minister, who was a bachelor, decided to marry. After several unsuccessful adventures with frivolous females he tired of the game and "began unexpectedly to cast a loving eye upon me, whom he had brought up cleverly to his hand." Silence takes us into her confidence: "There is certainly scarce any part of a man's life in which he appears more silly and ridiculous, than when he makes his first onset in courtship. The awkward manner in which my master first revealed his intentions, made me, in spite of my reverence to his person, burst out into an unmannerly laughter. However, having asked his pardon, and with much ado composed my countenance, I promised him I would take his proposal into serious consideration, and speedily give him an answer."

The answer was yes. This unexpected match astonished the country round about and furnished a topic of discourse for a long time. The couple live happily together in the "height of conjugal Love and mutual endearments for near seven years," bring two girls and a boy into the world, and then inexorable death strikes once more, leaving Silence a widow. She writes: "I have now remained in a state of widowhood for several years, but it is a state I never much admired, and I am apt to fancy that I could be easily persuaded to marry again, provided I was sure of a good-humored, sober, agreeable companion. But one, even with these few good qualities, being hard to find, I have lately relinquished all thoughts of that nature."

With this qualified invitation to suitors, Silence concludes her personal saga. She finishes the letter with a declaration of her character beginning, "Know then, That I am . . ." In the list of "I ams" we find, "I am a mortal enemy to arbitrary government and unlimited power. I am naturally very jealous for the rights and liberties of my country; and the least appearance of an incroachment on those invaluable priviledges, is apt to make my blood boil exceedingly." The year 1776, when the rebel Benjamin Franklin will be 70 years old, is over a half century away, but the lad of 16 is ready. Silence sums up her characteristics: "To be brief: I am courteous and affable, good humored (unless I am first provoked,) and handsome, and sometimes witty."

Silence has prefaced the account of her history with the excuse that people evaluate what is said not by the content but by who says it. She hopes that now the reader will be more willing to accept her further utterances, for she has a great deal to say on many subjects. In all her studies she has treasured up much useful knowledge which she feels it her civic duty to communicate to the public. She knows that she can't please all tastes at once so she plans to issue "peace-meal" her views on a variety of subjects. Her range of subjects is remarkably broad. There are eleven more Dogood letters, for a total of fourteen, covering such diverse subjects as Harvard College and writing elegies.

In Franklin's satire on Harvard College, Silence is pondering whether to send her son William to Harvard. Like other early American colleges, Harvard in 1722 trained mainly ministers and therefore the *Courant,* which was opposed to ministerial rule and to the Mathers, who were associated with Harvard, was not likely to be sympathetic. In addition, there was the town and gown division. Franklin represented the tradesmen, or leather apron men, as he called them, who were envious of the privileged scholars. In this letter, Silence is considering her problem when she falls asleep and has a dream. In her dream she travels through the countryside hearing everywhere about the famed Temple of Learning, where a great company of youth from all parts of the country are going, though some might be little better than dunces and blockheads. She enters the large and stately edifice where upon a magnificent throne sits Learning, in an awful state. At the foot of the throne are Madam Idleness attended by her maid Ignorance. The students who enter the temple try to climb the throne to Learning but it is difficult and most are satisfied to sit at the foot with the two lesser ladies. Each of those who does ascend, with help, seems satisfied with his learning even though the "Beetle-Scull" might be as ignorant as ever. Those who finished usually followed the beaten path to the Temple of Theology, though some took to merchandising, traveling, or to nothing. Many lived as poor as churchmice, being unable to dig, ashamed to beg, and as for living by their wits, found it impossible. As Silence concluded her dream she reflected on the folly of parents who, blind to their children's dullness and insensible to the solidity of their skulls, send them to the Temple of Learning simply because they can afford it. And there, for lack of ability, "they learn little more than how to carry themselves handsomely, and enter a room genteely, (which might as well be acquir'd at a dancing-school,) and from whence they return, after abundance of trouble and charge, as great blockheads as ever, only more proud and self conceited."

In the 250 years since Silence Dogood's essay appeared, Harvard students often have suffered criticism, but it is unlikely they ever received a more thorough drubbing than this one at the hands of young Benjamin Franklin. Years later, however, Franklin made peace with the Mathers, and in 1753 Harvard was kind enough to honor its former critic with an honorary degree of Master of Arts, even though he had never studied there or at any other college.

Many of the Dogood essays are related to women's affairs and problems. This 16-year-old lad, seeing the world through the eyes of the widow Dogood, had remarkable empathy for women and their problems. In her next publication, Silence reveals a letter from a reader of the *Courant* charging "the fair tribe" with the vices of pride and idleness. Silence vigorously defends her sex and counters that men are guilty of drinking and swearing, and while she admits to women's faults, she insists that there is no vice in which men are not equally guilty. In a following letter, however, she takes her own sex to task for their folly in the pride of apparel. She disdains "those airy mortals, who have no other way of making themselves considerable but by gorgeous apparel." She is particularly disturbed by a fashion presently reigning among her sex: "the most immodest and inconvenient of any the art of woman has invented, namely, that of hoop-petticoats." She finds that hoop petticoats answer neither the ends of necessary nor ornamental apparel. As she describes them, "These monstrous topsy-turvy mortar pieces are neither fit for the church, the hall, or the kitchen; and if a number of them were well mounted on Noddles-Island, they would look more like engines of war for bombarding the town, than ornaments of the fair sex." While Silence has little hope of persuading her sex to relinquish this extravagant foolery she will leave it to them to consider whether women, who pay no taxes, ought to take up more room on the King's Highway in such outfits than the men, who yearly contribute to the support of the government. This piece generated comment, first in the form of a letter to the *Courant* and then in an eight-page article bearing the impressive title, "Hoop-Petticoats, Arraigned and Condemned by the Light of Nature, and Law of God."

Concerning women's problems, Silence receives a petition from a repentant virgin, Margaret Aftercast, who describes her tragic situation:

"1. That your petitioner being puffed up in her younger years with a numerous train of humble servants, had the vanity to think, that her extraordinary wit and beauty would continually recommend her to the esteem of the gallants; and therefore as soon as it came to be publickly known that any gentleman addressed her, he was immediately discarded.

"2. That several of your petitioners humble servants, who upon their being rejected by her, were, to all appearance in a dying condition, have since recovered their health, and been several years married, to the great surprize and grief of your petitioner, who parted with them upon no other conditions, but that they should die or run distracted for her, as several of them faithfully promised to do.

"3. That your petitioner, finding herself disappointed in and neglected by her former adorers, and no new offers appearing for some years past, she has been industriously contracting acquaintance with several families in town and country, where any young gentlemen or widowers have resided, and endeavoured to appear as conversable as possible before them: She has likewise been a strict observer of the fashion, and always appeared well dressed. And the better to restore her decayed beauty, she has consumed above fifty pound's worth of the most approved cosmeticks. But all won't do.

"Your petitioner therefore most humbly prays, That you would be pleased to form a project for the relief of all those penitent mortals of the fair sex, that are like to be punished with their virginity until old age, for the pride and insolence of their youth.

Silence wishes she had the faculty of matchmaking for the benefit of Margaret and others, but unfortunately, she tells us, her extreme modesty and taciturnity forbid an attempt of this nature. Instead she proposes relief in a mutual Friendly Society, which turns out to be a plan for old maid's insurance in which any virgin attaining the age of 30 would receive a lump sum of 500 pounds cash. Silence stipulates exceptions, namely those who have made a practice of discarding "humble servants" and those who have refused several good offers of matrimony. And finally her last condition, that no woman who, after having received the payment, has had the good fortune to marry, shall entertain any company with praises of her husband for a period of over one hour's duration. The first offense would require returning half the money and a second offense, the remainder.

As a postscript to one of her letters Silence announces that she has left her seat in the country and has come to Boston to complete her observations on the vices of that town. It was on a pleasant moonlit evening in Boston when Mrs. Dogood first ventured abroad on her quest. As she walked along and tuned in on the conversation of one group of young people, she was startled to hear that she, herself, was the topic of conversation. One of the females in the group pretended to know her, telling the others, "that I [Silence] was a Person of ill character, and kept a criminal correspondence with a gentleman who assisted me in writing." But one of the "Gallants" cleared Silence of this charge by saying, "that tho' I wrote in the character of a woman, he knew me to be man." One can imagine young Franklin's great delight in deceiving his readers by telling them the truth, which they are not expected to believe. But the speaker comments further that the man who is responsible for the Widow Dogood's utterance should be endeavoring to reform himself rather than spending his wit in satirizing others.

Franklin, who loved ships and would have become a sailor had not his father vetoed that notion, now turns to nautical terminology in describing Silence's next encounter that evening: "I had no sooner left this set of ramblers, but I met a crowd of Tarpolins and their doxies, linked to each other by the arms, who ran . . . [at] the rate of six knots an hour and bent their course toward the Common. Their eager and amorous emotions of body, occasioned by taking their mistresses in tow, they called wild steerage: And as a pair of them happened to trip and come to the ground, the company were called upon to bring to, for that Jack and Betty were foundered. But this fleet were not less comical or irregular in their progress than a company of females I soon came up with, [and here either the widow of a country minister or the candlemaker's 16-year-old son shows an unexpected knowledge of the real world] who, by throwing their heads to the right and left, at everyone who passed by them, I concluded came out with no other design than to revive the spirit of love in disappointed batchelors, and expose themselves to sale to the first bidder.''

In her night's ramble Silence observed pensive youths with mournful looks and a slow pace, crying out on the cruelty of their mistresses, and others with a more rapid pace and cheerful air whispering, "I'm certain I shall have her! This is more than I expected! How charmingly she talks!''

Silence sums up:

> "Upon the whole I conclude, That our night-walkers are a set of people, who contribute very much to the health and satisfaction of those who have been fatigued with business or study, and occasionally observe their pretty gestures and impertinencies. But among men of business, the shoemakers, and other dealers in leather, are doubly obliged to them, inasmuch as they exceedingly promote the consumption of their ware: And I have heard of a shoemaker, who being asked by a noted rambler, Whether he could tell how long her shoes would last; very prettily answered, That he knew how many days she might wear them, but not how many nights; because they were then put to a more violent and irregular service than when she employed herself in the common affairs of the house.''

The vice of drunkenness receives the attention of Mrs. Dogood in one of her letters to the *Courant*. For the widow of a clergyman, she is amazingly tolerant of drinking, as long as it is in moderation. She observes that liquor assists those who want the talent of a ready utterance, . . . "much study and experience, and a little liquor, are of absolute necessity for some tempers, in order to make them accomplished orators." Moderate use of liquor works like a well-regulated anger to make someone eloquent who ordinarily can talk only in broken sentences. Hence, notes Silence, women are generally the most eloquent because they are the most passionate: "It has been said in the praise of some men . . . that they could talk whole hours together upon anything; but it must be owned to the honour of the other sex, that there are many among them who can talk whole hours together upon nothing.''

Silence's tolerance of drinking did not extend to the case of the drunkard who, she stated, retained only the shape of a man while he acted the part of a beast. She was interested in the change of persons' dispositions when intoxicated. Some men became profane when drunk (Franklin, himself, was so recorded on one occasion, although he was normally a moderate drinker) but others, who were the most profligate wretches when sober, became mighty religious in their cups. She reports that drunkards themselves have invented numberless words and phrases to cover their folly. "They are seldom known to be drunk, tho' they are very often boozey, cogey, tipsey, fox'd, merry, mellow, fuddl'd, groatable, confoundedly cut, see two moons, are among the Philistines, in a very good humour, see the sun, or, the sun has shone upon them; they clip the King's English, are almost froze, feavorish, in their altitudes, pretty well entered, &c."

Frustrated poets frequently become critics of other people's poetry and such is the case with young Franklin. In a comic burlesque, Silence focuses her attention on a very special form of poetry, the New England funeral elegy. In this latter essay, Silence discusses an elegy which is clearly terrible poetry but she pretends it is excellent and heaps praise on it. Then she gives her own recipe for making a New England funeral elegy. She begins by expressing her opinion that New England lacks good poetry not because the people are devoid of ability or education, but because they do not receive sufficient encouragement and praise in their effort. She is determined to correct this fault and do her patriotic duty in praising worthy New England poetry. She comes upon a piece entitled "An Elegy upon the much Lamented Death of Mrs. Mehitebell Kitel Wife of Mr. John Kitel of Salem." With lavish use of hyperbole, she describes it as the most "Extraordinary" piece ever written in New England. The language is so soft and easy, the expression so pathetic, the verse so charming and natural that it is almost beyond comparison. No English elegies may be compared with this in respect to the elegance of style or smoothness of rhyme. And as for the affecting part, Silence leaves it to the reader to judge if any other lines would sooner make them draw their breath and sigh, if not shed tears, than these following:

> Come let us mourn, for we have lost a wife, a daughter, and a sister,
> Who has lately taken flight, and greatly we have missed her.

In another place:

> Some little time before she yielded up her breath,
> She said, I ne'er shall hear one sermon more on earth.

She kist her husband some little time before she expired,
Then leaned her head the pillow on, just out of breath and tired.

But Silence is especially awed by the threefold application in the first line, *a Wife, a Daughter, and a Sister*. The line in the celebrated Watts, namely, *GUNSTON the Just, the Generous, and the Young*, is nothing compared to it. The latter only mentions three qualities of one person deceased, which therefore could raise grief but for one. Whereas the former ("our most excellent Poet") gives the reader an idea of the death of three persons, which is three times as great a loss as the death of one, and consequently must raise three times as much grief and compassion in the reader.

Silence apologizes that space prohibits her from discussing even half the excellent qualities of this elegy. But she must somehow honor the author who has invented a new species of poetry that was never known before and has no name. It cannot be called epic, lyric, or any known name, therefore, in remembrance and honor of the dead she will call it *Kitelic*. The term caught on, and for some time later local writers used this term in referring to bad poetry.

Now, Silence notes, since it is certain that most New England elegies are wretchedly dull and ridiculous, she submits her own recipe for a New England funeral elegy, which was left her for a legacy by her late reverend husband:

"For the subject of your Elegy. Take one of your neighbours who has lately departed this life; it is no great matter at what age the party died, but it will be best if he went away suddenly, being killed, drowned or frozen to death.

"Having chose the person, take all his virtues, excellencies, &c. and if he have not enough, you may borrow some to make up a sufficient quantity: To these add his last words, dying expressions, &c. if they are to be had; mix all these together, and be sure you strain them well. Then season all with a handful or two of melancholly expressions, such as, dreadful, deadly, cruel cold death, unhappy fate, weeping eyes, &c. Have mixed all these ingredients well, put them into the empty scull of some young Harvard; (but in case you have never a one at hand, you may use your own,) there let them ferment for the space of a fortnight, and by that time they will be incorporated into a body, which take out, and having prepared a sufficient quantity of double rhymes, such as, power, flower; quiver, shiver; grieve us, leave us; tell you, excell you; expeditions, physicians; fatigue him, intrigue him; &c. you must spread all upon paper, and if you can procure a scrap of Latin to put at the end, it will garnish it mightily; then having affixed your name at the bottom, with a *Mœstus Composuit,* you will have an excellent elegy.

THE BUSY BODY PAPERS

It will be recalled that the *Busy Body Papers* were written when Franklin was a young printer in Philadelphia and had been foiled in his plan to publish a newspaper by Samuel Keimer, who learned of his plan and beat him to the punch. The Busy Body letters were submitted to Bradford's newspaper, *The Mercury,* as a counter-blow by Franklin to divert attention from Keimer's *Gazette.*

These letters are a series of light, satirical essays begun by Franklin and continued by his friend Joseph Breitnal. In the first letter the author describes himself as a moral critic (*censor morum*) for the public welfare, since he is concerned with the growing vices and follies of his country folk. Observing that, "what is every body's business is no body's business," he has decided to take "no body's business" wholly into his own hands. He becomes a busy body, a general meddler—"because I am naturally enclined to be meddling with things that don't concern me." He will expose whatsoever he finds "nonsensically ridiculous or immorally dishonest." Why is he doing it? "Purely for the good of my country." Besides, he rashly informs Mr. Bradford, who is publishing these essays in his newspaper, that his paper is "frequently very dull," and supposedly needs something new to stimulate the readers. Realizing that people do not like to be told of their faults, he assures the readers "if any are offended at my publickly exposing their private vices, I promise they shall have the satisfaction in a very little time of seeing their good friends and neighbours in the same circumstances."

In *Busy Body No. 2* Franklin lives up to his role as a moral critic treating the subjects of ridicule and satire. "Among the tribe of laughers I reckon the pretty gentlemen that write satire . . . taking an advantage of the ill taste of the town, to make themselves famous for a pack of paultry low nonsense, for which they deserve to be kicked rather than admired. . . ." He takes these to be the most incorrigible of his readers and anticipates "they will be squibbing at the Busy Body himself."

Busy Body No. 3 treats the subject of virtue and takes a swipe at Franklin's adversary, Keimer, by contrasting two characters. One, called Cato, is a simple fellow and a paragon of virtue. The other, a caricature of Keimer, is Cretico, of whom the Busy Body says: "Thou sowre philosopher! . . . Thou art crafty, but far from being wise." He gives Cretico some friendly advice: "Neglect those musty authors; let them be covered with dust and moulder on their proper shelves: and do thou apply thy self to a study much more profitable, the knowledge of mankind, and thy self."

Readers might have recognized the sour philosopher as Samuel Keimer and doubtless this was Franklin's intention. Despite the Busy Body's disclaimer, "if any bad characters happen to be drawn in the course of these papers, they mean no particular person," Keimer nevertheless perceived himself as Cretico although he coyly wrote, "I have been seriously considering . . . which I would choose to be, Cato or the Cretico." However, he decried "the odiousness of defamation and scandal" and warned the Busy Body of the ill effect of his gross descriptions.

In *Busy Body No. 4,* Franklin enjoys his favorite game of writing a fictitious letter to the editor and then answering it himself. He presents a letter which, he says, "I regard the more for that it comes from one of the fair sex." The lady has a problem:

> I am a single Woman, and keep a shop in this town for a livelyhood. There is a certain neighbour of mine, who is really agreeable company enough, and with whom I have had an intimacy of some time standing; But of late she makes her visits so excessively often, and stays so very long every visit, that I am tired out of all patience. I have no manner of time at all to my self; and you, seem to be a wise man, must needs be sensible that every person has little secrets and privacies that are not proper to be exposed even to the nearest friend. Now I cannot do the least thing in the world, but she must know all about it; and it is a wonder I have found an opportunity to write you this letter.

The lady explains that she likes her neighbor and doesn't wish to offend her by sending her away. Besides, she is a good customer. But there are complications.

> But, alas, Sir, I have not yet told you half my afflictions. She has two children that are just big enough to run about and do pretty

mischief: These are continually along with Mamma, either in my room or shop. . . . Sometimes they pull the goods off my low shelves down to the ground, and perhaps where one of them has just been making Water; My friend takes up the stuff, and cries, Eh! THOU LITTLE WICKED MISCHIEVOUS ROGUE!—but it has done no great damage; 'tis only wet a little; and so puts it up upon the shelf again. Sometimes they get to my cask of nails behind the counter, and divert themselves, to my great vexation, with mixing my ten-penny and eight-penny and four-penny together. I endeavour to conceal my uneasiness as possible, and with a grave Look go to sorting them out. She cries, Don't thee trouble thy self, Neighbour: Let them play a little; I'll put all to rights my self before I go.

But things are never so put to rights but that I find a great deal of work to do after they are gone. Thus, Sir, I have all the trouble and pesterment of children, without the pleasure of calling them my own. And they are now so used to being here that they will be content no where else. If she would have been so kind as to have moderated her visits to ten times a day, and stayed but half an hour at a time, I should have been contented, and I believe never have given you this trouble. But this very morning they have so tormented me that I could bear no longer. For while the mother was asking me twenty impertinent questions, the youngest got to my nails, and with great delight rattled them by handfuls all over the Floor. And the other at the same Time made such a terrible din upon my counter with a hammer, that I grew half distracted.

In her confusion she cut the apron she was making out of shape and spoiled a piece of her best muslin. She pleads:

Pray, Sir, tell me what I shall do . . . But I have twenty things more to tell you besides all this; There is a handsome gentleman that has a mind to make love to me, . . . but he can't get the least opportunity to: O dear, here she comes again; I must conclude Yours, PATIENCE

It is understandable that poor Patience has run out of patience, and the Busy Body sympathizes with her, but without solving her problem he takes readers to Turkey to observe how its people cope with guests who stay too long. Quoting "an author of unquestionable veracity" he writes:

When you visit a person of quality and have talked over your business, . . . he makes a sign to have things served in for the entertainment, which is generally, a little sweetmeat, a dish of sherbet, and another of coffee; all which are immediately brought in by the servants, and tendered to all the guests in order, with the greatest care and awfulness imaginable. At last comes the finishing part of your entertainment, which is, perfuming the beards of the company.

This ceremony may perhaps seem ridiculous at first hearing; but . . . I will say this in its vindication, that it's design is very wise and useful. For it is understood to give a civil dismission to the visitants; intimating to them, that the master of the house has business to do, or some other avocation, that permits them to go away as soon as they please; and the sooner after this ceremony the better. By this means you may, at any time, without offence, deliver your self from being detained from your affairs by tedious and unseasonable visits; and from being constrained to use that piece of hypocrisy so common in the world, of pressing those to stay longer with you, whom perhaps in your heart you wish a great way off for having troubled you so long already.

The fifth paper was announced as designed to be "a terror to evil-doers" but was actually a preposterous jest, in which the censor of morals became a moral policeman determined to reform local transgressors.

There are little follies in the behaviour of most men, which their best friends are too tender to acquaint them with: There are little vices and small crimes which the law has no regard to, or remedy for: There are likewise great pieces of villany sometimes so craftily accomplished, and so circumspectly guarded, that the law can take no hold of the actors. All these things, and all things of this nature, come within my province as Censor, and I am determined not to be negligent of the trust I have reposed in my self, but resolve to execute my office diligently and faithfully.

The Busy Body assures his readers that he takes no delight in raking into the dunghill lives of vicious men, and so as not to alarm the many people whose past may embarrass them, he graciously grants a reprieve for all crimes an offenses committed from the year 1681 up to the date of his first paper.

I shall take no notice who has, (heretofore) raised a fortune by fraud and oppression, nor who by deceit and hypocrisy; what woman has been false to her good husband's bed, nor what man has, by barbarous usage or neglect, broke the heart of a faithful wife, and wasted his health and substance in debauchery; what base wretch has betrayed his friend, and sold his honesty for gold, nor what yet baser wretch, first corrupted him and then bought the bargain: All this, and much more of the same kind I shall forget and pass over in silence; but then it is to be observed that I expect and require a sudden and general amendment.

And so that people will not think they can conceal their evil-doing and thereby escape being exposed, the Busy Body reveals a letter from a reader who has wonderful powers of discovering iniquity however it may be hidden.

"I rejoice Sir, at the opportunity you have given me to be service-able to you, and by your means to this Province. You must know, that such have been the circumstances of my life, and such were the marvellous concurrences of my birth, that I have not only a faculty of discovering the actions of persons that are absent or asleep; but even of the devil himself in many of his secret workings, in the various shapes, habits and names of men and women. And having traveled and conversed much and met but with a very few of the same perceptions and qualifications, I can recommend my self to you . . . My father's father's father (for we had no grandfathers in our family) was the same John Bunyan that writ that memorable book *The Pilgrim's Progress*, who had in some degree a natural fac-ulty of Second Sight. This faculty . . . was enjoyed by all his De-scendants, but not by equal talents.

Indeed the talent might have become extinct in his family had not his father been a traveler. A trip to New England apparently helped to revive this power, for the reader's older brother, who was born there, had so much of this faculty that he was able to detect witches in their occult performances.[1] Sharing with New England a natural atmosphere for supernatural phenomena were the Highlands of Scotland, where the second-sighted reader, himself, was born. The soil, climate and as-tral influences in Scotland apparently all combined to concentrate this faculty in his person, so he was now able to sit closeted in his room and through his inner vision continually see numbers of men, women and children distances away and everything they were doing. Not one to waste such a remarkable talent for doing good, he offers his services to the Busy Body. The Busy Body apologizes for concealing the name

[1] This is a jibe at the Salem and other witch trials in New England which Cotton Mather helped to prosecute. B. F. would return to the subject in his newspaper.

of his correspondent, but the life and safety of someone with such unusual powers must be secured. To illustrate this necessity for secrecy, Franklin tells a little story, which he had borrowed from *The Spectator* of Addison and Steele:

> I remember the fate of my poor monkey: He had an illnatured Trick of grinning and chattering at every Thing he saw in petticoats. My ignorant country neighbours got a notion that Pugg snarled by instinct at every female who had lost her virginity. This was no sooner generally believed than he was condemned to Death; By whom I could never learn, but he was assassinated in the night, barbarously stabbed and mangled in a thousand places, and left hanging dead on one of my gate posts, where I found him the next morning.

The Busy Body now asserts his plan of not only being a moral censor but a censor of all writing, which must receive his approval and the payment to him of a small fee. In case any of his readers take this outrageous plan seriously, he adds an amendment which indicates his humorous intent. This liberal amendment permits publication of all satirical writings about the Busy Body himself without censorship or payment of fees, "which indulgence," he adds, "the small wits in and about this city are advised gratefully to accept and acknowledge."

Breitnal wrote the rest of the series, except for No. 8, which was Franklin's last appearance as the Busy Body. This number ridicules those who pursue bizarre, get-rich-quick schemes in preference to hard work at their regular trades. The Busy Body claims to receive a proposal from an astrologer for the two of them to utilize the powers of the Busy Body's second-sighted friend to seek buried treasure and become the richest men of the Province. The astrologer, Titan Pleiades, is a thin disguise for Titan Leeds, the real life astrologer and almanac writer whom Franklin takes on as an adversary a few years later. Note the high falutin' salutation of the letter.

> 'To Censor Morum, Esq; Busy-Body General of the Province of Pennsylvania, and the Counties of Newcastle, Kent, and Sussex, upon Delaware. Honourable Sir:
> I judge by your lucubrations, that you are not only a lover of truth and equity, but a man of parts and learning, and a master of science. As such I honour you. Know then, Most Profound Sir, that I have from my Youth up, been a very indefatigable student in, and admirer of that divine science, astrology. I have read over Scot, Al-

bertus Magnus, and Cornelius Agrippa above 300 times; and was in hopes by my knowledge and industry, to gain enough to have recompenced me for my money expended, and time lost in the pursuit of this learning.

You cannot be ignorant, Sir, (for your intimate Second-sighted correspondent knows all things) that there are large Sums of money hidden under ground in divers places about this town, and in many parts of the country; but alas, Sir, notwithstanding I have used all the means laid down in the immortal Authors before mentioned, and when they failed, the ingenious Mr. P———d———l with his Mercurial Wand and Magnet, I have still failed in my purpose. This therefore I send to propose and desire an acquaintance with you, and I do not doubt, notwithstanding my repeated ill-fortune, but we may be exceedingly serviceable to each other in our discoveries. And that if we use our united endeavours, the time will come when the Busy-Body, his Second-sighted Correspondent, and your very humble Servant; will be three of the richest men in the Province. And then, Sir, what may not we do? A Word to the Wise is sufficient. I conclude with all demonstrable Respect Yours, and Uraniana's votary,

TITAN PLEIADES.

Upon receiving this proposition the Busy Body rushes to his second-sighted friend who assures him that there is no longer any silver or gold hid underground in the Province, not even one ounce. He himself had long since dug up the pirates' treasure and used it for charitable purposes. The second-sighted friend is concerned that so many honest laboring people have caught the get-rich-quick bug and are exhausting themselves and ruining their families in pursuing the imaginary hidden treasure. He gives us a glimpse of their frantic activities:

They wander thro', the woods and bushes by day to discover the marks and signs. At midnight they repair to the hopeful spot with spades and pickaxes. Full of expectation they labor violently, trembling at the same time in every joint, thro' fear of certain malicious demons who are said to hunt and guard such places. At length a mighty hole is dug, and perhaps several cartloads of earth thrown out, but alas, no cag or iron pot is found, no seaman's chest crammed with Spanish pistoles, or weighty pieces of eight!

Then they conclude, that thro' some mistake in the procedure, some rash word spoke, or some rule of art neglected, the guardian spirit had power to sink it deeper into the earth and convey it out of their reach. Yet when a man is once thus infatuated, he is so far from being discouraged by ill success that he is rather animated to double his industry, and will try again and again in a hundred different places in hopes at last of meeting with some lucky hit that shall at once sufficiently reward him for all his expense of time and labor.

The belief in pirates' gold is so strong, we are told, that you can hardly walk half a mile out of town in any direction without seeing several pits dug by gold-struck citizens. There seems to be such a peculiar charm in this method of acquiring riches that if the sands of the Schuylkil River "were so mixed with small grains of gold, that a man might in a day's time with care and application get together to the value of half a crown,[1] I make no question but we should find several people employed there, that can with ease earn five shillings a day at their proper trades."

In this piece Franklin seems to be advising fortune hunters of generations to come, the '49ers of the last century and the stock speculators of this one. He recognizes the universal attraction in the pursuit of precious metals but observes that certain, if not sudden, wealth is to be considered in less glamorous occupations:

> There is certainly something very bewitching in the pursuit after mines of gold and silver, and other valuable metals. And many have been ruined by it. A sea captain of my acquaintance used to blame the English for envying Spain their mines of silver, and too much despising or overlooking the advantages of their own industry and manufactures. For my part, says he, I esteem the banks of Newfoundland to be a more valuable possession than the mountains of Potosi; and when I have been there on the fishing account, have looked upon cod pulled up into the vessel as a certain quantity of silver ore, which required only carrying to the next Spanish Port to be coined into pieces of eight; not to mention the National Profit of fitting out and employing such a Number of ships and seamen.

> Let honest Peter Buckrum, who has long without success been a searcher after hidden money, reflect on this, and be reclaimed from that unaccountable folly. Let him consider that every stitch he takes when he is on his shopboard, is picking up part of a grain of gold that will in a few day's time amount to a pistole; And let Faber think the same of every nail he drives, of every stroke with his plain. Such

---

[1] A crown was worth 5 shillings.

thoughts may make them industrious, and of consequence in time they may be wealthy. But how absurd is it to neglect a certain profit for such a ridiculous whimsey: To spend whole days at the George [tavern] in company with an idle pretender to astrology, contriving schemes to discover what was never hidden, and forgetful how carelessly business is managed at home in their absence. To leave their wives and a warm bed at midnight and fatigue themselves with the violent exercise of digging for what they shall never find, and perhaps getting a cold that cost their lives, or at least disordering themselves so as to be fit for no business beside for some days after. Surely this is nothing less than the most egregious folly and madness.

I shall conclude with the words of my discreet friend Agricola, of Chester County, when he gave his son a good plantation "My Son, says he," I give thee now a valuable parcel of land; I assure thee I have found a considerable quantity of gold by digging there. Thee mayst do the same. But thee must carefully observe this: Never to dig more than plow deep.

PART TWO

Franklin in Public Life

9

FRANKLIN BECOMES A PUBLIC MAN

THOMAS CARLYLE CALLED BENJAMIN FRANKLIN the father of all Yankees. Although Carlyle overestimated Franklin's influence, there is no denying the profound effect of Franklin's activities in shaping his country.

After making his mark as a printer, the young Philadelphian was soon influencing public opinion with his newspaper and almanac. At the same time he went into business, selling stationery, business forms, books, and then added other assorted items. The latter included ink, pencils, sealing wax, and, from time to time, Spanish wine, linseed oil, cheese, cod fish, compasses, his brother's homemade soap and his mother-in-law's salves and ointments. His faithful and industrious wife, Deborah, helped with the shop while her husband was busy with writing and printing.

No sooner had Franklin set up in business than he received an unsolicited visit from a local citizen, which he vividly recollected years later:

> There are croakers in every country always boding its ruin. Such a one then lived in Philadelphia, a person of note, an elderly man with a wise look and very grave manner of speaking. His name was Samuel Mickle. This gentleman, a stranger to me, stopped one day at my door and asked me if I was the young man who had lately

opened a new printing house. Being answered in the affirmative, he said he was sorry for me because it was an expensive undertaking and the expense would be lost, for Philadelphia was a sinking place, the people already half bankrupts or near being so—all appearances of the contrary, such as new buildings and the rise of rents, being to his certain knowledge fallacious, for they were in fact among the things that would soon ruin us. And he gave me such a detail of misfortunes now existing, or that were soon to exist, that he left me half-melancholy. Had I known him before I engaged in this business, probably I never should have done it. This man continued to live in this decaying place and to declaim in the same strain, refusing for many years to buy a house there because all was going to destruction, and at last I had the pleasure of seeing him give five times as much for one as he might have bought it for when he first began his croaking.

No doubt Franklin had another laugh when, 37 years after this visit, his daughter in Philadelphia wrote to him in England that Samuel Mickle's daughter was to be married, adding "she has a fine fortune." Despite his pessimism Sam Mickle had done very well for himself as had the recipient of his doleful tidings.

Franklin's success was no accident. He had ability, he was hard working, and he was willing to take a risk. As soon as he obtained enough capital from the success of his business he set up partnerships in the printing business in South Carolina, New York, and Connecticut. Through his contacts and his writings he got contracts as public printer for many of the colonies. In fact, he was so successful that he was able to retire only 20 years after Sam Mickle's memorable visit.

Franklin's unusual success has been a subject of interest to many millions of Americans wishing to emulate it. It was made of many parts. Franklin stressed industry and frugality, which indeed he practiced. But these qualities alone were not enough; one must have the *appearance* of them as well. Thus Franklin played the part that would win him public esteem in Quaker Pennsylvania. He dressed simply, avoided tavern and pool room, and never went fishing or shooting. He admits a book sometimes "debauched" him from his work, "but that was seldom, snug, and gave no scandal." Actually, Franklin was an avid reader and rose at 5 o'clock to provide time for reading before starting work at 8 in the morning. To make a public demonstration of his hard-working nature, he sometimes loaded up the paper he bought for his business on a wheelbarrow and wheeled it through the streets of Philadelphia in view of all the citizens.

The Junto, a club Franklin formed at this time, which may be said to be a forerunner of the Rotary, Kiwanis, and other businessman's clubs, played a part in his success. The main purposes of this club were self-improvement and fellowship, but the rules also provided that members would assist each other as they could in furthering their businesses. These contacts were valuable to Franklin and did bring him work, as he acknowledges, but indirectly they did much more for him. Franklin was never satisfied to live the life of a simple trades-man. His need for friendship was great and his intellect was outgoing and insatiable. He selected young men like himself for this club and it soon became a vital part of his life. The members read books and dis-cussed stimulating subjects of politics, science, morals, and phi-losophy.

One of the subjects the Junto discussed in 1729 was the need for more paper money in Pennsylvania. The wealthy creditors opposed it, fearing it would cause inflation, but the tradesmen and merchants like Franklin thought it would stimulate commerce. Franklin wrote and printed a pamphlet making a case for the paper currency, which won the battle in the Legislature. Those who favored this view saw to it that Franklin got the contract for printing the money, which was very profitable for him. Franklin always felt that his position was correct but he was sensitive to the problem of inflation, which was rampant in Colonial America and he admitted that there were limits to the dis-tribution of paper money. If we were to have a paper currency he felt it should be an honest one that holds its worth. "Were we about to order a true Standard Yard . . . and a true Standard Peck . . . no man in his senses would propose the yard to be made of a knit garter, and the peck of a ribb'd stocking." A five dollar bill should not be worth four dollars, and calling it five dollars does not make it so. "Values will be as they are valued . . . and not as we call them."

In the Junto, Franklin relaxed his policy about avoiding taverns and idleness for in the name of fellowship he heartily drank rum and wine and sang together with his companions. He even composed some drinking songs:

The Antediluvians were all very sober
For they had no wine, and they brewed no October; [ale]

All wicked, bad livers, on mischief still thinking,
For there can't be good living where there is not good drinking
                              Derry down.

'Twas honest old Noah first planted the vine,
And mended his morals by drinking its wine;
He justly the drinking of water decry'd;
For he knew that all mankind, by drinking it, dy'd.
                              Derry down.

From this piece of history plainly we find
That water's good neither for body or mind;
That virtue and safety in wine-bibbing's found
While all that drink water deserve to be drowned.
                              Derry down.
So for safety and honesty put the glass round.

In *Poor Richard,* Franklin had said of his poetry: "Souse down into prose again, my muse; for poetry's no more thy element, than air is that of the flying-fish, whose flights, like thine, are always short and heavy." Now he turned to songs, which technically might not be considered poetry. Another song that Franklin composed about the time was committed to writing some 40 years later when he was ambassador to France. In this song the singer exhorts his cohorts to seek happiness in love, riches, or power. But they know better; that happiness is not to be found in any of these things but only in friends and wine, to which the singer finally assents. The expression, "bear the bell," means win the prize:

Fair Venus calls; her voice obey;
In beauty's arms spend night and day.
The joys of love all joys excell,
And loving's certainly doing well.

Chorus

Oh! no!
Not so!
For honest souls know
Friends and a bottle still bear the bell.

Then let us get money, like bees lay up honey;
We'll build us new hives and store each cell.
The sight of our treasure shall yield us great pleasure;
We'll count it and chink it and jingle it well.

Chorus. Oh! no! etc.

If this does not fit ye, let's govern the city;
In power is pleasure no tongue can tell.
By crowds though you're teased, your pride shall be pleased,
And this can make Lucifer happy in hell.

Chorus. Oh! no! etc.

Then toss off your glasses and scorn the dull asses
Who, missing the kernel, still gnaw the shell;
What's love, rule, or riches? Wise Solomon teaches
They're vanity, vanity, vanity still.

Chorus

That's true!
He knew!
He'd tried them all through;
Friends and a bottle still bore the bell.

In the Junto, the members discussed morality and how to achieve it, but Franklin, who had a passion for self improvement, was determined to do something about it. His goal was high; no less than his own moral perfection. He made a list of moral virtues, 13 in all, and he kept a daily account of his conduct in each virtue in a notebook he carried with him. While he never achieved his goal of perfection, his careful self examination helped him break some old habits and correct some errors he saw in himself. The virtue of Order gave him the most trouble. Order with regard to a place for things like papers was extremely difficult for him to acquire since he had an excellent memory and it conveniently substituted for an orderly system. He made so little progress in trying to rectify this matter that he was almost ready to give up and content himself with a faulty character in this respect. He compared himself to the man buying an ax from a smith. The man desired to have the whole surface as bright as the edge, and the smith consented to grind it bright for him if he would turn the wheel. He agreed and turned while the smith pressed the broad face of the ax hard and heavily on the stone, which made turning very fatiguing. Every now and then the man left the wheel to see how the work was coming; finally saying he would take the ax as it was, without further grinding. ''No,'' said the smith, ''turn on, turn on; we shall have it bright by and by; as yet 'tis only speckled." "Yes," said the man, "but I think I like a speckled ax best."

At first Franklin's list only contained 12 virtues. But a Quaker friend informed him that he was generally thought of as proud and that in his conversation he could be overbearing and insolent. He determined to cure himself of this vice and made humility the 13th virtue on his list. He could not boast of much success in acquiring this virtue but he was able, at least, to give the appearance ot it. He became less dogmatic in his conversation and instead of asserting his opinion he adopted expressions such as "I imagine" and "It so appears to me at present." As a result he found his conversations more pleasant and the modest presentation of his opinions procured them a more ready reception than before. Franklin concluded, however, that there is "no one of our natural passions so hard to subdue as pride; disguise it, struggle with it, beat it down, stifle it, mortify it as much as one pleases, it is still alive and will every now and then peep out and show itself . . . For even if I could conceive that I had completely overcome it, I should probably be proud of my humility."

But Franklin did not fret over his inability to achieve moral perfection, for he reasoned that such extreme nicety might be a kind of foppery in morals which might make him appear ridiculous. Besides it would not be wise; "A man without faults is a hateful creature," attracting envy and enmity. "A benevolent man," he thought, "should allow a few faults in himself, to keep his friends in countenance." He might have concluded from this reasoning, "I think I like a speckled character best."

Further evidence of Franklin's self improvement was his study of foreign languages. He started with French and then undertook Italian. An acquaintance who was also studying that language would often tempt Franklin to play chess with him. Finding that took too much of his study time, he finally refused to play any more, except on the condition that the victor in every game should have the right to impose a task, either in the grammar to be learned, or in translations, etc. The loser was on his honor to perform his task before the next meeting. "And as we played pretty equally, we thus beat one another into that language."

His love for books led Franklin to propose that the Junto members pool their books and keep them at Junto headquarters so that the combined library would be available to all members. Books were meant to be read, not kept for prestige. Franklin satirized this class of book collector under the name of Pollio:

> Pollio, who values nothing that's within,
> Buys books as men hunt beavers—for their skin.

The scheme he proposed was tried but had some problems so he came up with another plan—a lending library open to subscription by all citizens. This was the first lending library in America and was a great success, serving as a model to many others that would follow and raise the intellectual level of Americans. To the Junto he proposed other plans, which led to an efficient police force and the first fire department in Philadelphia. He published a paper on the education of youth in Pennsylvania, which led to an academy being established in Philadelphia that eventually became the University of Pennsylvania.

Franklin's reputation as a public spirited citizen was now well recognized in Philadelphia. When a physician friend conceived the idea of establishing a hospital, there being none to this date in America, he met with little success. Wherever he went to obtain assistance he was asked, "Have you consulted Franklin on this business, and what does he think of it?" When he described the plan to Franklin, the latter not only subscribed to it himself but heartily agreed to procure subscriptions from others. He promoted it in the newspapers and money started to come in but then lagged. He knew that voluntary contributions would not be enough; there would have to be help from the government, so he prepared a petition to the Assembly. It ran into a snag because the country members felt it would serve only the city people, who they thought should have to pay for it. Besides, they doubted that the city people would support it. When Franklin stated that he could raise 2000 pounds from voluntary donations, they rejected that as impossible. This led Franklin to his scheme. He wrote a bill stating that the House would provide 2000 pounds for the hospital only if such an amount should be raised first by contributors. The members who were in opposition to the grant now conceived that they might get credit for being charitable without the expense, and voted for its passage. As soon as the bill had passed, Franklin began again to solicit funds from the public, using the argument that now every man's donation would be doubled. The subscription accordingly exceeded the necessary amount and with the Assembly's grant a handsome building was erected and became a useful and flourishing institution.

As soon as this was accomplished, a minister called upon Franklin to ask his assistance in procuring funds for a new meeting house. Since Franklin did not wish to wear out his welcome with his fellow citizens by constantly dunning them, he absolutely refused the request. The minister then requested a list of names of generous citizens. Again Franklin refused, not wishing to take advantage of these good people by marking them for solicitation by other beggars. The minister finally asked Franklin to give him, at least, his advice. "That I will readily do. In the first place, I advise you to apply to all those who you know will give something; next, to those who you are uncertain whether they will give anything or not, and show them the list of those who have given; and lastly, do not neglect those who you are sure will give nothing, for in some of them you may be mistaken." The minister laughed, thanked Franklin, and said he would take his advice. He did so, for he asked everybody; and he obtained a much larger sum than he had expected, with which he erected a capacious and elegant meeting house.

In one case Franklin's generosity found him to be a donor rather than a solicitor for charities. Franklin was among a group of people boarding a boat going to New York when the canoe taking them to the boat overturned, throwing the passengers into the water. All were picked up safely and when they arrived in New York Franklin generously treated them to a liberal entertainment at a tavern. One of the passengers claimed to have been instrumental in saving Franklin's life, although it was never in danger and, besides, Franklin was an excellent swimmer. But the man used this excuse and his being poor to dun Franklin for money every time he saw him in the years that followed. Franklin always gave him something, and over the years it came to a considerable sum. The man died but to Franklin's consternation he received a letter of supplication from the widow. Franklin lamented, "He seems . . . to have left me to his widow as part of her dowry."

When a friend who was in financial straits came to him for help, Franklin was most sympathetic and gave the man the money he needed. But Franklin told him he was not giving him the money, only lending it to him. He was sure that a man with his good character would fall into better circumstances and then he would be able to pay off his debts. And then, when he met with another honest man in similar distress, he must pay his debt to Franklin by lending this sum to that man, and urging him to discharge the debt in the same way. Hopefully, the money would thus go through many hands before meeting with a knave who would stop its progress. Franklin acknowledged, "This is a trick of mine for doing a deal of good with a little money. I am not rich enough to afford much in good works, and so am obliged to be cunning and make the most of a little."

One of Franklin's greatest public accomplishments in Pennsylvania was the establishment of a militia for defense of the Province. It was not easy since the Quakers, who had a majority in the Assembly, were pacifists and the Proprietors in England were not anxious to spend any of their money on the Province. Making no headway through official channels he proposed a militia formed through a voluntary association of citizens, and in typical Franklin manner he organized a campaign that put it across. He published articles in his newspaper and an anonymous pamphlet, *Plain Truth,* in which he spelled out the danger. England was at war with Spain and France, and there had been rumblings in the northern colonies and privateer attacks near Philadelphia with the threat of more. The Indians on the frontier might be persuaded by the French to cause trouble. And Pennsylvania had no militia, no forts, no cannon for defense. "The way to secure peace is to be prepared for war," he wrote. And he reminded his readers of the saying, "One sword often keeps another in the scabbard." After the literature came a meeting, with Franklin explaining his plan and handing out subscriptions to sign. Within a few weeks there were over 10,000 subscribers, the people had provided themselves with arms, and formed themselves into companies and regiments. Franklin then proposed a lottery to defray the cost of building a battery and furnishing it with cannon. A few old cannon were bought from Boston, but these not being enough he tried to borrow some from Governor Clinton of New York. With three of his associates Franklin called on Clinton. Clinton refused them peremptorily; but then at dinner with his Council, where there was great drinking of Madeira wine, he softened a bit and agreed to lend them six cannon. After a few more bumpers he advanced to ten, and finally he very goodnaturedly conceded eighteen fine cannon complete with carriages. Franklin was chosen colonel of the Philadelphia regiment, but not feeling fit for that position he declined the honor. When their battery was completed and cannons were in place, he took his turn of duty as a common soldier.

To encourage the support of the ministers and their congregations in this venture, Franklin suggested the Governor and Council proclaim a fast day to implore the blessing of heaven on their undertaking. They approved but had no precedent from which to draw the proclamation. Franklin's experience in Puritan New England where a fast was proclaimed every year came in handy, and he drew up the paper in the accustomed style. It was very effective and even persuaded many of the Quakers.

Among the Quakers, particularly the younger ones, many became convinced that bearing arms for defense was acceptable even though they were uncompromisingly opposed to offensive war. One of the old Quakers, James Logan, who staunchly supported Franklin's efforts, told him an anecdote about his old master, William Penn. He had come over from England with Penn, serving as his secretary. It was wartime and their ship was chased by an armed vessel. The captain prepared for defense but told Penn and his Quakers that he did not expect their assistance and they might retire into the cabin, which they did. All except Logan, that is, who chose to remain on deck and was quartered to a gun. The armed vessel proved not to be an enemy, so there was no fighting. Nevertheless William Penn severely rebuked his young secretary for staying on deck and undertaking to defend the vessel contrary to Quaker principles. This reproof being given in front of the whole company piqued the secretary, who answered: "I being thy servant, why did thee not order me to come down? But thee was willing enough that I should stay and help to fight the ship when thee thought there was danger."

This conflict between religion and duty provided the Quakers in the Assembly continual embarrassment. When grants were requested by the Crown for military purposes they evaded when they could, and when they could not they tried to disguise their compliance by granting the money "For the King's use" without inquiring how it was used. When the funds were not demanded directly by the Crown other phrases had to be invented. For example, when powder was needed for the garrison at Louisburg which the government of New England solicited from Pennsylvania, the Quakers could not grant money to buy powder for that was an ingredient of war, but they voted funds for the purchase of bread, flour, wheat, "or other grain." The Governor understood that "other grain" meant gunpowder and there was never any objection to his use of the money to purchase that commodity.

When Franklin was concerned that the lottery for the battery might not be successful he said to one of the members of the Fire Company, "If we fail, let us move the purchase of a fire engine with the money; the Quakers can have no objection to that. And then we will buy a great gun, which is certainly a 'fire engine'."

As a newspaperman and an involved citizen Franklin had great interest in political affairs. Yet he withheld himself as a participant in the political arena. Had not *Poor Richard* warned of people who take such an interest in government they don't keep their own place in order:

> There's many men forget their proper station,
> And still are meddling with th' administration.
> Thus spending too much thought on state affairs.
> The business is neglected which is theirs.
> So some fond traveller gazing at the stars
> Slips in next ditch and gets a dirty arse.

But Franklin found a cozy niche for himself where he could observe the government in action but not have to take sides on every public issue, which could make him enemies and hurt his business. He got himself the job of Clerk of the Assembly, which let him hear all the speeches and be paid a salary besides. The speeches, he discovered, could be very long and tiresome and he found himself a hobby making mathematical puzzles of magic squares and circles while the debates droned on. The position of Clerk helped him secure profitable government business like the printing of votes, laws, and paper money; therefore he felt threatened when a new member promoted a candidate for his job. He had learned an old maxim, "He that has once done you a kindness will be more ready to do you another than he whom you yourself have obliged," and he put it to a test. Having learned that the new member had in his library a very scarce and curious book, he wrote him a note requesting the favor of borrowing it for a few days. The member sent it immediately and Franklin returned it in a week with another note earnestly expressing his sincere appreciation for the favor. When they next met he spoke to Franklin, which he had never done before, and manifested a readiness to help the young clerk on all occasions, with the result that they became great friends and Franklin had no trouble retaining his position.

Franklin's life was quite full with this position, his newspaper, the almanac, the shop, the Junto, the Freemasons, and good works. But he found time to invent a furnace that would heat houses efficiently without filling them with smoke and to conduct electrical experiments which were to bring him honorary degrees from three American colleges and even greater fame abroad. He formed the American Philosophical Society, the first scientific association in America, and he applied for and obtained the post of Deputy Postmaster-General of the Colonies. He laid out 300 pounds to cover contingent fees and charges for obtaining this position but advised his London friend who was handling the transaction that "the less it costs the better, as 'tis for life only, which is a very uncertain tenure."

As soon as he was financially able, Franklin retired from active business. He had other ambitions than accumulating wealth, as he wrote his aging mother: "I would rather have it said 'he lived usefully' than 'he died rich.' " No gentleman by birth, with no chance of a family inheritance, had there been one, his being "the youngest son of the youngest son for five generations back," he could now live the life of a gentleman and be free to do whatever he pleased. He chose to enter politics, where he conceived he could enlarge his power of doing good. He ran for a seat in the Assembly where as a clerk he had to listen to debates without taking part in them, and was elected every year for ten years. On Franklin's taking a seat in the House, his son was appointed to the vacant position of Clerk.

In the Pennsylvania legislature he was quickly drawn into the controversy with the Governor, who was under the control of the hereditary Proprietors, the sons of William Penn. The Penns, who lived in London, had large land holdings in Pennsylvania, and as was their right under the charter given by the Crown to their father, they appointed the Governor. No longer being Quakers and public spirited like their father, their interest was simply in drawing as much income as possible from the Province. When money had to be raised for defense, a difference arose over the taxing of all properties, including those of the Proprietors, with the Assembly insisting and the Governor resisting. As Franklin noted, only one word separated them. The money bill declared that all estates were to be taxed, those of the Proprietaries not excepted. The Governor's amendment would substitute the word "only" for "not." This was in Franklin's mind a small but very material alteration, and one which was a constant source of conflict. The messages and responses between the parties often were tart and sometimes indecently abusive. Yet the personal relations between the Governor and Franklin, who wrote the answers for the Assembly, were very cordial. One afternoon, at the height of the public quarrel, the two met on the street and the Governor invited Franklin to dinner. In the gay conversation over wine the Governor jokingly remarked that he liked the idea of Sancho Panza in Don Quixote who when offered a government, requested that it be composed of blacks, so if he did not agree with his people he might sell them. One of the Governor's friends said, "Franklin, why do you continue to side with these damned Quakers? Had not you better sell them? The Proprietor would give you a good price." Franklin replied, "The Governor has not blacked them enough."

The Governor did his best to blacken the Assembly, but they wiped off the coloring as fast as he laid it on, and returned it thick upon his own face, according to Franklin's account. Under the Assembly's pressure on the one side and on the other, under bond to the Proprietors not to concede, the Governor broke under the strain and quit, as did many other governors to follow. Franklin, who was the leader of the forces in the Assembly also felt the stress. He complained to a friend that he was heartily sick of the situation and if it weren't for his ability to influence a good measure occasionally he would not serve again, since both sides expected more from him than they should, blamed him sometimes for not doing what he was not able to do, and for not preventing what was not in his power to prevent. "The Assembly rides restive; and the Governor, tho' he spurs with both heels, at the same time reins-in with both Hands, so that the public business can never move forward; and he remains like St. George in the Sign, always on horseback, and never going on." This reminded Franklin of the old catch:

> There was a mad man,
> He had a mad wife
> And three mad sons beside,
> And they all got upon a mad horse
> And madly did they ride.

Franklin may have felt like General Shirley, the commander of the English forces in America at this time, who was happy to be replaced by another commander. Franklin met Shirley in New York at a party for the incoming general. It was a big affair and some chairs had been borrowed, among them a very low one in which Shirley was seated. Franklin commented, "They have given you, sir, too low a seat." He replied "No matter, Mr. Franklin, I find a low seat the easiest!"

Referring to the Proprietors, Franklin stated, "if I have offended them by acting right, I can, whenever I please, reverse their displeasure by acting wrong." But the wound was never healed. He said, "We know that whatever our distresses are, the Proprietor has no bowels; he never relents." The opposition did its best to win Franklin to its side. They had his son appointed Governor of New Jersey but Ben remained as determined as ever. One of the governors flatly tried to buy him off with "adequate acknowledgements and recompenses." He assured Franklin he wanted harmony and no one could be more serviceable to that end than himself. The Governor ordered a decanter of Madeira and the more he drank the more profuse were his solicitations and promises. Franklin's answer was that his circumstances, thanks to God, were such as to make these favors unnecessary to him.

An anecdote comes down about Franklin's ability to stand up to such pressure. He had been outspoken on some issue which aroused the opposition of rich and influential men. His friends were alarmed and urged him to desist, whereupon Franklin invited them to dinner the following night. At the dinner Franklin's wife served nothing but pudding and water. He then thanked his friends for their advice but said he had no intention of following it: "He who can subsist upon sawdust pudding and water, as can Benjamin Franklin, needs not the patronage of any man."

10

THE SAGE AND THE SAVAGES

THE WISDOM OF FRANKLIN'S ACTIVITIES FOR Pennsylvania's defense was not immediately apparent because peace came unexpectedly and everything quieted down for a few years. But in 1754 the French and Indian Wars introduced a decade of sporadic fighting in the colonies with feverish preparation for defense, and as might be expected Franklin was in the midst of it. The British government, not approving of Franklin's plan for the unified defense of the colonies for fear that they would become too strong and independent in a military way, chose instead to send over General Braddock with two regiments of regular English troops to dispatch the Indians and the French. The Pennsylvania Assembly, as a gesture of good will, sent Franklin to meet him. Braddock was anxious to get on with the job but he was unable to obtain enough wagons to convey the stores and baggage for the campaign. Franklin was asked if he could obtain the wagons, horses, and supplies of food. With some difficulty, he did produce them but only after giving his personal bond as guarantee for their safe return.

General Braddock became very friendly with Franklin and discussed his plan of attack with him. He was blusteringly confident, planning to take Fort Duquesne (now Pittsburgh) in three or four days, then proceed on to take Niagara and Frontenac. Franklin thought Braddock was a brave man and might have made a good officer in a European war, but he had too high an opinion of his regular troops and too low an opinion of both Americans and Indians. Franklin was concerned that Braddock's Army, in tracking through the woods over a narrow road, would make a long line that the Indians could cut like a thread into pieces. Braddock smiled at this. "These savages may indeed be a formidable enemy to your raw American militia, but upon the King's regular and disciplined troops, Sir, it is impossible they should make any impression." Franklin had provided the General with an Indian interpreter plus guides and scouts who could have been of great use to him if he had treated them decently, but he slighted and neglected them and they gradually left him.

The campaign was a disaster. The troops were ambushed and 714 out of 1,100 picked men were killed. The bewildered remnant fled leaving all their supplies, including the wagons for which Franklin stood personally responsible. "This whole transaction," noted Franklin, "gave us Americans the first suspicion that our exalted ideas of the prowess of British regulars had not been well founded." The General himself, mortally wounded, was brought off the field, where he died in a few days. As his aide-de-camp reported to Franklin, the General was completely silent the first day and that night his only words were "Who could have thought it?" He was silent the second day, and then in his last minutes said, "We shall better know how to deal with them another time."

Franklin now found himself being sued by the farmers for the wagons he had guaranteed and he would have been ruined if General Shirley, who took command after Braddock, had not made good the money. Many of his expenses, however, could not be presented until much later and when these did not get paid Franklin protested to Lord Loudon, General Shirley's successor. Franklin stated that he had charged no commissions or fees for his service and it was not just for him to have to wait any longer. "Oh, Sir," Lord Loudon replied, "you must not think of persuading us that you are no gainer. We understand better these affairs and know that everyone concerned in supplying the army finds means in the doing it to fill his own pockets." Franklin's assurance that he had not pocketed a farthing was brushed aside and he never did receive payment. Disgusted with Loudon, whose conduct of the war Franklin described as frivolous, expensive, and disgraceful beyond conception, he wondered how such a man could come to be entrusted with such important business as the conduct of a great army, "but having since seen more of the great world . . . my wonder is diminished."

The crushing defeat of Braddock had no more effect on the Governor of Pennsylvania than "the miracles of Moses had on the heart of Pharaoh." But when the news reached England, the Proprietors were forced to make a compromise and a militia bill was quickly passed and funded. Thereupon the Governor prevailed upon Franklin to take care of the northwestern frontier, by raising troops and building a line of forts. The frontier was then less than a hundred miles from Philadelphia, and when the village of Gnadenhütten near the Moravian settlement of Bethlehem was burned and the inhabitants were massacred by a war party of Shawnee, the Government became uneasy. With fifty cavalrymen Franklin set out for Bethlehem, Easton, and Reading. Easton was in a state of terrified disorder but Bethlehem surprised Franklin by having such a good defense posture. A quantity of arms and ammunition had been purchased from New York; in addition, people had piled up small paving stones by the windows of their high stone houses for the women to throw down on the heads of invading Indians. Franklin's surprise at this was occasioned by his knowledge that the Moravians had obtained an act of Parliament exempting them from military duties, and he had supposed they were conscientiously scrupulous about bearing arms. Their leader explained that bearing arms was not one of their established principles but at the time of the act of Parliament it was thought to be a principle with many of their people. On the present occasion, however, they found to their surprise it was adopted by only a few.

At Bethlehem Franklin recruited more men and dispatched groups of them to various outposts to build stockades. He, himself, with 130 men, 70 skilled axmen, a doctor, a chaplain, plus horses and wagons set out for Gnadenhütten. Just before they left he was met by eleven farmers who had been driven off their farms by Indians. They wanted to go back and get their cattle and requested guns and ammunition, which Franklin gave them. Gnadenhütten was twenty miles from Bethlehem and Franklin's party got caught in the rain along the way. It was fortunate they were not attacked, Franklin said, for they could not keep their gunlocks dry. The Indians, he observed, were more dexterous in contrivancies for that purpose. That day the Indians had met the eleven poor farmers whose guns would not go off, the priming being wet from the rain, and killed ten of them. On the second day

Franklin's men reached Gnadenhütten, where they planned their fort and set the axmen to work chopping down trees. The trees fell so fast that Franklin, the efficiency expert, took out his watch and timed two men cutting a pine. It took them just 6 minutes to cut down a 14-inch tree, and all that were needed were cut in only five hours. By evening they had enclosed their camp with a strong breastwork and provided themselves with a shelter from the weather. It rained so hard every other day that the men could not work, yet the stockade, 125 feet long by 50 feet wide, which Franklin apologized for calling a fort, was completed in a week. They hoisted their flag and sounded their guns to warn any Indians in earshot.

The efficiency expert was also a psychologist. He concluded from watching the men that they were most contented when they were employed. The days they worked they were goodnatured and cheerful, but on the idle days they were quarrelsome and mutinous, finding fault with their food and everything else. This put him in mind of a sea captain whose rule it was to keep his men constantly at work. On one occasion the mate told him that they had completed their work and there was nothing left for them to do, "Oh," he replied, "make them scour the anchor."

They saw no Indians but saw the imprints of their bodies where they had been secretly lying in the grass, watching the men build the fort. Since it was midwinter the Indians had needed a fire to keep warm but they could not afford to reveal their position. To accomplish this they had made small fires with charcoal placed in the bottom of holes three feet deep. These gave no visible light, sparks or smoke yet allowed them to keep their feet warm, an essential matter with Indians.

The chaplain of the troop was a zealous Presbyterian minister who had complained to Franklin that the men were not attending prayers. When the men enlisted they were promised a gill of rum a day. They received half of it in the morning and half in the evening and were always prompt in coming for it. Franklin remarked to the chaplain that it might be below the dignity of his profession for him to act as steward of the rum. "But if you were to deal it out, and only after prayers, you would have them all about you," he predicted. The chaplain liked the idea, gave it a try, and "never were prayers more generally and punctually attended."

With everything at the fort under control Franklin returned to

Bethlehem where he rested up for a few days. The first night, being in a good bed, he had trouble sleeping since he had become accustomed to the hard floor of the fort where he slept wrapped only in a blanket or two. While at Bethelehem he took an interest in the practices of the Moravians and was especially intrigued by the way they arranged marriages. The leaders who were acquainted with the dispositions of the respective young people, he was told, could best judge what matches were suitable. Franklin objected, "If the matches are not made by the mutual choice of the parties, some of them may chance to be very unhappy." "And so they may," answered the Moravian elder, "if you let the parties choose for themselves"—which, indeed, Franklin could not deny.

When Franklin arrived in Philadelphia he was happy to learn that his plan for a voluntary militia was doing so well. The officers met him and chose him to be colonel of the regiment, and this time he accepted. He had 1,200 men and a company of artillery with six brass field pieces that the men could fire twelve times a minute. The first time he reviewed his regiment, they accompanied him to his house and saluted him with some rounds fired in front of his door, which knocked over several pieces of his electrical apparatus and shattered the glass in them. His new honor proved to be as brittle, for all the commissions were rescinded by the repeal of the militia law in England.

This expedition to the frontier was not Franklin's first encounter with Indians. In 1723 delegates of eight Indian nations, with their squaws and children, had arrived in Boston for conferences with the Massachusetts Assembly. Wherever they went crowds gathered around them and it is not likely that the young apprentice missed this treat. Much later, in commenting on the greater politeness of the Indians, he compared this brazen crowding around Indians by white people with the Indian's practice of hiding behind bushes to satisfy their curiosity in observing visitors to their camps. He was so interested in Indian affairs that during his business career he printed and sold the accounts of treaties made with the Indians from 1736–1762, and these documents remain a valuable record of those historical proceedings.

In 1753 the Governor commissioned Franklin and two others to make a treaty with the Indians of the Six Nations, Delawares, Shawnee, Miami, and Wyandots. The Indians were troubled by the pressure they were feeling from the expansion of the French on the west and the English Colonies on the east. They didn't have the confidence in the new white leaders that they had had in William Penn, who had treated them honestly and generously, and they wanted assurances from the English Americans that they would keep on their side of the mountains. The Colonials wanted peace with the Indians and needed them as a buffer between themselves and the French.

They met at Carlisle, Pennsylvania, where the Indians showed up with nearly a hundred men, women, and children. The negotiations could not proceed until after lengthy ceremonial formalities insisted upon by the Indians, which included the acceptance by them of gifts from the white men of blankets, belts, bolts of cloth, guns and ammunition, wampam, and rum. The Indian spokesman, an Oneida chief, eloquently appealed to white men to return to the peace they had once enjoyed. He used an old Indian expression which became one of Franklin's favorites. In exhorting all of the assembled Indian and whites for continued union and friendship he said, "Let us keep the chain from rusting." Franklin's friends in England and France remembered his encouraging them to follow the Indians' advice always to "keep the chain of friendship bright and shining."

Franklin recognized that on the one hand the Indians were "savages," simple childlike creatures; yet on the other hand, from their very simplicity arose wisdom that was lost on more sophisticated people. At the Carlisle conference the Indians demanded the rum they knew had been brought for them, but the commissioners, who were afraid they would get drunk and disorderly, refused. When the Indians complained, they were promised there would be plenty of rum after the business was finished. When that time arrived, the Indians claimed and received their rum. That evening, hearing a great rumpus, the commissioners went out to investigate and found that the Indians were all drunk and had made a great bonfire in the middle of the square. Men and women were quarreling and fighting, their dark-colored, half-naked bodies could be seen in the flickering light of the bonfire as they ran after and beat one another with firebrands. This sight, accompanied as it was by horrid yelling, was a scene that Franklin speculated as closely resembling a vision of hell as one could imagine.

At midnight some of the Indians came thundering at the door of the commissioners demanding more rum, but they did not get it. The next day they sent three of their old counselors to apologize for their misbehavior. The orator acknowledged the fault but blamed it on the rum, and then tried to excuse the rum by saying, "The Great Spirit who made all things made everything for some use, and whatever use he designed anything for that use it should always be put to. Now, when he made rum, he said, 'Let this be for Indians to get drunk with.' And it must be so.''

Then Franklin soberly observed that if it were the design of Providence "to extirpate these savages in order to make room for cultivators of the earth, it seems not improbable that rum may be the appointed means." He noted further that it had already annihilated all the tribes who formerly inhabited the seacoast.

The following year at Albany, New York, Franklin again had an occasion to meet and confer directly with the Indians of the Six Tribes. It was at this conference that he proposed his plan of union of the colonies for their mutual defense, only to see his plan whittled away by the delegates of the other colonies. As a skillful bargainer he accepted these deletions, commenting that "when one has so many different people with different opinions to deal with . . . one is obliged sometimes to give up some smaller points in order to obtain the greater." But as he saw the union itself slipping away due to petty jealousies among the colonies, he thought of what he earlier had written: "It would be a very strange thing if six nations of ignorant savages should be capable of founding a scheme for such an union, and be able to execute it in such a manner that it has subsisted for ages, and yet that a like union should be impracticable for ten or a dozen English Colonies, to whom it is more necessary."

As Franklin got to know the Indians, he gained more respect for them and appreciation of their customs. He didn't look down on them as heathen savages to be converted and domesticated, but as a different people with a way of life to be understood and even admired. They didn't have debtors' prisons like the English, or any jails at all, Franklin noted, because with them personal liberty was so highly valued. Debts of honor were generally paid since it was a disgrace to be dishonest. He deplored the cheating of Indians by white traders and urged instead gaining the Indians' friendship and military support by fair trading with low prices. Every Indian, he argued, is a disciplined soldier and soldiers of this kind are needed in America where European discipline is of no value. The Indians have been to the cities and have been shown the advantages of civilized arts and sciences but have no desire to adopt them. They live on the spontaneous production of nature by hunting and fishing, and they find it an easier and better life. The proof is that even when young white persons of either sex, who have been taken prisoner by the Indians and lived with them are ransomed, they return to the woods at their first opportunity. The Indians have few and only natural wants, which are easily supplied; but we have infinite artificial wants, and with no less craving for them. All this was said by Franklin long before Thoreau was born and thought of Walden.

If the Indians set so little value on what we prize so highly, what use would they have for our schools? Franklin relates an incident that occurred during a treaty.making session with Virginia and Six Nations at Lancaster, Pennsylvania, in 1744. After the parley the spokesman for Virginia offered to give a dozen Indian youths a free education at William and Mary College in Williamsburg, where they could be instructed in all the learning of the white people. According to the rules of politeness of the Indians, their answer was deferred since it might be thought that they treated the matter lightly and without proper respect if they answered without lengthy deliberation. On the next day, their speaker rose and expressed the Indians' deep sense of the kindness of the Virginia government for making this offer and then explained why they must refuse it:

> We know that you highly esteem the kind of learning taught in those colleges, and that the maintenance of our young men, while with you, would be very expensive to you. We are convinced, therefore, that you mean to do us good by your proposal; and we thank you heartily. But you, who are wise, must know that different nations have different conceptions of things; and you will therefore not take it amiss, if our ideas of this kind of education happen not to be the same with yours. We have had some experience of it; Several of our young people were formerly brought up at the colleges of the Northern Provinces; they were instructed in all your sciences; but, when they came back to us, they were bad runners, ignorant of every means of living in the woods, unable to bear either cold or hunger, knew neither how to build a cabin, take a deer, or kill an enemy, spoke our language imperfectly, were therefore neither fit for hunters, warriors, nor counsellors; they were totally good for nothing. We are however not the less obliged by your kind offer, tho' we decline accepting it; and, to show our grateful sense of it, if the gentlemen of Virginia will send us a dozen of their sons, we will take great care of their education, instruct them in all we know, and make men of them.

The incident is true; the offer was made and refused, as noted in the records, but the details are Franklin's creation.

When Franklin arrived in France in 1776, his reputation had preceded him and he was accepted as a great sage. The French people were eager to hear what he would tell them about the savages of America. Their late philosopher, J. J. Rousseau, had expounded his concept of the noble savage, in which he declared that wisdom and goodness resided in such simple people and wickedness was just a corruption of civilization. Would Franklin support such ideas? He was not one to disappoint his friends: "Savages we call them," he said, "because their manners differ from ours, which we think the perfection of civility; they think the same of theirs. Perhaps, if we could examine the manners of different nations with impartiality, we should find no people so rude as to be without any rules of politeness; nor any so polite as not to have some remains of rudeness." Franklin thought that the politeness of the Indians in conversation might have been carried to excess since it would not permit them to contradict what, in their presence, has been asserted to be the truth. He acknowledged the wisdom of this policy in permitting them to avoid disputes, but he personally found it difficult to know what they really thought. The missionaries, especially, complained about this conduct. The Indians would listen with great patience to the truths of the Gospel explained to them and give their usual tokens of assent and approval. You would think they were convinced. No such thing. It was just politeness.

As a case in point, Franklin told his French companions a little story about the Indians and the Swedish missionary.

A Swedish Minister, having assembled the chiefs of the Susquehanah Indians, made a sermon to them, acquainting them with the principal historical facts on which our religion is founded; such as the fall of our first parents by eating an apple, the coming of Christ to repair the mischief, his miracles and suffering, etc. When he had finished, an Indian orator stood up to thank him. "What you have told us," says he, "is all very good. It is indeed bad to eat apples. It is better to make them all into cider. We are much obliged by your kindness in coming so far, to tell us these things which you have heard from your mothers. In return, I will tell you some of those we have heard from ours. In the beginning, our fathers had only the flesh of animals to subsist on; and if their hunting was unsuccessful, they were starving. Two of our young hunters, having killed a deer, made a fire in the woods to broil some part of it. When they were about to satisfy their hunger, they beheld a beautiful young woman descend from the clouds, and seat herself on that hill, which you see yonder among the Blue Mountains. They said to each other, it is a spirit that has smelt our broiling venison, and wishes to eat of it; let us offer some to her. They presented her with the tongue; she was pleased with the taste of it, and said, 'Your kindness shall be rewarded; come to this place after thirteen moons, and you shall find something that will be of great benefit in nourishing you and your children to the latest generation.' They did so, and, to their surprise, found plants they had never seen before; but which, from that ancient time, have been constantly cultivated among us, to our great advantage. Where her right hand had touched the ground, they found maize; where her left hand had touched it, they found kidney beans; and where her backside had sat on it, they found tobacco.''

The good missionary, disgusted with this idle tale, said, ''What I delivered to you were sacred truths; but what you tell me is mere fable, fiction, and falsehood.'' The Indian, offended, replied, ''My brother, it seems your friends have not done you justice in your education; they have not well instructed you in the rules of common civility. You saw that we, who understand and practise those rules, believed all your stories; why do you refuse to believe ours?''

Certain unique characteristics of the Indians seemed to delight Franklin's fancy. He told Abbé Morellet that the Indians accept a fact at its face value and never attempt to seek its cause. This is the case for even an extraordinary occurrence such as that when an Indian in Philadelphia came to see him make a demonstration of lighting brandy with an electric spark. ''These white men are clever,'' said the Indian, without the least evidence of surprise or reflection.

Franklin's respect for the Indian was best illustrated by the great dignity with which he received Scotosh, son of the half-king of the Wyandot nation, when Franklin was president of the Pennsylvania Assembly in 1786. Scotosh, who was on his way to New York with his retinue, passed through Philadelphia and paid his formal respects to the head of that state. Chief Scotosh, with three strings of white wampum in his hand and by his side a white French trader acting as interpreter began his speech with the greeting, ''My Brothers.'' His first information was that among his people all was good. Then with great gravity he gave Franklin the first string of wampum. He began again with ''My Brothers,'' and noted that near Niagara Falls there are some bad Indians, but none of them were his people. Another wampum ceremony followed and another ''My Brothers.'' Then he explained that he was glad that the measuring of the Indian country might be delayed because he was afraid the bad people would do mischief and the measurers would be killed. Then he presented the third string of wampum. This was the message the Chief officially delivered on behalf of his father. Speaking for himself, he thanked his white brothers for making a clear road so that he could come with convenience and without danger. The Indians will do the same for you, he said, when you have occasion to visit our country. He asked for a response to the message from his father on how the mischief he feared might be prevented.

Although Scotosh had asked for the reply as soon as possible, Franklin did not want to be rude so he let him wait for two days while he "deliberated." Then, armed with three strings of wampum, Franklin responded in the same ceremonial fashion as the Chief, punctuating each statement with the saluation, "Our Brother," and closing with a string of wampum. He first expressed pleasure on behalf of the Assembly that all was well with the Wyandots. He was happy that none of them was among the bad people near the Falls, who would probably soon suffer for their evil action. On the matter of measuring land, this is far beyond the limits of Pennsylvania, under the direction of that great council, Congress. Since Scotosh was going to New York where Congress was seated, Franklin assured him that his friendly advice would be welcomed. He then gave Scotosh some white man's money for traveling expenses and a letter to a friend in New York introducing Scotosh and requesting accommodations and courtesies for him. Franklin concluded his speech by assuring the Chief, "we should endeavor always to keep the road between us open, clear, and safe."

As a humanitarian, Franklin saw the injustice of the white man's treatment of the Indian. He said: "It has appeared to me that almost every war between the Indians and whites has been occasioned by some injustice of the latter toward the former." Franklin tells of a meeting between Conrad Weiser, the Indian who served as interpreter for Pennsylvania, and his old friend Canassatego. The latter is inquiring about the white man's custom of assembling every seventh day in the great house; what is it for? "They meet there," says Conrad, "to hear and learn good things." Canassatego was skeptical, "If they met so often to learn good things, they would certainly have learnt some before this time. But they are still ignorant. You know our practice. If a white man is travelling thro' our country, enters one of our cabins, we all treat him as I treat you; we dry him if he is wet, we warm him if he is cold, we give him meat and drink . . . we spread soft furs for him to rest and sleep on; we demand nothing in return. But if I go into a white man's house at Albany, and ask for victuals and drink, they say, 'Where is your money?' and if I have none, they say, 'Get out, you Indian dog.' You see they have not yet learned those little good things, that we need no meetings to be instructed in, because our mothers taught them to us when we were children.''

Franklin was no romantic visionary like Rousseau; he was a product of the real world, a keen observer who had a strong feeling for justice. He deplored the war between Georgia and the Creek Indians. The land under dispute should have been purchased from the Indians, who would usually sell at bargain rates, he told the Governor of Georgia in 1787. The distress and expense caused by such wars make it cheaper as well as more honest to buy the Indian lands rather than take them by force.

Franklin's sympathetic attitude toward the Indians was acquired over the years with his involvement in Indian affairs. Perhaps the greatest single event in influencing this position was his confrontation with the Paxton Boys. The decade of the French and Indian War had caused deep hatred between the frontier people and the Indians. Fearing for their actual survival, the Indians had been fierce and brutal in their primitive manner of fighting. The English Colonials responded in kind by putting a bounty on the scalps of Indian men, women, and children. General Amherst even conceived of biological warfare on the Indians by sending them blankets inoculated with smallpox.

In Lancaster County, Pennsylvania, a gang of Scotch-Irish settlers known as the Paxton Boys vented their fury on a nearby village of domesticated Christian Indians, murdering the six who were present. The fourteen remaining were locked up in the workhouse for their protection by the authorities, but the Paxton Boys broke in and ruthlessly put them all, old and young, to the ax. There was little expression of public outrage on the part of the white citizens: as they looked at it, Indians were Indians. In fact many people in Pennsylvania actually favored the action, sharing the hatred of the red men.

Franklin's outcry was a voice in the wilderness. He reacted strongly, putting his righteous indignation into words in a stirring pamphlet, "A Narrative of the Late Massacres in Lancaster County." He described these Indians' long history of peaceful association with their white neighbors. The tribe had welcomed William Penn with presents of venison, corn, and skins and entered into a treaty of friendship. This treaty has been frequently renewed ''and the chain brightened, as they express it." He recounted the slaughter, plainly describing in brutal detail how the savage mob hacked to pieces the innocent, defenseless people.

"If an Indian injures me, does it follow that I may revenge that injury on all Indians?" he argued. "The only crime of these poor wretches seems to have been that they had a reddish-brown skin and black hair . . . If it be right to kill men for such a reason, then, should any man with a freckled face and red hair kill a wife or child of mine, it would be right for me to revenge it by killing all the freckled red-haired men, women, and children." He reminded his fellow citizens that even barbarians practice their barbarism only against their enemies, not against their friends. The perpetrators of this wicked slaughter he labelled Christian white savages, and predicted they would hear the shrieks of their victims and be haunted by their ghosts.

The pamphlet won the support of thinking people but aroused the ire of the opposition. With their appetite only whetted by their unpunished crimes, the fanatical Paxton gang grew into a frenzied mob of 500 men and began to move toward Philadelphia, determined to wipe out the 140 Moravian and Quaker Indians sheltered there. The authorities were thrown into a panic; without a militia Philadelphia was defenseless in the face of such a mob. The Governor sent for British troops from Carlisle to guard the Indians and, despite his personal antagonism, he called on Franklin to organize the local defense. In fact, as Franklin put it, he "did me the honor, in an alarm, to run to my house at midnight, with his councillors at his heels, for advice, and made it his headquarters." Franklin mustered eight companies and a battery of artillery to add to the three companies of British regulars who had arrived. The Governor asked Franklin to take command of the militia but he preferred to take his position in the ranks.

When the boisterous rioters arrived at the outskirts of Philadelphia they were challenged, and Franklin, as spokesman, with three other men went out to meet them. Backed up by solid military strength, his arguments became suddenly convincing and the insurgents dispersed quietly without a struggle. This was one of Franklin's finest hours. He wrote to an associate, "your old friend was a common soldier, a councillor, a kind of dictator, an ambassador to a country mob, and, on his returning home, nobody again." Like every great man, to his wife he was only a husband.

11

THE COLONIAL AGENT IN LONDON

IN 1757 BENJAMIN FRANKLIN ARRIVED IN LONDON AS colonial agent for the Province of Pennsylvania. Relations between the colonists and the hereditary Proprietors of Pennsylvania in England were bad and getting worse, so the Assembly dispatched Franklin to London to obtain concessions from them. Although he had expected his trip to be brief, his mission kept him in England for five years on this trip and eleven years on a succeeding trip.

Although Franklin worked hard and well on his assignment, which expanded in later years when a number of other colonies appointed him their agent as well, he failed to obtain the concessions he sought. The Proprietors were not interested so much in the goodwill of the colonists as in extracting as much money as they could from their American holdings. Franklin tried to go over their heads to the administrators of the royal government and to Parliament but he found either general indifference, or a feeling that the colonists should be taxed more heavily. There was a great deal of corruption in the government, which appalled Franklin and blocked the effectiveness of his diplomacy. And although he made many friends among those Englishmen who admired him for himself and his accomplishments, many of the titled aristocracy in high positions regarded him with disdain because of his common birth and ancestry.

Franklin returned to America in 1762 and began travelling over the country inspecting post offices in his official capacity as Deputy Postmaster General for the Colonies. In 1764 he was returned to London to petition the King for a change from proprietary to royal government. At that time Franklin was under the impression that the young King, George III, was a person of great moral integrity who would govern the Americans honestly and fairly. Franklin was to be disappointed by the King as he had been by the Proprietors and Parliament. The colonists were pressing for greater political and economic freedom and received instead greater restraint of their trade, imposition of new taxes, and the stationing of British troops in America. These actions inflamed the colonists, causing reactions by them, counteractions by the British, and further deterioration of relations, eventually leading to war. During these years Franklin was busy in England trying to persuade the government and the English people of the justice of the American position. However, in 1775, after being publicly rebuked by the British government and dismissed from his post as postmaster, he returned to America, joined the Continental Congress, and next year signed the Declaration of Independence.

In 1776 he left on another overseas mission, this time sent to represent the United States in France. Franklin remained in France during the Revolutionary War and a few years afterwards, until 1785. In France he was a diplomat, a money raiser, and in the eyes of the French people, a great, wise man engaged in a noble cause. On returning home from France he became President of the State of Pennsylvania, hosted the Constitutional Convention, worked on his autobiography, and died in 1790 at the age of 84.

Politics and government service occupied the greater part of Franklin's adult life. One can recount his accomplishments in this field—the Albany Plan of Union, the Articles of Confederation, his service as Ambassador to France, and his influence on the peace treaty with England—but we are primarily concerned with his peculiar brand of politics, namely politics with a wink. Franklin took part in the grave deliberations that accompanied the founding of his country and thanks to him they were not quite so grave.

One of the legitimate complaints of the colonists against the English rulers was in response to the incompetent governors and military leaders the government sent to America. These men were not skillful professionals but more often misfits, relatives, and cronies of the officials in power. It was Franklin's misfortune to meet up with such a public servant when preparing to leave for London on his first mission. He had booked passage on a packet boat from New York and sent ahead his luggage and supplies for the two to three month voyage when the General of the British Forces in America, Lord Loudon, arrived in Philadelphia and asked Franklin to assist him in negotiations between the Assembly and the Governor. These negotiations were deadlocked over the matter of whether the Proprietor's holdings could be taxed for defense costs like all other property in the colony. Consenting to Loudon's plea, Franklin succeeded in getting the Assembly to yield in this one instance. Franklin was now free to proceed with his voyage, but in the meantime the packet had sailed with his provisions. His only recompense, he lamented, was His Lordship's thanks for his service, while all the credit for the accomplishment went to Loudon.

Franklin had to provide for new provisions and another ship from New York. He spoke to Loudon, who as Commanding General during wartime, had to give his permission for the ships to sail. There were two ships at New York bound for England and Loudon informed Franklin that one was to sail very soon. Concerned that he not miss her, Franklin requested the precise time of departure. Loudon's answer was, "I have given out that she is to sail on Saturday next, but I may let you know, *entre nous,* that if you are there by Monday morning you will be in time, but do not delay longer." Having an unexpected delay at a ferry, it was Monday noon before Franklin arrived, and since the wind was fair he was afraid the ship might have sailed. He was much relieved to discover she was still in the harbor and would not depart until the next day.

"One would imagine that I was now on the very point of departing for Europe," Franklin wrote, "I thought so; but I was not then so well acquainted with His Lorships character, of which indecision was one of the strongest features." The ship did not sail on the next day, or the next week, or the next month. It was the beginning of April when Franklin hurried to New York but the end of June before he was on his way. Before sailing the ships had to await the General's letters, which were always to be ready tomorrow. The passengers were very impatient, particularly the merchants who had orders for fall goods. Yet they could do nothing but wait for his Lordship's letters, which were not ready. And yet, Franklin observed, whoever visited General Loudon found him always at his desk, pen in hand, and they concluded, "he must needs write abundantly."

One day Franklin visited the General to pay his respects, and met a messenger from Philadelphia, named Innis, who had arrived with a message from the Governor. He also delivered to Franklin some letters sent from his friends in Philadelphia, which occasioned Franklin to inquire when he would return so that he might carry back some letters Franklin would give him. He replied that he was ordered to return to the General's quarters at 9 for the General's reply to the Governor, and then would set off immediately. Franklin, therefore, made sure to put his letters for Philadelphia in Innis' hands the same day. Two weeks later Franklin met Innis again in the same place and addressed him.

> "So you are soon returned, Innis!"
> "Returned! No, I am not gone yet."
> "How so?"
> "I have called here by order every morning these two weeks past for His Lordship's letter, and it is not yet ready."
> "Is it possible, when he is so great a writer, for I see him constantly at his scritoire [writing desk]."
> "Yes," says Innis, "but he is like St. George on the signs, always on horseback, and never rides on."

The packets were finally permitted to sail down to Sandy Hook to join the Royal Fleet anchored there, and the passengers thought it best to be on board, so after all this time they would not be left behind if, by a sudden order, the ships should sail. They were detained at Sandy Hook for six weeks longer, consuming their sea stores and having to procure more. At last the fleet sailed and Franklin's ship was permitted to break away and steer for England. Two other packets, however, were obliged to sail with the fleet to Canada where for some time Loudon gave the men military exercises on sham forts in preparation for besieging Louisburg, but then changed his mind and returned to New York with the packets and their passengers. During Loudon's absence the French and Indians took Fort George and many defenders of the garrison were massacred.

Franklin, himself so decisive a person, was exasperated at Loudon's indecision. He had never before wasted so much time in his life. During his long wait he had his wife send him books on chess, which helped him fill the time more productively. Although one of his life-long resolutions was to maintain an unruffled disposition under all conditions, the compulsory indolence was too frustrating for him and according to a report by the captain to Loudon, "Franklin got drunk one day and talked plain language."

It was difficult for Franklin to imagine how a man like Loudon could be given a part of such great responsibility, but after he went to England and saw the inefficiency and general corruption in the government he was so longer surprised. Of the Parliament he wrote: "For as most of the members are bribing or purchasing to get in, there is little doubt of selling their votes to the minister . . . to reimburse themselves. Luxury introduces necessity . . . this brings most of the Commons as well as the Lords to market; and if America would save for three or four years the money she spends in fashions, fineries, and fopperies of this country, she might buy the whole Parliament, minister and all." When a committee of the government issued a report favorable to the Proprietors but ruinous to the colonists of Pennsylvania, Franklin made his appeal in a letter to the Prime Minister, William Pitt, who Franklin believed to be fair and reasonable. In a postscript to the letter he referred to the committee: "Between you and I it is said that we may look upon them all to be a pack of d——d r——ls [damned rascals], and unless we bribe them all higher than our adversaries can do, and condescend to every piece of dirty work they require, we shall never be able to attain common justice at their hands." This was an audacious statement for Franklin to make in writing to the Prime Minister; therefore to make it less official he ran his pen over it making two big crosses, which did not hide the words but made it unnecessary for Pitt to give it his official acknowledgment. Whether or not Pitt agreed with Franklin's assessment of the committee he certainly must have been amused by it. Pitt was later to befriend America and to defend Franklin against attack by his opponents, but he himself was disliked by the King and lost his high post.

England, in Franklin's eyes, was rich and corrupt, as contrasted to poor and virtuous America. In dealing with politicians, he said he took pains to speak the exact truth. "That is my only cunning; and the politicians are so corrupt that I always fool them by this means." Morality, he maintained, "was the single rational design for individual happiness as it was the sole guarantee of public happiness." After speaking at length on this theme, he concluded by assuring his companions, "If rascals knew all the advantages of virtue, they would become honest out of rascality."

Franklin was contemptuous of the government, which seemed oblivious to reason and justice. Years later Benjamin Rush recalled Franklin saying that "the ministry read history not to avoid blunders but to adopt and imitate them," and that "he could have purchased the independence of America for one-tenth of the cost of defending it, such was the venality of the British court." Writing to an English friend, he indicated in plain language his feelings about the temper of the government: "The taking of Havana [from Spain in the Seven Years War] . . . is a conquest of the greatest importance and will doubtless contribute a due share of weight in procuring us reasonable terms of peace; if John Bull does not get drunk with victory, double his fists, and bid all the world kiss his a——e." In a letter to a newspaper he lectured John Bull on his bad conduct toward his family:

> Give me leave, Master John Bull, to remind you that you are related to all mankind; and therefore it less becomes you than any body to affront and abuse other nations. But you have mixed with your many virtues, a pride, a haughtiness, and an insolent contempt for all but yourself, that I am afraid will, if not abated, procure you one day or other a handsome drubbing. Besides your rudeness to foreigners, you are far from being civil even to your own family. The Welsh you have always despised for submitting to your government: But why despise your own English, who conquered and settled Ireland for you; who conquered and settled America for you? Yet these you now think you may treat as you please because, forsooth, they are a conquered people. Why despise the Scotch, who fight and die for you all over the world? Remember, you courted Scotland for one hundred years and would fain have had your wicked will of her. She virtuously resisted . . . but at length kindly consented to become your lawful wife. You then solemnly promised to love, cherish, and honor her as long as you both should live; and yet you have ever since treated her with utmost contumely, which you now begin to extend to your common children. But pray, when your enemies are uniting in a Family Compact against you, can it be discreet in you to kick up in your own house a family quarrel?

This letter bore the signature Homespun. No doubt it relieved Franklin to express himself in the papers since he was not able to do so at court. The homely metaphorical style is so characteristic of Franklin that although the following letter in an English newspaper in

1766 is not known for certain to have been written by Franklin, the style and content have caused it to be included in his writings: "A certain judge . . . declared from the bench as his opinion that every man had a legal right to chastise [beat] his wife if she was stubborn and obstinate; but then he observed that his right ought to be exercised with great lenity and moderation."

"It seems our lawyers are of opinion," the author states, "that England has an indisputable right to correct her refractory children of North America. But then, as the judge observed, it ought to be done with temper and moderation, lest, like an unskillful surgeon, we should exasperate and inflame the wound we ought to mollify."

Franklin's agitation and determination during this period of anti-American policy by the government is indicated on his learning that three of his friends had been dismissed by the government from their appointed jobs as justices of the peace. He commented: "They do not, I dare say, sleep a jot the worse for their dismission. These are times in which 'The post of honor is a private station.' But those times, I think, will not long continue: At least nothing in my power shall be wanting to change them." In the same letter he predicted that the Stamp Act would pass despite his efforts in opposing it. The Stamp Act, a tax imposed on all documents in America, was considered unjust by Americans because it was an internal tax imposed by the government in England and America had no representation in Parliament. Thus the famous American cry "Taxation without Representation" was heard and grew louder as more taxes were levied from England. As Franklin predicted, the Stamp Act did pass and caused a storm of protest in America as well as the boycott of British goods. It was suggested that the Americans might be calmed and the prestige of Parliament maintained if the new act was administered so as to require tax stamps on such items as cards and dice but not on all public documents. This proposal was rejected by Franklin as not likely to be accepted, but one of the members of Parliament encouraged him to suggest other alternatives that would preserve the tax but remove America's objection to it. "I must confess," said Franklin, that I have thought of one amendment; if you will make it, the act may remain and yet the Americans will be quieted. It is a very small amendment too; it is the change of only a single word." "Aye," said the member, "What is that?" "It is in that clause where it is said that 'from and after the first day of November, one thousand seven hundred and sixty five, there shall be paid, etc.' The amendment I would propose is, for one, read two, and then all the rest of the act may stand as it does.''

British manufacturers, merchants, and shippers trading with America were losing business due to the American boycott resulting from the Stamp Act and Franklin organized them in favor of its repeal. They carried petitions for repeal to all the trading towns in the kingdom. Finally, under this pressure, the House of Commons agreed to hear witnesses on the harm this act was said to be doing. The star witness was Franklin, himself, the most famous American in England. He knew he would be sharply questioned by anti-American members so he carefully prepared for his examination. The examination was a smashing success: he out-dueled his adversaries and his friends asked him the very questions that he had coached them to ask. One of them asked whether Franklin might have a small amendment that would make the Stamp Act palatable to Americans but Franklin evaded the question, thinking the answer "too light and ludicrous for the House." A month later the Stamp Act was repealed.

The stakes had been high for Franklin. When the Stamp Act was passed, his enemies at home spread the word that he had sold out to the British. Franklin discounted them, calling them "the bird and beast people" with their "pecking, snarling, and barking." At first he felt that the malice of his enemies was harmless, saying, "All their arrows shot against us have been like those Rabelais speaks of, which were headed with butter hardened in the sun." But they roused a mob of rioters in Philadelphia who tried to burn his house down, and would have done it had not his wife bravely held them off at rifle point. Fortunately, not all his opponents were so violent. Lord Clare, whom he had made look silly in the debate over the Stamp Act, invited Franklin to his house for dinner. He told Franklin that during his examination in Commons he had answered some questions a little pertly, yet he liked him for the spirit he showed in the defense of his country. At dinner they each drank a bottle and a half of claret and, at parting, Franklin confided to his son, "he hugged and kissed me, protesting he never in his life met with a man he was so much in love with."

For a man constantly in the forefront of public affairs Franklin made relatively few enemies. He had a warm, genial personality and avoided altercation but privately he held strong opinions about certain people. Describing the appearance of a man who had betrayed him, Franklin wrote, "He certainly was intended for a wise man; for he has the wisest look of any man I know; and if he would only nod and wink, and could but hold his tongue, he might deceive an angel." Of another, he said, "I made that man my enemy by doing him too much kindness. Tis the honestest way of acquiring an enemy. And since 'tis convenient to have at least one enemy, who by his readiness to revile one on all occasions may make one careful of one's conduct, I shall keep him an enemy for that purpose."

During the troubled times before the Revolution, Lord Hillsborough became head of the American affairs department of the Government. Franklin said his character was made of "conceit, wrongheadedness, obstinacy, and passion," and he "perplexed and embarrassed" American affairs by his "senseless management." Hillsborough, for his part, described Franklin as "a fractious, turbulent fellow, always in mischief, a republican, enemy to the king's service, and what not." In view of this clash of personalities, consider the following unexpected meeting of the two: "I went down to Oxford with . . . Lord Le Despencer," Franklin related. "That same day Lord Hillsborough called upon Lord Le Despencer, whose chamber and mine were together in Queens College. I was in the inner room shifting and heard his voice but did not see him, as he went down stairs immediately with Lord Le Despencer, who mentioned that I was above, he returned directly and came to me in the plesantest manner imaginable. 'Dr. Franklin,' says he, 'I did not know till this minute that you were here, and I came back *to make you my bow!* I am glad to see you at Oxford, and that you look so well, etc.' In return for this extravagance, I complimented him on his son's performance in the theatre, though indeed it was but indifferent, so that account was settled. For as people say when they are angry, If he strikes me, I'll strike him again; I think sometimes it may be right to say, If he flatters me, I'll flatter him again. This is *lex talionis,* returning offences in kind."

After the Stamp Act was repealed there was a proposal to force Americans to pay for the cost of the stamps that were printed in anticipation of their future sales. In response, an aroused Franklin shot off a letter to the press. "Shall we then keep up for a trifle the heats and animosities that have been occasioned by the Stamp Act, and lose all the benefit of harmony and good understanding between the different parts of the empire which were expected from a generous total repeal? . . . Where are the officers to be found who will undertake to collect

it? Who is to protect them while they are about it?'' These were some
of the questions and arguments Franklin marshalled against this proposition. ''The whole proceeding,'' he went on, ''would put one in mind
of the Frenchman that used to accost English and other strangers on
the Pont-Neuf with many compliments and a red hot iron in his hand.
'Pray Monsieur Anglois,' says he, 'Do me the favor to let me have the
honor of thrusting this hot iron into your backside?' 'Zoons, what does
the fellow mean! Begone with your iron or I'll break your head!'
'Nay, Monsieur,' replies he, 'if you do not choose it, I do not insist
upon it. But at least, you will in justice have the goodness to pay me
something for the heating of my iron.' ''

Whenever America was attacked, Franklin rushed to the defense,
no matter how trivial the matter might seem on its face. He saw
through attempts by the opposition to belittle America so that it would
be easier then to take actions against her. As an example, a writer
representing the government's viewpoint, using the pseudonym of *Vindex Patriae*, had made aspersions on the Americans' diet implying that
an American boycott on such imports as tea would be ineffectual.
Franklin tried to correct any misimpressions *Vindex* may have made:

> Vindex Patriae, a writer in your paper, comforts himself and the
> India Company with the fancy that the Americans, should they re-
> solve to drink no more tea, can by no means keep that resolution,
> their Indian corn not affording ''an agreeable, or easy digestible
> breakfast.'' Pray let me, an American, inform the gentleman, who
> seems quite ignorant of the matter, that Indian corn, take it for all in
> all, is one of the most agreeable and wholesome grains in the world;
> that its green ears roasted are a delicacy beyond expression; that
> *samp,* * *hominy, succotash,* and *nokehock* made of it are so many
> pleasing varieties; and that a *johnny* or *hoecake* hot from the fire is
> better than a Yorkshire muffin. But if Indian corn were as disagree-
> able and indigestible as the Stamp Act, does he imagine we can get
> nothing else for breakfast? Did he never hear that we can have oat-
> meal in plenty for water gruel or *burgoo;* as good wheat, rye and

* For those unacquainted with these delectable American specialties, samp is a coarse
hominy or a porridge or mush made from it. Hominy is hulled and dried corn, whole or
ground, eaten when boiled, as in the case of hominy ''grits'', a breakfast staple in the
South. Succotash is whole kernel corn mixed with beans. Nokehock is corn meal used in
many ways in food preparation such as corn bread or johnny cake, a corn cake cooked
on a griddle. Burgoo is a thick gruel or porridge, frumenty is hulled wheat boiled in
milk and flavored with sugar and spices.

barley as the world affords to make *frumenty;* or toast and ale; that there is plenty of milk, butter, and cheese; that rice is one of our staple commodities; that for tea we have sage and bawm in our gardens, the young leaves of the sweet white hickory or walnut and, above all, the buds of our pine, infinitely preferable to any tea from the Indies; while the islands [Jamaica, etc.] yield us plenty of coffee and chocolate? Let the gentleman do us the honor of a visit in America and I will engage to breakfast him every day in the month with a fresh variety, without offering him either tea of Indian corn.

Was the manifold abundance of America and the resourcefulness of its people ever so proudly described? Franklin, who had written again as Homespun, wanted to make it clear that although America was a part of the British Empire, she could, if necessary, go it alone. And more and more as the years went by; the political events seemed to bring that eventuality closer to reality. As more British troops were sent to America, Franklin worried about the explosive mixture of armed soldiers and angry people: "I am in perpetual anxiety lest the mad measure of mixing soldiers among a people whose minds are in such a state of irritation may be attended with some sudden mischief. For an accidental quarrel, a personal insult, an imprudent order . . . or twenty other things may produce a tumult, unforeseen . . . in which such a carnage may ensue as to make a breach that can never afterward be healed."

As official hostility toward America became manifest in the government, it turned as well against America's agent, whose position now was very close to that of an ambassador. There were efforts to buy him off, which he spurned, and then to force him to resign his position of Deputy Postmaster General of the Colonies, which he refused. He told his sister, "My enemies were forced to content themselves with abusing me plentifully in the newspapers and endeavoring to provoke me to resign. In this they are not likely to succeed, I being deficient in that Christian virtue of resignation." If they wanted his office they would have to take it, which they eventually did. To friends in America who had heard rumors that he had accepted bribes for a high position in the government, he assured them, "there is not the least foundation for such a report; that far from having any promise of royal favor, I hear of nothing but royal and ministerial displeasure; which, indeed, as things at present stand, I consider as an honor."

America had friends in England but, as Franklin noted, they were now in disgrace, as he was. He received from a friend a packet of letters which had been sent privately by the Governor of Massachusetts to the government in England, calling for more troops and controls in America. Franklin sent these letters to a confidant in Massachusetts for the information of the local leaders, so that they would understand that these provocations were coming from their own shores and would not be so angered at the government. He strictly forbade their being made public, but these orders were ignored and when the government learned that the letters had been stolen the government ministers were enraged. A friend of Franklin's was accused of the theft and was involved in a duel. To save the man's life and honor, Franklin boldly admitted his part in sending the letters to America, but steadfastly refused to say how he got them.

The thunder now crashed over him. He was accused of treason but denied it, saying, "I am not conscious of any treasonable intention, and I know that much violence must be used with my letters before they can be construed into treason, yet having lately seen two of my actions, one my endeavor to lessen the differences between the two countries, the other to stop a dangerous quarrel between individuals, and which I would have thought and still think to be good actions, I am not to wonder if less than a small lump in my forehead is voted a horn." In the newspapers he was termed "Old Traitor Franklin," and called the same in verse.

> "Thou base, ungrateful, cunning, upstart thing!
> False to thy country first, then to they King."

At a public hearing on the subject of the stolen letters Franklin was villified and grossly abused by the government prosecutor. He did not respond, explaining that he had often been censured for the part he took in public affairs and had generally submitted in silence. When the censure was just, he felt he should "amend rather than defend," and when it was undeserved he felt that time would vindicate him. Yet he did not forget the humiliation he suffered. Nine years later when he was on his way to sign the Treaty of Paris which ended the Revolutionary War, he wore the coat he had worn the day he had been castigated by the English prosecutor. His fellow American, Silas Deane, asked him, "Why do you wear that old coat today? Franklin's terse answer was, "To give it a little revenge."

Franklin had tried his best to seek an accommodation between the government and the colonies but neither side was in the mood to yield to the other. He was not in favor of rebellion noting, "between friends every affront is not worth a duel, between nations every injury not worth a war, so between the governed and the government, every encroachment on rights is not worth a rebellion." He believed that America's strength was in her expanding wealth and rapidly growing population. After fighting had begun, he bolstered this contention with statistics: "Britain, at the expense of three million, has killed 150 Yankees this campaign, which is 20,000 pounds a head . . . During the same time 60,000 children have been born in America. From these data . . . [one] will easily calculate the time and expense necessary to kill us all." Time was on America's side and she must not be premature in pressing her case. Yet, under the circumstances, he found himself quoting the Italian adage, "Make yourselves sheep and the wolves will eat you." He had had enough. He felt his usefulness as agent for America was over, and in 1775, after more than a decade on this assignment, he returned home. As he prepared to leave, Strahan tried to persuade him to stay in England, saying that America would soon be filled with trouble and covered with blood. According to "Parson" Weems (author of the fable of young Washington and the cherry tree), who met Franklin about this time, Franklin replied emphatically to Strahan's pleading, saying, "No, sir! Where liberty is, there is my country!"

Now just one year short of the biblical span of three score and ten, Franklin had visions of retiring from public life when he reached Philadelphia. But while he was on shipboard, blood was spilled at Lexington and Concord and the die was cast. As soon as he arrived, Pennsylvania chose him as a representative to the Second Continental Congress. There he joined forces with George Washington, John Adams and Thomas Jefferson, was appointed to many important committees, and was made Postmaster General of America. The latter appointment was especially gratifying to Franklin, since he had been rudely ousted from his Postmaster position by the English. After the War of Independence had begun, he referred to this removal: "Since the suppression of my office I have received no further income from it, but neither has the King." When he was Deputy Postmaster under the Crown he used his right of franking letters by writing on the back, "Free. B. Franklin." However, reacting to the injustice he felt, he now changed the order of the words and wrote, "B. Free Franklin."

In Congress, Franklin, who was a good writer but a poor orator, preferred to remain silent. The young Jefferson, whose interests and temperament were much like Franklin's, was quick to note this characteristic of the older man. Years later he reflected: "I served with General Washington in the legislature of Virginia before the Revolution, and during it with Dr. Franklin in Congress. I never heard either of them speak ten minutes at a time, nor to any but the main point which was to decide the question. They laid their shoulders to the great points, knowing that the little ones would follow of themselves." John Adams, a spirited debater, whose personality was totally opposite to Franklin's, was puzzled that Franklin was appointed to all the important committees and he to few of them, especially when Franklin was observed, "from day to day sitting in silence, a great part of the time fast asleep in his chair."

But Adams was to serve with both Franklin and Jefferson on the most important committee that the Congress ever appointed, the one to draw up the Declaration of Independence. Jefferson was selected to do the writing because, it has been said, he had a grave and lofty style suitable to the serious occasion, whereas Franklin's style was homely, intimate, and confidential. Another story goes further to say that Franklin was not chosen to write the Declaration because the Founding Fathers were afraid he might slip a joke into it. Such an occurrence might have been possible, for he did insert some levity into the serious speech he made later on the closing of the Constitutional Convention. But in speculating on momentous events we tend to search for romantic explanations, when usually the reasons have more mundane foundations. It appears more probable that Jefferson was given the writing job because he was the youngest member of the committee and might be prevailed upon to do the hard work that no one else wanted to do. Jefferson did his job well and the other committee members made only minor alterations in the draft. One of Franklin's changes was to substitute the words "self evident" for Jefferson's "sacred and undeniable" in that phrase of the Declaration of Independence, "We hold these truths to be self evident: That all men are created equal . . ."

Although Franklin, Adams, and the two other committee members were generous in accepting Jefferson's version without much alteration, such was not the case when the draft reached the Congress. Jefferson, who listened with pain to the members' proposals for carving up his proud creation, received consolation from Franklin. Jefferson related the incident:

> When the Declaration of Independence was under the consideration of Congress, there were two or three unlucky expressions in it which gave offence to some members. The words "Scotch and other foreign auxiliaries" excited the ire of a gentleman or two of that country. Severe strictures on the conduct of the British king, in negotiating our repeated repeals of the law which permitted the importation of slaves, were disapproved by some Southern gentlemen, whose reflections were not yet matured to the full abhorrence of that traffic. Although the offensive expressions were immediately yielded these gentlemen continued their depredations on other parts of the instrument. I was sitting by Dr. Franklin, who perceived that I was not insensible to these mutilations. "I have made it a rule," said he, "whenever in my power, to avoid becoming the draughtsman of papers to be reviewed by a public body. I took my lesson from an incident which I will relate to you. When I was a journeyman printer, one of my companions, an apprentice hatter, having served out his time, was about to open shop for himself. His first concern was to have a handsome sign-board, with a proper inscription. He composed it in these words, 'John Thompson, Hatter, makes and sells hats for ready money,' with a figure of a hat subjoined; but he thought he would submit it to his friends for their amendments. The first he showed it to thought the word 'Hatter' tautologous, because followed by the words 'makes hats,' which show he was a hatter. It was struck out. The next observed that the word 'makes' might as well be omitted, because his customers would not care who made the hats . . . He struck it out. A third said he thought the words 'for ready money' were useless, as it was not the custom of the place to sell on credit. Every one who purchased expected to pay. They were parted with, and the inscription now stood, 'John Thompson sells hats.' 'Sells hats!' says his next friend. 'Why nobody will expect you to give them away, what then is the use of that word? It was stricken out, and 'hats' followed it, . . . as there was one painted on the board. So the inscription was reduced ultimately to 'John Thompson' with the figure of a hat subjoined."

An anecdotal account of the signing of the Declaration given by some of the Franklin biographers has John Hancock, the first to sign, saying, "We must be unanimous; there must be no pulling different ways; we must all hang together." "Yes," Franklin agreed, "we must indeed all hang together, or most assuredly we shall all hang separately.''

Even after independence was declared Franklin was still willing to talk peace. Lord Howe, a well-intentioned English moderate, had contacted Franklin while he was still in London in the hope that he might reconcile the differences between the government and America. He asked Franklin to draw up a plan for conciliation which he (Howe) might take to the ministry. Franklin felt sure it would do no good, but Howe tried to impress on him the infinite service he would be doing for the nation and the great merit in doing so good a work. Franklin recorded Howe saying, ''that he should not think of influencing me by any selfish motive, but certainly I might with reason expect any reward in the power of the government to bestow. This to me was what the French call *spitting in the soup*.'' Nevertheless, Franklin did draw up a proposal for harmony but, as he had expected, the government was not interested. Now, the very same Howe came to America as Admiral of the British Fleet to put down the rebellion. At this late date he still cherished a hope for peace and sent a messenger to Congress asking that some of its members be sent to New York City, which his brother, General Sir William Howe, had just taken in battle from General Washington. Congress sent Franklin, John Adams, and Edward Rutledge of South Carolina. It was on this trip that Franklin and Adams were confined to a small room at an inn and Franklin instructed the reluctant Adams on the value of fresh air (*See Chapter 21*).

Like the previous meeting with Howe, this one was doomed to failure since Howe was operating only on his own goodwill and did not represent the British government, which would not even recognize the existence of any American government. Howe readily admitted that he had no authority to receive the Americans except as private persons to which Adams replied, ''Your lordship may consider me in any light you please; and indeed I should be willing to consider myself . . . in any character which should be agreeable to your lordship *except that of a British subject*.'' In view of Britain's military might Howe did not consider the rebellion had any chance of success. Yet, if America should fall, he said he would lament it like the loss of a brother. Franklin responded with an air of confidence, ''My Lord, we will use our utmost endeavors to save your lordship that mortification.''

A new nation would require official symbols and Congress set

Franklin, Adams, and Jefferson to the task of devising a seal for the United States. Congress rejected most of their recommendations but kept their Latin motto, *E Pluribus Unum* (one out of many). The recommendation for the reverse side was a design proposed by Franklin. It pictured "Pharaoh sitting in an open chariot, a crown on his head and a sword in his hand, passing through the divided waters of the Red Sea in pursuit of the Israelites. Rays from a pillar of fire in the cloud, expressive of the Divine presence and command, beaming on Moses, who stands on the shore and, extending his hand over the sea, causes it to overflow Pharaoh. Motto: 'Rebellion to tyrants is obedience to God.' "

In her battle for independence America would need help. She needed munitions, naval vessels, and most of all, credit to purchase supplies. Where would she get such assistance? The most likely place to look would be England's traditional enemy, France, and Congress dispatched Silas Deane to France for this purpose. Franklin gave Deane letters of introduction to several of his friends in France. One of them wrote to Franklin telling him how sympathetic the French were to America and their desire to help. Congress then decided to send additional Commissioners to France, and Franklin and Jefferson were elected. Jefferson could not go because of his wife's illness so Arthur Lee, who was then in England, was appointed in his place. When Franklin's election was announced, Dr. Benjamin Rush turned to him with concern for his personal safety and health, for he was now a few months short of 70 and beside the danger of the sea voyage there was the real possibility of being captured by the British navy and hanged as a traitor. Franklin brushed aside Rush's fears, rejoining philosophically, "I am old and good for nothing; but as the storekeepers say of their remnants of cloth, I am but a fag-end and you may have me for what you please. Perhaps the best use such an old fellow can be put to is to make a martyr of him."

12

A PATRIOT WITH HUMOR

WHEN THE 70-YEAR-OLD FRANKLIN ARRIVED IN FRANCE he thought his usefulness was about over but, in fact, he was never before so successful, never so much admired. He had many problems to face—with the British enemy, with jealous colleagues from home, and with the burden of a formidable diplomatic responsibility. He had requests from the Congress for war supplies and goods of all kinds and had to find the materials, arrange credit, and secure ships to run the blockade of the English navy. These requests were on top of his formal duties with the French ministers and the French royal court. Although he did an amazing job for one man, he sometimes despaired of being able to serve all of these functions. Writing to his nephew Jonathan Williams, who was in France trying to obtain shipping for America-bound goods, he was grieved to hear that the ships from Brest could not take these goods, and added: "At this distance from the ports, and unacquainted as I am with such affairs, I know not what to advise about getting either the clothing or the small arms and powder at L'Orient . . . and yet everybody writes to me for orders, or advice, or opinion, or approbation, which is like calling upon a blind man to judge of colors."

In communicating to Arthur Lee he indicated further the range of his instructions: "By this packet, indeed, we have some fresh instructions . . . that, in case France and Spain will enter the war, the United States will assist the former in the conquest of the British Sugar Islands, and the latter in the Conquest of Portugal.'' The U.S. would have to provide six frigates manned with not less than 24 guns each and two million dollars in provisions, for which she would only desire the British holdings in America. ''We are ordered to borrow if we can 2,000,000 pounds on interest. . . . We are also ordered to build six ships of war.'' And then he remarked, ''It is a pleasure to find things ordered which we were doing without orders.''

Franklin's home, which served as his offices as well, was besieged with persons seeking commissions as officers in the U.S. army. He had to turn most of them away since his government had little money and greater needs for it than adventurers and fortune hunters. There were exceptions however, like Lafayette and von Steuben. The Prussian military officer, Baron von Steuben, became a hero in the Revolutionary War, converting Washington's rag-tail army of farmers and merchants in the depths of despair at Valley Forge into the finely disciplined fighting force that ultimately defeated the better-equipped, professional army fielded by the British General.

Von Steuben, who had served as an aide to Frederick the Great before he came to America, had the best military training then possible to obtain. At the time he was interviewed by Franklin he held only the rank of captain, and knowing that Congress would not be much impressed with him as a mere captain, Franklin wrote to Washington that he was sending him a lieutenant-general in the service of the King of Prussia, whom he had attended in all his campaigns. Congress was highly pleased with such an acquisition and immediately dispatched von Steuben to Washington at Valley Forge.

As part of his diplomatic duties Franklin had to make a formal appearance at the royal court of King Louis XVI and Queen Marie Antoinette. William Carmichael of Maryland, one of the Americans in Paris, observed: ''He had great influence at the Court of France. He seldom goes to court, but when he does, everything he says flies by the next post to every part of the kingdom.'' Franklin's major objective was to obtain money and military support from the French king, but this was particularly difficult before the French were openly allied to America, since they did not wish to be drawn into the fight until they were ready. Therefore, though sympathetic, they were hesitant about giving the aid that America so badly needed. A Frenchman seated next to Franklin at a dinner said to him, "One must admit, Monsieur, that it is a great and superb spectacle which America offers us today." To which Franklin replied, "Yes, but the spectators do not pay."

Although the French strongly favored America over their old enemy, England was powerful and had to be respected. The French were afraid to be on the losing side and English propaganda therefore stressed America's weakness. Lord Stormont, the English ambassador to France is said to have reported that six battalions of Washington's army had laid down their arms, and a Frenchman hearing this asked Franklin if the story was "a truth." "No, Monsieur," Franklin responded, "it is not a truth, it is only a Stormont." The story became so wellknown that in Paris the word Stormont soon became synonymous with lie.

Franklin was a superior propagandist but when it came to spying, the English were not to be outdone. The Americans in France were constantly spied upon and their letters intercepted. An American woman living in France warned Franklin that he was surrounded by spies. He thanked her for the information and said he had no doubt she was correct. But since he knew it to be impossible to keep from being watched by spies, he observed one rule to prevent any inconvenience from such practices, namely "to be concerned in no affairs that I should blush to have made public, and to do nothing but what spies may see and welcome." He then concluded, "If I were sure therefore that my valet-de-place was a spy, as he probably is, I think I should not discharge him for that, if in other respects I liked him."

The battle with the British had its skirmishes in France, not with swords but with words. When a royal edict was issued abolishing slavery in France, Franklin remarked, "Who would have thought a few years since that we should see a king of France giving freedom to slaves, while a king of England is endeavoring to make slaves of freemen?" An anecdote in a newspaper of the time tells of the coming together in France of Franklin and Edward Gibbon, author of *A History of The Decline and Fall of the Roman Empire*. Franklin stopped at an inn and on being informed that Gibbon was there, sent his compliments and requested the pleasure of spending the evening with Gibbon. In reply, Franklin received a card saying that despite Mr. Gibbon's regard for the character of Dr. Franklin as a man and a philosopher, he could not reconcile it with his duty to his king to have conversation with a rebel. Franklin answered with a note declaring that though Mr. Gibbon's principles had compelled him to withhold the pleasure of his conversation, Dr. Franklin had still such a respect for the character of Mr. Gibbon as a gentleman and a historian that when in his writing the history of empires, he should come to write the Decline and Fall of the British Empire, as he was soon expected to do, Dr. Franklin would be happy to furnish him with sufficient materials in his possession.

When Franklin heard that General Sir William Howe, had taken his home town of Philadelphia, he regarded it as a tactical blunder on the Britisher's part and haughtily retorted, "You mean, sir, Philadelphia has taken Sir William Howe."

The immense personal popularity of Franklin and that of his mission, caused him to be invited to all the French court parties. At these, according to Jefferson, he sometimes met the old Duchess of Bourbon who, like Franklin, loved to play chess. As they were pretty evenly matched, they always enjoyed playing together. "Happening once to put her king into prize, the Doctor took it. 'Ah,' said she, 'We do not take kings so.' 'We do in America,' said the Doctor."

"At one of the parties,' Jefferson continues, "the Emperor Joseph III,* then at Paris incognito under the title of Count Falkenstein, was overlooking the game in silence, while the company was engaged in animated conversation on the American question. 'How happens it, Monsieur le Compte,' said the Duchess, 'that while we all feel so much interest in the cause of the Americans, you say nothing for them?' 'I am a king by trade,' said he."

While Franklin was negotiating in Paris, according to a story by Jeremy Bentham, he sometimes went into a cafe to play chess. A crowd usually assembled to see the famous American. Upon one occasion, Franklin was losing the game, when, quite composed, he took the king from the board, put it in his pocket and continued to play. The opponent looked up, and seeing that Franklin was in earnest, he began, "Sir!" "Yes, Sir, continue," said Franklin, "and we shall soon see that the party without a king will win the game."

To add to his troubles with the English there were the difficulties Franklin had with his own countrymen. His fellow commissioners

* There is apparently a misprint in Jefferson's Works, for Joseph III should be Joseph II. Joseph II was Holy Roman Emperor at this time and made this secret visit to France to see his sister, Queen Marie Antoinette.

were envious of the great attention and personal tribute he received from the French. But even his daughter in America distressed him, by asking that he send her from Paris some long black pins, plus lace and feathers. This greatly irritated him, since he was adamant that Americans must sacrifice their luxuries for the war effort. He compared the request to her having put salt on his strawberries and he advised her to follow his example in practicing frugality: "If you wear your cambric ruffles as I do, and take care not to mend the holes," he said, "they will come in time to be lace; and feathers, my dear girl, may be had in America from every cock's tail."

The problem he had with the other American Commissioners in Paris, with whom Franklin nominally shared equal rank and responsibility, were more serious. Silas Deane and Franklin got along well but Arthur Lee (brother of Richard Henry Lee of Virginia) was suspicious of Deane and jealous of Franklin. Lee wrote to Congress that Deane was guilty of embezzling some funds he had handled, and he thought Franklin was either oblivious to this corruption or implicated in it. He hoped that both Deane and Franklin would be recalled, leaving him in charge of the American affairs in Europe. Congress did recall Deane but the charges against him were never proved or disproved since all his records were in France. In the meantime, Congress had appointed two more Commissioners, William Lee, brother of Arthur Lee, to be stationed in Berlin and Ralph Izard, from South Carolina, to Tuscany. Since the governments to which they were assigned did not recognize the United States, the new Commissioners resided in Paris and joined sides with Arthur Lee against Franklin. Of Lee, Franklin wrote, "in sowing suspicions and jealousies, in creating misunderstandings and quarrels, in malice, subtilty, and indefatigable industry, he has I think no equal."

Lee tried to get at Franklin by casting suspicion on the honesty of Franklin's nephew, Jonathan Williams, who served as financial aide in the American service in France and was later to become the first Superintendent of West Point. Franklin made no attempt to shield him by virtue of his family relationship. He answered Lee: "I have no desire to screen Mr. Williams on account of his being my nephew; if he is guilty of what you charge him with, I care not how soon he is deservedly punished and the family purged of him; for I take it that a rogue living in [a] family is a greater disgrace to it than one hanged out of it."

When he got wind of a move by the Lees and Izard to remove him, he commented: "I since hear that a motion has been made in Congress by a Carolina member for recalling me; but without success; and that A. Lee has printed a pamphlet against me. If my enemies would have a little patience that may soon see me removed without their giving themselves any trouble as I am now 75."

Congress did not remove Franklin but sent John Adams to replace Deane. Adams heard the complaints from both sides and quickly concluded that there should be a single Commissioner, an assessment in which Franklin concurred. Congress accepted the recommendation and, with the advice of the French minister to Congress, selected Franklin. The Lees and Izard were recalled and parted with Franklin in a respectful and civil manner. Franklin never let on that he knew of their agitation in Congress against him. He had always tried to maintain restraint and avoid disputes, but when Arthur Lee sent him a particularly annoying letter, he told Lee that he had pity for his sick mind and if he didn't control his temper he would go insane. He added in closing, "God preserve you from so terrible an evil . . . and for his sake pray suffer me to live in quiet." It is unlikely that Franklin sent Lee this letter for the next day he wrote Lee a long letter attending to the questions Lee had raised, but still quite candid, telling Lee that instead of answering his angry letters he had burned them. Actually he may not have sent either letter, for in his second letter he referred to both letters and said he did not believe he would send them unless exceedingly pressed by Lee, "for of all things I hate altercation."

Even after they returned to America, the Lees and Izard continued to bitterly malign Franklin in speeches and writings. He said of them: "It is enough for good minds to be affected at other people's misfortunes; but they, that are vexed at everybody's good luck can never be happy. I take no other revenge on such enemies than to let them remain in the miserable situation in which their malignant natures have placed them." In a way, however, he did take revenge on Izard by writing a satirical piece entitled, "Petition of the Letter Z." Izard had felt insulted and slighted because Franklin had failed to request his advice on some diplomatic matter and he had complained to Franklin. Making much of this minor incident, Izard joined the Lee faction. Purporting to be a selection from *The Tatler*, the "Petition" is directed to The Worshipful Isaac Bickerstaff, Esquire, Censor-General, and satirizes Izard and his sensitive feelings:

The petition of the letter Z, commonly called Ezzard, Zed, or Izard, most humbly showeth;

That your petitioner is of as high extraction, and has as good an estate, as any other letter of the alphabet;

That there is therefore no reason why he should be treated as he is, with disrespect and indignity;

That he is not only actually placed at the tail of the alphabet, when he had as much right as any other to be at the head; but is by the injustice of his enemies totally excluded from the word WISE; and his place injuriously filled by a little hissing, crooked, serpentine, venomous letter, called S, when it must be evident to your worship, and to all the world, that W, I, S, E, do not spell Wize, but Wise.

Your petitioner therefore prays, that the alphabet may by your censorial authority be reversed; and that in consideration of his long-suffering and patience he may be placed at the head of it; that s may be turned out of the word Wise; and the petitioner employed instead of him . . .

Mr. Bickerstaff, having examined the allegations of the above petition, judges and determines, that Z be admonished to be content with his station, forbear reflections upon his brother letters, and remember his own small usefulness, and the little occasion there is for him in the Republic of Letters, since S whom he so despises can so well serve instead of him.

Unfortunately, Adams and Franklin also became disenchanted with each other, although they continued to work together and were outwardly cordial. Adams acknowledged Franklin's greatness in philosophy and his tremendous popularity in France, but Adams had what one writer euphemistically termed "the instinct of self" and he was most uncomfortable in Franklin's shadow. He felt the same way about Washington, as indicated by his letter to Benjamin Rush: "The history of our revolution will be one continued lie from one end to other. The essence of the whole will be that Dr. Franklin's electrical rod smote the earth and that sprung General Washington. That Franklin electrified him with his rod—and thence forward these two conducted all the policy, negotiations, legislatures, and war."

Adams and Franklin were both sincere, courageous, able men but their personalities and styles were entirely different. Adams was vocal, aggressive, and abrupt; Franklin was quiet, amiable, and gentle in his approach. Dissatisfied with Franklin's easy manner of dealing with the

French government, Adams visited Vergennes, the French foreign minister, and vociferously demanded more money for America. Vergennes was so put out with Adams that he announced he would henceforth deal with no other American than Franklin. An adept diplomat, Franklin was able to get the continued aid from the French that was of such great importance in winning the war. But in his dealings in France circumstances unhappily brought Franklin closer together with Adams than with any of the other founding fathers. He gave a description of Adams that was later adopted by Jefferson, who had his own troubles with Adams. Franklin said of Adams that he was "always an honest man, often a great man, but sometimes positively mad." *

Adams' antagonism toward Franklin is exhibited in the following excerpt from Matthew Ridley's journal. Ridley, agent for Maryland, had been in Amsterdam making a loan for his state, after which he called on the American Representatives in Paris.

> 1782. Tuesday, Oct. 29th. Called to see Mr. Adams,—dined with him. He is much pleased with Mr. Jay. Went in the morning to see Dr. Franklin. Did not know of Mr. Adams' arrival. Spoke to Mr. A. about making his visit to Dr. F. He told me it was time enough. Represented to him the necessity of a meeting. He replied that there was no necessity; that, after the usage he had received from him, he could not bear to go near him. I told him whatever the differences were, he would do wrong to discover any to the world, and that it might have a bad effect on our affairs at this time. He said the Dr. might come to him. I told him it was not his place; the last comer always paid the first visit. He replied the Dr. was to come to him, he was first in the commission. I asked him how the Dr. was to know he was there unless he went to him. He replied that was true, he did not think of that, and would go. Afterwards, when pulling on his coat, he said he would not, he could not bear to go where the Dr. was. With much persuasion I got him at length to go. He said he would do it, since I would have it so; but I was always making mischief, and so I should find."

There were many minor problems that occupied Franklin the diplomat. He received a letter from Vergennes containing an appeal from a man who called himself a lieutenant-colonel in the Continental Mili-

---

* This was Jefferson's recollection. Franklin's actual words were, "always an honest man, often a wise one, but sometimes, and in some things, absolutely out of his senses."

tia. The man had landed in jail and demanded the return of a check taken from him which had been signed by Franklin. According to Franklin, the man was no officer but an imposter, who had been around Paris several years pretending to be an American business man and fleecing ignorant Frenchman who believed him. When he first got into trouble, Franklin helped him with money but now he regretted it. He apologized to Vergennes on behalf of the fellow, explaining that he was a young man of very little understanding, who fell in with a set of sharpers and joined them, "having neither good sense enough to be an honest man nor wit enough for a rogue."

Regarding another American embezzler, one Thomas Digges, who ran off with a large sum he had been given for the relief of American prisoners in England, Franklin was not so apologetic. "We have no name in our language for such atrocious wickedness," he declared. "If such a fellow is not damned, it is not worth while to keep a devil." David Hartley, one of Franklin's English friends who was a member of Parliament, worked with Franklin to obtain the exchange of American prisoners of war. In writing to Franklin he hoped that out of gratitude (to France for help in the war) America would not throw herself into the arms of France. Franklin replied: "America has been forced and driven into the arms of France. She was a dutiful and virtuous daughter. A cruel mother-in-law turned her out of doors, defamed her, and sought her life. All the world knows her innocence and takes her part; and her friends hope soon to see her honorably married."

Franklin liked to employ metaphor in expressing his tender concern for his country. When David Hartley proposed a family compact between England, France, and America, Franklin responded, "America would be as happy as the Sabine girls, if she could be the means of uniting in perpetual peace her father and her husband." Thinking of America as a young woman, he said, "the heavens, jealous of her beauty, had visited her with the scourge of civil war." Upon the British surrender after the battle of Yorktown, he regarded America in terms of a young giant, "the infant Hercules in his cradle has now strangled his second serpent . . ." And when the subject of European alliances for the newly independent United States arose, he felt strongly "that a young state like a young virgin should modestly stay at home and wait the application of suitors for an alliance with her." He projected optimistically, "Our virgin is a jolly one; and though at present not very rich, will in time be a great fortune."

He was always ready to defend America. When an English lady friend called him a rebel, he reacted with vigor. "You are too early, Hussy, (as well as too saucy) in calling me rebel; you should wait for the event which will determine whether it is a rebellion or only a revolution. Here [France] the ladies are more civil; they call us *les insurgens* . . . And methinks all other women who smart under the tyranny of a bad husband ought to be fixed in revolution principles, and act accordingly." As we see, Franklin could be accused not only of being a dangerous revolutionary; he was, worse yet, a woman's liberationist. Franklin's only unfulfilled wants were victory and peace. He had everything else anyone could desire. "I enjoy health, competence, friends, and reputation. Peace is the only ingredient wanting to my felicity."

Victory came but the treaty of peace did not follow for over a year. When it came, he with John Adams and John Jay negotiated and signed for America, while David Hartley signed for Great Britain. Hating the bickering and backbiting associated with the treaty making, he observed to Adams that the Biblical aphorism, "Blessed are the peace-makers," must be reserved for the other world, for in this they are frequently cursed.

In the preliminary negotiations leading to the peace treaty Adams and Jay were suspicious that their allies, the French, would try to win concessions from the English to favor their own interests to the detriment of American interests. They wanted to disregard their instructions from Congress and deal directly with the English without the French being present. As a result of his friendly, successful diplomacy with the French, Franklin did not share this desire. Furthermore, he had another important matter on his agenda, to obtain another large loan from the French, which he did want to jeopardize. But his compatriots, who distrusted his French position, were insistent and he had to go along on their terms, without the French.

In the hard bargaining with the English representatives Adams fumed and threatened, Jay appealed to reason, and Franklin told anecdotes. Under this balanced barrage the opposition gradually disintegrated and the Americans won their objectives. Yet the British negotiators, Oswald, Strachey, and Fitzherbert, were hesitant about signing. Fitzherbert pretended to believe that Oswald did not have the power to sign. According to Frank Monoghan in his biography of Jay, Adams then indicated that his colleagues were in no hurry and would wait until the articles could be approved by the British ministry. While the Britons were considering this point, Monoghan continues, Franklin executed a bit of perfect strategy. Stating he was anxious to have another messenger go to London, he pulled from his pocket a small bundle of papers. He said he was pleased that there would be an opportunity to insert an article re-paying Americans for the loss of effects seized by the British Army "entirely out of the consequences of any military irregularities." Since there was ample proof of these losses, it was only proper that they should be paid. The Britons were obviously befuddled; and the Americans hurried to support Franklin. Adams recounted a damaging tale about General Gage at Boston; Jay contributed several incidents; and Laurens, having just arrived, contributed a story of plunder in Carolina. Franklin then proceeded to enumerate property that had been carried off in Philadelphia. Hearing all this, Oswald, Strachey and Fitzherbert retired to an adjoining room and returned briefly with the announced opinion that Oswald had full powers to sign. Dining with Adams that evening, Matthew Ridley found him in fine spirits.

"May I ask if you would like to have some fish, Mr. Adams?"

"No, thank you," said Adams laughingly. "I've had a pretty good meal of them today."

In this mellow mood Adams even went so far as to praise his fellow-negotiator. Ridley reports, "Mr. A. is well satisfied with Dr. F——'s conduct, and says he has behaved well and nobly, particularly this day."

When the preliminary articles of the treaty were obtained, it fell upon Franklin rather than his associates, who were already in disfavor with the French, to break the news to Vergennes and make the necessary apologies. Franklin had been on very good terms with Vergennes, and this was a very difficult position for him to be in, particularly with the loan coming up. But he had no choice and dutifully accepted the burden. First he notified Vergennes that the preliminary articles had been settled and then sent him a copy of the treaty that had just been signed. Vergennes was tight-lipped, saying only that the Americans had done very well for themselves. It was when Franklin pressed for the loan, however, that Vergennes rendered his rebuke: "I am at a loss, Sir, to explain your conduct and that of your colleagues on this occasion. You have concluded your preliminary articles without any communication between us, although the instructions from Congress prescribe that nothing shall be done without the participation of the King . . . You are wise and discreet, Sir; you certainly understand what is due to propriety; you have all your life performed your duties. I pray you to consider how you propose to fulfill those which are due to the King? . . . When you shall be pleased to relieve my uncertainty, I will entreat the King to answer your demands." In polite, diplomatic language Vergennes was saying, "Now, talk your way out of this one, if you can."

Franklin tried. He first assured Vergennes that nothing agreed to in the preliminaries was contrary to the interests of France. Further, as Vergennes must be aware, the agreement just signed would not officially be valid until a peace treaty had been made between France and England. Having thus argued that no harm had really been done, Franklin disarmingly acknowledged the guilt of the Americans in failing to consult Vergennes, but allowing it to be only the neglect of propriety. He insisted it was not from want of respect of the King, "whom we all love and honor." Franklin said he hoped that the great work which had been so nearly brought to perfection would not be ruined by this single indiscretion. "And certainly," he said, now bringing up the loan, "the whole edifice sinks to the ground immediately if you refuse on that account to give us any further assistance." He went on to affirm every American's debt to France and to proclaim that no other king was ever more beloved and respected by his subjects than the French king was by the people of the United States. After these honeyed phrases came a bold note in a different key. "The English, I just now learn," he blurted as if someone had suddenly come to the door with a urgent message, "flatter themselves that they have already divided us." He then added with an adroitness that must have made Vergennes laugh dryly, "I hope this little misunderstanding will therefore be kept a secret, and they will find themselves totally mistaken." The following week in a letter to the American financier Robert Morris, Franklin explained that there was a "little misunderstanding" with the French but it was "got over," and the first installment of the loan of six million livres was already on its way to the United States.

With the treaty signed and the loan in hand Franklin turned for a while from public duties to attend to the mountain of personal correspondence that had accumulated. He wrote an American friend, "I . . . rejoice with you in the peace God has blessed us with and in the prosperity it gives us a prospect of . . . We are now friends with England and all mankind. May we never see another war! For in my opinion *there never was a good war, or a bad peace.*" This profound comment, which Franklin underlined for emphasis, was to live on as one of the world's great quotations.

Seeing peace restored, Franklin proclaimed: "America has only to be thankful and to persevere. God will finish his work and establish their [Americans] freedom. And the lovers of liberty will flock from all parts of Europe with their fortunes to participate with us in that freedom." Considering these immigrants, he painted an America of opportunity, not of luxury: "Our country offers to strangers nothing but a good climate, fertile soil, wholesome air, free governments, wise laws, liberty, a good people to live among, and a hearty welcome. Those Europeans who have these or greater advantages at home would do well to stay where they are." And as a true democrat, he stated: "Much less is it advisable for a person to go thither who has no other quality to recommend him but his birth. In Europe it has indeed its value, but it is a commodity that cannot be carried to a worse market than to that of America, where people do not inquire of a stranger, 'What is he?' but 'What can he do?' " It is unlikely that the spirit of America has ever since been more concisely stated.

The peace achieved, Franklin was beginning to hanker for home. But first he had a chance to set straight his good friend the Abbé Raynal. The Abbé had guests at a dinner party, half of whom were Americans and the other half French. He had an absurd theory, then accepted in Europe, that animals and even man physically degenerated as a result of living in America. During the dinner he got around to this subject and expounded on it with his usual eloquence. As Jefferson relates it, Franklin did not argue the scientific merits of the theory or even try to correct the Abbé with his generous powers of persuasion. Instead, he proposed a simple experiment.

"We are here one-half Americans and one-half French," he said, "and it happens that the Americans have placed themselves on one side of the table, and our French friends are on the other. Let both parties rise and we will see on which side nature had degenerated."

"It happened that the Abbé's American guests were . . . of the finest stature and form," relates Jefferson, "while those of the other side were remarkable diminutive. And the Abbé himself, particularly, was a mere shrimp."

13

WITH MY VIZARD ON

THE FRENCH NOVELIST HONORÉ DE BALZAC ONCE DECLARED, "The hoax is a work of Franklin, who invented the lightning rod, the hoax, and the republic. Balzac was overstating, but it is true that Franklin was happiest when he was masquerading, "with my vizard on," as he put it. From the age of 16, when he created the widow Dogood, to the year of his death at 84 when he concocted a speech he attributed to Sidi Mehemet Ibrahim of Algiers, he assumed many literary disguises. Franklin was the hidden playwright behind his characters and on occasion found himself actually acting out their roles. Some of his hoaxes served no other purpose than entertainment but usually they permitted Franklin to be social critic or political propagandist.

As social critic Franklin lampooned witch trials in a newspaper story in his *Pennsylvania Gazette* in 1730. The story purports to recount a gathering of 300 people at Mt. Holly, New Jersey, to determine the guilt of persons accused of witchcraft. It is a good-humored satire in which the reporter views the proceedings with wide-eyed innocence. The accused persons have been charged with "making their neighbor's sheep dance in an uncommon manner and with causing hogs to speak and sing psalsms," which the reporter tells us brings amazement and great terror to the King's good and peaceable subjects. How will the guilt of the accused be determined? By tested and true methods, of course. The accused will be weighed in scales against a Bible and if they are guilty the Bible will be heavier. Or, if they are bound with rope and put into the river and they float, they are proved guilty. However, if they sink and survive they are free to enjoy their innocence.

The accused, anxious to prove their innocence, voluntarily offered to undergo the trials. They had, however, one condition, that their most violent accusers would be tried with them. It was agreed and the time and place of the trial was advertised around the county. The accused were a man and a woman and the accusers the same. Using the scale test first, a huge Bible was provided and the scales were fixed on a gallows erected for that purpose opposite the Justice's house so that the Justice's wife and the rest of the ladies might see the trial without mingling with the mob. Then, out of the house came a tall, grave man carrying the holy writ, stopping before the accused wizard, who was put on the scale. A chapter out of the Book of Moses was read over the accused and the Bible was put on the other scale. To the great surprise of the spectators, flesh and bones came down plump, and far outweighed the great, good book. In the same manner the others were tried and their lumps of mortality were too heavy for Moses and all the prophets and apostles.

The accusers and the mob, not satisfied with this experiment, insisted on the trial by water. Accordingly a most solemn procession was made to the mill pond where the accused and accusers were stripped, allowing the women only their shifts. They were bound hand and foot and placed on the water from a barge. The male accuser being thin and spare sank slowly but the rest all floated lightly on the water. A sailor on the barge jumped on the back of the accused man trying to drive him down but he came right up again. The female accuser was ducked a second time but she floated as lightly as before. She declared that the accused had bewitched her to make her float, and she wanted to be ducked again a hundred times, to duck the devil out of her. The accused man was now not so confident of his innocence as before, saying, *"if I am a witch it is more than I know."*

The more thinking part of the spectators were of the opinion that any person so bound and placed in the water, unless they were mere skin and bones, would float until their breath was gone and their lungs filled with water. But it being the general belief of the populace that the women's shifts and garters helped to support them, it is said they are to be tried again the next warm spell, naked.

We may now smile at this account but it should be recalled that witch trials were not uncommon in early America and those at Salem, Massachusetts in 1692, in which Cotton Mather played a large part, sentenced nineteen people to death for witchery and 150 more to prison. As late as 1722 a woman was tried for witchcraft in England. The belief in witches and demonology was well established in the popular and religious culture, even though enlightened people like Franklin could ridicule it. Franklin's hoax is not credible today but in 1731 a respected English publication, the *Gentleman's Magazine,* picked up the story from the *Gazette* and printed it as fact.

Another social protest of the young Franklin in the form of a hoax is the *Speech of Polly Baker.* Franklin may not have been a champion of woman's rights as we define them today but he fought injustice where he found it, and in his day the treatment of women by the law left something to be desired. Polly Baker is a simple woman who has had five illegitimate children and each time has been tried and severely punished for bastardy. In this trial for the same offense she stands before the bar and pleads for justice:

> May it please the honorable bench to indulge me in a few words: I am a poor unhappy woman who has no money to see lawyers to plead for me, being hard put to it to get a tolerable living. I shall not trouble your honors with long speeches; for I have not the presumption to expect that you may . . . be prevailed upon to deviate . . . from the law in my favor. All I humbly hope is that your honors would charitably move the Governor's goodness in my behalf, that my fine may be remitted. This is the fifth time, gentlemen, that I have been dragged before your court on the same account . . . This may have been agreeable to the laws . . . but . . . I take the liberty to say that I think this law by which I am punished is both unreasonable in itself and particularly severe to me, who have always lived an inoffensive life . . . and [I] defy my enemies to say I have ever wronged man, woman, or child.
>
> I have brought five fine children into the world at the risk of my life; I have maintained them well by my own industry, without burdening the township, and would have done it better if it had not been for the heavy charges and fines I have paid. Can it be a crime . . . to add to the number of the King's subjects in a new country that re-

ally wants people? . . . I should think it a praiseworthy rather than a punishable action. I have debauched no other woman's husband, nor enticed any youth . . . [I would] be stupefied to the last degree not to prefer the honorable state of wedlock to the condition I have lived in. I always was and still am willing to enter into it. I defy any person to say I ever refused an offer of that sort: On the contrary, I readily consented to the only proposal of marriage that was even made me, which was when I was a virgin. But too easily confiding in the person's sincerity that made it, I unhappily lost my honor by trusting in his; for he got me with child and then forsook me. That very person you all know; he is now become a magistrate of this country. I must now complain of it as unjust and unequal, that my betrayer and undoer should be advanced to honor and power in the government that punishes my misfortunes with stripes and infamy.

If mine, then, is a religious offense, leave it to religious punishments. You have already excluded me from the comforts of your church communion. Is that not sufficient? You believe I have offended heaven, and must suffer eternal fire. Will not that be sufficient? What need is there, then, of your additional fines and whipping? But how can it be believed that heaven is angry at my having children, when to the little done by one towards it God has been pleased to add his divine skill and admirable workmanship in the formation of their bodies, and crowned it by furnishing them with rational and immortal souls. Forgive me, gentlemen, if I talk a little extravagantly on these matters; I am no divine, but if you gentlemen must be making laws, do not turn natural and useful actions into crimes.

But take into your wise consideration the great and growing number of bachelors in the country, many of whom have never sincerely and honorably courted a woman in their lives: and by their manner of living leave unproduced (which is little better than murder) hundreds of their posterity to the thousandth generation. Is not this a greater offence against the public good than mine? Compel them then, by law, either to marriage or to pay double the fine of fornication every year.

What must poor young women do who cannot force themselves upon husbands, when the laws take no care to provide them any; and yet severely punish them if they do their duty without them—the duty of the first and great command of nature and of nature's God, increase and multiply. A duty which nothing has been able to deter me. But for its sake I have hazarded the loss of the public esteem and have frequently endured public disgrace and punishment. And therefore [I] ought, in my humble opinion, instead of a whipping, to have a statue erected to my memory.

According to the information Franklin gives in the introduction, Polly's speech had such a profound effect that the court dispensed with her punishment and one of the judges married her the next day. This was Franklin's most famous hoax. It appeared first in an English newspaper and in a few weeks newspapers and magazines all over the British Isles copied it. As soon as the English papers reached America, Polly's story was picked up and it swept through the American press.

The Gentleman's Magazine ran the story and supplied the further information that Polly and the judge who married her had 15 children, in addition to her original five. In the following issue a correspondent was concerned because some people had insinuated that the speech in Polly's name was entirely fictitious. To set the record straight he volunteered the information that he had been in New England two years before and had the pleasure of personally seeing the celebrated Polly Baker, then near 60 years of age but a comely woman and the wife of Paul Dudley of Roxbury, Massachusetts. This account brought another letter which refuted the imputation that Paul Dudley was married to Polly Baker. Dudley, who was Chief Justice of Massachusetts, was long married to a daughter of Governor Winthrop with whom he had no children, and the editor published an apology to Justice Dudley for the unintentional libel he had unwaringly printed.

But this did not terminate the Polly Baker story. It was revived in American newspapers over the years and appeared in a work on marriage, fornication, and divorce entitled *Social Bliss Considered*. Later, in France, the Abbé Raynal cited it as an outstanding example of social injustice and vindication in his popular book, *Philosophical and Political History*, and still other versions appeared in French. Finally, in the works of Thomas Jefferson there is told the following story:

"The Doctor and Silas Deane were in conversation one day at Passy [Franklin's home near Paris when he was ambassador to France] on the numerous errors in the Abbé Raynal's book, when the Abbé himself happened to step in. Silas Deane said to him, 'The Doctor and myself, Abbé, were just speaking of the errors of fact into which you have been led.' 'Oh, no Sir,' said the Abbé, 'that is impossible. I took the greatest care not to insert a single fact for which I had not the most unquestionable authority.' 'Why,' says Deane, 'there is the story of

Polly Baker and the eloquent apology you have put into her mouth. I know there never was such a law in Massachusetts.' 'Be assured,' said the Abbé, 'you are mistaken, and that that is a true story. I do not immediately recollect indeed the particular information on which I quote it, but I am certain that I had it for unquestionable authority.' Doctor Franklin, who had been for some time shaking with unrestrained laughter . . . said, 'I will tell you, Abbé, the origin of that story. When I was a printer and editor of a newspaper, we were sometimes slack of news, and to amuse our customers I used to fill up our vacant columns with ancedotes and fables and fancies of my own, and this Polly Baker is a story of my making on one of these occasions.' The Abbé, without the least disconcert, exclaimed with a laugh, 'Oh very well, Doctor, I had rather relate your stories than other men's truths.' ''

For a man so sensitive to social justice we may be surprised to learn that Franklin owned Negro slaves and even traded in them. In all fairness to him and other founding fathers who were slaveholders, we must make our judgment not on today's customs but on those prevailing in the 18th Century, when very few people considered slavery immoral or unjust. But as Franklin grew older and saw the miserable treatment of the Indians by the colonists and the exploitation of the colonists by the English, it is not surprising that he recognized the inhumanity of slavery. He not only recognized the problem, but as was usual for him, he was prepared to do something about it. Thus, in his later years, we find Franklin not only fervently opposed to slavery but the president of the first abolition society in America. In the last public act of his life, Franklin signed a memorial to the U.S. House of Representatives to employ the power vested in it by the newly-adopted Constitution to discourage the traffic in the human species.

In the debate in Congress over this memorial, James Jackson of Georgia made a speech opposing the memorial, which was published in the *Federal Gazette*. Shortly thereafter, a letter signed Historicus, commenting on the speech appeared in that newspaper. Jackson's eloquent speech put Historicus in mind of a similar one made about 100 years earlier by Sidi Mehemet Ibrahim, a member of the Divan of Algiers "which may be seen in Martin's account of his consulship, anno 1687." This speech (which no one was ever able to find) opposed granting a petition of the sect called Erika (purists), who argued that, because they were unjust, piracy and slavery should be abolished. The speech is a parody on Jackson's speech, the Erika substituting for the Quakers and the white, Christian slaves taken by the Algerian pirates substituting for the Negro slaves. This piracy and enslavement of Americans and Europeans inflamed the people, thus making the comparison most persuasive.

The arguments are very practical ones. If we cease capturing and enslaving Christians, reasons Sidi Mehemet, who will cultivate our lands, perform the labor in the city, and in our families? "Must we not then be our own slaves?" We must have more compassion for our own Muslims than for these Christian dogs, he pleads. Step by step, he makes the same points as Jackson, but employing them as arguments on behalf of enslaving white men. In place of the Bible he quotes from the Koran to prove that slavery is acceptable. Sidi Mehemet's speech convinced the Divan that the plundering and enslaving of Christians were unjust, but since it was in the interest of the state to continue the practice, the petition was rejected. Because like motives produce like actions, Historicus fears it is predictable that the present petition to Congress to abolish the slave trade will have a similar fate. Franklin was right; it would take not petitions but a civil war to end slavery in America.

Many of Franklin's protests were directed not inward at social ills but outward at the British government. In these cases, Franklin's wit was pointed and sharp. Such a protest is Franklin's response to the action of the government in exporting convicted criminals to the colonies. The colonies tried to pass local laws to prevent this objectionable dumping of undesirables in their midst but these laws were disallowed by Great Britain, with the excuse "that these laws are against the public utility, as they tend to prevent the *improvement* and *well peopling* of the colonies." Anonymously, Franklin turned his satire on this "benevolent" reasoning:

> Such a tender parental concern in our mother country for the welfare of her children calls aloud for the highest returns of gratitude and duty . . . 'Tis something to show a grateful disposition.
>
> It has been said that these thieves and villains introduced among us spoil the morals of youth . . . and perpetuate many horrid crimes. But let not private interests obstruct public utility. Our mother knows what is best for us. What is a little housebreaking, shoplifting, or highway robbing; what is a son now and then corrupted and hanged, a daughter debauched and poxed, a wife

stabbed, a husband's throat cut, or a child's brains beat out with an axe, compared with this *"improvement* and *well peopling* of the colonies!"

In some of the uninhabited parts of these provinces there are numbers of these venomous reptiles we call rattlesnakes; felon-convicts from the beginning of the world. These, whenever we meet with them, we put to death . . . I would humbly propose that this general sentence of death be changed for transportation. In the Spring of the year, when they first creep out of their holes, they are feeble, heavy, slow, and easily taken; and if a small bounty were allowed per head, some thousands might be collected annually and transported to Britain. There I would propose to have them carefully distributed in St. James Park, in the Spring Gardens and other places of pleasure about London; in the gardens of all the nobility and gentry throughout the nation, but particularly in the gardens of the Prime Ministers, the Lords of Trade and Members of Parliment, for to them we are most particularly obliged.

. . . And may not the honest rough British gentry, by a familiarity with these reptiles, learn to creep, and to insinuate, and to slaver, and to wriggle into place (and perhaps to poison such as stand in their way), qualities of no small advantage to courtiers! In comparison of which "improvement and public utility," what is a child now and then killed by their venomous bite, . . . or even a favorite lap dog?

I would only add that this exporting of felons to the colonies may be considered as a trade as well as a favor. Now all commerce implies returns . . . and rattlesnakes seem the most suitable returns for the human serpents sent us by our mother country. In this, however, as in every other branch of trade, she will have the advantage of us . . . For the rattlesnake gives warning . . . which the convict does not.

This piece appeared in the *Pennsylvania Gazette* in 1751 but Franklin was to return to the same subject in another piece he submitted to the same paper 36 years later. The United States was now free but the English claimed debts on the new country and restrained her shipping. In this second letter, Franklin reminded his readers of that phrase "for the better peopling of the colonies", and the "tenderness" of the mother country in emptying her jails into the colonies for that purpose. He carries on with his irony: "We are therefore much in her debt on that account and, as she is of late clamorous for the payment of all we owe her . . . I am for doing . . . what is in our power. The felons she planted among us have produced such an amazing increase that we are now enabled to make ample remittance in the same commodity. And since . . . many of our vessels are idle through her restrains on our trade, why should we not employ those vessels in transporting the felons to Britain?''

Franklin also proposes that English ships coming to America be required to carry back to Britain at least one felon for every fifty tons of her burden. ''Thus we shall not only discharge sooner our debts, but furnish our old friends with the means of better peopling . . . their promising new colony of Botany Bay.'' Botany Bay was the site of Captain Cook's first landing in Australia in 1770. And, as if in response to Franklin's idea, the British established a penal settlement at Botany Bay in 1788, one year after the publication of his article.

As agent for the colonies in England, Franklin presented their grievances to the government. Getting nowhere through direct negotiation, Franklin hoped he might persuade the English public of the injustice of the government's policies. He published an unsigned satire, ''Rules by Which a Great Empire May Be Reduced to a Small One'', in which the American grievances were dramatically displayed. Franklin begins: ''An ancient sage boasted that though he could not fiddle, he knew how to make a great city of a little one. The science that I, a modern simpleton, am about to communicate is the very reverse.'' He makes the point that extensive empires are troublesome to govern leaving the ministers no time for fiddling. In his homespun way he compares a great empire to a great cake, which is most easily diminished at the edges. He therefore advises the ministers to get rid of the remotest provinces first, and the next will follow, etc. So that this separation will be sure to occur, the provinces should not enjoy the same rights as the mother country. ''By carefully making and preserving such distinctions, you will (to keep to my simile of the cake) act like a wise gingerbread baker who . . . cuts his dough half through in those places where, when baked, he would have it broken to pieces''. In eighteen additional steps, Franklin outlines to the new government minister to whom the letter is directed how he may mistreat, infuriate, and alienate the colonists, all of his examples which are presented in mock humor, being the very injustices of which the colonists have complained and which eventually led to the revolution. Finally, Franklin says that if the minister will only practice those few excellent rules he will that day be rid of the trouble of governing these colonies and ''all the plagues attending their commerce and connection from henceforth and forever.'' The letter is signed Q.E.D. This article was a scathing criticism of government policy and a prediction that such policy would surely lead to a rupture, but it produced no move for conciliation by the king and his ministers.

A second satire, placed in a newspaper, was an outrageous hoax, an "Edict by the King of Prussia," that similarly enumerated the American grievances. Franklin was a guest at the estate of Lord Le Despencer when the newspaper with the story appeared, as he recounts the incident: "Mr. Whitehead was there too, who runs early through all the papers and tells the company what he finds remarkable. He had them in another room, and we were chatting in the breakfast parlor when he came running in to us out of breath, with the paper in his hand. 'Here!' says he, 'here's news for ye! Here's the King of Prussia claiming a right to this kingdom!' All stared, and I as much as anybody; and he went on to read it. When he had read two or three paragraphs, a gentleman present said, 'Damn his impudence, I dare say we shall hear by next post that he is upon his march with one hundred thousand men to back this.' Whitehead, who is very shrewd, soon after began to smoke it [out], and looking in my face said, 'I'll be hanged if this is not some of your American jokes upon us.' The reading went on, and ended with abundance of laughing and a general verdict that it was a fair hit."

The Edict is an official looking document in which King Frederick of Prussia makes demands of taxes, customs duties, trade restrictions, and limitations on manufactured goods on Great Britain. These demands are based upon the fact that the island of Britain was settled by Germans and they never have been emancipated from the mother country. The demands and restrictions are the same that the British government has imposed on America. Franklin has put the shoe on the other foot, making vivid the inequity of the government's position. As an afterthought, Frederick announces he will favor our said colonies in Britain with all the thieves, murderers, etc., "whom we, in our great clemency, do not think fit here to hang, shall be emptied out of our jails into the said island of Great Britain, for the better peopling of that country." In a final thrust, Franklin, posing as Frederick, argues the justice and reasonableness of his demands and regulations, since they were copied from those the British government itself has imposed upon its own colonies in America and Ireland. The day after publication of the Edict, Franklin sent his clerk out to pick up extra copies but they were sold out.

The efforts of the peacemakers were to no avail and military hostilities commenced between Britain and her American colonies. There was also another war, the propaganda war, and it found Franklin in the front lines. The fight against their own people was not very popular with the English; therefore the government found it expedient to hire mercenaries in the form of Hessian soldiers, which action was even less popular. Franklin capitalized on this sentiment in his satire, "The Sale of the Hessians." In this devastating hoax, a German nobleman, the Count de Schaumbergh is writing from Rome to Baron Hohendorf, the commander of the Hessian troops in America. The Count has been wintering in Italy and has just received news of the crushing defeat of the Hessians in the battle of Trenton:

> . . . I have learned with unspeakable pleasure the courage our troops exhibited at Trenton, and you can imagine my joy on being told that of the 1950 Hessians engaged in the fight, but 345 escaped. There were just 1,605 men killed, and I cannot sufficiently commend your prudence in sending an exact list of the dead to my minister in London. This precaution was the more necessary, as the report sent to the English ministry does not give but 1,455 dead. This would make 483,450 florins instead of 643,500 which I am entitled to demand under our convention.
>
> I trust . . . that you will not have tried . . . to recall [save] the life of the unfortunates whose days could not be lengthened but by the loss of a leg or an arm . . . I am sure they would rather die than live in a condition no longer fit for my service . . . there is no wiser course than to let every one of them die when he ceases to be fit to fight. You did right to send back to Europe that Dr. Crumerus who was so successful in curing dysentery . . . you know that they pay me as killed for all who die from disease.
>
> I am about to send you some new recruits. Don't economize them. Remember glory before all things. Glory is true wealth. There is nothing degrades the soldier like the love of money. He must care only for honor and reputation, but this reputation must be acquired in the midst of dangers. A battle gained without costing the conqueror any blood in an inglorious success, while the conquered cover themselves with glory by perishing with their arms in their hands. Do you remember that of the 300 Lacedaemonians who defended the defile of Thermopyle, not one returned? How happy should I be could I say the same of my brave Hessians!

The Count admits that the Lacedaemonian king, Leonidas, died with them, but things have changed, he says, and it is no longer the custom for princes to fight in America for a cause for which they have no concern. And to whom should they pay the thirty guineas per man if he did not stay in Europe to receive them? He must replace the men who are lost, but grown men are becoming scarce so he will send boys. He consoles himself that the scarcer the commodity the higher the price. It isn't that he is a mercenary person, but his trip to Italy has been very expensive, and he has made arrangements to produce an Italian grand opera which he does wish to give up. He is obviously a religious man, for in the last sentence of the letter he says, "Meantime I pray God, my dear Baron de Hohendorf, to have you in his holy and gracious keeping."

This piece may seem heavy handed but Franklin based it upon inglorious facts. The Prince of Anspack (Franklin's Count de Schaumbergh), who recruited his subjects against their wishes, found it necessary to disarm and fetter them and, with the help of his guard, drive them to the seaside where they were shipped to America. On his return through Holland, Franklin states, the Prince was publicly hooted by mobs in every town. The King of Prussia humored himself by charging the Princes a toll per head for the men they drove through his dominions, the same as paid for cattle, since they were sold as such. In a letter Franklin wrote from France in 1777, he commented; "The people of this country are almost unanimously in our favor." Without doubt, the action of the German Princes and Franklin's propaganda helped bring this about.

An artfully contrived bit of literary deception for propaganda purposes was produced by Franklin in the form of a supplement to the *Boston Independent Chronicle*. The material purports to be taken from a letter from Captain Gerrish of the New England Militia, who has captured a quantity of animal pelts from Indians fighting for the English:

> The possession of this booty at first gave us pleasure; but we were struck with horror to find among the packages eight large ones containing scalps of our unhappy country-folks taken in the three last years by the Senneka Indians from the inhabitants of the frontiers . . . and sent by them as a present to Col. Haldimand, Governor of Canada . . . to be by him transmitted to England. They were accompanied by the following curious letter to that gentleman.
>
> At the request of the Senneka chiefs, I send you herewith to your excellency . . . eight packs of scalps, cured, dried, hooped, and painted, with all the Indian triumphal marks, of which the following is invoice and explanation.

The grisly contents of all eight packages are described in realistic detail, numbers 5 and 8 being the most gruesome examples:

> No. 5 containing 88 scalps of women; hair long, braided in the Indian fashion, to show they were mothers; hoops blue; skin yellow ground, with little red tadpoles, to represent, by way of triumph, the tears of grief occasioned to their relatives; a black scalping knife or hatchet at the bottom to mark their being killed with those instruments. Seventeen others, hair very gray; black hoops; plain brown color; no mark, but the short club or casse-tête, to show they were knocked down dead, or had their brains beat out.
>
> No. 8 This package is a mixture of all varieties above-mentioned; to the number of 122; with a box of birch bark containing 29 little infants scalps of various sizes; small white hoops; white ground; no tears; and only a little black knife in the middle to show they were ripped out of their mother's bellies.
>
> With these packs, the Chiefs send to your excellency the following speech, delivered by Conejogatchie in Council . . .
>
> 'Father, we send you herewith many scalps, that you may see we are not idle friends.'
>
> (A blue belt.)
>
> 'Father, we wish you to send these scalps over the water to the great King that he may regard them and be refreshed; and that he may see our faithfulness in destroying his enemies . . .'
>
> (A blue and white belt with red tassels)

After each brief speech another belt of wampum was presented by the Chief in accordance with Indian ceremony. He wished to inform the King that the King's enemies are many and growing fast in number. "They were formerly like young panthers; they could neither scratch nor bite . . . But now their bodies are become as big as the elk and strong as the buffalo; they have also got great and sharp claws. They have driven us out of our country for taking part in your quarrel."

What to do with these scalps? Captain Gerrish said it was first proposed to bury them but since Lt. Fitzgerald was planning to go to Ireland, it was thought he might carry them to England and some dark night hang them on the trees in St. James Park where the King and Queen could see them from their palaces in the morning. This suggestion was not approved; it being proposed instead to send one of every kind to the King for his museum, some of those of women and little children to the Queen, the rest to be distributed among the members of Parliament, with a double quantity to the bishops.

This chilling humor reminds us that Franklin had read and greatly admired Jonathan Swift and his caustic wit. Franklin felt very bitter toward the English. He sent John Adams a copy of his hoax, saying, "I send enclosed a paper, of the veracity of which I have some doubt as to the form, but none as to the substance, for I believe the number of people actually scalped in this murdering war by the Indians to exceed what is mentioned." And referring to the King, he wrote, "and that Muley Ishmael (a happy name for a prince as obstinate as a mule) is full as black a tyrant as he is represented in Paul Jones' pretented letter." To complete his deception, Franklin did the printing on his own press copying the type and the paper of the Boston newspaper for his supplement and even inserting advertisements to ensure the semblance of authenticity.

The "Paul Jones pretented letter" was actually the work of Jones' fellow American and close friend, Ben Franklin. Under instructions from Franklin, the American Fleet Commander, John Paul Jones, with his tiny ragged navy had the audacity to raid the coasts of England and capture English ships in retaliation for like British action against America. Sir Joseph York, British minister at the Hague, had angrily called Jones a pirate; a charge Franklin answered in Jones' name.

He first defines a pirate as the enemy of all mankind, and then explains that he is an enemy to no part of mankind except England. A pirate, he continues, makes war for the sake of rapine, "Ours is a war in defense of liberty." America is defending her property that the English would have taken with an armed force in violation of her rights. "Yours, therefore, is a war of rapine . . ." he tells York. Has Sir Joseph forgotten the principle of Hambden's lawsuit with Charles I that, "what an English king has no right to demand, an English subject has a right to refuse?" Franklin lists the violations of the King against Americans and finally concludes that George III, due to his bloody deeds, is the greatest tyrant who has ever lived. "Let us view one of the worst and blackest of them, Nero." He put to death a few of his courtiers, etc. "Had George III done the same and no more, his crime, though detestable as an act of lawless power, might have been as useful to his nation as that of Nero was hurtful to Rome, considering the different characters and merits of the sufferers."

He concludes, "It afflicts me, therefore, to see a gentleman of Sir Joseph York's education and talents, for the sake of a red riband and a paltry stipend, mean enough to style such a monster [King George] his master, wear his livery, and hold himself ready at his command even to cut the throats of fellow subjects. This makes it impossible for me to end my letter with the civility of a compliment, and obliges me to subscribe myself simply, JOHN PAUL JONES, whom you are pleased to style a pirate.''

In the Jones letter Franklin expressed himself well—too well for a sea dog. Horace Walpole, the English writer, asked a friend, ''Have you seen in the papers an excellent letter by Paul Jones to Sir Joseph York? Dr. Franklin, himself, I should think, was the author. It is certainly from a first-rate pen, and not a common man-of-war.''

Not all of Franklin's impostures were created for the sake of persuasion; some were crafted only for entertainment by their fun-provoking author. Among these was the ''A Parable against Persecution.'' The parable tells the story of Abraham and an old stranger from the wilderness who passes Abraham's tent. Abraham graciously entreats him to come in, eat, and spend the night. But when Abraham discovers that the man does not bless God but worships a god of his own, Abraham turns him out into the wilderness. God calls to Abraham and scolds him saying, ''Have I borne with him these 398 years, and nourished him, and clothed him, notwithstanding his rebellion against me; and couldst not thou, who art thyself a sinner, bear with him one night?'' Repentant, Abraham goes out and finds the man and showers him with hospitality. ''And God spake unto Abraham saying, For this thy sin, shall thy seed be afflicted four hundred years in a strange land; but for they repentance will I deliver them; and they shall come forth with power, and with gladness of heart, and with much substance.''

This story, in its original form, came from Persian literature and was related in an English book, where Franklin saw it and liked it since it reinforced his own feelings of tolerance. He substituted Abraham and biblical language in the story, had it printed and bound up in his own Bible and read it to audiences as the fifty-first chapter of Genesis. Only a few friends knew his trick and many of his listeners searched their Bibles in vain for these passages. One of his great pleasures was to read it by heart out of his open Bible, he knew it so well, and listen with great solemnity to the learned remarks of the scripturians upon it, which he recalled were ''sometimes very diverting.'' He said, ''I was always unwilling to give a copy of the chapter for fear it would be printed, and by that means I should be deprived of the pleasure I often had of amusing people with it.'' But he softened and gave a copy to his friend Lord Kames, who gave it general circulation by including it in his book, *History of Man,* much to Franklin's disappointment.

John Baskerville is today considered one of the foremost among those who have advanced the art of printing. He produced new types which were much superior in distinctness and elegance to those previously employed. Yet his contemporaries asserted that the quality of his printing owed more to the paper and ink than to his new type. As a printer, Franklin was elated by Baskerville's work and sent a copy of a Baskerville printing of Virgil as a gift to Harvard. He visited Baskerville in Birmingham and later wrote him a letter about the reaction to his new type: "Let me give you a plesant instance of the prejudice some have entertained against your work." Franklin then related his talk with a literary man who maintained that Baskerville would be the cause of all English readers going blind. The letters of his type, the man declared, were too thin and narrow and hurt the eye, and he could never read a line of them without pain. "I thought," Franklin said to him, "that you were going to complain of the gloss of the paper some object to." "No, no," says he, ". . . it is the form and cut of the letters themselves; they have not that height and thickness of the stroke, which makes the common printing so much the more comfortable to the eye." "You see," said Franklin to Baskerville, "This gentleman was a connoisseur." Franklin tried to defend Baskerville but the man knew what he felt, and furthermore some of his friends had made the same observation.

"Yesterday he called to visit me," Franklin continued, "when, mischievously bent to try his judgment, I stepped into my closet, tore off the top of Mr. Caslon's specimen, and produced it to him as yours." Franklin told the man he had been examining it since the two had talked but could find no trouble with it. "He readily undertook it, and went over the several founts, showing me everywhere that he thought instances of that disproportion, and declared that he could not then read the specimen without feeling very strongly the pain he had mentioned to me." Franklin spared him the embarrassment of the fact that these were the types he had been reading all his life and the very ones his own book was printed with. Franklin remarked to Baskerville, ". . . and yet [he] never discovered this painful disproportion in them till he thought they were yours."

An interesting postscript is that after Franklin was back in Philadelphia Baskerville printed this letter without Franklin's knowledge as an advertisement, making it an early example of the use of the personal letter as a testimonial in advertising. It was fortunate that he did, for it functioned in preserving this amusing document, which otherwise might have been lost to us.

Although Franklin was usually in the role of the imposter, on one occasion he was on the receiving end of a friendly canard. During his term as minister to France, Franklin was continually plagued by people who wanted something from him, and was particularly annoyed by the many letters soliciting money. He did his best to meet these requests but the more he satisfied, the more he received. According to Claude-Anne Lopez in *Mon Cher Papa,* Franklin's friends, the Brillons, knowing of his frustration over these solicitations, imitated such a letter to "His Excellency" and Franklin fell into the trap. After he read the first few lines "begging the kindness of his highness," he threw the letter on his table, sighing impatiently, ". . . always demands of money. It is bad to have the reputation of being charitable. We expose ourselves to a thousand importunities and a good deal of expense as a punishment for our pride, nay our vanity, which lets our small benefactions be known, whereas Our Lord has given us the good and political advice to keep our right hand from knowing what our left hand has done." When he read the rest of the letter, however, and saw at the end "the dear names" of the members of the Brillon family, he kissed the signatures with affection. He enjoyed the joke on himself as much as the rest, saying that his pleasure had been increased by the realization that the letter begged not for money but only for friendship.

Where fun was concerned, no subject was sacred to Franklin, even science. When all Paris and Franklin, too, were in a state of happy agitation over the invention of the gas balloon, he penned a letter to the press under the guise of a lady correspondent with an invention of her own: "Our chemists, it is said, are sparing no effort to discover a kind of air both lighter and less expensive . . . to fill our aerostatic machines [balloons]. But it is really singular that men as enlightened as those of our century should be forever searching . . . for what nature offers everywhere and to everybody, and that an ignorant woman such as me should be the first to think of the solution. . . . If you want to fill your balloons with an element ten times lighter than inflammable air, you can find a great quantity of it, and ready made, in the promises of lovers and of courtiers and in the sighs of our widowers; in the good resolutions taken during a storm at sea, or on land during an illness; and especially in the praise to be found in letters of recommendation.''

The following science hoax continues in much the same manner on the subject of gases. This bagatelle did not appear in the published works of Franklin but in small privately printed editions of his ''surreptitious'' writings, and has, threfore, not become very well known. Even Carl Van Doren's famous biography of Franklin barely mentons it. Titled, ''To the Royal Academy of Brussels,'' or sometimes called ''Perfumes,'' its fragrance was a little too pungent for the publishers. The piece is a parody on the stuffy, pompous writings of many learned academicians and the abstract, erudite subjects they select to write about. To leaven the satire, Franklin makes his arguments with the majestic sweep and grandeur deserving of his profound subject, yet he sprinkles it with a liberal supply of puns for the reader who may not be so impressed with his serious bearing. The Royal Academy had the practice of proposing an annual prize question which in this case is a mathematical one, namely, ''Given any single figure, one is asked to inscribe there the greatest number of times another smaller figure, which is also given.'' Franklin found this question lacking in the essential property of a prize question, that of utility. ''Permit me then humbly to propose one of that sort for your consideration,'' he requests, and then explains that among the functions of the human body the digestion of food creates gases that not only are offensive but highly dangerous when forcibly retained, and he asks for the discovery of a drug that can be mixed with food to remove disagreeable odors, and possibly make them ''as agreeable as perfumes.''

Lest his question should be considered impossible, Franklin assures the Academicians that there already exists knowledge on varying that smell. The man who dines on stale meat and onions will produce a stink that no one can tolerate, while he that dines only on vegetables shall have a breath that will not disturb the most delicate nose; ''and if he can manage so as to avoid the report, he may anywhere give vent to his griefs, unnoticed. We know that lime arrests the fetid air arising from putrid matter, then perhaps a glass of limewater taken with meals will have the same effect on the air issuing from our bowels? Asparagus gives our urine a disagreeable odor, and a pill of turpentine bestows on it the smell of violets. Why then, he asks, should it be thought impossible to find the means of making a perfume of our wind than of our water?

Franklin considers the immortal honor to be expected by the inventor of this perfume. In contrast, he observes how little actual importance to mankind have been those discoveries in science that have hitherto made philosophers famous:

> Are there twenty men in Europe at this day the happier, or even the easier, for any knowledge they have picked out of Aristotle? What comfort can the vortices of Descartes give to a man who has whirlwinds in his bowels! The knowledge of Newton's mutual attraction of the particles of matter, can it afford ease to him who is racked by their mutual repulsion, and the cruel distensions it occasions? The pleasure arising to a few philosophers from seeing, a few times in their life, the threads of light untwisted and separated by the Newtonian prism into seven colors, can it be compared with the ease and comfort every man living might feel seven times a day by discharging freely the wind from his bowels? Especially if it be converted into a perfume.

What infinite satisfaction must it bring to the benevolent person, Franklin contemplates, to know how much that he has added to the pleasure and happiness of so many people by means of this. The generous soul, who now offers his guests their choice of Claret or Burgundy, Champagne or Madeira would then inquire whether they choose musk or lily, rose or bergamot. "And surely such a liberty of ex-pressing one's scent-iments and pleasing one another is of infinitely more importance to human happiness than that liberty of the press." In conclusion, Franklin asserts, that in terms of universal and continual utility, the science of the above-mentioned philosophers, even with the addition of the mathematical prize question of the figure and the figures inscribed in it, "are altogether scarcely worth a fart-hing."

The last word is dropped below the line of type and printed by itself so that it serves as the signature (and an appropriate one) to the letter. Franklin sent this piece to Dr. Richard Price in England for his amusement. On second thought, he said to Price, "you are a mathematician, I am afraid I have judged wrong in sending it to you. Our friend Dr. Priestly, however, who is apt to give himself *airs* and has a kind of right to everything his friends produce upon that subject may perhaps like to read it, (and then Franklin's little joke) and you can send it to him without reading it." Price did read it, as he was meant to do, and replied that he and Priestly were both amused by its pleasantry and ridicule.

14

TO TELL A WHOPPER

AMERICANS LOVE THE TALL STORY, THE TEXAS TALE, the Liar's Club yarn about the huge fish that got away. Franklin was no different and some of his whoppers rank with the best.

One of them was inspired by the ignorance and gullibility of the English in regard to America, making them victim to propagandists' anti-American reports. With tongue in cheek, Franklin commented in a letter to an English newspaper that the world had grown too incredulous. Not all news articles that seem improbable are mere inventions, he averred, some are serious truths.* Formerly everything printed was believed, but now the reverse is true. People doubt the authority of newspapers, the predictions in almanacs, and the next step might even be a disbelief in the well-vouched-for accounts of ghosts and witches.

"Englishmen are too apt to be silent when they have nothing to say; too apt to be sullen when they are silent; and when they are sullen, to hang themselves." Fortunately, however, travelers who write about their voyages supply them with abundant funds for conversation.

The stories from America, he noted, are doubted by superficial

---

* This letter, in fact, was a "mere invention." It was written in response to an earlier letter in the same newspaper by "an ingenious correspondent that calls himself *the* Spectator." The Spectator was none other than Franklin himself.

readers who do not believe that Americans can establish industries to compete with England. They claim that American sheep have so little wool there is not sufficient to produce a pair of stockings a year for each inhabitant. "Let us not be amused by such groundless objections. The very tails of the American sheep are so laden with wool that each has a car or wagon on four little wheels to support and keep it from trailing on the ground." Would they caulk their ships, fill their beds, even litter their horses with wool if it were not plentiful and cheap?

Now, as for the account in the papers that the Canadians are making preparations for a cod and whale fishery in the upper lakes [an actual report in an English newspaper told of a whale fishery on Lake Ontario] ignorant people may object that the lakes are fresh water and that cod and whale are salt water fish. "But let them know, Sir, that cod, like other fish when attacked by their enemies, fly into any water where they think they can be the safest; that whales when they have a mind to eat cod, pursue them wherever they fly; and that the great leap of the whale in that chase up the fall of Niagara is esteemed by all who have seen it as one of the finest spectacles in nature!"

In France, a young scholar and close friend of Franklin named Cabanis seems to have been taken in by a bizarre story Franklin told him about a curious bird in America. In a book he wrote after Franklin's death, Cabanis mentions having heard Franklin tell several times of a sort of bird that he had seen in the forests of America which had two horned tubercles at the joint of its wings, like the horned screamer and the horned lapwing. At the death of this curious bird, according to Franklin's report to Cabanis, the two tubercles become the sprouts of two vegetable stalks, which grow at first by sucking the juice from its cadaver, and subsequently attach themselves to the earth to live like plants and trees. It is clear that Franklin never told him that this story was just a joke, for in his book Cabanis states that the learned naturalists to whom he spoke about this fact "ignore it absolutely." "Therefore," he gravely comments, "in spite of the great veracity of Franklin, I cite it with a great deal of reserve, and I draw from it no conclusion."

Franklin's fertile imagination and his ability to formulate a story to serve his purpose is illustrated in another bird tale related by John Adams. "Dr. Franklin told me," says Adams, "that before his return to America from England in 1775, he was in company . . . with a number of English noblemen, when the conversation turned upon fables, those of Aesop, La Fontaine, Gay, Moore, etc, etc." One of those present said he thought that the subject was exhausted. He did not believe anyone could now find an animal, beast, bird, or fish that he could work into a new fable with any success. The whole group appeared to agree, except Franklin, who was silent. The gentleman insisted that Franklin give his opinion. With submission to their lordships, Franklin said he believed the subject was inexhaustible and that many new and instructive fables might be made out of such materials. "Can you think of any one at present?" Franklin replied, "If your lordship will furnish me a pen, ink, and paper, I believe I can furnish your lordship with one in a few minutes." The paper was brought, and he sat down and wrote:

> Once upon a time, an eagle scaling round a farmer's barn and spying a hare, darted down upon him like a sunbeam, seized him in his claws and remounted with him in the air. He soon found that he had a creature of more courage and strength than a hare, for which, not withstanding the keenness of his eyesight, he had mistaken a cat. The snarling and scrambling of the prey was very inconvenient, and what was worse, she had disengaged herself from his talons, grasped his body with her four limbs so as to stop his breath, and seized fast hold of his throat with her teeth. Pray, said the eagle, let go your hold and I will release you. Very fine, said the cat, [but] I have no fancy to fall from this height and be crushed to death. You have taken me up, and you shall stoop and let me down. The eagle thought it necessary to stoop accordingly.

The moral was so applicable to England and America that it was agreed the fable was original, and it was highly applauded by the company. A shorter version of this fable was inserted in an English newspaper in 1770. It appeared along with another fable which attempted to show in a humorous way that Britain's unjust taxation policies of America would be resisted and would not work:

> A herd of cows had long afforded plenty of milk, butter, and cheese to an avaricious farmer who grudged them the grass they subsisted on. At length, [he] mowed it to make money of the hay leaving them to shift for food as they could. And yet [he] still expected to milk them as before, but the cows, offended at this unreasonableness, resolved for the future to suckle one another.

As Franklin himself had pointed out, not all news articles that seem improbable are mere inventions. After all, truth is stranger than fiction. And truth, liberally embellished and elasticized, might be even stranger still. Consider, if you will, a news article that appeared in the *Pennsylvania Gazette,* dated August 27, 1730:

> From Woodbury Creek, on the other side of the river, we hear that on Sunday night last a servant man belonging to one Tatcham got out of bed at midnight, and telling a lad who slept with him that he was going on a long journey and should never see him more, he went into the orchard and hanged himself on a tree. But it seems the rope broke in the operation and towards morning he found himself alive on the ground to his no small surprise. He then went and hid himself in the barn among some straw for several hours, while his master and the rest of the family were searching and inquiring after him to no effect. At length having procured a better rope, he hanged himself again in the barn, and was there accidentally found by the maid in the afternoon. When he was cut down there appeared no sign of life in him, nor were any means used to recover him. But by the time the coroner and his inquest were got together and come to view his body, he was upon his legs again and is now living.

Proverbs and epigrams were very useful in influencing prudent behavior and Franklin made abundant use of them in his almanac. A good story could also be very effective in this way and, for a journalist concerned with filling his columns, it had the added advantage of length. In *Poor Richard* for 1757 even the bored reader could not help but be intrigued by an article entitled, "How to make a Striking Sundial, by which not only a man's own family, but all his neighbors for ten miles round may know what o'clock it is (when the sun shines) without seeing the dial." The instructions follow:

> Choose an open space in your yard or garden on which the sun may shine all day without any impediment from trees or buildings. On the ground mark out your hour lines, as for a horizontal dial . . . On the line for one o'clock place one gun; on the two o'clock line two guns, and so of the rest. The guns must all be charged with powder, but ball is unnecessary. Your gnomon or style [the part of the sundial that casts a shadow] must have twelve burning glasses annexed to it, and be so placed . . . that the sun shining through the glasses . . . shall cause the focus or burning spot to fall on the hour line of one . . . at one o'clock, and there kindle a train of gunpowder that shall fire one gun. At two o'clock, a focus shall fall on the fire line of two, and kindle another train that shall discharge two guns successively; and so on for the rest.
> Note, there must be 78 guns in all.

Thirty-two pounders will be best for this use; but 18 pounders may do and will cost less, as well as use less powder.

Note also, that the chief expense will be the powder, for the cannon once bought will, with care, last 100 years.

Note moreover, that there will be a great saving of powder on cloudy days.

Following this description, there is message with a moral from the author: "Kind reader, methinks I hear thee say, 'That it is indeed a good thing to know how the time passes, but this kind of dial, notwithstanding the mentioned savings, would be very expensive and the cost greater than the advantage.' Thou art wise, my friend, to be so considerate beforehand; some fools would not have found out so much till they had made the dial and tried it. Let all such learn that many a private and many a public project are like this Striking Dial, great cost for little profit."

Concerned as he was with economics, Franklin was upset by the runaway inflation in America during the Revolutionary War, especially as it affected the welfare of salaried men, women, and orphans. He saw as the only consolation to the evil of this depreciation of money brought about by the over-supply of paper currency, the fact that the public debt was thereby proportionately diminished. In a letter written in France, he described this reduction in the public debt by depreciation of the currency as a kind of imperceptible tax, every one having paid a part of it in the fall of the money's value. Having discussed this subject in a very serious manner he suddenly took off on a flight-of-fancy on paper currency.

This effect of paper currency is not understood on this side of the water. And indeed the whole is a mystery even to the politicians—how we have been able to continue a war four years without money, and how we could pay with paper that had no previously fixed fund appropriated specifically to redeem it. This currency as we manage it is a wonderful machine. It performs its office when we issue it; it pays and clothes troops, and provides victuals and ammunition. And when we are obliged to issue a quantity excessive, it pays itself off by depreciation.

It is no wonder that Franklin's thoughts were on economics. He had to find the money to support the American army, which he was able to do with the help of the French government. As a man of humble beginnings in a new country, he viewed with some disapproval the lavish spending of the French upper classes. He was particularly critical of the expensive velvets and lace worn by the men and their elaborate, curled wigs powdered heavily with flour. Franklin once commented to Turgot, the French Minister of Finance, "You have in France an excellent means of making war without spending money. You need only agree not to have your hair curled and not to use powder as long as the war shall last. Your wig makers will form an army, and you can maintain them with the fees you will save. And the grain which would otherwise be used to make powder will serve to feed them."

In contrast to the French dandies, consider Franklin's appearance in France. He gave a description of himself to an Englishwoman in 1777:

> I will describe myself to you. Figure me in your mind as . . . very plainly dressed, wearing my thin gray straight hair that peeps out under my only coiffure, a fine fur cap, which comes down my forehead almost to my spectacles. Think how this must appear among the powdered heads of Paris! I wish every gentleman and lady in France would . . . follow my fashion, comb their own heads as I do mine, dismiss their *friseurs* and pay me half the money they paid to them. . . . I could then enlist those *friseurs,* who are at least 100,000 and with the money I would . . . make a visit with them to England and dress the heads of your ministers and privy counsellors, which I conceive to be at present a little disarranged.

One of Franklin's many talents was the ability to recognize talent in others. Among his recruits from Europe who became famous in the service of America were Tom Paine, Baron Von Steuben, and the Marquis de Lafayette. After the fighting in America was over, Lafayette returned to France and a warm friendship was kindled between the most popular American in France and the most popular Frenchman in America. Lafayette notified Franklin of the birth of his new daughter, two months premature but healthy, saying, "Every child of mine . . . is a small addition to the number of American citizens." He compared her early birth to the American Revolution, which was brought about earlier than it should have been but did very well. "They ask me what name my daughter is to have. I want to present her as an offering to my western country." And so he named her after one of the united states, Virginia.

Franklin informed Lafayette of his pleasure at the happy news.

Commenting on the name of Virginia, Franklin wrote, "In naming your children I think you do well to begin with the most ancient state. And as we cannot have too many of so good a race I hope you and Madam Lafayette will go through the thirteen." Not one to ignore economy even in ordinary affairs, Franklin continued, "But as that may be . . . too severe a task for her delicate frame, and children of seven months may become as strong as those of nine, I consent to the abridgement of two months for each. And I wish her to spend the twentysix months so gained in perfect ease, health, and pleasure." Back to the names of the states again, he says, "While you are proceeding, I hope our states will (some of them) new-name themselves. Miss Virginia, Miss Carolina, and Miss Georgiana will sound prettily enough for the girls, but Massachusetts and Connecticut are too harsh even for the boys, unless they were to be savages."

When Franklin left France and died several years later, his French friends remembered him with fondness and recorded numerous anecdotes about him. One which became very popular relates a story about his travels in America. Riding all day on horseback in very cold weather Franklin arrived at a tavern. Shivering and numb with cold, he made his way toward the fireplace but it was surrounded with men and the seats were all taken. No one moved to offer him a place. He then called out in a loud voice for a basket of oysters to be taken outside to his horse. The men in the tavern were overcome with curiosity to see the oysters opened and given to the horse. Franklin then sat himself down and relaxed in one of the vacated seats beside the fire. When the men came back to tell him that the horse would not eat the oysters, Franklin replied, "In that case, give the horse some hay and bring the oysters to me."

PART THREE

The Women and the Man

15

AN AMERICAN IN PASSY

FRANKLIN'S ENORMOUS POPULARITY WAS A PHENOMENON IN France in the latter part of the 18th century. Before he took up residence in Paris in 1776 Franklin was already known as the wizard of electricity and, through translations of "The Way to Wealth" from *Poor Richard's Almanac,* he was recognized as a sage as well. Rousseau's concept of the noble savage, which ascribed purity and wisdom to primitive man, had just become popular; and since the wise, lightning-taming Franklin came from a primitive land, he was heralded as the living embodiment of this concept. Disembarking from the ship after a stormy, winter voyage he had a walking stick, fur cap, no wig, and rough, simple clothes. This costume, so different from the fancy frills and laces the Frenchmen were then wearing, completed his image as the noble savage in the eyes of the public. Quick to recognize that such a favorable reputation would be useful to his mission, he continued to go wigless and wear simple clothes, leading many Frenchmen to mistakenly believe he was a Quaker. Wherever he went, people crowded around to see this phenomenon, the "noble savage" from America. Those who did not know his identity, noticed his plain clothes and asked, "Who is this old peasant who has such a noble air?"

In writing to his sister, Franklin confirmed the report she had heard of his unusual popularity in France. "Few strangers," he wrote, "have the good fortune to be so universally popular." Clay medallions of his likeness were displayed everywhere in Paris. They were worn as lockets and in rings or were set in the lids of snuff boxes. These along with prints, busts, and pictures were sold in incredible numbers; as he observed to his daughter, they "made your father's face as well known as that of the moon." If he did anything that would oblige him to run off, he told her, his *phiz* would give him away wherever he would show it. "It is said by learned etymologists that the name *doll* . . . is derived from the word IDOL. From the number of *dolls* now made of him," Franklin said of himself, "he may be truly said . . . to be *i-doll-ized* in this country." The French king may have been annoyed at the competition he was receiving for, when the Queen's favorite companion, the Countess Polignac, expressed uninhibited enthusiasm for this American hero, he sent her a chamber pot with Franklin's likeness on it. To accommodate the flood of requests for his portrait and sculpture, Franklin sat posing so often that he became sick of the boredom of it. Yet, acquiescing to another portrait-sitting request for a friend he couldn't refuse, he said, "Cheer me up, or you will have of me the saddest of portraits."

Whether it was because of his overwhelming popularity or despite it, Franklin was very happy in France. He said he enjoyed "the sweet society of a people whose conversation is instructive, whose manners are highly pleasing, and above all nations of the world, have in the greatest perfection the art of making themselves beloved by strangers." As evidence, he cited the civility of this nation where your first acquaintances find out what you like and tell others; "If you like mutton, dine where you will find mutton." Somebody let it be known that he loved ladies and then everybody presented him their ladies (or the ladies presented themselves) to be embraced, that is to have their necks kissed. "For as to kissing of lips or cheeks it is not the mode here, the first is reckoned rude and the other may rub off the paint." The French ladies, Franklin found, have however a thousand other ways of rendering themselves agreeable, by their various attentions and their sensible conversation. " 'Tis a delightful people to live with." "In Paris where the mode is to be sacredly followed," he once joked, "I was once very near making love to my friend's wife."

He found the French men guilty of some frivolities, but harmless ones. They dressed their hair so that hats could not be worn, but employed instead the *chapeau bras,* a hat meant not to be worn but to be carried under the arm, a fashion this practical Yankee considered utterly ridiculous. They also filled their noses with snuff, but these things were not vices in Franklin's judgment, only the tyranny of custom. "In short," he concluded, "there is nothing wanting in the character of a Frenchman that belongs to that of an agreeable and worthy man."

At first Franklin had trouble with the French language. His inability to understand spoken French caused him to make a real blunder. He told of a meeting where there were many speeches and, not being able to understand the rapidly spoken words, he watched the lady beside him and applauded when she did. To his embarrassment, he learned later from his grandson, he had been applauding praises of himself, and in his desire to be congenial had applauded more loudly than anybody else.

Even after he became competent in speaking French, Franklin was never comfortable with the French manner of speaking. The volubility of the French and their animated conversation, with participants freely plunging in rather than patiently waiting for the first speaker to finish his discourse, made him uneasy. He complained, "If you Frenchmen would only talk no more than four at a time, I might understand you . . ." He explained the problem to his fellow Americans, "if you do not deliver your sentence with great rapidity you are cut off in the middle of it by the impatient loquacity of those you converse with, and never suffered to finish it." He illustrated the point with a story of a French bishop who entered a group where another ecclesiastic was talking so long and incessantly that the newcomer could not get in a word of his own. The bishop finally cried out, "He is lost if he spits."

In contrast, Franklin's quiet nature startled and fascinated the French. His silence was invariably interpreted as deep contemplation and wisdom, the natural endowments of a great philosopher. An anecdote concerning this quality of the man, perhaps exaggerated, is recorded by the French political philosopher Bailly. A neighbor of Franklin, he paid a call on his fellow scientist. After entering the room Bailly kept silent, respectfully waiting for his host to begin the conversation. Eventually he offered Franklin a pinch of tobacco which the latter refused with a smile and a gesture. After two hours of silence, Bailly got up to leave and Franklin's only words as he accompanied him to the door were "fort bien." Bailly loved to tell this story, confirming the legend in France of Franklin's reticence.

As a public official, it was important for Franklin to be able to write French and he made an earnest effort toward that end. He wrote exercises of his own in French and sent them to his friends for correction with his apology: "I am conscious that I have written here a great deal of very bad French; it may disgust you who write that charming language with so much purity and elegance. But if you can finally decipher my awkward and unfit expressions you will perhaps have at least that kind of pleasure that one has in solving enigmas or discovering secrets."

Madame Brillon, Franklin's good friend, was his principal instructor in the French language. She carefully edited his writings for errors but discounted his concerns about them. "What you call your bad French often gives spice to your narration by the construction of your sentences and by the words which you invent," she told him. She advised him to laugh at the grammarians, "If your French is not very pure, it is at least very clear!" And she assured him, as she knew it would please him to know, that it was always very good French to say, "Je vous aime."

He thanked his instructor for having accepted with such good grace his poorly written messages which he did not finish because he did not have the time to look up all those masculine and feminine words in the dictionary, nor the modes and tenses in the grammar. Coyly, he wrote "masculines" (instead of "masculins") and "feminins" (for "feminines"), purposely reversing the gender of the French word endings to emphasize his dissatisfaction with such problems which did not exist in English. "For sixty years, now," he went on, taking a new turn, "masculine and feminine things—and I am not talking about modes and tenses—have been giving me a lot of trouble. I once hoped that at the age of 80 I would be liberated from that. But here I am, four times 19, which is very close to 80, and yet those French feminines still bother me.

They did indeed. With Puritan disapproval mingled with male envy, John Adams observed that Franklin "at the age of seventy odd, has neither lost his love of beauty nor taste for it . . ." And one of Franklin's close friends in France, the Abbé de la Roche, noted that at dinner parties given in his honor women flocked to see him. They would speak to him for hours on end without realizing that he understood little of what they said. "In spite of the time they wasted," commented the Abbé, "he greeted each one of them with a kind of amiable coquettishness that they loved.'' Among Franklin's female acquaintances in France was Madam Le Roy, the wife of his scientist friend, whom he teasingly referred to as his ''little pocket wife'' because of her size. She made history as one of the first women to go up in a balloon.

There was the Countess Houdetot, the recipient of Rousseau's virtuous but tormented love as revealed in his famous *Confessions*. One of the most influential women of her time, who kept one of the leading salons in Paris, she sought out Franklin and lent her influence to assist the American cause. She honored him on the grounds of her estate in a spring festival with great ceremony, consisting of poetry praising liberty, and toasting him and his great achievements. She had him plant a tree to commemorate symbolically the memorable event. In another ceremony, the most beautiful of three hundred young women placed a crown of laurel on his gray head and kissed both his cheeks. Death can hold no terror, the old man must have thought, if heaven is like this.

There was Mademoiselle de Passy, who lived in a splendid chateau near his residence and who was considered one of the most beautiful young women in France. According to Adams, Franklin called her, ''his favorite and his flame and his mistress, which flattered the family and did not displease the young lady.'' When she married the Marquis de Tonnerre (*tonnerre* meaning lightning), his friends asked him how it was that ''with all your lightning rods you couldn't keep lightning from hitting Mademoiselle de Passy?''

There was Mademoiselle Le Veillard, the young daughter of his ardent admirer, the mayor of the village of Passy, where Franklin lived. Probably just in her early teens she had a crush on the old man, who could charm ladies of all ages. She once left a note, ''Mademoiselle Le Veillard came by to have the honor to be kissed by Monsieur Franklin.'' And she wrote him, ''You told me that when you would write that you loved me a little, it would mean a lot. As for me, I tell you that I love you a lot. I hope you will not conclude, therefore, that I love you a little . . . for . . . I assure you that when I say a lot, that is exactly what I mean.''

There was Madam Foucault, the married daughter of Franklin's host and landlord, Chaumont. After Franklin had returned to the United States, his grandson who was still in France, conveyed the love of the Chaumont family. He added, ''and the beautiful Madam Foucault accompanies hers with an *English* kiss.'' In his reply Franklin sent his love to the family and thanked Madam Foucault for sending him the kiss. But he lamented that it had grown cold in transit and "I hope for a warm one when we meet." Monsieur Brillon mentioned her in writing to Franklin: "We saw her yesterday. She is marvelously plump once again and has just acquired new curves. Very round curves, very white, they seem to have a quality most essential in the eyes of amateurs such as you . . . It would be possible, I bet, to kill a flea on them . . ."

It was however, the eldest of the Chaumont girls, nicknamed "la mere Bobie," who meant the most to Franklin. She took charge of his household ordered the food, kept his accounts, and earned the title, "my wife." It was a title of endearment which he had fondly conferred upon various women before and did not suggest but, rather, by this humorous avowal, actually negated any implication of romantic attachment. She did her job well and he showed her the tender appreciation that won her affection. When he was prepared to leave France she wrote to him at the ship appealing to him to reconsider. She invited him to come back to his old room and assured the aged widower, "you will never find in the other hemisphere a wife who loves you more than yours." In his response from America he recalled the happy times he spent with the Chaumonts but regretted that those days could never return. With deep feeling he released her from her "vows" saying "as I am already in another world, you are free to choose a better husband, an event I wish with all my heart."

Soon after Franklin arrived in Paris he moved in with the Chaumonts in the village of Passy, on the outskirts of Paris on the way to Versailles. Passy, now swallowed up by Paris, was then a country place of farms and woods and grand chateaus. Such was the Hotel de Valentinois, the residence of the Chaumonts overlooking the Seine River, a mansion with spacious grounds and terraces. When he first arrived and visited Franklin there, Adams was in a stew over the magnificence of the place and the extravagance of Franklin for taking such plush accommodations at public expense. He may have been mollified upon learning that Franklin and Deane occupied one of the pavillions free of charge, as a guest of Chaumont, who was partisan to America in her struggle for freedom. Chaumont was a merchant prince who helped Franklin equip the American forces with ships and uniforms and eventually bankrupted himself in the process. Though their affairs were entangled with financial knots and every kind of problem, the friendship of Franklin and Chaumont remained firm throughout the whole period.

Living with Franklin in the pavillion was the small staff with which he conducted his diplomatic affairs. While Adams was dismayed at Franklin's heavy social schedule and the little time he seemed to take for official duties, his intimate friend Cabanis marveled at his relaxed efficiency: "Franklin's most original trait, that would have made him unique in any century, was his art of living . . . He would eat, sleep, work whenever he was fit . . . so that there never was a more leisurely man, though he certainly handled a tremendous amount of business. No matter when one asked for him, he was always available. His house in Passy, where he had chosen to live because he loved the country and fresh air, was always open to visitors . . . Let it not be said that he unloaded his work on his secretaries, for he had only one secretary, his own grandson . . . besides, he and his grandson occasionally used the help of an ordinary transcriber. Such was the staff of the Minister Plenipotentiary of the United States."

When la mere Bobie eventually gave up her supervision of the Franklin household, these duties were assumed by a house manager named Finck. The arrangement with Finck was very simple. For a flat fee each month he would provide the meals, pay the bills, etc., thus relieving Franklin of the details of household affairs. Unfortunately, it didn't work out as Franklin had planned. Finck was always complaining, as Franklin told Madam Helvetius, "even if he has signed twenty times that he is fully satisfied, he will never rest and . . . will confront you with a list of demands. He will abuse you if you don't give in, and even if you do he will complain just the same." When Franklin left for America, Finck ran off without paying any of the shopkeepers and tried to put the blame on Franklin and his grandson. When last heard of, Finck was successfully evading the police and enjoying himself with gambling and prostitutes. Upon receiving the news, Franklin simply remarked, "he was fairly paid in money for every just demand he could make against us, and we have his receipts in full. But there are knaves in the world whom no writing can bind . . . He was continually saying of himself, 'I am an honest man, I am an honest man.' But I always suspected he was mistaken, and so it proves."

In her delightful book, *Mon Cher Papa,* Claude-Ann Lopez propounds an interesting question. She wonders how Franklin, surrounded as he was by a house manager who was a thief, a secretary who was a spy, and a grandson who was a playboy, ever accomplished what he did. She might also have wondered how he did it when he spent so much time playing chess. Franklin felt it desirable for the goodwill it generated among the people of influence in France to attend the many social gatherings to which he was invited. To escape the boredom of the small talk and the petty gossip, he found an escape in chess, which fascinated him. He had a passion for the game and would call for the chessboard and play for hours. He often played with Madam Brillon, and Madam Foucald learned to play just to please him. When he played he was so absorbed in the game, he was lost to the world. On one occasion his "pocket wife," Madam LeRoy, was actually left out in the rain when he and her husband were busily playing chess late into the night. On another occasion he played with Le Veillard at Madam Brillon's while she was soaking in her tub. Although discreetly hidden from view, she was unable to remove herself and was too polite to ask her guests to leave even though they played for hours. The next day Franklin apologized for his indiscretion and said, "never again will I consent to start a game in your bathing room."

An anecdote concerning Franklin's preoccupation with chess was passed down by the Chaumonts and preserved in writing by Chaumont's grandson. According to the account, every free evening he had Franklin would spend with the Chaumonts in the central part of the mansion, of which he occupied one of the wings. One evening he began a game of chess in the apartment of Madam Chaumont with the priest who was the Chaumonts' son's tutor. When the lady was ready to retire, the participants moved their game to Franklin's wing where they continued to play until all the candles were used up. Not ready to quit, Franklin sent the priest off to find a fresh supply of candles. "May the goddess of night protect you in your adventurous journey," Franklin called to the departing priest as he himself, in the last flickers of candlelight took advantage of his opponent's absence to plan how to out-maneuver him. When the abbé returned without the candles, Franklin asked, "What is the problem? Has the goddess of night failed to answer my prayer or has Mercury sent one of his imps to our grounds?" "It is not a matter of night and robbers," said the abbé, "but Phoebus or at least Aurora with her rosy fingers who reigns at this moment." And with a dramatic move he pulled the blinds and flooded the room with sunlight. "You are right, it is daytime," said Franklin. "Let's go to sleep."

Among his circle of friends two of Franklin's greatest admirers were abbés. They were the Abbé de la Roche and the Abbé Morellet, who resided along with the young physician, Cabainis, on Madam Helvetius' estate. Madam Helvetius and Madam Brillon were the Parisian ladies Franklin was most interested in and he visited them and their friends on a regular schedule each week. With Madam Brillon, who was an outstanding musician, the emphasis was on music, including the playing of the armonica, an instrument Franklin had invented. With Madam Helvetius and her abbés, the emphasis was on sparkling conversation accompanied by sparkling wines. Madam Helvetius was the widow of a philosopher and the abbés and Cabanis were scholars, creating an intellectual milieu in which Franklin was right at home. Although the abbés were priests, they were so in name only, having long since dropped their ecclesiastical activities. It was therefore a jest born of irony when, in departing from France, Franklin wrote Madam Helvetius from shipboard, "Wish me a good crossing and tell the good abbés to pray for us, that, after all, being their profession."

The Abbé de la Roche was a lover of books and Franklin, as a former printer and publisher, enjoyed going over the abbé's collection of first editions and discussing with him the valuable books in his library. (When Franklin returned to the United States he brought many trunkloads of books with him and had the largest personal library in America at that time.) The abbé, who had observed Franklin regularly for eight years, admired him in many ways, one of which was for his amazing capacity for work. Franklin, as the abbé knew him, could work eight days straight taking only cat-naps in his chair and would "find a new morning" after only an hour or two of sleep. And at the age of 80 he could still swim across the Seine at Passy. But what was even more remarkable to the abbé was that Franklin, who held a high diplomatic post, had only one manservant, saying when asked about his frugality, "with two you get only half of one, and with three hardly any at all."

The Abbé Morellet had met Franklin some years earlier when he was visiting in England and Franklin was agent for the colonies. They immediately liked each other and struck up a friendship despite the language barrier. Morellet, like Franklin, was a man-of-the-world with wide-ranging interests and appetites. They shared interest in economics, philosophy, and humanitarian ventures. There was a joke in Madam Helvetius' group that Abbé de la Roche loved only his books while Abbé Morellet cared only for cream and specious reasoning. Actually Morellet enjoyed not only cream but all good food and especially good wine. It was this reputation for specious reasoning and wine drinking that challenged Franklin, something of a hand at specious reasoning himself, to write this merry bagatelle and address it to the Abbé Morellet:

> You have often enlivened me, my very dear friend, with your excellent drinking songs; in return, I desire to edify you by some Christian, moral and philosophical reflections upon the same subject.
>
> "In vino veritas," says the wise man; "truth is in wine."
>
> Before Noah, men, having only water to drink, could not find the truth. So they went astray; they became abominably wicked and were justly exterminated by the water which they loved to drink.
>
> This good man Noah, having seen that all his contemporaries had perished by this bad drink, took an aversion to it; and God, to quench his thirst, created the vine and revealed to him the art of making wine of it. With the aid of this liquor he discovered more truth; and since his time the word to divine [1] has been in use, commonly signifying to discover by means of wine . . . Therefore, since this time all excellent things, even the deities, have been called divine or divinities.

He then refers to the biblical miracle at Cana where the wine for the marriage ceremony had run out and Jesus supplied more by converting water into wine.

> We speak of the conversion of water into wine, at the marriage of Cana, as a miracle. But this conversion is performed every day by the goodness of God before our eyes. Behold the water which falls from the skies upon our vineyards; there it enters into the roots of the vines to be changed into wine; a constant proof that God loves us, and that he loves to see us happy. The particular miracle was performed only to hasten the operation, upon an occasion of sudden need which required it.
>
> It is true that God has also taught men to bring back wine into water. But what kind of water? Brandy [2] (*eau de vie*); in order that they might thereby themselves perform the miracle of Cana in case of need, and convert the common water into that excellent species of wine called punch. My Christian brother, be benevolent and beneficent like him, and do not spoil his good beverage.
>
> He has made wine to rejoice us. When you see your neighbour at

---

[1] *divin* in French, making a pun on the French word for wine, *vin*.

[2] *brandy* in French is *eau de vie*, "water of life."

table pouring wine into his glass, do not hasten to pour water into it. Why do you wish to mix the truth? It is likely that your neighbour knows better than you what suits him. Perhaps he does not like water: perhaps he only wishes to put in some drops of it out of regard to the fashion: perhaps he does not wish another to observe how little of it he puts into his glass. Therefore, offer water only to children. It is a false complaisance and very inconvenient. I say this to you as a man of the world, but I will finish, as I began, like a good Christian, by making a religious remark to you, very important, and drawn from Holy Writ, namely that the Apostle Paul very seriously advised Timothy to put some wine into his water for his health's sake; but that not one of the apostles nor any of the holy fathers have ever recommended putting water into wine.

Just in case the good abbé is not yet convinced that men were meant to prefer wine over water, Franklin has a postscript complete with sketches (drawn by his grandson) giving evidence from nature that could hardly be denied.

P. S. To confirm you still more in your piety and gratitude to Divine Providence, reflect upon the situation which he has given to the elbow. You see in figures 1 and 2 that the animals which ought to drink the water that flows upon the earth, if they have long legs have also long necks, in order that they may reach their drink without the trouble of falling on their knees. But man, who was destined to drink wine, ought to be able to carry the glass to his mouth. Look at the figures below: if the elbow had been placed near the hand, as in figure 3, the part A would be too short to bring the glass to the mouth; if it had been placed nearer the shoulder, as in figure 4, the part B would have been so long, that it would have carried the glass quite beyond the mouth: thus would we have been tantalized. But owing to the present situation, represented in figure 5, we are in a condition to drink at our ease, the glass coming exactly to the mouth. Let us adore then, glass in hand, this benevolent wisdom; let us adore and drink.

But Franklin's activities were by no means confined to his friends in the neighborhood of Passy. He frequently met with Vergennes in Paris or travelled to the royal court at Versailles. He was elected to membership in many learned and scientific societies and attended some of their meetings. He was admitted to membership in the Masonic Lodge of the Nine Sisters and was later chosen to be its Grand Master. When Voltaire, shortly before his death, returned to Paris in triumph after twenty-eight years absence, he was initiated into this

Lodge and entered on the arm of Franklin. The two great philosophers were popular heroes in France and were jointly recognized when they appeared at the Academy of Sciences. The incident was faithfully recorded by John Adams:

> Voltaire and Franklin were both present, and there presently arose a general cry that Monsieur Voltaire and Monsieur Franklin should be introduced to each other. This was done, and they bowed and spoke to each other. This was no satisfaction; there must be something more. Neither of our philosophers seemed to divine what was wished or expected; they however took each other by the hand. But this was not enough. The clamor continued until the explanation came out: They must embrace in the French manner. The two aged actors upon this great theater of philosophy and frivolity then embraced each other by hugging one another in their arms and kissing each others' cheeks, and then the tumult subsided. And the cry immediately spread throughout the kingdom, and I suppose all over Europe: Isn't it charming to see Solon and Sophocles embracing.

John Jay, who was later to become the first Chief Justice of the United States, had served with Franklin in the Continental Congress and during the war had been American Minister to Spain. When Jay came to Paris to help draw up the peace treaty, Franklin invited him and his family to stay with him in his house at Passy. Jay respected and admired Franklin and the two men got along very well. When he had to make a trip to England he left his wife and children in Franklin's care. Franklin liked to tease Mrs. Jay and she enjoyed it too. He made a demonstration for her with two pieces of magnetized steel, one representing her and the other her husband. When they were close, he showed her, her piece drew Jay's to her. But when Jay was far away, and closer to a third piece, representing an English lady, the latter had the greater attraction. During Jay's absence their slave girl ran away and when she was located she refused to come back. Franklin advised Mrs. Jay not to force her return but give her a few weeks to think it over. She did, and before the month was up the girl reconsidered and decided to return.

In 1780, when Jay was still in Spain, Franklin wrote from France that he hoped that Spain would not take advantage of the distress of the United States to try to pressure her into giving up any rights to the Mississippi. "Poor as we are," he wrote, "yet as I know we shall be rich, I would rather agree with them to buy at a great price the whole of their right on the Mississippi, then to sell a drop of its waters. A neighbor might as well ask me to sell my street door.'' But he had good news from America to relate to Jay. ''The spirit of our people was never higher.'' There were ''vast exertions preparatory for some important action.'' And there was harmony and affection between the troops of France and the U.S. And, further, he informed Jay, ''I shall now be able to pay up your salaries complete for the year . . .'' ''If you find any inclination to hug me for the good news of this letter,'' he concluded, ''I constitute and appoint Mrs. Jay my attorney, to receive in my behalf your embraces.''

Shortly after this letter to Jay, Franklin received a letter from William Carmichael, who had left France to join Jay in his efforts to obtain aid from Spain. Carmichael had a favor to ask. The Prince and Princess had come from Spain to France. Would Franklin meet them and pay his respects? Franklin replied, ''I was able to pay my respects and to thank the Princess for their civilities to my compatriots at Madrid.'' Carmichael made another request on behalf of the royal couple. We are not told what it was but Franklin's attempt to comply with it proved embarrassing to the old philosopher. He wrote Carmichael, ''By the mistake of my man, who it seems had inquired for the Princess instead of the Prince, I was shown into a dressing room where a lady was at her toilet; and not knowing at first who it was, and expecting the Prince, I was a little puzzled till he came.'' Apparently, the parties recovered without international repercussions.

When Mrs. Jay wrote to Franklin asking him for one of the many prints the French had done of him when he was in vogue, he replied modestly and then described something of the French customs of the time.

> Mrs. Jay does me the honor in desiring to have one of the prints that have been made here of her countryman. I send what is said to be the best of five or six. . . . The verses at the bottom [extolling Franklin] are truly extravagant. But you must know that the desire of pleasing, by a perpetual rise of compliments in this polite nation, has so used up all the common expressions of approbation that they become flat and insipid, and to use them almost implies censure. Hence music that formerly might be sufficiently praised when it was called *bonne,* to go a little farther they call *excellente,* then *superbe, magnifique, exquise, celeste,* all which being in their turns worn out. There only remains *divine,* and when that is grown as insignificant as its predecessors, I think they must return to common speech and

common sense. As from vying with one another in fine and costly paintings on their coaches, since I first knew this country, not being able to go further in that way they have returned lately to plain carriages painted without arms or figures, in one uniform color.

While Franklin was in France, the Space Age arrived with the advent of the manned balloon and, as might be expected, he was an enthusiastic observer and promoter of this new scientific development. Although the connection was just coincidental, it is noteworthy that he was his country's first Postmaster General and he was the first person to receive an international airmail letter. This letter, written to him in England in 1783, was hand-carried by two daredevil balloonists in the first international flight, across the English Channel, and delivered to him at Passy. It seems a fitting circumstance that one of the balloonists was an American Tory from Boston, John Jefferies, and that now, with the war over, there was nothing to detract from the jubilant reception he was to receive from Franklin and his friends.

Although in those days Paris had its crazes which were short lived, like ballooning and Mesmer's mystic medicine, and the fad of Franklin worship, yet this American's substantial popularity held steadfast over the whole period of his stay. Adams reluctantly acknowledged years later that not only was Franklin known to kings, nobility, clergy and philosophers but there was scarcely a peasant, a coachman, a lady's chambermaid or a scullion in the kitchen who did not know his name and consider him a friend of humankind. When he departed from France, the King furnished him the royal litter, a large carriage pulled by mules, to take him to the coast. Franklin's friends, who had tried to convince him to stay, came to see him off. "A very great concourse of the people of Passy" surrounded the carriage according to his grandson, and "a mournful silence reigned about him, and was only interrupted by a few sobs." In the procession following the royal litter were two coaches carrying his two grandsons and friends who accompanied him along the way. There was also a wagon carrying 27 pieces of luggage, with an additional 128 boxes of household goods following by barge down the Seine. It was a triumphal send-off with some people walking behind the procession and others cheering as the philosopher passed by.

Thomas Jefferson, who was present to witness the scene of Franklin's departure, remarked, "When he left Passy, it seemed as if the village had lost its patriarch." When Franklin asked to be relieved so that he could return home, Congress sent Jefferson to take over his position as Minister to France. Jefferson arrived almost a year before Franklin left so the two men, who previously had served together in Congress, now had time to become personally well acquainted.

Of all of the founding fathers of America, none hit it off so well together as Franklin and Jefferson. They were peas in a pod, with sweeping interests in science, government, and the arts; and the strongest conviction in their democratic attitudes and liberal outlooks toward religion and human behavior. No American admired Franklin more than Jefferson, and Franklin showed his mutual feeling for the younger man by entrusting a manuscript copy of his autobiography to him when Jefferson visited him in Philadelphia a month before his death. Jefferson described Franklin as, "the greatest man and ornament of the age and country in which he lived." He adopted as his personal seal a motto which Franklin had proposed for the great seal of the U. S., "Rebellion to Tyrants is Obedience to God."

In France, Franklin introduced Jefferson to the circle of the Countess Houdetot and his friends at Passy, who soon became Jefferson's friends. Jefferson observed, "There appeared to me more respect and veneration attached to the character of Dr. Franklin in France than to any other person in the same country, foreign or native." What was his secret that made Franklin so personally likeable and successful? Jefferson thought he had discovered it. "Never contradict anybody," Franklin told him. "It was one of the rules which, above all others, made Dr. Franklin the most amiable of men in society. If he was urged to announce an opinion, he did it rather by asking questions, as if for information, or by suggesting doubts."

Since they were in regular personal contact there was no need for the two men to correspond while in France; thus, unfortunately, we do not have much of a record of their conversations and activities together, but we are indebted to Jefferson for preserving a number of the entertaining anecdotes about Franklin. Jefferson noted that his succession of Franklin at the court of France, "was an excellent school of humility." When he met people for the first time in France and they asked him if he were the one who had come to replace Franklin, he delighted the Frenchmen with his reply, "I am only his successor," he protested, "No one can replace him."

16

THE ROMANTIC IMPULSE

IN HIS ENTERTAINING LITTLE BOOK, WHICH CLAIMS TO DESCRIBE Benjamin Franklin's career in the field of Venus and is significantly titled, *The All-Embracing Franklin,* A. S. W. Rosenbach agrees that Americans are justly proud of Franklin for his many accomplishments, but thinks that the one distinction of which Franklin himself was evidently most proud has been unfortunately neglected. According to Rosenbach, "His many amorous adventures, his gallantries, his winning ways with the fair sex, his love epistles have not been set down in the way they deserve. If they were as well known as his experiments in electricity or his feats of statesmanship we would be even prouder of him than we are today." On this note, Rosenbach concludes that Franklin must be regarded as "America's upstanding genius."

Whether Franklin deserves such an accolade each reader must decide for himself. "Parson" Weems described Franklin as one who with "equal ease could . . . charm alike the lightnings and the ladies." Certainly Franklin was at ease in the company of women and at his witty best in his exchanges with them. There is little record of his verbal repartee but we have many letters that give us a peep into this personal domain. Do they reveal him to be the inventor of sex as well as the stove and bifocal glasses? Perhaps, as we parade the evidence in these chapters, we may be able to provide some insight into his romantic life and style.

Franklin had a romantic link with five women: two American, one English, and two French. The first was Deborah Read, the girl he married. On her part it was laugh at first sight. She couldn't help laughing when she saw him coming down the street with rolls under each arm and one in his mouth. She thought better of him later, but then he went off to England neglecting to write, and her family urged another marriage on her. That marriage was no laughing matter, for her husband turned out to be a bigamist, and when discovered, ran off. Soon afterward, Franklin returned, renewed his interest, and their marriage followed. Their first child, William, was illegitimate. Whether he was the issue of a premarital affair with another woman, or whether Deborah was pregnant from her ill-fated, illegal marriage remains a mystery. No matter; William was accepted and reared as their own child, receiving a good education and eventually becoming the Governor of New Jersey. He also produced an illegitimate son, who was to grow up and have an illegitimate child of his own. Whether this threefold occurrence in three succeeding generations was genetic or mere happenstance remains to be determined, but it has been waggishly referred to as a dynasty of bastards.

Franklin had another son, Francis, who died young of smallpox and a daughter, Sarah (Sally), who brought him grandchildren, all legitimate, and cared for him in his old age when he returned from France. Deborah was a hearty soul who took care of the children and the house and helped Ben build his business: "She assisted me cheerfully in my business, folding and stitching pamphlets, tending shop, purchasing old linen rags for the paper makers, etc." The young printer told others: "Win a prudent wife, if she does not bring a fortune, she will help to make one." It was good advice, for long after Deborah's death Franklin disclosed: "Frugality is an enriching virtue; a virture I never could acquire myself. But I was lucky enough to find it in a wife, who thereby became a fortune to me." In the early days the Franklins were frugal indeed, as revealed in this engaging story of their new-found affluence.

> We kept no idle servants, our table was plain and simple, our furniture of the cheapest. For instance, my breakfast was [for] a long time bread and milk (no tea),* and I ate it out of a twopenny earthen

* Tea was a luxury in those days.

porringer, with a pewter spoon. But mark how luxury will enter families and make progress in spite of principle. Being called one morning to breakfast, I found it in a china bowl, with a spoon of silver! They had been bought for me without my knowledge by my wife, and had cost her the enormous sum of three-and-twenty shillings, for which she had no other excuse or apology to make but that she thought *her* husband deserved a silver spoon and china bowl as well as any of his neighbors.

Although, as their wealth increased, the Franklins' silver and china collection expanded greatly, Debbie continued to do her own spinning and knitting and when, in the protest over the Stamp Act the colonists boycotted British goods, Franklin was proud to announce that he was clothed from head to foot in woolen and linen of his wife's manufacture.

Deborah was a warm-hearted person but she was quick to anger. She was continually battling neighbors and relatives who spoke of "her turbulent temper." She frequently got angry with William and was overheard calling him "the greatest villain on earth," expressing her feeling according to the observer, with invectives, "in the foulest terms I ever heard from a gentlewoman." How did Franklin react to such a wife? As a man who hated altercation, he avoided confrontation where he could, and where he could not he developed the art of diplomacy that was to serve him so well in his political career. When the next door neighbor, who was Deborah's second cousin, and a lawyer by profession, asked Franklin to arbitrate his dispute with Deborah, Franklin jokingly replied that as an attorney he ought to choose a better court to bring his action. "Would you submit to the decision of a husband, a cause between you and his wife? Don't you know that all wives are in the right?" Franklin recommended chivalry and concession on the part of the neighbor, considering the sex of the adversary, and he quoted Socrates, "in differences among friends, they that make the first concessions are the wisest."

When a man wanted to discuss some business matters, Franklin invited him to come over to the house, explaining that his dame being away made him "quite the master of the house." If Deborah, like Bridget Saunders, was sometimes a scold, one had to be philosophical and weigh everything in the balance. He had written on shrewish wives: "Women of that character have generally sound and healthy constitutions, produce a vigorous offspring, are . . . special good housewives and very careful of their husband's interest. As to the noise attending all this, 'tis but a trifle when a man is used to it.'' He reasoned, ''You can bear with your own faults, and why not a fault in your wife.'' He practised what *Poor Richard* preached, ''Keep your eyes wide open before marriage, half shut afterwards.'' Deborah was not beautiful, she did not have the education or the graceful charm that he was later to find so exciting in other women, but she was a loyal and dutiful wife, and he expressed his appreciation of her qualities in a drinking song he wrote for his friends at the Junto. A few of the nine verses follow.

> Of their Chloes and Phyllises poets may prate
> I sing my plain country Joan
> Now twelve years my wife, still the joy of my life
> Blest day that I made her my own.
> > My dear friends, etc.*

> Not a word of her face, her shape, or her eyes,
> Of flames or of darts shall you hear;
> Tho' I beauty admire 'tis virtue I prize,
> That fades not in seventy years.

> Am I laden with care, she takes off a large share,
> That the burden ne'er makes me to reel,
> Does good fortune arrive, the joy of my wife,
> Quite doubles the pleasures I feel.

> In raptures the giddy rake talks of his fair,
> Enjoyment shall make him despise,
> I speak my cool sense, that long experience,
> And enjoyment have changed in no wise.

> Were the fairest young princess, with million in purse
> To be had in exchange for my Joan,
> She could not be a better wife, mought be a worse,
> So I'd stick to my Joggy [Joan] alone.
> > My dear friends,
> I'd cling to my lovely old Joan.

When Franklin was out building forts to protect the frontier from Indians, his Debby was busy in the kitchen cooking meat and mince pies for the men at the front. Her ''pappy,'' as she called him, wrote her from Gnadenhütten to thank her. ''We have enjoyed your roast

---

* Refrain of ''My dear friends'' with last line repeated after each verse.

beef and this day we began on the roast veal. All agree that they are both the best . . . of the kind. Your citizens that have their dinners hot and hot know nothing of good eating. We find it in much greater perfection when the kitchen is four score miles from the dining room.''

When he went to England as agent for Pennsylvania she sent him apples, cranberries, buckwheat and hams. In turn he sent her many gifts including lace, cloth, clothes of the latest London fashion, and prayer books with large print so that she would ''be reprieved from the use of spectacles in church a little longer.'' He sent her a box of china items and wrote, ''I almost forgot among the china, to mention a large fine jug for beer, to stand in the cooler. I fell in love with it at first sight; for I thought it looked like a fat, jolly dame, clean and tidy, with a neat blue and white calico gown on, good natured and lovely, and put me in mind of somebody.''

They began their letters with the salutation, ''My dear child'' and she would sometimes write, ''My dearest dear child.'' He would close with, ''Your affectionate husband'' or ''Your loving husband.'' In one letter in which he was cross at her for not writing he added a postscript saying, ''I have scratched out the loving words, being writ in haste by mistake when I forgot I was angry.''

With regard to faithfulness in writing, the shoe was usually on the other foot. She was the one to be upset by the absence of his letters. In his letter of June 10, 1758, from London he acknowledged, ''I have before me your letters of Jan. 15, 22, 29 and 31. Feb. 3, 4, and 6, March 12, April 3, 9, 17 and 23, which is the last . . . It is impossible to get out of your debts.'' At another time he wrote, ''I know you love to have a line from me by every packet, so I wrote though I have little to say.'' His intentions may have been good, but with many activities near at hand he was frequently neglectful.

In his letter of June 10, he mentioned a cloak and black silk he had sent her, a hat and cloak and a pair of buckles with French paste stones for Sally. He got pleasure from looking at Sally's picture and he was having an artist make copies of the pictures of the other members of the family. Debby was praised for having avoided engaging in political disputes. ''If your sex can keep cool,'' he advised her, ''you may be a means of cooling ours the sooner . . .'' She had disposed of the apple trees very properly, he agreed, and he sympathized with her on the loss of the walnuts. He referred to her spinning in a most complimentary way; "I could not find the bit of thread you mention to have sent me of your own spinning; perhaps it was too fine to be seen?" He explained that he had not sent the tools for Josey Croker because he thought Josey would be coming to England to get experience working in the best shops, but if Josey is about to be married this would not be advisable and the tools will be sent immediately. (It turned out Josey didn't need the tools after all; he had been killed by Indians two weeks earlier.) For his electrical experiments Franklin had run a wire from his lightning rod into the house and had two bells connected to it to give notice when the rod was electrified. In reference to this, he wrote her, "if the bells frighten you, tie a piece of wire from one bell to the other, and that will conduct the lightning without ringing or snapping . . . Though I think it best the bells should be at liberty to ring, that you may know when the wire is electrified, and if you are afraid may keep at a distance." Although Deborah had the distinction of living in the first house in the world to have an electric alarm system, it somehow failed to spark her enthusiasm.

In Franklin's letter of June 10 we find this puzzling statement: "Your answer to Mr. Strahan was just what it should be; I was much pleased with it. He fancied his rhetoric and art would certainly bring you over." William Strahan, a London publisher and Frankin's long-time friend, had tried to induce Deborah to join her husband in England. He had written her in reference to her husband, "I never saw a man who was, in every respect, so perfectly agreeable . . . Now madam as I know the ladies here consider him in exactly the same light I do, upon my word I think you should come over with all convenient speed to look after your interest; not but that I think him as faithful to his Joan, as any man breathing, but who knows what repeated and strong temptation may in time . . . accomplish." This encouragement, Strahan felt, would bring Deborah to her husband's side but Franklin knew differently. He told Deborah that Strahan had offered to lay him a considerable wager that his letter would bring her over, but, "I tell him I will not pick his pocket, for I am sure there is no inducement strong enough to prevail with you to cross the seas." Franklin was right. Deborah's fear of the ocean did not permit her to end the long years of loneliness and separation during his two tours of duty in England. After Strahan received Deborah's answer he wrote to Franklin's partner in Philadelphia, "I am sorry she dreads the sea so much

. . . There are many ladies here that would make no objection to sailing twice as far after him.''

Was Franklin pleased with Deborah's answer because it proved him to be correct, or because she was not coming? He may have meant the former, for he wrote her, "I meet with persons of worth, and the conversation of ingenious men give me no small pleasure; but at this time of life, domestic comforts afford the most solid satisfaction and my uneasiness at being absent from my family, and longing desire to be with them, make me often sigh in the midst of cheerful company." And when he left England in 1762 to come home, he assured Strahan he would be back to settle in England if only he could prevail on Mrs. Franklin to accompany him. On the other hand, it cannot be denied that Debby, coarse and turbulent as she was, would not have been an asset to Franklin in his diplomatic maneuvers with sophisticated Londoners, where social amenities were so important. And if he were so attractive to the opposite sex as Strahan suggested, her presence might have caused them to be repelled rather than attracted.

Her letters to Franklin were rambling accounts of local events, and her spelling, though not likely to win a contest, had a certain quaint charm. "I am a shamed of maney of our sittisons but I think you air informed by better handes than I am. I am to one [own] I did not write by the laste packit all thow I did in quier when it wold saile." This letter told she had some visitors who "dranke tee with us and we had the beste buckwheat kakes that ever I maid. They sed I had ought dun [outdone] my one [own] ought doings."

Deborah died of a stroke in December, 1774, while Benjamin was still in England. From 1757 until her death she and her husband had less than two years together. She had begged him to return and he promised to do so, but one political crisis followed another on the road to war and he didn't arrive home until May, 1775.

Several years before he left for England a young lady sent Franklin a gift of homemade cheese. He thanked her for it and added that Mrs. Franklin was very proud that a young lady should have so much regard for her old husband as to send him this present. He noted that he and Mrs. Franklin talk of her every time the cheese is brought to the table. "She is sure you are a sensible girl . . . and talks of bequeathing me to you as a legacy; but I ought to wish you a better, and hope she will live a hundred years, for we are grown old together, and if she has any faults I am so used to them that I don't perceive them, as the song says," and he quoted a stanza from his "Plain Country Joan":

> Some faults we have all, and so may my Joan,
>   But then they're exceedingly small;
> And now I'm used to 'em, they're just like my own.
>   I scarcely can see 'em at all.

"Indeed I begin to think she has none, as I think of you; and since she is willing I should love you as much as you are willing to be loved by me, let us join in wishing the old lady a long life and a happy [one]."

The young lady was Catherine Ray of Rhode Island, whom Franklin met on a trip to Boston in 1754 on postoffice business. She was 23, he was approaching 50, and they started a friendship and correspondence that would last until he died thirtyfive years later. Catherine, or Katy, as he called her, lived with her parents on Block Island and was visiting mutual relatives in Boston when she met this fascinating man, Franklin. They took a trip together by horseback in which they visited her married sister on the way to her home. The details of the trip are not known except as he referred to "those hours and miles that we talked away so agreeably, even in a winter journey, a wrong road, and a soaking shower." He had asked her for "favors" (kisses), which she refused. Whether he was teasing, serious, or not quite sure, we have no way of knowing but she was in no way offended. On the contrary, she was apparently infatuated with him for she wrote him several letters which, contrary to his habit, he appears to have destroyed. No doubt his heart must have skipped a few beats, but his normal caution and concern for his reputation caused him to discourage any further romantic inclination.

In his first letter he speaks of their parting when he stood on shore and watched her boat travel toward Block Island. "It gives me great pleasure to hear that you got home safe and well that day. I thought too much was hazarded when I saw you put off to sea in that very little skiff, tossed by every wave . . . I stood on the shore and looked after you, till I could no longer distinguish you even with my glass; then returned to your sister's, praying for your safe passage . . . I left New England slowly, and with great reluctance . . . I almost forgot I had a home . . . then, like an old man who begins to think of heaven, I begun to think of and wish for home. And as I drew nearer, I found the attraction stronger and stronger, my diligence and speed increased with my impatience. I drove on violently and made such long stretches that a very few days brought me to my own house and to the arms of my good old wife and children, where I remain, thanks to God, at present well and happy.''

This description of his devotion to his old wife and family could hardly have been expected to inflame her passions. But he added, teasingly, "Persons subject to the hyp [hypochondria], complain of the northeast wind as increasing their malady. But since you promised to send me kisses in that wind, and I find you as good as your word, 'tis to me the gayest wind that blows and gives me the best spirits. I write this during a northeast storm of snow, the greatest we have had this winter. Your favors come mixed with the snowy fleeces which are pure as your virgin innocence, white as your lovely bosom—and as cold." This is all the romance his prudence will permit. He quenches the embers with his next sentence, "But let it warm towards some worthy young man, and may heaven bless you both with every kind of happiness.''

Catherine was an intelligent girl who was quick to interpret his message. But she knew she had found a wonderful person in Franklin and she was not going to let him go. She transferred his role from suitor to father confessor and counselor in matters of the heart. In this way he was able to assist her with his wisdom and experience and at the same time, vicariously enjoy the pulsating experience of young love. When she had a suitor who was profuse in his ardor but sparing in declaring his intention of marriage, Franklin sympathized with her and quoted the song about the girl with an overattentive suitor—she ''had rather be married than plagued with him so." The wisdom he had to offer her, however, was that the ultimate decision would have to be hers alone, saying, "I only pray God to bless you in your choice.''

Later, when he was in England, Katy wrote to Deborah for similar advice on a young man but Benjamin forbade her to give it. On her part, Katy wrote him freely what was on her heart and in her mind: "I have said a thousand things that nothing should have tempted me to have said to anybody else, for I knew they would be safe with you.'' On his part, he encouraged her to write freely everything she should think fit without concern that anyone else would see her letters. In one letter she had written: "Tell me you . . . love me one thousandth part so well as I do you" and "absence rather increases than lessens my affection.'' He would not wish to limit such pleasant sentiments expressed by her, but his replies would have to be more guarded, as he commented, ''I say less than I think,'' for he knew that ''expressions of warm friendship . . . between persons of different sexes are liable to be misinterpreted by suspicious minds.'' But he wasn't always as circumspect as he intended to be for in the following letter he says; ''I commend your prudent resolutions in the . . . [not] granting of favors to lovers. But if I were courting you, I could not heartily approve such conduct . . . You have spun a long thread, 5022 yards! It will reach almost from Block Island hither. I wish I had hold of one end of it, to pull you to me.'' He seems now to have remembered the ''suspicious minds'' and tempers his remarks. ''But you would break it rather than come. The cords of love and friendship are longer and stronger, and in times past have drawn me farther, even back from England to Philadelphia. I guess that some of the same kind will one day draw you out of that island.''

Some years earlier Katy had met a Spaniard named Laureano who fell in love with her but had to return to Spain. He sent her a letter on his arrival in Spain which Katy asked Franklin to translate. The lovesick Spaniard professes his love for Katy, expresses his melancholy without her, and is mainly concerned about her retaining her virtue in his absence. He gives her fatherly advice not to put her trust in men and asks her to beg God to make her a saint. In this instance, Franklin broke his rule on advising her on the merits of particular suitors. He honored the Spaniard for loving her as a credit to his good taste and judgment, but told her to forget him and choose some worthy young Englishman. Like the Spaniard, Franklin has fatherly advice for Katy. When she gets a good husband she should stay at home and nurse the children, and live like a Christian. She should spend her spare hours in some worthy activity like learning arithmetic. He explains some details of this study. ''You must practice *addition* to your husband's estate by industry and frugality; *subtraction* of all unnecessary expenses; *multiplication* (I would gladly have taught you that myself, but you . . . wouldn't learn) he will soon make you a mistress of it. As to *division*, I say with brother Paul, 'Let there be no divisions among ye.' '' Referring to Katy's sister with two children as being acquainted with the rule of two, he hoped Katy would become as expert in the rule of three so that when he would have the pleasure of seeing her again, he would find her ''like my grape vine, surrounded with clusters, plump, juicy, blushing, pretty little rogues, like their mama.'' She had sent him some sugar plums, adding the cryptic message, ''they are, everyone, sweetened as you used to like.'' He knew how to interpret the message for in a postscript to his letter he acknowledged receipt of the sugar plums and remarked they were ''so sweet from the cause you mentioned, that I could scarce taste the sugar.'' On that happy trip they took together, did she carry sugar plums with her, and did he insist she sweeten each with a kiss before he took it? Alas, this is mere conjecture; the fact must remain like the origin of the pyramids, among the great unsolved mysteries of the past.

Their correspondence continued. She hoped he would come again to Boston but he assured her that his involvement in public affairs made that unlikely. He suspected that her trip to Boston to see her sister must have some other explanation. ''Don't hide your heart from me,'' he joked, ''You know I can conjure.'' He asked her to present his best compliments to all their mutual friends and relatives, naming each one and then saying, ''in short, to all that love me. I should have said all that love you, but that would be giving you too much trouble.'' This alternating teasing with gallantry was a style he would develop and expand in his communication with other women in years to come. When Franklin went to England, Katy wrote to Deborah asking advice about a suitor. In this case it may have been the one she accepted, William Greene, a farmer of Warwick, Rhode Island, who was to become Chief Justice of the State Supreme Court and then Governor. In 1763, when Franklin arrived home from his first period of duty in England, Katy had two girls and was pregnant again. He had already instructed her in the rule of three; now he had some instruction in addition. Humorously attributing this instruction to Deborah, he wrote, ''She joins with me in congratulating you on your present happy situation. She bids me say she supposes you proceeded regularly in your arithmetic and that, before you got into multiplication you learnt addition, in which you have had occasion to say, one that I carry, and two makes three. And now I have writ this, she bids me scratch it out again. [But] I am loathe to deface my letter, so e'en let it [stand].''

He assured her that although he had been in most parts of England and had travelled to Scotland, Flanders, and Holland he was not much altered, at least in his esteem and regard for his Katy. He made a trip to Boston with his daughter and stopped at Warwick on the way. He fell from his horse and received Katy's tender care and attention. They did not see each other again until he returned home from England in 1775 and travelled to Massachusetts to see Washington. He took Catherine's son Ray back to Philadelphia with him, where he watched over the boy while he attended the Philadelphia Academy. Franklin and Katy saw each other briefly when the Greenes visited the Franklins at Philadelphia in 1776 but Benjamin was so busy with the affairs of Congress he had little time to spare with them. This was their last meeting but not the end of their association. They not only corresponded but kept in touch through Franklin's sister Jane, who was friendly with Catherine and who took refuge with the Greenes when the British besieged Boston during the war. The warm feeling of Franklin and Katy for each other survived long absences, politics, and war. When Franklin returned from England in 1775, he wrote: "I long much to see once more my native country and my friends there, and none more than my dear Katy and her family. Mr. Greene I hope will allow an old man of 70 to say he loves his wife, it is an innocent affection." He promised if he could find time to visit New England and "you may be assured the honest old soul, as you call him, will not pass your door." The next year she wrote him: "Mr. Greene is most all the while gone but comes home with a smile and I smile again. Is [that] not as you used to tell me? I impute [a] great part of the happiness of my life to the pleasing lessons you gave me in that journey."

In December, 1787, Catherine sent Franklin a bag of sweet corn with the hope that he would have as much pleasure eating it as she had in sending it. She knew he would be pleased to hear Ray was very smart in the farming way, with ten to sixteen hands at work putting up a monstrous stone wall. Franklin acknowledged receipt of the corn, which he enjoyed. He was happy to hear that her son, his young friend Ray, was "smart in the farming way." He thought farming was the most honorable of occupations, as being the most independent. "The farmer," he noted, "has no need of popular favor, nor the favor of the great. The success of his crops depending only on the blessing of God upon his honest industry." At the age of 83 Franklin looked back and found his life tolerably happy, and he would have no objection living it over again. He concluded his letter with a thought for Katy, "Among the felicities of my life I reckon your friendship, which I shall remember with pleasure as long as that life lasts."

When Franklin arrived in England in 1757 he was alone, a wide ocean away from friends and family. But not for long. As a convivial person who craved congenial companionship, Franklin soon acquired many friends and even a surrogate family. Friends found him a place to live in London near the government offices where he had business. He resided with his son William and two servants in four rooms on the second floor of a house on Craven Street. The house was owned by Margaret Stevenson, a widow who had an 18-year-old daughter named Mary, or Polly, as she was more often called. This was Franklin's home and adopted family for the fifteen years he remained in England prior to the American Revolution. The family was later increased by Sally Franklin, a 13-year-old English cousin whose father brought her to London and was persuaded to leave her there to obtain her schooling. She was like a second daughter to Franklin. And then there was another child, his grandson, William Temple Franklin, William's illegitimate son, who was born in England and raised by Franklin.

Polly Stevenson spent much of her time away from home, living with an old aunt, and we are indebted to that separation for the correspondence between Polly and Franklin during those years in London. At first his letters were simply paternal and domestic. He hoped to arrange a match between Polly and William, but William was a gay blade doing the town and had no interest in Polly, to his father's disappointment. Polly was a fine girl and an intelligent one, with great curiosity for even such non-domestic subjects as science. This curiosity the philosopher felt an urge to satisfy. He sent her books to read and answered her questions on the working of barometers and the preservation of timbers from insect damage. He wrote her six pages, clearly and carefully explaining the effect of the tide in rivers, and concluded with an apology for not finishing the letter with the usual compliment: "After writing six folio pages of philosophy to a young girl, is it necessary to finish such a letter with a compliment? Is not such a letter of itself a compliment? Does it not say she has a mind thirsty after knowledge and capable of receiving it, and that the most agreeable things one can write to her are those that tend to an improvement of her understanding? It does indeed say all this, but then it is still no compliment; it is no more than plain honest truth . . . So if I would finish my letter in the mode, I should yet add something that means nothing, and is merely civil and polite. But being naturally awkward at every circumstance of ceremony, I shall not attempt it. I had rather conclude abruptly with what pleases me more than any compliment can please you, that I am allowed to subscribe myself, Your affectionate friend, B. Franklin.''

How would a young girl respond to such a letter and compliment from a distinguished philosopher and friend? Like this: "Such a letter is indeed the highest compliment. What you concluded it with, I should think too far strained to be sincere, if I did not flatter myself [that] it proceeded from the warmth of your affection, which makes you see merit in me that I do not possess. It would be too great vanity to think I deserve the encomiums you give me, and it would be ingratitude to doubt your sincerity. Continue, my indulgent friend, your favorable opinion of me, and I will endeavor to be what you imagine me.''

Encouraged by such an astute reply from one so young, Franklin described to her one of his most interesting experiments. He had taken a number of little pieces of different colored cloth samples from a tailors pattern card and had laid them on the snow on a bright sunshiny morning. In a few hours the black piece, having been most warmed by the sun, was sunk deep in the snow, the blue almost as deep, the light blue less deep, and all the other colors sinking in accordance with the lightness of their color, the white one having remained on the surface of the snow, not having sunk at all. "What signifies philosophy that does not apply to some use?" he asked. Might we not learn from this experiment, he suggested, that white clothes would be more practical for hot, sunny weather than black clothes? That soldiers and sailors who labor in the sun should have white uniforms and summer hats should be white to repel the heat, thus reducing headaches and fatal heat stroke? To think that the clothes of a good part of the world's teeming population could be changed by a few swatches of cloth lying on the snow!

From philosopher-instructor Franklin's role with Polly gradually expanded to pseudo-suitor. "Hearing that you was in the park last Sunday," he wrote her, "I hoped for the pleasure of seeing you . . . but though I looked with all the eyes I had, not excepting those I carry in my pocket, I could not find you." When he was planning to take Polly to the theater to see *School for Lovers* the theater happened to be closed. He commented: " 'Tis a pity that you are so desirous of studying in that school it should not be open. I would almost venture to undertake reading to you a few lectures on the subject myself." Dr. Hawkesworth was a successful essayist and editor who was a mutual friend of Franklin and Mary Stevenson. They teased each other about him. Mary had written that Hawkesworth was a "dangerous man" because of his persuasiveness. Hawkesworth had written to Franklin; "I have just received a line from the Virgin Mary, and I dine with her at Kensington on Friday. I hope there will be no jealousy in heaven for my wife will be of the party." Franklin wrote to Polly: "I begin to see a rival in Dr. Hawkesworth. But, what is uncommon with rivals, the more he likes you, and you him, the more, if possible, I shall esteem you both."

What could be more romantic to a woman than receiving on her birthday poetry written to her by a dear friend. She had made him a pair of garters, sending it with verses attached, and now he was balancing the account with verses of his own. They are preceded with an explanation and apology: "A muse, you must know, visited me this morning! I see you are surprised as I was. I never saw one before. And I shall never see another. So I took the opportunity of her help to put the answer into verse, because I was some verse in your debt ever since you sent me the last pair of garters. The muse appeared to be no housewife. I suppose few of them are. She was dressed (if the expression is allowable) in an undress, a kind of slatternly negligee neither neat and clean nor well made—and she has given the same sort of dress to my piece. On reviewing it I would have reformed the lines and made them all of a length, as I am told lines ought to be. But I find I can't lengthen the short ones without stretching them on the rack, and I think it would be equally cruel to cut off any part of the longer ones. Besides, the superfluity of *these* make up for the deficiency of *those,* and so from a principle of justice I leave them at full length that I may give you, at least in one sense of the word, good measure."

It was Polly's 27th birthday and she had indicated something about getting old and not celebrating the event, for Franklin challenges this notion:

> No hospitable man, possessed of generous wines,
> While they are in his vaults, repines
> That age impairs the casks; for well he knows
> The heavenly juice
> More fit for use
> Becomes, and still the older better grows . . .

Not only was Polly a friend to teach, and counsel, and tease, but her girl friends, Misses Blunt and Barwell, became his friends as well to beseech jokingly for kisses, and they in turn returned his affection. Polly's mother, too, was captured in Franklin's gay orbit. When Mrs. Stevenson went away for several days, Franklin wrote advising her to return immediately, thus letting her know her importance to him, but pretending for the fun of it that just the opposite was true. He assured her that everything was proceeding smoothly in her absence; the house was very quiet and he would be even happier if Nanny and the cat would follow their mistress and leave him to the enjoyment of an empty house, in which he would never be disturbed by questions of whether he intended to dine at home and what he would have for dinner, or by a mewing request to be let in or let out. "This happiness however is perhaps too great," he imagined, "to be conferred on any but saints and holy hermits. Sinners like me (I might have said us) are condemned to live together and tease one another. So concluding, you will be sentenced to come home tomorrow . . ."

Unlike her daughter, Margaret Stevenson disliked writing letters so Franklin always transmitted her love when he wrote to Polly. In one letter he expressly made a point of Mrs. Stevenson's apology for not writing. "My dear Polly's good mama bids me write two or three lines by way of apology for her so long omitting to write. She acknowledges the receiving two agreeable letters lately from her beloved daughter . . . The reasons for her not writing are that her time all day is fully taken up during the daylight with the care of her family and—laying abed in the morning. And her eyes are so bad that she cannot see to write in the evening—for playing at cards. So she hopes that one who is all goodness will certainly forgive her, when her excuses are so substantial. As for the secretary, he has not a word to say in his own behalf though full as great an offender, but throws himself upon mercy."

When Franklin was off traveling around England, he received a teasing letter from Polly referring to her mother and answered it. "The account you give me of a certain lady's having entertained a new gallant in my absence did not surprise me for I have been used to rivals, and scarcely ever had a friend or a mistress in my whole life that other people didn't like as well as myself." As to the identity of the rival he did a little deduction. Having seen in the papers that Prince Charles had left Rome on a long journey, nobody knew where, there was no doubt "that it was he, who had taken the opportunity of my absence to solace himself with his old friend."

So happily established with an admiring assemblage of women, it was an understandably sad occasion when in 1762 Franklin left his second home to return to his first. He expressed it poignantly to Polly: "It will be yet five or six weeks before we embark and leave the old world for the new. I fancy I feel a little like dying saints, who in parting with those they love in this world, are only comforted with the hope of more perfect happiness in the next." He regretted that the marriage that he had envisioned for his son and Polly did not materialize and she would not "become his own in the tender relationship of a child." But he nevertheless made his touching goodbye to her in that relationship. "Adieu, my dearest child: I will call you so. Why should I not call you so since I love you with all the tenderness, all the affection of a father? Adieu. May the God of all goodness shower down his blessings upon you . . ."

But the span of an ocean did not terminate the friendship of Franklin and Mary Stevenson. She wrote him the news of herself and his old friends. He replied that he was happy to have his American friends and family about him and even happier to know that he was not forgotten by his dear friends in England. He missed those good, interesting people. "Of all the enviable things England has," he recalled, "I envy it most its people. Why should that petty island, which compared to America is but a stepping stone in a brook, scarce enough of it above water to keep one's shoes dry; why, I say, should that little island enjoy in almost every neighborhood more sensible, virtuous and elegant minds than we can collect in ranging 100 leagues of our forests. But, 'tis said, the arts delight to travel westward." Franklin expressed both a fact and a prophecy and he was correct in both. England had great minds like Horace Walpole, Edmund Burke, James Boswell, Charles Fox, Jeremy Bentham and others with whom Franklin became acquainted, apart from the Stevenson circle. And so he could not have been greatly disappointed when in 1764 he was returned again to England.

Once again in London, he found his old lodgings and old friends and picked up where he had left off. Polly had a problem and sought advice from her wise counselor. Her old aunt, with whom she had stayed, was crotchety and unreasonable and poor Polly, her miserable victim, had walked out. Franklin's reply has been characterized by James M. Stifler, who published the Franklin-Stevenson correspondence, as "a lovely letter of shrewd analysis of human feelings, calm advice, and a spiritual exhortation that many a bishop could not have surpassed.'' Franklin commiserated with Polly in her difficult situation, expressed his confidence in her good sense, and told her she need not follow his advice if she did not agree with it. Then he made a compassionate analysis of the disposition of the cantankerous old aunt: ''Her temper, perhaps, was never of the best, and, when that is the case, age seldom mends it. Much of her unhappiness must arise from thence, and since wrong turns of the mind by time are almost as little in our power to cure as those of the body, I think with you that her case is a compassionable one.'' He urged Polly to return, to invent amusements for the unhappy old woman, to be pleased when she accepted them and to be patient when she peevishly rejected them. He explained that, ''nothing is more apt to sour the temper of aged people than the apprehension that they are neglected; and they are extremely apt to entertain such suspicions.'' He impressed on Polly that ''nothing can contribute to true happiness that is inconsistent with duty,'' and that as God governs, proper action will be rewarded. ''I pray him to direct you.'' Polly went back to her aunt and, as predicted, she did receive her reward some years later when she desperately needed it.

In 1767, accompanied by Dr. Pringle, Franklin went traveling on the continent, and thanks to his correspondence with Polly we know how French ladies of that time put on their makeup. Polly would be interested in such things and Franklin was interested in everything. ''As to rouge,'' he carefully observed, ''they don't pretend to imitate nature in laying it on. There is no gradual diminution of the cheek to the faint tint near the sides . . . I have not had the honor of being at any lady's toilette to see how it is laid on, but I fancy I can tell you how it is or may be done. Cut a hole of three inches in diameter in a piece of paper; place it on the side of your face in such a manner as that the top of the hole may be just under your eye; then with a brush dipped in the color paint face and paper together, so that when the paper is taken off there will remain a round patch of red exactly the form of the hole. This is the mode, from the actresses on the stage upward through all ranks of ladies to the princesses of the blood.''

''You see I speak of the Queen,'' Franklin wrote in his letter from France, ''as if I had seen her—and so I have . . . We went to Versailles last Sunday and had the honor of being presented to the King.'' Franklin was obviously very flattered at being received by the King of France but he wanted Polly to be sure of where his loyalty lay. ''No

Frenchman shall go beyond me,'' he boasted, ''in thinking my own king and queen the very best in the world, and the most amiable.'' Even eminent philosophers, as history proves, are subject to change their minds.

Franklin loved to travel. ''Travelling is one way of lengthening life,'' he ventured, ''at least in appearance. It is but a fortnight since we left London, but the variety of scenes we have gone through makes it seem equal to six months living in one place. Perhaps I have suffered a greater change, too, in my own person than I could have done in six months at home. I had not been here six days before my tailor and perruquier had transformed me into a Frenchman. Only think what a figure I make in a little bag wig and with naked ears! They told me I was become twenty years younger and looked very gallant.''

In those days the receiver of a letter rather than the sender paid the cost of postage. In closing this letter from France, Franklin told Polly, ''this letter shall cost you a shilling, and you may consider it cheap, when you reflect that it has cost me at least fifty guineas to get into the situation that enables me to write it. Besides I might, if I had stayed at home, have won perhaps two shillings of you at cribbage.''

In the summer of 1769 Franklin visited France again and on his arrival received a gay, intoxicated letter from Polly in London. ''Welcome to England! my dear, my honored friend.'' She discussed some things on her mind, then catching herself, remarked, ''How strangely I let my pen run on to a philosopher! But that philosopher is my friend, and I may write what I please to him.'' Finally, she broke the news that had produced her ebullient mood. ''I met a very sensible physician yesterday . . . He must be clever because he thinks as *we* do. I would not have you or my mother surprised if I should run off with this young man . . . I was so much pleased with him . . . though I assure you he has made no proposal. How I rattle! This flight must be owing to this new acquaintance, or to the joy of hearing my old one is returned to this country.'' Franklin might guess which produced her enlivened spirits. In his reply he assured her, ''I have reason to be jealous of this same, insinuating, handsome young physician; but as it flatters more my vanity . . . to suppose you were in spirits on account of my safe return, I shall turn a deaf ear to reason in this case, as I have done with success in twenty others.''

Several months later the young physician, William Hewson, made his proposal and Polly turned to her philosopher friend for guidance.

As he had done with Katy Greene before, he left her to her own sound judgment, saying "I shall be confident, whether you accept or refuse, that you do right." She accepted. Polly and her physician were married and were very happy together. Franklin was named godfather to their first child, a boy, and Polly wrote how much the child resembled him. Franklin was delighted with her news of his godson, how many teeth he had cut, and so on. Polly's reference to his resemblance to his godfather in his taking air baths in his birthday suit, prompted Franklin to say, "His being like me in so many particulars pleases me prodigiously; and I am persuaded there is another which you have omitted, though it must have occurred to you while you were putting them down." This comment has been characterized by A. O. Aldridge as "an anatomical allusion neither esoteric nor very delicate."

Franklin was a forerunner of the permissive school in bringing up children and advised Polly to let the boy have everything he liked. This advice was not given lightly; it was based on his scientific theory of child development: "I think it of great consequence while the features of the countenance are forming; it gives them a pleasant air, and, that being once become natural and fixed by habit, the face is ever after the handsomer for it, and on that much of a person's good fortune and success in life may depend. Had I been crossed as much in my infant likings and inclinations as you know I have been of late years, I should have been, I was going to say 'not near so handsome,' but as the vanity of that expression would offend other folks' vanity, I change it . . . and say, 'a great deal more homely.' "

Polly had a second son and then a daughter. When her mother urged her to wean the baby girl, Polly pleaded with her by saying that Franklin would be very angry if she didn't let the baby suck for a year. Her mother had no response, for absent or present, the Doctor's opinion was her law. Always sensible in matters of health, Franklin objected to the tight corsets that even little girls were made to wear. Polly wrote: "My girl was highly pleased with your telling me I do right to keep her without stays. Her reflection upon it when she was going to bed last night was, "It is very curious grandmama should want me to wear stays when her best friend, the one she thinks most of, says you do right to keep me without."

In the home on Craven Street Franklin was the undisputed head of the household and in his jocular way liked to play the king at court. He once entertained his friends with a newspaper he wrote on a few days' occurrences in the Stevenson home, in which he mimicked the papers that reported the gossip of the royal court and Parliament. Since it was forbidden to make public reports of the latter events, these papers masked the news so as to conceal individual's names but leave no doubt as to their identity. This family frolic, staged in such a ridiculous, pompous manner with all its domestic nonsense, must have added to the hilarity and gleeful spirits that already permeated "Franklin's kingdom." Under the title of *Craven Street Gazette,* the paper treats with gentle satire the events of four days in September, 1770, when Margaret Stevenson was away and Polly with her husband moved in to take care of the household. Franklin enjoyed himself, pretending his gross mistreatment by the new administration, as excerpts from the paper show:

> *Saturday:* This morning Queen Margaret,[1] accompanied by her first maid of honour, Miss Franklin,[2] set out for Rochester. Immediately on their departure, the whole street was in tears—from a heavy shower of rain. It is whispered, that the new family administration, which took place on her majesty's departùre, promises, like all other new administrations, to govern much better than the old one.
>
> We hear that the great person (so called from his enormous size),[3] is grievously affected at the late changes, and could hardly be comforted this morning though the new ministry [4] promised him a roasted shoulder of mutton and potatoes for his dinner.
>
> It is said, that the same great person intended to pay his respects to another great personage [5] this day at St. James's, it being coronation-day; hoping thereby a little to amuse his grief; but was prevented by an accident, Queen Margaret, or her maid of honour, having carried off the key of the drawers, so that the lady of the bedchamber [6] could not [find] a laced shirt for his highness.[7] Great clamours were made on this occasion against her majesty.
>
> Other accounts say that the shirts were afterwards found, though too late, in another place. And some suspect that the wanting a shirt from those drawers was only a ministerial pretence to excuse picking the locks, that the new administration might have everything at command.
>
> *Sunday:* Dr. Fatsides [8] made 469 turns in his dining-room, as the

---

[1] Margaret Stevenson
[2] Sally Franklin
[3] Franklin ridiculing himself
[4] Polly
[5] King George III
[6] Nanny, the maid
[7] Franklin
[8] Franklin

exact distance of a visit to the lovely Lady Barwell,[9] whom he did not find at home; so there was no struggle for and against a kiss, and he sat down to dream in the easy-chair, that he had it without any trouble.

Monday: It is currently reported that poor Nanny had nothing for dinner in the kitchen, for herself and puss, but the scrapings of the bones of Saturday's mutton.

Tuesday: This morning my good Lord Hutton called at Craven-Street House, and inquired very respectfully and affectionately concerning the welfare of the Queen. He then imparted to the big man [10] a piece of intelligence important to them both, and but just communicated by Lady Hawkesworth, *viz.* that the amiable and delectable companion, Miss D[orothea] B[lount],[11] had made a vow to marry absolutely him of the two whose wife should first depart this life. It is impossible to express the various agitations of mind appearing in both their faces on this occasion. Vanity at the preference given them over the rest of mankind; affection to their present wives, *fear* of losing them, hope, if they must lose them, to obtain the proposed comfort; jealousy of each other in case both wives should die together, etc., etc., etc.,—all working at the same time jumbled their features into inexplicable confusion. They parted at length with professions and outward appearances indeed of enduring friendship, but it was shrewdly suspected that each of them sincerely wished health and long life to the other's wife; and that however long either of these friends might like to live himself, the other would be very well pleased to survive him.

The public may be assured that this morning a certain great personage [12] was asked very complaisantly by the mistress of the household if he would choose to have the blade-bone of Saturday's mutton that had been kept for his dinner to-day, broiled or cold. He answer'd gravely, 'If there is any flesh on it, it may be broiled; if not, it may as well be cold.' Orders were accordingly given for broiling it. But when it came to table, there was indeed so very little flesh, or rather none, (Puss having dined on it yesterday after Nanny) that if our new administration had been as good economists as they would be thought, the expense of broiling might well have been saved to the publick, and carried to the sinking fund. It is assured the great person bears all with infinite patience. But the nation is astonished at the insolent presumption, that dares treat so much mildness in so cruel a manner!

[9] Miss Barwell, Polly's friend
[10] Franklin
[11] Polly's friend
[12] Franklin

Now, returning to the old tricks he employed in another *Gazette,* Franklin called on one of his favorite newspaper practices, the counterfeit letter to the editor followed by the counterfeit response. The "weighty" subject for discussion is none other than the great person himself and his miserable treatment:

> To the Publisher of the *Craven-Street Gazette.*
>
> Sir: I make no doubt of the truth of what the papers tell us, that a certain great person is half-starved on the blade-bone of a sheep (I cannot call it of mutton, there being none on it) by a set of the most careless, worthless, thoughtless, inconsiderate, corrupt, ignorant, blundering, foolish, crafty, and knavish ministers, that ever got into a house and pretended to govern a family and provide a dinner. Alas for the poor old England of Craven Street! If they continue in power another week, the nation [13] will be ruined. Undone, totally undone, if I and my friends are not appointed to succeed them. I am a great admirer of your useful and impartial paper; and therefore request you will inset this without fail, from
>
> Your humble servant, INDIGNATION.

And then for the spurious response:

> To the Publisher of the *Craven-Street Gazette.*
>
> Sir: Your correspondent, Indignation, has made a fine story in your paper against our Craven Street Ministry, as if they meant to starve his highness, giving him only a bare blade-bone for his dinner, while they riot upon roast venison. The wickedness of writers in this age is truly amazing. I believe that if even the Angel Gabriel would condescend to be our minister, and provide our dinners, he could scarcely escape newspaper defamation from a gang of hungry, ever-restless, discontented, and malicious scribblers.
>
> It is, Sir, a piece of justice you owe our righteous administration to undeceive the publick on this occasion, by assuring them of the fact, which is, that there was provided and actually smoking on the table under his royal nose at the same instant, as fine a piece of ribs of beef roasted as ever a knife was put into, with potatoes, horseradish, pickled walnuts, etc., which his highness might have eaten of if so he had pleased to do. And which he forbore to do merely from a whimsical opinion that beef doth not with him perspire well, but makes his back itch, to his no small vexation, now that he has lost the little Chinese ivory hand at the end of a stick,

[13] Himself

commonly called a scratch back, presented to him by her Majesty. This is the truth, and if your boasted impartiality is real, you will not hesitate a moment to insert this letter in your next paper.

I am, tho' a little angry at present, A HATER OF SCANDAL.

As may be noted in the last line of the above letter, Franklin spelled the word "though" in the abbreviated way "tho'." This is because as a busy writer he used many abbreviations (most of which have been spelled out in this book for the purpose of clarity), but also because he was disturbed by the lack of relationship between the spelling and the sound of so many words. He even went so far as to develop a phonetic alphabet for spelling reform, which he revealed to Polly. She answered him in a letter using his new alphabet but raised some objections to it. One objection was that with the new spelling the etymologies of words would be lost and we could not derive their meanings. Franklin doubted that we look to etymologies of words for their present meanings. "If I should call a man a knave and a villain," he said, "he would hardly be satisfied with my telling him that one of the words originally signified only a lad or servant, and the other an under-ploughman or the inhabitant of a village."

Franklin also answered Polly's objection that with the new spelling all the books already printed would be useless. He believed that people would learn to read the old writing as educated Italians learn to read Latin, which was the language of their ancestors. But if the spelling of the words had not changed from the Latin the pronunciation of the Italian words would have no relation to their spelling. When an Italian sounds the word *Vescovo* (bishop in Italian), he would have to write *Episcopus* (bishop in Latin). Franklin indicated similarly that if we had continued the Saxon spelling and writing, English people would have the same difficulty in learning their language as Chinese have in learning theirs. With Franklin's simplified spelling there would be no unsounded letters, or letters with different sounds, as occurs in English and makes it so hard for foreigners to learn. He might have mentioned but didn't, the possible spelling of fish as *ghoti*, using the *gh* as sounded in *enough*, the *o* in *women*, and the *ti* in *caution*. Although Franklin was logical enough to desire phonetic spelling for the English language, he was wise enough to know that the spelling reform he desired would not be publicly accepted, and did not attempt to promote it. He was correct in his assumption, for the many later calls for spelling reform such as proposed by George Bernard Shaw and Theodore Roosevelt generated very little enthusiasm.

Polly was so happy, with her philosopher friend, her husband, and her children. Then in 1774, tragedy struck with terrible suddenness; her husband got an infected finger and died four days later. How would she care for her children and herself? The answer came in the reward Franklin assured her would be hers if she would do her duty and return to her aunt. He may have been speaking of a spiritual reward but he was thinking of a material one as well, Aunt Tickell's inheritance, which Polly received in her hour of need.

In 1775 Franklin returned to America, but he did not forget Polly, nor she him. She wrote to him in America and in France, and at his invitation she and her children spent several lovely months with him in the chateau at Passy during his last year in France. Finally, yielding to his encouragement, Polly became an American, bringing her family to Pennsylvania in 1786. During his final illness she read to him, relieving him so much from his agony that he was able to quote poetry to her. He thought back over their friendship and saw it as "all clear sunshine, without the least cloud in its hemisphere."

Was Polly Stevenson at any time Franklin's mistress? There—we said it—the question that many may have been thinking but were afraid to ask. Could Franklin have been Margaret Stevenson's lover? These are tantalizing questions, for we don't know the answers but must speculate from the evidence we have. Carl Van Doren sees Polly's relationship to Franklin as a daughter and Mrs. Stevenson as a sister. Alfred Owen Aldridge, on the other hand, sees Polly in the role of ingenue, combination daughter and flirt, while Mrs. Stevenson played the part of mother and wife to him (hopefully, not at the same time). Both men are authorities distinguished for their scholarship on Franklin. Aldridge quotes Franklin as calling Mrs. Stevenson "my little wife," but that is hardly proof, for he used that term to refer to Strahan's 11-year-old girl, and the Chaumont daughter in France. He also referred to the diminutive Madam Le Roy as "my pocket wife." Cited also by Aldridge are Strahan's letter to Deborah to come over and take her rightful place. But did the other women Strahan referred to, who might find Franklin so attractive, include Margaret Stevenson? The evidence, from the few letters we have from Mrs. Stevenson to Franklin and vice-versa, seems hardly convincing that they were lovers. How about Polly? In 1767, the American artist Charles Willson

Peale was in London studying painting and called on Franklin at his lodgings on Craven Street. He came unannounced and found Franklin "sitting with a young lady on his knee." Was it Polly? Peale drew a sketch of the scene before him which is described by Charles C. Sellers, author of *Benjamin Franklin in Portraiture*, as showing a gentleman with a girl on his lap "in amorous reciprocation." Peale remembered the incident, noting in his diary that the Doctor was very friendly to him and showed him "experiments he was then making." But was the girl in the sketch Polly? Unfortunately we cannot tell, and are left to the questionable resources of our own fertile imaginations.

Sketch by Charles Willson Peale of Franklin with young lady.

17

A MAN OF LETTERS

LETTERS, AS MUST NOW BE EVIDENT, WERE Franklin's favorite mode
of literary expression. Not only personal messages, but his essays,
charades, bagatelles, propaganda pieces, and scientific papers were
written in letter form. Even his autobiography is written as a letter.
Franklin was best on a one-to-one basis with people and the letter was
personal and natural for him, like speaking to someone in the next
chair. His was a quiet, reflective temperament and in letters he could
take time to collect his thoughts and polish his phrases. Letters did not
require a rigid style but allowed him to be his informal self, taking
whatever liberties he wished. This informal style is illustrated in the
letter he sent to Madam LeVeillard making amends for her husband's
absence. When Franklin left France in 1785, his friend LeVeillard accompanied him to the English Channel where Franklin took the boat to
Southampton to get his ship for America. At the last minute, LeVeillard decided to go along to England and left to Franklin the explanation to his wife: "You know, my dear friend," Franklin wrote her,
"that your husband, a while ago, tried to convince me to remain in
France. Now the tables are turned and I am trying to persuade him to
come with me to America; and I have great hopes of succeeding, for I
have already prevailed upon him to go as far as England." Then, to
tease her, he called on his favorite electrical joke. "Perhaps, since you

are so far away and I am so close, we will see your power of attraction diminished and mine reinforced so that I shall be able to drag him along." But he was not forgetting her; he had an alternative plan for her. "In such a case, I don't see any better solace for you than taking a lover, and in order to conduct this affair with more prudence and decency, I recommend Monsieur le Curé. He is a good and worthy priest whom I esteem infinitely. If you don't like this suggestion, follow us and bring along your amiable children. Thus, I shall acquire the whole family to live with me in America, which would give me infinite pleasure."

Some of Franklin's letters are of interest because of what they reveal not so much about him but about the developing country in which he lived. In a letter to Richard Jackson, a member of Parliament and Pennsylvania's agent in England, Franklin painted a verbal picture of the development of the western frontier town of Pittsburgh. In it, he characterizes the nature of the local people in a subtle way by referring to the rental price of the brewery and their choice of a clergyman:

> There are now some considerable little towns on the line of communication between this place and Fort Pitt; and the town under that fort has, they say, at least 200 log houses. There is a brewery, would you think it, near the town, that lets for 100 pounds a year. Smiths, carpenters, taylors, shoemakers, and most other common trades are in the town; and the inhabitants, on some mistaken intelligence of a design among the Indians to attack the place, formed two good companies of militia. Their fuel is chiefly stone coal, brought from just across the Monongahela, and sold in the town at twopence a bushel. I cannot call it pittcoal, because it is not dug out of pits, but broke off the cliff into boats in the river; the vein 3 feet thick. The government, civil as well as military, is in the commanding officer, Col. Bouquet, whose will is the law; and as he is a very good man it is a very good government. The people have balls for dancing and assemblies for religious worship, but as they cannot yet afford to maintain both a clergyman and a dancing-master, the dancing-master reads prayers and one of Tristram Shandy's sermons every Sunday.

In this letter Franklin goes on to discuss the considerable trade that was carried on there with the Indians and how General Amherst had unwittingly insulted the Indians by failing to bring them presents. He explained that it was a custom of the Indians when they met with another nation or tribe always to exchange presents; and since they considered the white man to be wealthy by their standards, they took his behavior to be a sign of contempt.

The letter was an art form for Franklin. He took pleasure in demonstrating originality in little things, as in the excuse for ending a letter or in the complimentary close. In a long letter written from Philadelphia in August, 1745, he found a legitimate, if ingenious, excuse for concluding, *viz:* "The impertinence of these mosquitoes to me, now I am in the humor of writing, prevents a great deal of mine [impertinence] to you, so that for once they are of some use in the world." A year later he wrote a long philosophical letter in his shop and finally excused himself with: "The din of market increases upon me and that, with frequent interruptions, has I find, made me say some things twice over and, I suppose, forget some others I intended to say. It has however one good effect, as it obliges me to come to the relief of your patience, with your humble servant, B. Franklin." In this conclusion, it will be noted he played a favorite game of trying to incorporate the complimentary close and signature into the body of the letter so that there is a natural flow of meaning without a break. After a very personal, delicate letter to Katy Greene, he used the elements of sudden discord and contrast to bring down the curtain, with "Adieu. The bell rings and I must go among the grave ones, and talk politics."

He usually needed an excuse for the delinquence in his correspondence to his many friends. To one friend he wrote, "I beg you'd excuse the delay, and desire you would remember in my favor the old saying, 'They who have much business must have much pardon.' " To his niece, he wrote from France, "The difficulty, delay, and interruption of correspondence with those I love is one of the great inconveniences I find in living so far from home: but we must bear these and more with patience if we can; if not, we must bear them as I do with impatience." The niece, Elizabeth Hubbard Partridge, was the recipient of some of Franklin's most delightful letters. In one of them he mentioned sending her from Paris a china figure she had requested, probably of him, and he closed with the statement, "I send with it a couple of fatherly kisses for you and your amiable daughter, the whole wrapped up together in cotton to be kept warm."

It was Franklin's homespun, familar style that, in an age of formalism, made his letters unique. Writing to Richard Jackson about the American colonies, he said, "I have, with you, long entertained a fondness for Connecticut. The country and the people are both a good deal to my taste; but Pennsylvania is my darling.'' He is said to have pictured New Jersey as "a barrel with bungs at both ends.'' When, during the wars with the French and Indians, the English were putting pressure on the colonies for a larger share of the defense, Franklin urged the Pennsylvania Assembly to make a significant gesture of compliance. It did, sending General Amherst 1,000 men for his offensive against the Indians. Franklin wrote to inform Jackson, noting that Pennsylvania had been previously reckoned backward in such measures, but in this case had responded more generously than any of the other colonies. He hoped that Jackson would let this action by Pennsylvania be broadcast to her favor in England and "let us be praised a little by way of encouragement,'' he suggested, "to be good boys for the future.'' Could this quotation have emanated from Washington, Adams, Jefferson, Madison or other early American statesmen? In his editing of the Franklin-Jackson correspondence, Van Doren indicated that "only Franklin'' would have expressed himself "and let us be . . . good boys'' on such a serious matter. After he returned to the United States from France, Franklin was soon in debt to many of his French friends in terms of correspondence. He sent this quick note, with its inventive form, to let them know that he hadn't forgotten them and that he still cared. It was addressed to Abbé de la Roche but was meant for Madam Helvétius and all her satellites, who are mentioned, as follows:

> Dear Sir,
>
> I hope soon to be in a situation when I can write largely and fully to my friends in France, without the perpetual interruptions I now daily meet with. At present I can only tell you that I am well,
>
> and that I esteem you,
> and l'Abbé Morellet,
> and M. Cabanis,   infinitely
> and love dear Mme.
>   Helvétius,
>
> Adieu. Yours most affectionately,
>
>   B. Franklin.

The letters Franklin wrote to William Strahan, the English printer, well illustrate some of the points of his style that have been mentioned. When Franklin was in Philadelphia between his two terms of service in England, Strahan sent him a series of letters describing political events in England that were so vivid and clear that Franklin was glowing in his praise. Then he added, "If I were king . . . I should certainly make you the historiographer of my reign. There could be but one objection. I suspect you might be a little partial in my favor. But your other qualifications for an historian being duly considered, I believe we might get over that." Strahan modestly replied to Franklin's praise saying jokingly that this was evidence that his friend's judgment was failing. Franklin used this little joke of Strahan's to take off on a flight of fancy of his own. "You tell me," Franklin wrote, "that the value I set on your political letters is a strong proof that my judgment is on the decline. People seldom have friends kind enough to tell them that disagreeable truth. . . . And indeed I learn more from what you say than you intended I should, for it convinces me that you have observed that decline for some time in other instances . . . but you have kept the observation to yourself till you had the opportunity of hinting it to me kindly under the guise of modesty. . . . I will confess to you another circumstances that must confirm your judgment of me, which is that I have of late fancied myself to write better than I ever did. And farther, that when anything of mine is abridged in the papers or magazines, I conceit that the abridger has left out the very best and brightest parts. These, my friend, are much stronger proofs, and put me in mind of Gil Blas's patron, the homily maker."

It was true that Franklin, like all writers, was sensitive to editing of his work. After one editor got through abridging his article, Franklin said sorrowfully, "He has drawn the teeth and pared the nails of my paper, so that it can neither scratch nor bite. It seems only to paw and mumble." The Gil Blas referred to, is the main character in a French novel translated by Smollet. In his adventures in Spain, Gil is asked by the Archbishop of Granada to advise him if he sees any signs of failing power in him. After a stroke of apoplexy the patron preached a homily and Gil dutifully told him it was inferior. The Archbishop responded that he had never done better and summarily dismissed the young man.

When Franklin was ready to depart for England in 1757, he wrote to Strahan to let him know. They had never met before but did business together and were friends through correspondence. "Our Assembly talk of sending me to England speedily," Franklin wrote, "Then look out sharp, and if a fat old fellow should come to your printing house and request a little smouting [part-time work], depend on it, 'tis your affectionate friend and humble servant. [B. Franklin]." He incorporated the complimentary close in this letter as he did in a more famous letter during the Revolutionary War. In 1775 Strahan, as a member of Parliament, had voted with the government, declaring the Americans to be rebels. Franklin was angry and wrote the following letter:

> Mr. Strahan,
>   You are a member of Parliament and one of that majority which has doomed my country to destruction. You have begun to burn our towns and murder our people. Look upon your hands! They are stained with the blood of your relations! You and I were long friends. You are now my enemy, and I am
>
>   Yours,
>   B. Franklin

Franklin never sent the letter. Having expressed himself, he put the letter aside and instead sent Strahan a friendly letter to which he received a friendly answer. Although Strahan remained loyal to the King, the friendship of the two withstood the strain and they continued their correspondence over a period of fifty years.

There was one kind of letter writing which was the bane of Franklin's existence when he was ambassador to France. This was writing letters of recommendation. He was constantly besieged by strangers who insisted that their fortune would be made or their honor would be saved, if only he would certify in a letter whatever they told him about themselves. Many wanted a commission in the American army and asked for letters recommending them to Congress and to Washington. Franklin's response to a letter he received from a man named Lith, which reached him shortly after his arrival in France, shows both his frustration and patience in dealing with this nuisance. In his letter Franklin tells Lith: "You express yourself as astonished, and appear to be angry that you have no answer to a letter you wrote me of the 11th of December, which you are sure was delivered to me." He explained that on that date he had just landed in France and had received no such letter. He did get one from Lith in January which he did not answer. The reason, he said, might displease him, but whoever writes to a stranger should observe three points: "(1) That what he proposes be practical. (2) His propositions should be made in explicit terms so as to be easily understood. (3) What he desires should be in itself reasonable." According to Franklin's letter, Lith was negligent in all these points. First, he wanted a safe voyage to America, when that was impossible, and second, without too much expense, but didn't state what he could afford. Lastly, he wanted letters to Congress and General Washington, which Franklin didn't believe reasonable "to ask of one who knows no more of you than your name is Lith and you live at Bayreuth." "I doubt not your being a man of merit, and knowing it yourself you may forget that it is not known to everybody. But reflect a moment, Sir, and you will be convinced that if I were to make a practice of giving letters of recommendation to persons of whose character I knew no more than I do of yours, my recommendations would soon be of no authority at all." Franklin thanked him for his offer to be of service to America but assured him that numbers of experienced officers who had volunteered had to be turned away. Rather than take so long, so expensive, and so hazardous a voyage, Franklin suggested he take the advice of friends and stay at home.

There were many others. One wanted Franklin to recommend him to be king of the new country in America. He wrote that since America had dismissed their king they would need another—himself. He was of an ancient Norman family whose line had never been bastardized. When he received no reply to his letter, he sent another with the generous proposal that if he were given a pension of 15,000 pounds he would remain at home and let the Americans govern themselves as they wished. In another case, a woman sent him a letter on behalf of a young man: "If you have in your country the secret of reforming a detestable creature who is the chief torment of his family, I beg you to send over the bearer of this letter. You will be performing a miracle worthy of yourself." Another letter soliciting Franklin's aid was from a monk who had lost a lot of money gambling and asked Franklin to help him retain his only treasure, his reputation. Franklin wrote on the letter, "wants me to pay his gaming debts, and he will pray for success of our cause." Franklin's enormous fame in Europe and his reputation for performing miracles no doubt led to so many people seeking his endorsement of their schemes. More for his own amusement than for actual use, and to relieve what he called "my perpetual torment," he prepared a model letter of recommendation useful for all strangers who made appeals to him.

> The bearer of this, who is going to America, presses me to give him a letter of recommendation, though I know nothing of him, not even his name. This may seem extraordinary, but I assure you it is

not uncommon here. Sometimes, indeed, one unknown person brings another, equally unknown, to recommend him; and sometimes they recommend one another. As to this gentleman, I must refer you to himself for his character and merits, with which he is certainly better acquainted than I can possibly be. I recommend him, however, to those civilities which every stranger of whom one knows no harm has a right to; and I request you will do him all the good offices, and show him all the favour that on further acquaintance you shall find him to deserve.

This form letter was in the pattern of the set speech he had written for himself when he travelled around the colonies as a young man. When he entered a tavern, his greeting was ready: "My name is Benjamin Franklin, I was born at Boston, am a printer by profession, shall return at such a time, and have no news—now what can you give me for dinner?"

The longest letter Franklin ever wrote was his autobiography. It was begun during a visit with the Shipleys and their five daughters at their country estate at Twyford in 1771. Franklin loved the Shipley family and they reciprocated. He captivated them with stories of his youthful adventures in America, which they insisted he put down in writing. They gave him pen and paper and he wrote about a third of his memoirs during that enjoyable three-week visit. As he departed in the coach the family waved farewell, that is except for the youngest, 11-year-old Kitty, who was going to school in London and accompanied Franklin on the day-long journey by horse carriage. When he arrived in London Franklin sent Mrs. Shipley a thank-you letter, but not of the ordinary perfunctory kind:

Dear Madam:
    This is just to let you know that we arrived safe and well in Marlborough Street, about 6, where I delivered up my charge.
    The above seems too short for a letter; so I will lengthen it by a little account of our journey. The first stage we were rather pensive. I tried several topics of conversation, but none of them would hold. But after breakfast we began to recover spirits, and had a good deal of chat. Will you hear some of it?

Would she like to hear some of it? We can imagine Franklin smiling at his little joke as he wrote that line. The 65-year-old statesman-philosopher and the 11-year-old schoolgirl carried on an animated conversation about the future of her sisters. She wanted to see them married, but to what kind of husbands? Informally, without quotation marks, Franklin presents both the narration and the conversation.

> We began with Georgiana. She thought a country gentleman, that loved travelling and would take her with him, that loved books and would hear her read to him. I added, that had a good estate and was a member of Parliament and loved to see an experiment now and then. This she agreed to; so we set him down for Georgiana, and went on to Betsy.
>
> Betsy, says I, seems of a sweet mild temper, and if we should give her a country squire, and he should happen to be of a rough, passionate turn, and be angry now and then, it might break her heart. Oh, none of 'em must be so; for then they would not be good husbands. To make sure of this point however, for Betsey, shall we give her a bishop? Oh no, that won't do. They all declare against the Church, and against the Army; not one of them will marry either a clergyman or an officer; that they are resolved upon. What can be their reason for that?

This news must have been a shock to the Shipleys, with the Bishop and his son both in church robes. Thankfully Kitty has an explanation which must provided relief and a chuckle as well.

> Why you know, that when a clergyman or an officer dies, the income goes with 'em; and then what is there to maintain the family? There's the point. Then suppose we give her a good, honest, sensible city merchant who will love her dearly and is very rich? I don't know but that may do.
>
> We proceeded to Emily, her dear Emily, I was afraid we should hardly find any thing good enough for Emily; but at last, after first settling that, if she did marry, Kitty was to live a good deal with her. We agreed that as Emily was very handsome we might expect an Earl for her. So having fixed her, as I thought, a countess, we went on to Anna Maria.
>
> She, says Kitty, should have a rich man that has a large family and a great many things to take care of; for she is very good at managing, helps my Mama very much, can look over bills, and order all sorts of family business. Very well; and as there is a grace and dignity in her manner that would become the station, what do you think of giving her a Duke? Oh no! I'll have the Duke for Emily. You may give the Earl to Anna Maria if you please: but Emily shall have

the Duke. I contested this matter some time; but at length was forced to give up the point, leave Emily in possession of the Duke, and content myself with the Earl for Anna Maria.

And now what shall we do for Kitty? We have forgot her, all this time. Well, and what will you do for her? I suppose that though the rest have resolved against the Army, she may not yet have made so rash a resolution. Yes, but she has; unless, now an old one, an old General that had done fighting, and is rich, such a one as General Rufane; I like him a good deal. You must know I like an old man, indeed I do, and somehow or other all the old men take to me; all that come to our house like me better than my other sisters. I go to 'em and ask 'em how they do and they like it mightily; and the maids take notice of it, and say when they see an old man come, there's a friend of yours, Miss Kitty. But then as you like an old General, hadn't you better take him while he's a young officer, and let him grow old upon your hands, because then, you'll like him better and better every year as he grows older and older. No, that won't do. He must be an old man of 70 or 80, and take me when I am about 30. And then, you know, I may be a rich young widow.

They chatted on all the way to town and she was very entertaining, Franklin assured Mrs. Shipley. But he now apologized for making his letter far too long as first it was too short. Then says he, "The Bishop would think it too trifling, so don't show it to him. I am afraid too that you will think it so, and have a good mind not to send it." But it tells that Kitty is well at school and that is his apology for sending it. He sends his love to the family, his best respects to the Bishop, and 1,000 thanks to Mrs. Shipley, herself, for all her kindnesses and the happy days he enjoyed at Twyford. We can imagine the Shipleys' pleasure in having such a congenial house guest who would take the trouble to write this entertaining letter.

Georgiana, the next youngest Shipley sister, received an unusual gift from Franklin. It was a gray squirrel from America. She named it Mungo and was very fond of it, but it escaped from its cage and was killed by a dog. When Franklin heard the sad news he sent Georgiana a letter of condolence.

I lament with you most sincerely the unfortunate end of poor Mungo. Few squirrels were better accomplished; for he had a good education, had travelled far, and seen much of the world. As he had the honour of being, for his virtues, your favorite he should not go, like common skuggs [squirrels], without an elegy or an epitaph. Let us give him one in the monumental style and measure, which, being neither prose nor verse, is perhaps the properest for grief; since to use common language would look as if we were not affected, and to make rhymes would seem trifling in sorrow.

EPITAPH

Alas! poor Mungo!
Happy wert thou, hadst thou known
Thy own felicity.
Remote from the fierce bald eagle,
Tyrant of thy native woods,
thou hadst nought to fear from his piercing talons,
Nor from the murdering gun
Of the thoughtless sportsman.
Safe in thy weird castle,
Grimalkin never could annoy thee.
Daily wert thou fed with the choicest viands,
By the fair hand of an indulgent mistress;
But, discontented,
Thou wouldst have more freedom.

Too soon, alas! dist thou obtain it;
And wandering,
Thou art fallen by the fangs of wanton, cruel Ranger!

Learn hence,
Ye who blindly seek more liberty,
Whether subjects, sons, squirrels or daughters,
That apparent restraint may be real protection;
Yielding peace and plenty
With security.

You see, my dear Miss, how much more decent and proper this broken style is, than if we were to say, by way of epitaph,

Here Skugg
Lies snug,
As a bug
In a rug.

and yet, perhaps, there are people in the world of so little feeling as to think that this would be a good-enough epitaph for poor Mungo.

If you wish it, I shall procure another to succeed him; but perhaps you will now choose some other amusement.

In 1786 Franklin wrote Kitty Shipley a bagatelle in letter form in response to an inquiry from her. He called it, "The Art of Procuring Pleasant Dreams." He began, "As a great part of our life is spent in sleep during which we have sometimes pleasant and sometimes painful dreams, it becomes of consequence to obtain one kind and avoid the other. If we can sleep without dreaming . . . painful dreams are avoided. If while we sleep we can have any pleasing dream it is as the French say, *autant de gagné,* so much added to the pleasure of life." From this introduction he plunged into a lecture on proper diet, sufficient exercise, and plenty of fresh air. On the latter subject, he commented, "It is observed of Methusalah who, being the longest liver, may be supposed to have best preserved his health, that he slept always in the open air. For when he had lived five hundred years, an angel said to him, 'Arise Methusalah and build thee a house, for thou shalt live yet five hundred years longer.' But Methusalah answered and said, 'If I am to live but five hundred years longer, it is not worth while to build me a house; I will sleep in the air as I have been used to do.' "

To avoid unpleasant dreams Franklin advised moderate eating and the use of thinner and more porous bed clothes, to allow the air to filter in and the "perspirable matter" to escape. However, should you be awakened and have trouble falling back to sleep, the Doctor prescribes the following procedures: "Get out of bed, beat up and turn your pillow, shake your bed clothes well, with at least twenty shakes, then throw the bed open and leave it to cool. In the meanwhile, continuing undressed, walk about your chamber until your skin has had time to discharge its load. . . . When you begin to feel the cold air unpleasant, then return to your bed and you will soon fall asleep and your sleep will be sweet and pleasant. All the scenes presented to your fancy will be, too, of the pleasing kind. I am often as agreeably entertained with them as by the scenery of an opera." Kitty responded that she was flattered that Franklin would take so much of his precious time to reply to her request, but where, she wanted to know, "do you read that Methusalah slept in the open air? I have searched the Bible in vain to find it." Apparently Miss Shipley was unaware of Franklin's extraordinary talent for inventing biblical quotations.

One may wonder how we have such an excellent record of Franklin's letters. The credit goes to Franklin himself. Every time he wrote a letter he made a copy which he saved along with the rough draft, in book form. He liked to refer to his many volumes of letterbooks to refresh his mind on what he had said on various subjects and to whom. But more than that, he had a sense of history, for he saved every invitation to dinner, every visiting card, every souvenir. Albert H. Smyth, who edited ten volumes of Franklin's works remarked, "No public man has ever more completely revealed himself or more copiously recorded the march of events in his time. His care in this respect is at once the delight and the despair of his biographer."

Unfortunately the record is not complete. When Franklin was in France during the War for Independence, the English plundered the papers he left at home, and six of eight letterbooks were lost. In Franklin's will he bequeathed his papers, including the autobiography, to his grandson, Temple, who had served as his secretary in France. He knew the papers would have monetary value and he wanted to assist the young man. Temple looked over the papers and took those manuscripts he thought important with him to London, intending to edit and publish the autobiography and papers. The world waited with eager anticipation for Franklin's memoirs. Years passed and still nothing happened. Jefferson was sure that Temple had been paid by the British government to suppress publication. In the meantime a poor French translation of the autobiography appeared, based upon the incomplete copy Franklin had sent his French friend, Le Veillard. From that an even poorer English translation of the French translation appeared. Still nothing from Temple. It was twenty-seven years before Temple published his edition of his grandfather's papers. He had not been bribed; he had just been incredibly indolent, confused, and wrapped up in other affairs.

Only a portion of the papers Temple held were actually published. These and the rest were put in a chest and deposited with a banking firm for safekeeping. Temple died in 1823 and his widow removed the chest from the vault, whereupon the papers disappeared for seventeen years. No one knew what she had done with them but they were eventually found loosely bundled up on the top shelf of a tailor's shop where Temple had lodged. Many were missing, but they had not gone to waste. The thrifty tailor was cutting them up for patterns for suits and dresses. For ten years the finder tried unsuccessfully to sell the papers, but in 1851 an American bookseller, Henry Stevens, purchased them. He immediately recognized their value and arranged them, repaired them, and listed them. Unbelievably, they became "lost" again. Before Stevens could sell or publish his collection he pledged them as security for a loan. The creditor withheld them from use by scholars and it was not until 1882 when his executors sold them at auction to the U.S. Department of State that their contents came into public view.

The autobiography that Temple Franklin published in 1817 was thought to be authentic. It was not. For one thing, Temple had prettied it up with 1,200 changes, substituting nice Latin words for Franklin's vigorous Anglo-Saxon expressions. For another, it was not the complete manuscript. Temple had Franklin's original manuscript, but finding the Le Veillard copy clearer, he exchanged copies, not realizing that the original had several pages not in the one he obtained. It was not until 1868, seventy-eight years after Franklin's death, when the American Minister to France, John Bigelow, discovered the original, that Franklin's autobiography, as he wrote it, was published.

While it is true that Temple's collection of Franklin's manuscripts came into public view in 1882, there were two exceptions. These were termed by 19th century critics as "explosive" and "too indecent to print." One was the essay on "Perfumes," which really was "explosive". The other was a letter known by the title, "Advice to a Young Man on the Choice of a Mistress" but is sometimes referred to simply as *the* letter. It too has a history. At the Department of State this letter "was kept very private", and when Bigelow wanted to add it to his edition of Franklin's works, Secretary of State Bayard protected the good name and reputation of the United States by refusing permission. The letter, nevertheless, did receive clandestine circulation through private printings in limited editions and was read aloud at men's dinner parties and smokers. It was not considered acceptable for general circulation until 1926, when it appeared in a popular biography.

The manuscript of the Mistress letter was acquired by a Chicago collector upon whose death it was given to the City of Chicago. After that it was purchased by the famed Philadelphia collector A. S. W. Rosenbach, who relates this account of his acquisition:

"The original manuscript came to me in a curious way. It was thought immoral in the chaste city of Chicago to which it had been bequeathed by the will of a discriminating citizen. Chicago being known for its purity, and not tolerating anything that is even slightly indelicate, offered it to me—at a price of course, for it did not hesitate to profit, like a frail sister, from its shame. I would sooner have this precious document, written entirely by the hand of Franklin, than many of the public monuments of that great western city.''

Franklin's letter is dated June 25, 1745, and is addressed merely to "My dear friend," indicating that it was really an essay in the form of a letter, probably meant for the entertainment of the Junto members, and not intended for any special recipient.

I know of no medicine fit to diminish the violent natural inclinations you mention; and if I did, I think I should not communicate it to you. Marriage is the proper remedy. It is the most natural state of man, and therefore the state in which you are most likely to find solid happiness. Your reasons against entering into it at present, appear to me not well-founded. The circumstantial advantages you have in view by postponing it, are not only uncertain, but they are small in comparison with that of the thing itself, being married and settled. It is the man and woman united that make the complete human being. Separate, she wants his force of body and strength of reason; he, her softness, sensibility and acute discernment. Together they are more likely to succeed in the world. A single man has not nearly the value he would have in that state of union. He is an incomplete animal. He resembles the odd half of a pair of scissors. If you get a prudent healthy wife, your industry in your profession, with her good economy, will be a fortune sufficient.

But if you will not take this counsel, and persist in thinking a commerce with the sex inevitable, then I repeat my former advice, that in all your amours you should prefer old women to young ones. You call this a paradox, and demand my reasons. They are these:

1. Because as they have more knowledge of the world and their minds are better stored with observations, their conversation is more improving and more lastingly agreeable.

2. Because when women cease to be handsome, they study to be good. To maintain their influence over men, they supply the diminution of beauty by an augmentation of utility. They learn to do a 1000 services small and great, and are the most tender and useful of all friends when you are sick. Thus they continue amiable. And hence there is hardly such a thing to be found as an old woman who is not a good woman.

3. Because there is no hazard of children, which irregularly produced may be attended with much inconvenience.

4. Because through more experience, they are more prudent and discreet in conducting an intrigue to prevent suspicion. The commerce with them is therefore safer with regard to your reputation. And with regard to theirs, if the affair should happen to be known, considerate people might be rather inclined to excuse an old woman who would kindly take care of a young man, form his manners by her good counsels, and prevent his ruining his health and fortunes among mercenary prostitutes.

5. Because in every animal that walks upright, the deficiency of the fluids that fill the muscles appears first in the highest part: The face first grows lank and wrinkled; then the neck; then the breast and arms; the lower parts continuing to the last as plump as ever: So that covering all above with a basket, and regarding only what is below the girdle, it is impossible of two women to know an old from a young one. And as in the dark all cats are gray, the pleasure of corporal enjoyment with an old woman is at least equal, and frequently superior, every knack being by practice capable of improvement.

6. Because the sin is less. The debauching a virgin may be her ruin, and make her for life unhappy.

7. Because the compunction is less. The having made a young girl miserable may give you frequent bitter reflections; none of which can attend the making an old woman happy.

8th and lastly. They are so grateful!!

Thus much for my paradox. But still I advise you to marry directly; being sincerely

Your affectionate friend,
BENJAMIN FRANKLIN

PART FOUR

Peregrinations of an Agile Mind

18

EVERYTHING MAKES ME
RECOLLECT SOME STORY

"THE DOCTOR IS ALWAYS SILENT UNLESS HE HAS some diverting story to tell, of which he has a great collection," reported Abigail Adams. To Franklin, conversation was like money, a medium of exchange, and he who contributes nothing gets nothing in return. Franklin gave people their money's worth, often with an entertaining story in the bargain. Anecdotes were to Franklin's oral expression what letters were to his writing. He was a natural anecdotist in what has become an American tradition of cracker barrel story-tellers. He told his daughter, "you know, everything reminds me of some story." And then he proceeded to tell her one. His excuse for telling a story was that it illustrated some point he was making, but one wonders whether in reality it was the other way around and the point was actually the excuse for telling the story.

Franklin had a story for every occasion. When his wife wrote him that his daughter had punished one of his granchildren quite severely, he replied that he was pleased that his wife had acted correctly and not interfered with their daughter's disciplining of her children. He was afraid that because of his wife's fondness for her grandchildren she might spoil them:

> There is a story of two little boys in the street; one was crying bit-
> terly; the other came to him to ask what was the matter. "I have

been," says he, "for a pennyworth of vinegar, and I have broken
the glass, and spilled the vinegar, and my mother will whip me."
"No, she won't whip you," says the other. "Indeed she will," says
he. "What," says the other, "ha'n't you then got ne'er a grand-
mother?"

When the Declaration of Independence was being debated by
Congress and Jefferson sat suffering in fear of its mutilation, Franklin
relieved his torment with his story of John Thompson, the hat seller
(see Chapter Twelve.) A similar story he liked to tell was of his own
experience when he was a member of the Pennsylvania Assembly. He
had carefully drawn up a proposal which he read to a group of people
at a public meeting in order obtain support for it. A carpenter who was
present took it into his hands and dividing the sheet into two, said of
one leaf, "this I think is enough and will answer."

Franklin was devoted to public life, having spent over fifty years
in public service. However, when he retired at the age of 82 and a
friend insisted on the need of the country for his services, he told him
the following story about "the harrow."

> A farmer, in our country, sent two of his servants to borrow one
> of a neighbor, ordering them to bring it between them on their shoul-
> ders. When they came to look at it, one of them, who had much wit
> and cunning, said: "What could our master mean by sending only
> two men to bring this harrow? No two men upon earth are strong
> enough to carry it." "Poo!" said the other, who was vain of his
> strength, "what do you talk of two men? One man can carry it. Help
> it on my shoulders and see." As he proceeded with it, the wag kept
> exclaiming, "Zounds, how strong you are! I could not have thought
> it! Why, you are a Samson! There is no such another man in
> America! What amazing strength God has given you! But you will
> kill yourself! Pray put it down and rest a little, or let me bear a part
> of the weight." "No, no," said he, being more encouraged by the
> compliments than oppressed by the burden; "you shall see I carry it
> quite home." And so he did. In this particular I am afraid my part of
> the imitation will fall short of the original.

"He that is prodigal of his hours," said *Poor Richard,* "is a
squanderer of money." Franklin believed people should be industrious
and not waste time, but he knew that they understood the reality of
money better than the abstraction of time. "If we lose our money it
gives us some concern. If we are cheated or robbed of it, we are

angry. But money lost may be found . . . time once lost can never be recovered. Yet we squander it as though . . . we had no use for it." To nail down his argument Franklin related this story: "I remember a notable woman who was fully sensible of the intrinsic value of time. Her husband was a shoemaker and an excellent craftsman, but never minded how the minutes passed. In vain did she inculcate to him that *time is money.* He had too much wit to apprehend her and it proved his ruin. When at the alehouse among his idle companions, if one remarked that the clock struck eleven, 'What is that,' says he, 'among us all?' If she sent him word by the boy that it had struck twelve; 'Tell her to be easy, it can never be more.' If, that it had struck one, 'Bid her be comforted, for it can never be less.' "

It should come as no surprise that Franklin advocated a firm fiscal policy, both for individuals and for a nation. During the Revolutionary War he wrote, "Nothing can recover our credit in Europe and our reputation but . . . punctual payment of the interest and the final regular discharge of the principal." He continued, "I hope we will never deserve . . . the reproof given to an enthusiastic knave in Pennsylvania, who being called upon for an old debt, said to the creditors: 'Thou must have a little more patience; I am not yet able to pay thee.' 'Give me then your bond,' says the creditor, 'and pay me the interest.' 'No, I cannot do that; I cannot in conscience either receive or pay interest, it is against my principle.' 'You have the conscience of a rogue' says the creditor: 'You tell me it is against your principle to pay interest; and it being against your interest to pay the principal, I perceive you do not intend to pay me either one or t'other.' "

The accumulation of wealth was desirable in Franklin's opinion, but not for its own sake. There had to be a justifiable social purpose. When he was in England he toured a factory in Norwich where his host very proudly stated, "Here is cloth for Italy; this is for Germany, this for the West Indies, and this for the American continent." Franklin observed in the factory that the workers were half-naked or wearing patched and tattered clothing. He approached his guide and asked: "And don't you make anything for Norwich?"

While he approved of the accumulation of wealth, he had little patience for ostentation. He told of a rich Quaker friend who lived all by himself in an enormous house. When Franklin saw the house he asked the man why, when he needed just a fraction of the space, did he bother to keep up this large house. The response was, "Because I have the means." On entering the dining room Franklin saw a table large enough to accommodate twenty-five people. When asked about it, the Quaker replied in the same way; he had the means. "In that case," said Franklin, "why don't you have a hat of the same size. You have the means!" In another anecdote he preaches the same kind of sermon.

> The gentleman in the story . . . had built a very fine house and thereby much impaired his fortune. He had a pride, however, in showing it to his acquaintances. One of them after viewing it all remarked [about] a motto over the door, "ŌIA VANITAS." "What," says he, "is the meaning of this ŌIA? It is a word I don't understand." "I will tell you," said the gentleman. "I had a mind to have the motto cut on a piece of smooth marble but there was not room for it between the ornaments. . . . I therefore made use of a contraction anciently very common in Latin manuscripts by which the m's and n's in words are omitted, and the omission noted by a little dash above which you see there. So that the word is *omnia,* OMNIA VANITAS [all is vanity]." "Oh," says his friend, "I now comprehend the meaning of your motto. It relates to your edifice and signifies that if you have abridged your Omnia, you have nevertheless left your Vanitas legible at full length."

In his own case, Franklin did not continue in the business world to pile up riches but retired for other pursuits as soon as he became financially independent. Another printer he liked to tell about conducted his affairs somewhat differently. He worked only half of each week. When Franklin commented that a full week's work would make it easier for him in the future, he replied that he had an uncle in London who meant to work hard for twenty years and then live like a gentleman. That, the young man said, was to become a gentleman by wholesale. For himself, he preferred the retail way, to have half a week now rather than a whole week twenty years from now.

Franklin had an aversion for the consumption of useless frivolities. Yet he didn't believe that luxuries were the evil they were represented to be by many people. "Is not the hope of one day being able to purchase and enjoy luxuries a great spur to labor and industry?" He argued that without such a spur people might be, through natural inclination, lazy and indolent. "To this purpose," he added, "I remember a circumstance," and he was launched into his story.

> The skipper of a shallop employed between Cape May and Philadelphia had done us some small service for which he refused pay. My wife, understanding that he had a daughter, sent her as a present

a new-fashioned cap. Three years after, this skipper being at my house with an old farmer of Cape May, his passenger, he mentioned the cap and how much his daughter had been pleased with it. "But," says he, "it proved a dear cap to our congregation." "How so?" "When my daughter appeared in it at meeting, it was so much admired that all the girls resolved to get such caps from Philadelphia; and my wife and I computed that the whole could not cost less than a hundred pounds." "True," says the farmer, "but you do not tell all the story. I think the cap was nevertheless an advantage to us, for it was the first thing that put our girls upon knitting worsted mittens for sale at Philadelphia, that they might have wherewithal to buy caps and ribbons there. And you know that that industry has continued, and is likely to continue and increase to a much greater value, and answer better purposes." Upon the whole, I was more reconciled to this little piece of luxury since not only the girls were made happier by having fine caps, but the Philadelphians by the supply of warm mittens.

It is seen that Franklin eased right into his stories without elaborate buildup or preliminaries. The story had to stand on its own merit. Further, he did not wish to diminish its impact by too-heavy advance billing. He chided his niece for the way she introduced a story she sent him. "Your story is well told and entertaining. Only let me admonish you of a small though common fault of story-tellers. You should not have introduced it by telling me how comical it was, especially a post before you sent the story itself. For when the expectation is raised too high, 'tis a disadvantage to the thing expected." The finish should also be done properly for greatest effect. Benjamin Rush jotted a number of sketchy notes about Franklin in his diary, one of them concerning ways of ending conversations. It attributes to Franklin the statement, "Four ways of winding up conversations, by stories of robbers, duels, murders, and in America, of snakes." The subject is intriguing and one wishes Rush had elaborated a little. But, lacking further detail, we will try to follow the formula and conclude this chapter with the kind of stories Franklin specified.

We have two of Franklin's anecdotes dealing with robbers. Anxious to dissuade his physician friend Dubourg from investing in a business of which he had no knowledge, Franklin told him the story of a man condemned for horse stealing. A professional horse thief who went to see the condemned man to find out how he came to be captured became aware after a few questions that the fellow was just a novice at the trade. When he admitted it was mere chance that brought him to take the horse, the professional replied angrily, "What the devil do you mean by stealing horses if you are not a real horse thief?"

The other story takes place when Franklin was American agent in England shortly before the war. He was responding to an official government spokesman who indicated that the Americans were his enemies and ludicrously tried to persuade the King that there was a great similarity in their characters and conduct, and his enemies, therefore, were the enemies of His Majesty and of all government. "This puts me in mind," began Franklin, and told his story of a chimney-sweeper condemned to be hanged for theft: The man was charitably visited by a good clergyman for whom he had worked. He said to the minister, "I hope your honor will take my part and get a reprieve for me, and not let my enemies have their will. Because it is upon your account that they have prosecuted and sworn against me." "On my account! How can that be?" "Why, sir, because as how, ever since they knew I was employed by your honor they resolved upon my ruin. For they are enemies to all religion, and they hate you and me and everybody in black."

In protesting the folly of dueling—which was later to take the life of his colleague in the Constitutional Convention, Alexander Hamilton—Franklin cited the case of a gentleman in a coffee-house who desired another patron to sit farther from him. " 'Why so?' 'Because, sir, you stink.' 'That is an affront, and you must fight me.' 'I will fight you, if you insist upon it; but I do not see how it will mend the matter. For if you kill me, I shall stink too. And if I kill you, you will stink, if possible, worse than you do at present.' "

On the subject of murder, Franklin relates the story of the two keepers of the Eddystone lighthouse. In 1775 his colleagues were discouraged by their many internal quarrels and he thought this story might bring them some comfort: The two keepers spent all winter together without seeing a living soul, their lighthouse perched on a solitary rock in the midst of storms. Each autumn all the provisions for the whole winter were brought to them since it was not possible to safely make the trip again till spring. One spring the relief party found only one man there. They asked him where the other man was and he answered that he must be up above; he had not seen him for six months. The men were about to arrest him for murder when they discovered he was innocent. The two keepers had quarreled but had settled their argument amicably by dividing the lighthouse so as not to bother one another. Thus, they had spent the winter in peace.

As to snakes, Franklin made use of them in his stories and writings. His forceful cartoon in 1754, the first political cartoon in America, showed a snake dismembered into a number of pieces, each representing one of the Colonies, with the caption "Join or Die." He had written a satirical piece in which he proposed repaying England's "favor" of sending criminals to America by sending rattlesnakes to England in return. And he told the fable of the two-headed snake to persuade Pennsylvania not to adopt a bicameral legislature. Not having another snake anecdote handy to finish with, we will try to make do with one about a piece of rope. Franklin had been working on a tiring political matter which wearied him and he hoped to be done with it. He said, "I begin to be a little of the sailor's mind when they were handing a cable out of a store into a ship, and one of them said, 'Tis a long, heavy cable. I wish we could see the end of it.' 'D——n me,' says another, 'if I believe it has any end. Somebody has cut it off.' "

19

ON GETTING ALONG WITH PEOPLE

FRANKLIN HAS BEEN REFERRED TO AS A PARAGON but it would be more correct to describe him as a polygon. A multi-sided individual involved in many disparate pursuits with many different people, he brought to each his characteristic trademark of wisdom sprinkled with wit.

A neighbor in Philadelphia had a vexing problem which he took to Franklin, seeking advice. It seemed that people would steal into his yard and tap a keg of beer which he kept there. What should he do to prevent it? Franklin's answer was simple: "Put a pipe [cask] of Madeira [wine] alongside it." He gave some better advice to Polly Stevenson on avoiding seasickness, in an account he gave her of his boat trip to France.

> At Dover . . . we embarked for Calais with a number of passengers who had never been before at sea. They would previously make a hearty breakfast because if the wind should fail we might not get over till supper time. Doubtless they thought that when they had paid for their breakfast they had a right to it, and that, when they had swallowed it, they were sure of it. But they had scarce been out half an hour before the sea laid claim to it, and they were obliged to deliver it up. So it seems there are uncertainties, even beyond those between the cup and the lip. If you ever go to sea, take my advice

and live sparingly a day or two beforehand. The sickness, if any,
will be lighter and soon over.

After a long letter in which he bemoans people's neglecting necessities due to the expense of vain luxuries, he ends as follows: "Almost all parts of our bodies require some expense. The feet demand shoes; the legs, stockings; the rest of the body, clothing; and the belly, a good deal of victuals. Our eyes, though exceedingly useful, ask . . . only the cheap assistance of spectacles, which could not much impair our finances. But the eyes of other people are the eyes that ruin us. If all but myself were blind, I should want neither fine clothes, fine houses, nor fine furniture."

Franklin understood the world and its shortcomings very well. In 1730, as editor of the *Gazette,* he wrote a column condemning dishonest merchants. "There are a great many retailers who falsely imagine that being historical * (the modern phrase for lying) is much for their advantage. And some of them have a saying, 'That 'tis a pity lying is a sin, it is so useful in trade.' " In a paper he wrote calling for reform of the overly severe criminal laws, he digressed to tell an anecdote about an inmate at Newgate prison who found that during the night somebody had taken the buckles out of his shoes. The fellow cried, "What the devil! Have we thieves among us? Let us search out the rogue and pump him to death."

But as with all good reformers, he had to take stock of the world as it was. He told about a Frenchman who was sentenced to be hanged for larceny. " 'Who ever heard,' the culprit asked, 'of a man worth 200,000 livres being hanged?' And he got off." In Paris during the war, Franklin wore no wig. Someone at a party said to him, "You must be deprived of wigs in Philadelphia?" To which he retorted, "We have a greater need of men than of wigs."

Franklin enjoyed all types of humor and had no prejudice against puns. He told a friend, "Your string of puns" made us 'very merry,' adding, "You will allow me to claim a little merit or demerit in the last, as having a hand in making you a punster." In his revealing portrait of Franklin, "Benjamin Franklin, Philosopher and Man," A. O. Aldridge tells of Franklin's participation in a ribald punning session. He attended a meeting of a men's group called the Tuesday Club, at which the secretary proposed that one of the members who was plan-

---

* probably the origin of our meaning for *lying:* 'telling a story.'

ning to leave the club, be "from a long standing . . . transmogrified in an honorary member." Another member objected, "Why, Mr. Secretary, you would not have us dock the gentleman. I suppose the member, however he may stand now at this juncture, is as long as ever." After much laughter, the president rejoined, "The longstanding members methinks are waggish." Franklin picked up the jest with the comment, "Longstanding members, I think gentlemen . . . are not so properly waggish, because if they stand they cannot wag."

In writing to a lawyer in Philadelphia he contrived some punning in Latin and deviously extracted a little Rabelaisian humor. "Your copy of Kempis [Thomas à Kempis, 15th century ecclesiastic], must be a corrupt one," he joked, "if it has that passage as you quote it, *in omnibus requiem quaesivi, sed non inveni, nisi in angulo libello* [Everywhere I have sought relaxation, but I have not found it, except in a corner with a book]. The good father understood pleasure (requiem) better, and wrote, *in angulo cum puella* [in a corner with a girl]. Correct it thus without hesitation. I know there is another reading, *in angulo puellae* [in the corner of a girl]; but this reject, though more to the point, as an expression too indelicate."

Franklin believed in a natural order in the universe. Men were meant to marry and raise families, and when he came to London he was disturbed by the prevailing custom of men delaying marriage in order to enjoy the bachelor's carefree life. He wrote to his friend Sargent, "The account you give me of your family is pleasing, except that your eldest son continues so long unmarried. I hope he does not intend to live and die in celibacy. The wheel of life that has rolled down to him from Adam without interruption should not stop with him. I would not have one dead unbearing branch of the genealogical tree of the Sargents. The married state is, after all our jokes, the happiest, being conformable to our natures. Man and woman have each of them qualities and tempers in which the other is deficient, and which in union contribute to the common felicity. Single and separate they are not the complete human beings: they are like the odd halves of scissors; they cannot answer the end of their formation." In his own case, he attempted to make the best of what was not a perfect marriage. When he heard people say they were tired of something and were ready to give up, he urged perseverance and said, "Well, do as married people do, tire and begin again."

He was fond of children and got along very well with them, as he did with people of all ages. He enjoyed their company and, in the case of his own children and grandchildren, he tended to be over-indulgent with them. The fact that William was not more like him and that Temple was a playboy may have been the result of his lack of sternness. In his old age, when he was very ill in bed, a friend reported that when his grandsons were playing very noisily outside, he would open his window and call to them: "Boys, can't you play without making so much noise. I am reading and it disturbs me very much." The servants said he never used an angry word to any of them. Franklin is quoted as saying: "Children should be treated like strangers who arrive from an unknown country and must be politely taught the customs of ours." In a letter to his sister, he revealed his sympathetic understanding of boys: "I have brought up four or five myself, and have frequently observed that if their shoes were bad they would say nothing of a new pair till Sunday morning just as the bell rung. If you asked them why they did not get ready, the answer was prepared, 'I have no shoes,' and so of other things, hats and the like. Or if they knew of anything that wanted mending, it was a secret till Sunday morning. And sometimes I believe they would rather tear a little than be without an excuse."

In a bagatelle to Madam Brillon, Franklin recalled an incident from his own childhood that taught him a lesson: "When I was a child of seven years old . . . I went directly to a shop where they sold toys for children, and being charmed with the sound of a whistle . . . gave all my money for it. When I came home, whistling all over the house, much pleased with my whistle but disturbing all the family, my brothers, sisters, and cousins, understanding the bargain I had made, told me I had given four times as much for it as it was worth, put me in mind what good things I might have bought with the rest of the money and laughed at me so much for my folly that I cried with vexation. And the reflection gave me more chagrin than the whistle gave me pleasure." Now for the lesson: "This however was afterward of use to me, the impression continuing on my mind; so that often when I was tempted to buy some unnecessary thing, I said to myself, 'Do not give too much for the whistle,' and I saved my money. As I grew up . . . and observed the actions of men, I thought I met many who gave too much for the whistle." Among his examples were an over-ambitious fortune-seeker, a miser, a spendthrift, and "a beautiful, sweet-tempered girl married to an ill-natured brute of a husband.'' He felt that a great part of the miseries of mankind were caused by the false estimates people put on the value of things—giving too much for the whistle. No austere moralist, but an understanding human being, Franklin concludes his piece: ''Yet I ought to have charity for those unhappy people when I consider that with all this wisdom of which I am boasting, there are certain things in the world so tempting . . . if they were put to sale at auction, I might very easily be led to ruin myself in the purchase and find that I had once more given too much for the whistle.'' In this confession, he is humorously referring to the beautiful but married recipient of his missive, Madam Brillon, as the cause of his possible weakness to temptation.

Franklin supervised the education of his son William, who studied law, his grandson Benny Bache, whom he directed into his own craft of printing, and his grandson William Temple Franklin, who served as his secretary in France and whom he hoped would make a career in government service. He once counseled Temple, ''You are now in that time of life which is the properest to store your mind with such knowledge as is hereafter to be ornamental and useful to you. I confide that you have too much sense to let the season slip. The ancients painted opportunity as an old man with wings to his feet and shoulders, a great lock of hair on the forepart of his head, but bald behind. Whence comes our old saying, 'Take time by the forelock'; as much as to say, when it is past there is no means of pulling it back again, as there is no lock behind to take hold for that purpose.''

A staunch advocate of education, Franklin stated, ''Learning, whether speculative or practical is . . . the natural source of wealth and honor.'' He wanted young people to acquire through education ''that benignity of mind which shows itself in searching for and seizing every opportunity to serve and to oblige, and is the foundation of what is called 'good breeding.' '' These were goals that he set for himself as well, and were largely responsible for his successful relationship with people.

He informed the Governor of Georgia how New England provided education in the sparsely populated frontier settlements. A township of sixty families first chose a spot for their town, where they cleared about twenty acres, round which they placed their houses, fifteen on a side. In the middle of the square they erected a church and a school, stockaded around as a fort in case of attack from Indians. "Behind each house was a garden plot, then an orchard, and then a pasture for a cow or two, and behind all, outwards, their corn field." Thus situated, one house could not be attacked without . . . giving alarm to the rest . . . "Then they had the advantage of giving schooling to their children, securing their morals by the influence of religion, and improving each other by civil society and conversation." In remote settlements in Pennsylvania, Franklin observed, the people did not have these advantages of education, "and we are in danger of bringing up a set of savages of our own color."

In regard to Negroes, Franklin found free Negroes not by nature "deficient in natural understanding" but, he explained, "they have not the advantage of education." As President for the Society for Abolition of Slavery, he set up a plan for the instruction of children of free blacks. They would either "attend regularly the schools already established in this city [integration], or form others . . . that the pupils may receive such learning as is necessary for their future situation in life."

Education to Franklin was necessary not only for earning a living, but for making a person able to appreciate the world about him. He referred to the latter as "ornamental" knowledge. Talking to a young man who was ready to take a trip to Italy, Franklin advised him to acquire some knowledge of the country first, because without prior knowledge he would learn little from travel. "To see monuments requires only eyes, but to appreciate them requires a judgment exercised by comparisons and enlightened by study." He was annoyed by the fact that in the formal education of his time so much attention was given to Latin and Greek. He wrote, "There is in mankind an unaccountable prejudice in favor of ancient customs," and he found these to be perpetuated even after the circumstances that had once made them useful ceased to exist. The *"chapeau-bras,"* or hat that Frenchmen still carried under their arm to be stylish although it was not meant to be worn was a favorite example, and he termed "the prevailing custom of having schools for teaching generally our children in these days the Latin and Greek languages . . . the *chapeau-bras* of modern literature."

Another custom which earned Franklin's aroused criticism was that of teaching children to use the right hand to the detriment of the left. One of his bagatelles, "A Petition of the Left Hand," is a vehicle for his ideas on the subject. In it, "The Left Hand" addresses herself to the superintendents of education:

> . . . There are twin sisters of us; and the two eyes of man do not more resemble, nor are capable of being upon better terms with each other than my sister and myself, were it not for the partiality of our parents who make the most injurious distinctions between us. From my infancy I have been led to consider my sister as being of a more elevated rank. I was suffered to grow up without the least instruction while nothing was spared in her education. She had masters to teach her writing, drawing, music . . . but if by chance I touched a pencil, pen, or a needle, I was bitterly rebuked. And more than once I have been beaten for being awkward . . .
>
> But conceive not, Sirs, that my complaints are instigated merely by vanity . . . If any indisposition should attack my sister . . . the gout, rheumatism, and cramp, without making mention of other accidents, what would be the fate of our poor family?

A letter, apparently written by Franklin, to a French newspaper addressed itself to this same subject.

> . . . For a long time people have been writing against the absurd practice of requiring children to use the right hand and making them almost inept in using the other, although nature has actually made us ambidextrous. Several mothers have so well realized the justice of these protests that they have overcome the ancient prejudice and no longer oppose this natural equality . . . One day a child who was scolded for not using the right hand exclusively, upon being corrected by his governess, gave her a brisk blow. The mother, who was present, instead of punishing him, said . . . "Oh dear, my son, always with the left hand!"

Education, in Franklin's view, should be provided for adults as well as children. He did not mean formal education but information in books and periodicals. He makes his point, finishing with a figure of speech taken from science, but familiar to every blacksmith.

> The ancient Roman and Greek orators could only speak to the number of citizens capable of being assembled within the reach of their voice. Their writings had little effect, because the bulk of the people could not read. Now by the press we can speak to nations, and good books and well written pamphlets have great and general influence. The facility with which the same truths may be repeatedly enforced by placing them daily in different lights in newspapers,

which are everywhere read, gives a great chance of establishing them. And we now find that it is not only right to strike while the iron is hot, but that it may be very practicable to heat it by continually striking.

In this regard, Franklin followed his own advice and it made him a very effective propagandist. There was one subject, however, which remained taboo for him in his writing. That was religion. One experience he had as a young printer taught him a lesson he never forgot. In an advertisement he printed about a ship-sailing there was a postscript, "No sea hens or black gowns will be admitted on any terms." Sea hens are a species of auk that make a great uproar in their nesting grounds. Black gowns everyone knew to be clergymen. What the postscript meant and why it was used is obscure. It seems to have been a prank, either by Franklin or the ad-maker, but it backfired on Franklin. The ministers in Philadelphia were furious. Franklin responded publicly in his own defense.

He began by admitting that he had made a mistake by not refusing the ad, but it was done and could not be revoked. He would offer a few particulars in his behalf by way of mitigation, and cleverly made a request of his readers: "I desire none of them [the particulars] may be read when the reader is not in very good humor." He explained that he committed the deed without malice, having received the ad with the postscript on it, which he thought was there merely to attract attention and had no real meaning. He had never heard of sea-hens before and though he knew that black gowns referred to the clergy he could not imagine that a trifling mention of their dress would cause any disturbance. He was friendly with many clergy and would not be so stupid as to cause them offense. If he had any malicious intent, why had he not before talked against the clergy which was generally known to be the easiest topic on which to be witty. He was paid five shillings for the ad and none of the people who were angry with him for printing it would have given him so much to let it alone. If all the people of different opinions in Pennsylvania would give him as much for not printing things as he could get by printing them, he would live a very easy life but there would be very little printed. Notwithstanding the rashness of youth, he assured his readers that he had a better record of avoiding offenses against either church or state than any other printer in the province. "And lastly," he stated, "I have printed above a thousand advertisements which made not the least mention of sea-hens or black gowns; and this being the first offense, I have the more reason to expect forgiveness. I shall take leave to conclude with an old fable . . ."

> A certain well-meaning man and his son were travelling towards a market town, with an ass which they had to sell. The road was bad; and the old man therefore rode, but the son went a-foot. The first passenger they met asked the father if he was not ashamed to ride by himself and suffer the poor lad to wade along through the mire; this induced him to take up his son behind him. He had not travelled far when he met others who said they were two unmerciful lubbers to get both on the back of that poor ass, in such a deep road. Upon this the old man got off, and let his son ride alone. The next they met called the lad a graceless, rascally young jackanapes, to ride in that manner through the dirt while his aged father trudged along on foot; and they said the old man was a fool for suffering it. He then bid his son come down and walk with him, and they travelled on leading the ass by the halter; till they met another company who called them a couple of senseless blockheads for going both on foot in such a dirty way, when they had an empty ass with them which they might ride upon. The old man could bear it no longer. "My son," said he, "it grieves me much that we cannot please all these people. Let me throw the ass over the next bridge, and be no further troubled with him."

Franklin emphasizes that although he has a disposition almost as complying as the old man in the fable, he will not imitate him: "I shall not burn my press and melt my letters."

Toward the end of his life Franklin found himself not the accused but the accuser of the press. In the early days of the new government of the United States, the leaders found themselves frequently under vicious attack by an abusive press. Washington was called a fool by nature, Franklin a fool from old age. Franklin referred to these malevolent critics as bug writers "who will abuse you while you are serving them, and wound your character in nameless pamphlets; thereby resembling these dirty stinking insects that attack us only in the dark, disturb our repose, molesting and wounding us, while our sweat and blood are contributing to their subsistence." In a letter, he told a friend, "You do well to avoid being concerned in the pieces of personal abuse so scandalously common in our newspapers . . . as would disgrace us." He thought strangers reading these papers would see Americans in terms of the story of the two quarrelers in a coffee house. They were hurling invectives at each other, using such words as rogue, villain, rascal, scoundrel, etc., when seeing a gentleman sitting nearby, they attempted to refer their dispute to him. "I know nothing of you or your affairs," said he, "I only perceive that you know one another."

In a satirical essay Franklin referred to the "Supremest Court," namely, the "Court of the Press." This court may judge, sentence, and condemn to infamy, with or without an inquiry or hearing, at its discretion, all private individuals and public bodies. This court is established for the benefit of about one citizen in 500 who shall have the privilege of accusing and abusing the other 499 parts at their pleasure. Any man who has a knack for scribbling and can procure a press and a huge pair of blacking balls may commission himself to daub his blacking balls in your face if you make the least complaint. This court is not governed by any of the rules of courts of law. The accused is not allowed to know the name of his accuser or to confront witnesses against him. Its authority is founded in an article of the Constitution which established "Liberty of the Press," but it seems more like the liberty of the press that criminals have before conviction by the common law of England, that is the liberty to be "pressed to death" or to be hanged. If you object when your character is torn to flitters you are charged with being an enemy of the liberty of the press. If this so-called liberty consists of the power of affronting, calumniating, and defaming one another, I, for my part, says Franklin, "shall cheerfully consent to exchange my liberty of abusing others for the privilege of not being abused myself."

Since in the Constitution, there is provision for checks in government, if we are not to infringe upon the liberty of the press there must be another liberty to check it. "I mean the liberty of the cudgel," says Franklin. In primitive society if one man affronted another he would return the insult with a box on the ear, without breaking any law. "My proposal then is to leave the liberty of the press untouched . . . but to permit the liberty of the cudgel to go with it *pari passu* [side by side]. Thus, my fellow citizens, if an impudent writer attacks your reputation, dearer to you perhaps than your life, and puts his name to the charge, you may go to him as openly and break his head. If he conceals himself behind the printer and you can nevertheless discover who he is, you may in a like manner waylay him in the night and give him a good drubbing.'' For offenses against the public rather than private individuals, Franklin would be more lenient. In such cases, he proposed, ''we should in moderation content ourselves with tarring and feathering, and tossing them in a blanket.''

Dealing with this subject of abuse by the press, he noted the inconsistence of the name, Philadelphia, meaning brotherly love, with the spirit of rancor, malice, and hatred by its newspapers. According to them, ''a petty fiddler, sycophant, and scoundrel'' was appointed judge of the Admiralty; ''an old woman and fomenter of sedition'' to be another of the judges, with ''two harpies'' for comptroller and naval officer. The President of the Assembly of Pennsylvania, who was elected by unanimous choice (Franklin himself), was described as ''an old rogue'' who gave his assent to the federal Constitution merely to avoid refunding money he had purloined from the United States.

A stranger reading these newspapers, Franklin indicated, would be led to believe ''that Pennsylvania is peopled by a set of the most unprincipled, wicked, rascally, and quarrelsome scoundrels on the face of the globe.'' Franklin found some consolation, however, in the obituaries that the newspapers printed. He told the editor of a Philadelphia paper, ''Though living, you give one another [Pennsylvanians] the characters of devils; dead, you are all angels! It is delightful, when any of you die, to read what good husbands, good fathers, good friends, good citizens, and good Christians you were, concluding with a scrap of poetry that places you with certainty, every one in heaven. So that I think Pennsylvania a good country to die in, though a very bad one to live in.''

20

SCIENCE CAN BE FUN

SCIENCE CAN BE FUN—IF YOU'RE LIKE Benjamin Franklin. Franklin was a serious scientist, but not all of the time. No matter how grave the activity he was involved in, his native humor, like water in a burlap sack, always leaked through.

Franklin had the natural prerequisites for a scientist: curiosity and inventiveness. When he was a boy he loved to swim and found he could greatly improve his propulsion through the water by attaching oval palettes to his hands and something like sandals to his feet. It's too bad that he didn't think of goggles for he surely would have enjoyed underwater exploration. But he did perform an experiment that sounds like great fun. While flying a kite he came to a pond which was nearly one mile across and deciding to take a dip, he tied the kite to a stake. Seeing the kite flying in the air while he was swimming he thought of combining both sports:

"I found that lying on my back and holding the stick in my hands, I was drawn along the surface of the water in a very agreeable manner. Having then engaged another boy to carry my clothes . . . to a place . . . on the other side, I began to cross the pond with my kite, which carried me quite over without the least fatigue and with the greatest pleasure imaginable."

Describing the event many years later to a scientist friend in

France, Franklin speculated that it might be possible to cross the English Channel from Dover to Calais in this manner. But on second thought he concluded the packet boat would still be preferable.

A boy so adept with a kite might go far one day, especially in the realm of science. As a young man returning home from England by ship, he demonstrated the qualities of a good scientist in his keen observation and careful notations. He observed that the brilliant colors of the dolphin disappear when the fish dies, but when it is cut in pieces for bait the pieces retain the original lustre and fine color. In the journal of his voyage he recorded that the flying fish with its finny wings and forked tail was able to fly for fifty yards straight forward at a height of a yard or two above the water before dropping back into the water. As the ship neared port he described a heron that lodged aboard. " 'Tis a long-legged, long necked bird, having as they say but one gut. They live upon fish, and will swallow a living eel thrice sometimes before it will remain in their body."

And most peculiar of all on that voyage was the gulf weed, which bore a fruit of the animal kind, very surprising to see. "It was a small shell fish [shaped] like a heart." These vegetable animals "were visibly animated, opening their shells every moment and thrusting out a set of unformed claws, not unlike those of a crab; but the inner part was still a kind of soft jelly." Life on shipboard was dull and boring for most of the passengers, but if you were a keen observer it could be full of strange wonders and delights.

As a philomath, Franklin predicted the weather and as a newspaperman he posed riddles. What would he have done with this riddle? On the evening of October 21, 1743, a man in Philadelphia was planning to observe an eclipse of the moon at 9 p.m. but it was obscured by a northeast storm which blew in about 7 p.m. Yet in Boston, 400 miles to the northeast, the storm hit at 11 o'clock that night and didn't interfere with the eclipse, according to the Boston newspaper. If the storm came from the northeast, why didn't it hit Boston first? This is what perplexed the man in Philadelphia, who liked to solve riddles as well as ask them. He wrote his brother in Boston and confirmed the facts. He obtained information from several Colonies between the two cities and made sure it was the same storm, learning that the farther the Colonies were from Philadelphia the later the storm reached them. The solution he proposed to the riddle is as follows:

If the air in a room is at rest and a fire is made in the chimney, the heated air in the chimney is lighter and rises, and the air next to the chimney flows in to replace it, and so on successively right back to the door. The motion (*i.e.,* the storm) proceeds backwards towards the door (*i.e.,* Boston) but the direction of the flow (*i.e.,* wind) is toward the chimney (*i.e.,* Philadelphia). Looking at the coastline of America he suggested that the air is heated over Florida and the Gulf of Mexico and rises, being replaced by the next colder, denser air successively to the north. The motion is directed to the northeast by the coastline and the inland ridge of mountains which lie in a northeast-southwest direction.

Thus, sitting in his chair in Philadelphia, Franklin very simply explained the fierce northeast storms that rage down, or shall we say up, the continent of North America. He said modestly: "If my hypothesis is not the truth, it is at least as naked. For I have not with some of our learned moderns disguised my nonsense in Greek, clothed it in algebra, or adorned it with fluxions [calculus.] You have it in *puris naturalibus.*"

Franklin had the uncanny ability to see right to the heart of a problem and to describe it simply and clearly. His description of his invention in 1740 of the famous Franklin stove, or Pennsylvanian Fire-Place as he called it, was so masterful that a Franklin biographer said he was "inclined to lay down the principle that the test of literary genius is the ability to be fascinating about stoves."

While Franklin went on to invent bifocal eyeglasses, chart the Gulf Stream, and theorize on the nature of light etc., his greatest contribution to science, as everyone knows, was in electricity. He did not sit in his chair and speculate on this mysterious new fluid; he built apparatus and conducted many experiments, the most celebrated being his demonstration that lightning was electricity. But unlike the famous kite, some of Franklin's experiments were designed not to draw lightning but to draw laughter.

One experiment, called the Golden Fish, describes the action of a piece of gold leaf cut in such a way as to move when electrified, like a fish: "For if you take it by the tail and hold it at a foot . . . from the prime conductor, it will . . . fly to it with a brisk but wavering motion, like that of an eel through the water." Near the prime conductor it continually shakes its tail like a fish so that it seems alive. If you turn its tail toward the prime conductor, "then it flies to your finger, and seems to nibble it.'' All this to the great entertainment of the spectators.

Then there was the counterfeit spider, with a body of burnt cork and legs of linen thread. It was suspended by fine silk thread over a table with two upright wires. With an electrified vial the spider is animated and immediately flies to the wire near the vial, bending its legs in touching it, then springing off to fly to the other wire, hopping back and forth for an hour or more in dry weather. We are assured by its creator that the little spider appeared perfectly alive to persons unacquainted with the trick.

To heighten the fun, a person was electrified with the help of the "electrised" bottle and a wire. There were sparks every time his face or hand was touched. And the trick called the electric kiss was not only electrifying but positively shocking:

> Let A and B stand on wax; . . . give one of them the electrised phial [vial] in hand; let the other take hold of the wire; there will be a small spark; but when their lips approach, they will be struck and shocked.

An experiment called The Conspirators went much further—it was a test of loyalty. A picture of the King ("God preserve him") is made into a magical picture, with gold leaf behind it. A moveable gilt crown is placed on the king's head and the picture is moderately electrified. Now if a person takes hold of the frame with one hand so that his fingers touch the gilding, and with the other hand tries to take off the crown, he receives a terrible blow and fails in the attempt. "If the picture were highly charged, the consequence might perhaps be fatal as that of high treason." A spark from the picture was found to make a hole through all 48 sheets of a quire of paper, even though this thickness of paper was shown to be good armor against a sword or even a pistol bullet. The canny operator, who proves his loyalty by touching the face of the picture and the crown without a shock, is careful to hold the picture by the upper end where the back of the frame has no gilt.

Although Franklin was careful not to get shocked, he was careless on one occasion and received a great blow. He was planning to kill a turkey by electrocution using two large glass jars which contained as much "electrical fire" as forty vials when, distracted by the conversation of the people present, he grabbed a wire and took the full charge through his own body. As a scientist, he dutifully took advantage of the accident to record the incident and describe his sensations. He had been knocked senseless, not feeling anything or hearing the loud crack reported by the visitors. On coming around he noted a swelling in his hand, a violent quick shaking of his body and a general numbness which gradually disappeared, leaving only a soreness in his breastbone. He was embarrassed by the event and remarked wryly that he meant to kill a turkey but nearly killed a goose. It put him in mind of the Irishman and the gunpowder, where the Irishman, "about to steal powder, made a hole in the cask with a hot iron."

In a scientific paper that he wrote that year he stated, "If any one should doubt whether the electrical matter passes thro' the substance of bodies, or only over and along their surfaces, a shock from an electrified large glass jar . . . will probably convince him." It was an experiment, he said, that he desired never to repeat. But he did repeat the experiment of the electrocution killing of fowl, recommending it from his own experience as painless. In addition, he and his associates agreed that it made the birds unusually tender. Fowl, in fact, was the special treat in an electrical party they planned to be held on the banks of the Schuylkill River: "Spirits . . . are to be fired by a spark sent from side to side through the river, without any other conductor than the water . . . A turkey is to be killed for our dinner by the electrical shock, and roasted by the electric jack, before a fire kindled by the electrified bottle: when the healths of all the famous electricians in England, Holland, France, and Germany are to be drank in electrified bumpers, under the discharge of guns from the electrical battery."

For the uninitiated, it should be explained that an electrical jack was a type of motor run by static electricity, used in this case as a rotisserie. A footnote explained that an electrified bumper is a small thin glass tumbler, nearly filled with wine and electrified. When it was brought to the lips it gave a shock, providing the person had no whiskers and did not breathe on the liquor.

Franklin was so besieged with curious spectators that he often had trouble conducting his experiments. He made duplicate sets of apparatus so that other persons could perform the demonstrations for themselves and the curiosity seekers. For one of these persons, a minister without a pastorate named Ebenezer Kinnersley, Franklin planned a series of entertaining lectures which Kinnersley gave in cities from

Boston to Philadelphia with great success. Another such person was Domien, a globe-circling priest of the Greek Church from Transylvania. Seeing that he needed some way of earning a living, Franklin similarly equipped and taught him. Domien went on his way to South Carolina, writing back from Charleston "that he had lived 800 miles upon electricity; it had been meat, drink, and clothing to him."

But it should not be construed from their entertaining appeal that Franklin's experiments were performed merely for entertainment. His work was serious, painstaking, and ingenious, with the results carefully observed and reported to other investigators around the world. In fact, these experiments, which he sandwiched in the few years between his business and political careers, were themselves responsible for transforming electricity from a novel curiosity into a science of its own. And the one experiment that had the greatest influence toward that end was Franklin's proof that lightning was electricity. Other men, including Isaac Newton, had noted the similarity between lightning and electricity but it remained for Franklin to provide the demonstration to convince the world that the fearful bolts from heaven were the same stuff that men could produce and capture in a bottle. Franklin's notebook listed 12 ways lightning and electricity appeared alike. If, in addition to these ways, lightning would be attracted to pointed metal rods as was the electric fluid, then it might be drawn out of the clouds and the similarity would be complete.

Thus came his call to action: *Let the Experiment be Made.* Franklin was no armchair philosopher; he was a modern experimental scientist. If it could be done, let it be done! And indeed it was done—by a French scientist. Surprising as it may seem, Franklin was not the first to pull the sparks out of the sky. But the credit is all Franklin's for it was his experiment, which he wrote up so precisely that it could be followed with complete success by another man he had never met thousands of miles away. Franklin had published his proposed experiment and was waiting for the high steeple to be erected on Christ Church in Philadelphia in order to conduct it, when the French received the description of it from England and carried out Franklin's experiment. The English scientists had ridiculed it until they heard of its startling success in France. The villagers in a French country town were the first astonished humans to hear the crackling sound and see the streaming electric fire drawn from a stormy sky through a pointed iron rod into an electric vial. The experiment was quickly repeated in

Paris where the King of France, who had been shown some of Franklin's other electric experiments and tricks by his scientists, was delighted and commanded that Mr. Franklin of Pennsylvania receive his thanks and compliments.

Not knowing of the French results, Franklin tired of waiting for the church spire and thought that a kite would do even better. It did, and he had the supreme pleasure of seeing the sparks fly to his knuckle from the key he tied to the kite string, thus assuring him that his theory was correct. He should have been even more pleased that he wasn't killed, for an investigator trying the experiment in Russia a year later was killed. When he got word of the French King's commendation, Franklin wrote to a friend: "The *Tatler* [an English periodical] tells us of a girl who was observed to grow suddenly proud, and none could guess the reason till it came to be known she had got on a new pair of garters. Lest you observe anything of the kind in me, I think I will not hide my new garters under my petticoats, but take the freedom to show it to you, in a paragraph of our friend Collinson's letter. I ought . . . not indulge this vanity; I will not transcribe the paragraph, yet I cannot forbear."

Collinson was Franklin's correspondent and supporter in London who conveyed the notice of the French king's honor to him. In Collinson's letter to Franklin, which the latter so "reluctantly" quoted, Collinson said, "I think, now I have stuck a feather in thy cap, I may be allowed to conclude in wishing thee long to wear it." After quoting the above, Franklin wrote: "On considering this paragraph, I fear I have not so much reason to be proud as the girl had; for a feather in the cap is not so useful a thing . . . as a pair of good silk garters." When the English scientists of the Royal Society came to admit that an American tradesman was capable of great discoveries they gave Franklin their highest award, the Copley gold medal. He gratefully accepted the honor and added, "I know not whether any of your learned body have attained the ancient boasted art of multiplying gold; but you have certainly found the art of making it infinitely more valuable."

Despite his great ability Franklin had his share of failures in his electrical research. He commented, "In going on with these experiments, how many pretty systems do we build, which we soon find ourselves obliged to destroy! If there is no other use discovered of electricity, this, however, is something considerable, that it may help to make a vain man humble." And despite his success in discovering the fundamental principles of electricity, as a practical man Franklin could not be satisfied until there was some "use discovered of electricity." He put it this way: "Nor is it of much importance to us to know the manner in which nature executes her laws: 'tis enough if we know the laws themselves. 'Tis of real use to know that china left unsupported will fall and break; but how it comes to fall, and why it breaks, are matters of speculation. 'Tis a pleasure indeed to know them, but we can preserve our china without it."

One use he made of his new discovery about lightning was to provide a convenient way to charge the electrical bottles for his experiments. He fixed an iron rod nine feet above his chimney which was connected to a wire leading to his chamber door, where it was divided in two and to the ends of each, six inches apart, was connected a little bell. Between the bells, suspended by a silk thread, was a little brass ball, "to play between and strike the bells when clouds passed with electricity in them." One night he was awakened by loud cracks of noise and opening his door he saw a dense white stream of electric fire as large as his finger passing from bell to bell and lighting up the staircase as with sunshine. Franklin was as excited as the bells. He happily wrote, "So we are got beyond the skill of Rabelais's devils of two years old who, he humorously says, had only learnt to thunder and lighten a little round the head of a cabbage." But the rod connected by a wire to the ground served another purpose; it protected the house from the destructive effect of lightning. Franklin was, as the philosopher Kant said, a new Prometheus who had stolen fire from heaven. Now he had tamed it as well. The terror that lightning struck in the hearts of people from fear of physical harm and divine rebuke could thus be diminished. Some of the preachers did not like his stealing their fire, if not their thunder, which they interpreted as a sign of God's wrath, but when their dire predictions failed to occur, the lightning rods appeared on colonial houses almost like television antennas in modern times.

Not only did Franklin's rod give its inventor great fame around the world, it served him in a very practical way as well: "My own house was one day attacked with lightning, which occasioned the neighbors to run in to give assistance, in case of its being on fire. But no damage was done, and my family was only found a good deal frightened with the violence of the explosion. Last year, my house being enlarged, the conductor [rod] was obliged to be taken down. I found, upon examination, that the pointed termination of copper . . . had been almost entirely melted. Thus . . . this invention has proved of use to the author of it, and has added this personal advantage to the pleasure he before received from having been useful to others.''

When friends asked him how they could be safe from lightning in a house without lightning rods, he answered: ''The safest place is in the middle of the room, sitting in one chair and laying the feet up in another. It is still safer to bring two or three mattresses or beds into the middle of the room and, folding them double, place the chair upon them; for they not being so good conductors as the walls, the lightning will not choose an interrupted course through the air of the room and bedding when it can go through a continued better conductor, the wall.''

With his success and acclaim there was bound to be dispute and jealousy. When a French experimenter attacked his theories, Franklin decided not to reply: ''I concluded to let my papers shift for themselves, believing it was better to spend what time I could spare from public business in making new experiments than in disputing those already made.'' When a powder-magazine in Europe had been exploded by lightning, the Royal Society was asked to recommend the best method for protecting British arsenals. A committee was appointed which recommended Franklin's system, with one of the members dissenting. The dissenter claimed that points on the rods would needlessly attract the lightning stroke and thought knobs should be used instead. He published two pamphlets in defense of his view and became violently angry when the committee, which included Franklin, ignored them. Franklin did not respond but again explained his position: ''I have never entered into any controversy in defence of my philosophical opinions; I leave them to take their chance in the world. If they are right, truth and experience will support them, if wrong, they ought to be refuted and rejected. Disputes are apt to sour one's temper and disturb one's quiet. I have no private interest in the reception of my inventions by the world, having never made nor propose to make the least profit by any of them.'' Franklin never did attempt to patent or exploit any of his inventions, although others did and some inventions, like the stove, were very profitable. He felt that like charity and good works they were his public contribution.

The dispute over points and knobs continued until after the Revolutionary War had begun, when none other than his royal highness,

King George III, entered into the scientific controversy against the traitor Franklin by ordering that pointed rods on the royal palace be replaced by blunt conductors. This action invoked Franklin's reaction: "The King's changing his pointed conductors for blunt ones is . . . . a matter of small importance to me. If I had a wish about it, it would be that he had rejected them altogether as ineffectual. For it is only since he thought himself and family safe from the thunder of heaven that he dared to use his own thunder in destroying his innocent subjects."

Some wits in England had the last say by picking up the dispute and translating it into verse.

> While you, great George, for safety hunt,
> And sharp conductors change for blunt,
>   The nation's out of joint:
> Franklin a wiser course pursues,
> And all your thunder fearless views,
>   By keeping to the point.

If by any chance you happened to have been near Collington, Maryland, sometime during April of 1755 and saw a heavy set man on horseback chasing a whirlwind and thrashing at it furiously with his whip you might have thought he was a madman. You would have been wrong; it was just Ben Franklin of Philadelphia doing one of his things. Franklin was in Maryland to confer with General Braddock when he made a social visit to Colonel Tasker at his country home. As they were out riding they saw in a vale below them a small whirlwind beginning in the road, which showed itself by the dust it raised. "It appeared in the form of a sugar-loaf, spinning on its point, moving up the hill toward us, and enlarging as it came forward." The part near the ground he estimated to be no bigger than a barrel but it widened upwards till it seemed at 40–50 high, to be 20–30 feet in diameter. "The rest of the company stood looking after it; but my curiosity being stronger, I followed it, riding close by its side."

As he inspected this unusual phenomenon at close range he recalled the common notion that its relative, the water-spout, could be broken with a rifle shot. Not having a rifle, he tried to beat the little whirlwind to death by striking it again and again with his whip, but to no effect. As it moved, the whirlwind grew in size and intensity picking up leaves and breaking branches with such a fury that Franklin no longer wondered why his whipping didn't subdue it. He continued to follow it and observe its course and development for three-quarters of a mile until the flying debris made it too dangerous to be near. He watched it until it left the woods and crossed an old tobacco field, where finding no dust or leaves to pick up, it gradually became invisible.

He rejoined the group who were commenting on the vast height of the leaves now over their heads due to the whirlwind. When Franklin asked Colonel Tasker if such whirlwinds were common in Maryland, he answered pleasantly: "No, not at all common; but we got this on purpose to treat Mr. Franklin." Franklin remarked to Collinson, "And a very high treat it was too . . ."

In recounting Franklin's many accomplishments in science and invention one should not lose sight of his deficiencies. Why didn't he invent the bicycle? The wheel had already been invented; why not two, connected in a line? It would have been so easy for him. The simple truth is that he never thought of it. He was too busy dabbling in politics, doing electrical tricks, and pouring oil on water. The ancients had a belief that oil calmed troubled waters. Was there any truth to it? Benjamin Franklin was just the man to find out. His attention was first attracted to the matter when he was at sea in a convoy of 96 ships and he observed that the wakes of two of the ships were unusually smooth compared to the others. He asked the captain for some explanation: "The cooks," said he, "have I suppose been just emptying their greasy water through the scuppers, which has greased the sides of those ships a little." The captain spoke with some contempt as if this was something anybody should know. Franklin had little regard for this explanation until he remembered reading as a youth Pliny's account of the practice of seamen of that time pouring oil into the sea to still the waves in a storm. He had smiled when he first read it but he did not smile now. This was not a matter for mere speculation; let the experiment be made!

He went to a pond and dropped oil on it. It spread with surprising swiftness on the water but it did not smooth the waves. He had applied the oil on the side toward which the wind was blowing and the wind drove the oil back upon the shore. Now he tried the experiment on the other side. To his huge pleasure the oil, not more than a teaspoonful, produced an instant calm over several square yards and gradually extended itself until a quarter of the pond, about half an acre, was as smooth as glass. In his experiments he noticed the sudden, forcible spreading of the drop of oil on the face of the water, which didn't occur when he dropped the oil on polished marble or glass. On water the oil spread to become so thin as to produce prismatic colors, and beyond that to become invisible but still having its smoothing effect on the waves. Franklin was describing for the first time the phenomenon of monomolecular films, the study of which was to win Dr. Irving Langmuir the Nobel prize in 1932. Langmuir is better known, however, for his Franklinian-style demonstration of rain-making by seeding clouds.

An odd occurrence was reported to Franklin that related to his previous observations with oil and water. A pupil of another investigator noticed that when he was about to clean up a little cup in which he had kept oil and threw upon the water some flies that had drowned in the oil, the flies began to move and turn around on the water as if they were alive. Franklin guessed that the cause was the same as he had previously observed with the drop of oil and to prove it he made artificial flies with bits of oiled chips and paper, which acted in the same way. In the scientific account of his experiments Franklin said that whenever he went into the country he took a little oil in the upper hollow joint of his bamboo cane with which he could repeat the experiment as the opportunity might offer. This is all he says about it, but thanks to the anecdotes about Franklin by his friends we learn one of the ways he performed the experiment. One day when Franklin and his friends were walking together in the country, according to the account, he stopped still and dramatically claimed that he could quiet the waves on a small stream that was being whipped by the wind. He went off two hundred paces above where the others stood, then made some magic passes over the water and waved his bamboo cane three times in the air. The incredulous audience stood in astonishment as they saw the waves gradually sink and the stream become like a mirror. What kind of a magician was this Franklin! After enjoying his sport, Franklin revealed the secret of his cane and explained the experiment.

One time when he was pouring oil on the water, a farmer seeing the results, imagined some kind of supernatural influence and asked in amazement, "Tell me, what am I to believe?" "Only what you have seen and nothing else," was Franklin's blunt answer. He later commented: "This man, being witness to something extraordinary was ready to believe the wildest absurdities—such is the logic of three-fourths of the human race." In the same vein, he lamented that there are everywhere people who "think of inventions as miracles: there might be such formerly, but they are ceased." The age of miracles was past, the miracles of these days were performed by men of science like himself.

What made a true scientist? According to Franklin, it was care and accuracy in making observations. He deprecated himself as having too strong a penchant for building hypotheses, too little patience for details. As in a recipe, every detail is important to the overall success. In writing to William Brownrigg, the English physician to whom he directed his correspondence about the oil-on-water experiments, he wondered if Mrs. Brownrigg had failed in making parmesan cheese, since nothing had been heard about it. He joked that as a lady scientist she would not be discouraged by one or two failures. Perhaps, he suggested, something was omitted from the recipe. He recalled a foreign gentleman who acquired a taste for plum pudding in England and brought home a recipe for making it, only to be dismayed at seeing it brought to the table in the form of a soup. The cook declared he had followed the recipe exactly, but when it came to be examined there was discovered a small but important omission. "There was no mention of the bag." Plum pudding, as every Englishman knew, was boiled in a cloth bag to keep it from falling apart.

Once Franklin took up his political duties as agent for Pennsylvania in England his activity as an experimentalist diminished, but he found a satisfying new role as a science-statesman. He served on committees of scientific societies and kept up a voluminous correspondence with scientists from many countries, assisting and encouraging them in their efforts. When, in 1783, the Montgolfier brothers launched the first airship, the hot air balloon, Franklin was the American Ambassador to France. France was soon agog with ballooning and Franklin was among the most enthusiastic, following all the developments and contributing to a fund to support such experiments. Montgolfier paid him a visit and reported his experiences personally, inviting Franklin to watch some new experiments. Franklin was also well acquainted with J. A. C. Charles, who made the first hydrogen-filled balloon and rose in it to great heights in the sky. Charles—for whom Charles' Law on the expansion of gases with heat is named—considered himself a disciple of Franklin, who in turn, so admired Charles' ability that he exclaimed, "Nature cannot say no to him!" When partisans of the Montgolfiers hot air balloon clashed with

Charles' hydrogen balloon enthusiasts, Franklin played the part of peacemaker saying the balloon was a baby, of which Montgolfier was the father and Charles the wet nurse. When, with all of Paris, Franklin was enchantedly watching a balloon ascension, a cynic who was indifferent to the general enthusiasm asked him disparagingly, "What good is it?" Franklin's famous answer that swept Paris was, "What good is a newborn baby?" In a similar statement, he said of the balloon, "It is a child; perhaps it won't amount to much, perhaps it will be very brilliant. We will have to see its education completed first."

Franklin did think of some uses for balloons. He predicted their advantage in warfare, allowing a combatant to survey the enemy on the ground. He also envisioned himself being transported comfortably in the basket of a balloon with a man or horse on the ground pulling him around. This sort of conveyance was appealing since he was then suffering from a kidney stone which pained him terribly when he drove over bumpy roads in a carriage. He imagined a balloon might be anchored in place and meat could be raised to it by pulleys, to be preserved in the cold upper atmosphere. Water could be frozen in the same way when ice was needed.

In the popular excitement over ballooning, the wife of Franklin's scientist friend LeRoy went up for a balloon ride with some ladies and Franklin wrote her: "How courageous of you to go up so high in the air! And how kind of you, once you were so close to Heaven, not to want to leave us all and stay with the Angels." Franklin loved to tease the ladies and he often alluded to science in so doing. In Paris where he was so popular, women ardently bid for his presence and attention. When one of them feigned jealousy and asked if he didn't love her the most, he called on both diplomacy and electricity, "Yes," he responded, "when you are the nearest to me, because of the force of attraction."

He might rely on geometry to make his point, as in the case of Madame Brillon who charged him teasingly about his unfaithfulness to her. He countercharged in the same vein that her charge had stripped him of the only virtue left to him as a lover, his constancy. "Now that is most unfair, for it as clear as the clearest Euclidian proposition that he who is constant to many shows more constancy than he who is constant to only one."

In England, he became friends with "Polly" Stevenson, the intelligent daughter of his landlady, and when she moved to the country he corresponded with her on many things, including science. When Polly mentioned the commonly-held opinion that all rivers run into the sea, he recognized the audacity of challenging such general opinions, "But we must hazard something," he said, "in what we think the cause of truth."

> "Now, if a river ends in a lake, as some do, whereby its waters are spread so wide as that the evaporation is equal to the sum of all its springs, that lake will never overflow; and if instead of ending in a lake, it was drawn into greater length as a river, so as to expose a surface equal in the whole to that lake, the evaporation would be equal, and such a river would end as a canal; when the ignorant might suppose, as they actually do in such cases, that the river loses itself by running under ground, whereas in truth it has run up into the air."

When Polly asked him to explain why the water in the country, though cold at the spring, became warm by pumping, Franklin thought it prudent for him to defer attempting an answer until she could assure him of the fact: "I own I should expect that operation to warm not so much the water pumped, as the person pumping." He said he learned this prudence for not attempting to give reasons before being sure of the facts from a woman who was in the company of some men who were viewing and considering something they called a Chinese shoe. They were earnestly disputing the manner of wearing it and how it would be possible to put it on, when she broke in and said politely, "Gentlemen, are you sure it is a shoe? Should not that be settled first?"

Franklin approved of the reading Polly was doing about insects. Superficial minds might think such a study mere trifling, but the world was much obliged to these creatures. The little silkworm brings employment to thousands of families, the bee yields delicious honey, and another insect produces the scarlet dye, cochineal. And he added, "The usefulness of cantharides, or Spanish flies, in medicine is known to all, and thousands owe their lives to that knowledge." Spanish fly, from cantharides, was a well-known aphrodisiac.

Like many other great men of science Franklin considered the mystery of light. Newton had proposed the corpuscular theory which, because of his great fame, had become the accepted view. Franklin didn't like it and in opposing it, wrote jokingly to a fellow sympathizer: " 'Tis well we are not, as poor Galileo was, subject to the Inquisition for philosophical heresy. My whispers against the orthodox doctrine . . . would be dangerous; your writing and printing would be highly criminal. As it is, you must expect some censure, but one heretic will surely excuse another.''

Newton's theory was that light existed as minute luminous particles that were emitted from the sun and other radiating bodies. Franklin was troubled by the prodigious swiftness with which these particles would have to be continually driven from the sun. ''Must not the smallest particle conceivable have, with such a motion, a force exceeding that of a 24-pounder discharged from a cannon?'' He was worried, too, that by this tremendous discharge of particles the sun would grow smaller and have less gravitational pull on the planets. Yet, there was no evidence that the planets had changed their ancient orbits. He argued that the travel of sound could be explained without having to imagine sonorous particles that were thrown off by a bell. Still, for all this speculation he had to admit, ''I am much in the dark about light.''

When it came to the down-to-earth matter of lighting, this was a different matter. Dissatisfied with the street lights of his day which burned oil so inefficiently as to produce more smoke than light, he designed a lamp which provided more air for burning the oil with a brighter flame, giving a saving in fuel as well. Having an aversion for waste, he criticized the habit of city dwellers of staying up late at night burning innumerable candles and then sleeping late the next morning when the light was free. He readily admitted that he, himself, was one of the worst offenders. Perhaps, as penance for this he wrote a piece for a Paris newspaper, called ''An Economical Project.'' It begins by calling attention to the introduction by two Frenchmen of a splendid oil lamp for lighting rooms. There was discussion by some people, however, whether the extra light it gave made up for the extra oil it consumed. At which point Franklin interjected, ''I was pleased to see this general concern for economy, for I love economy exceedingly.'' He says that he went home to bed several hours after midnight with his head full of the subject, but a sudden noise awakened him at 6 in the morning. He was surprised to find his room bathed with light and thought at first that a number of those new lamps had been brought into it, when on rubbing his eyes, he saw that the light came in from the windows. He got up to inspect and perceived the sun just rising over the horizon.

It seemed odd that he (the sun was referred to by the personal pronoun, he, in the 18th century) would be rising so early, so Franklin looked at his almanac, which verified the time as correct. He imagined that the people of Paris would be as much astonished as he was to hear of the sun's rising so early, especially when they are assured, "that he gives light as soon as he rises." Franklin says he is convinced of this fact. No, stating it more strongly, he is certain of it. He could not be more certain of it, he tells us, for he saw it with his own eyes. And like a true scientist, he repeated the experiment the three following mornings with precisely the same result.

Yet when he explained his discovery to others he could tell by their faces that they did not believe him. One learned scientist assured him that he must be mistaken as it is well known that there could be no light at that hour, therefore none could enter his room. Franklin must have been deceived, he reasoned, the open window instead of letting in the light must have let out the darkness. Franklin said he was a little puzzled by this line of argument but not convinced.

Franklin did some calculating. He figured that if he had not been accidentally awakened so early he would have slept six hours longer while the sun was shining, in exchange for six hours he was up the following night by candle-light. If all the families of Paris followed his example, the amount of candle wax used in these six hours per day would amount to over 64 million pounds in six months time! To prevent such a waste he would enforce the following regulations: 1) levy a tax on every window with shutters to keep the sun out 2) let no family use more than one pound of candles per week 3) permit no coach travel after sunset 4) ring the church bells at sunrise, and if that was not enough let cannon be fired in every street to wake the sluggards.

For this "great discovery" which he bestowed on the public Franklin asked no reward whatever. He only desired the honor of it. Yet he knew there are little, envious minds who would, as usual, deny him this. They would say that his invention was known to the ancients and would quote passages from old books to prove it. He would not dispute that the ancients could have had almanacs and knew when the sun would rise, but it does not follow "that they knew he gave light as soon as he rose. This is what I claim as my discovery."

Original as it was, this discovery is not likely to rank with Franklin's profound contributions to electricity, but we have honored his principle in a practice Franklin would have heartily approved. We call it Daylight Saving Time.

21

THE DOCTOR'S MERRY MEDICINE

AN OLD FRENCH ENGRAVING BEARS THE INSCRIPTION, "Benjamin Franklin, Doctor of Medicine." The engraver was in error; Franklin was not a medical doctor. His title of doctor resulted from the honorary degrees he received from Oxford University in England and St. Andrews in Scotland for his scientific achievements. But in his scientific investigations he did not neglect medical science, and a noted Franklin biographer states that "the study of medicine was one of Franklin's chief interests and . . . one of the least known."

Franklin was a member of the Royal Medical Society of Paris and the Medical Society of London. Many medical men were among his intimate friends, including Sir John Pringle, Court Physician in England, Jan Ingenhousz, Physician to Queen Maria Theresa and King Joseph II of Austria, and Vicq d'Azyr, Queen Marie Antoinette's doctor in France. Medical subjects appear prominently in all his writings. One of the first books he printed in his own shop was John Tennent's "Every Man his own Doctor; or the Poor Planter's Physician." In *Poor Richard's Almanac,* Franklin described various medicines, such as rattlesnake root that the Indians used for treating the bite of the venomous reptile. His report contained useful information, such as the method the Indians used to dispense this medicine: "they sometimes chew it and spit it in the patient's mouth."

In the *Pennsylvania Gazette* for May 19, 1737 Franklin inserted the following item: "We hear from Burlington County, that on the 11th inst. died there of a stoppage in his urine, Dr. John Browne, a gentleman of singular skill in the profession of surgery, which he practiced in these parts many years with great success." This doctor was also the innkeeper who had befriended the young runaway from Boston on his way to Philadelphia. Franklin remembered him in his autobiography, "our acquaintance continued as long as he lived," but now the doctor's time had run out (if not his urine) and he had to go (but couldn't).

As already noted, Franklin was the prime mover in founding the first hospital in America. He was also responsible for the first flexible catheter in American medical history. Franklin's brother John in Boston had a urinary problem and asked his advice. Benjamin first suggested the use of lime water and soap and then devised the catheter. He states, "I went immediately to the silversmith's and gave directions for making one (sitting by till it was finished) that it might be ready for this post." Furthermore, he provided John with directions for modifying it if necessary. What doctor today could be expected to give his patient better service?

In Franklin's youth, smoky chimneys were inevitable annoyances of domestic life. Shakespeare put a smoky house in the category of tedious things, along with a tired horse and a nagging wife. Franklin directed himself to the question, "How may smoky chimneys be best cured?" His lifelong interest in this subject is exhibited in his publications and his invention of the "Pennsylvanian fireplace." In 1744 he wrote, "We leave it to the physicians to say how much healthier thick-built towns and cities will be, now-half-suffocated with sulphery smoke, when so much less of that smoke shall be made, and the air breathed by the inhabitants consequently so much purer." We may thus ring up another first for Franklin—first in air pollution control.

Most middle-aged persons come to discover bifocal eye glasses, but Ben Franklin was the first one to do so because he invented them. His vision was getting worse and he simply did not want to be bothered having to switch spectacles for close and distant viewing so he had the glasses cut and half of each pair mounted together in the same frame. He found that his bifocals also improved his hearing: "Since my being in France," he wrote, "the glasses that serve me best at table to see what I eat, not being the best to see the faces of those on the other side of the the the table who speak to me; and when one's ears are not accustomed to the sounds of a language, a sight of the move-ments in the features of him that speaks help . . . so that I understand French better by the help of my spectacles.''

In his old age he did experiment with his hearing and discovered he could hear better when, with his hand, he bent his ear toward the speaker, and much better yet with the simple device of shaping his hand in the form of a cup and placing it beside his ear. Had he pat-ented that invention his heirs might have become fabulously wealthy.

In Franklin's time smallpox was the dread disease of the world and in 1736, at the age of 4, Franklin's son, Francis, died of it. While Edward Jenner's cowpox vaccine for smallpox was not developed until 1796, vaccination was known in America since 1720 when Cotton Mather had introduced it in Boston. Franklin was a fervent advocate of vaccination but he had not vaccinated his son because the boy had been sickly and he was waiting for him to recover before subjecting him to the inoculation of smallpox scabs, which was the process then used for vaccination. People sometimes died from smallpox incurred as a result of the vaccination and the question in the public's mind was whether vaccination was worth the risk. Over the years Franklin col-lected statistics which showed that vaccination, dangerous as it was, was still many times safer than getting the disease ''in the natural way.'' In 1759 he wrote a preface to Dr. William Heberdon's book, *Some Account of the Success of Inoculation for the Small-Pox,* in which he presented his statistics. Ingenhousz, respecting Franklin's knowledge, sought his advice before inoculating the young princes of the Imperial family of Austria.

In describing his Pennsylvania fireplace for heating houses Frank-lin defended his use of iron. The offensive smell of some iron stoves was not caused by the iron, he assured the reader, but arose from the unclean manner of using those stoves. ''Iron,'' he maintained, ''is always sweet, and every way taken is wholesome and friendly to the human body—except in weapons.'' But this was not so for lead. Franklin deserves credit for characterizing lead poisoning. Lead, when hot, yields a very unwholesome steam, he tells us in this treatise. But it was his diagnosis of a common though serious disease known as the ''dry belly ache'' or ''dry gripes'' for which Franklin earned his credit. The disease was caused by lead poisoning but its many origins obscured its true nature. In Jamaica rum, he traced the trouble to the lead pipes used in distillation of the rum. He told of a family in Europe affected with dry belly ache by drinking rain water which was collected from leaded roofs. There was no trouble until the trees grew up and shed their leaves on the roof, and he supposed (correctly) that an acid in those leaves corroded the lead. As a printer, Franklin had observed that men who handled hot lead type sometimes became paralyzed in their hands. When he and John Pringle were in Paris, they visited a hospital known for its treatment of the dry belly ache and obtained there a pamphlet which contained the names and occupations of the patients. Since he already suspected lead poisoning, Franklin carefully studied the list and showed that all the patients—glaziers, plumbers, painters, potters, letter founders, white lead makers—used lead in their work.

Franklin's experiments in electricity had fired the imagination of the world and it is no surprise that it was hoped and even expected that electricity would do wonders in medicine. It was described as "the pure physic of the skies" and was believed by many to be the most powerful of all medicines because it was the most nearly divine. The press was filled with stories of miraculous cures ascribed to this magical fluid. Franklin observed, however, that they were mostly in remote villages in Europe and were unsubstantiated. He was skeptical for he knew how susceptible to suggestion people are. But as the world's foremost "electrician" Franklin was pressed for treatment by sick people who desperately put their hope in this new wonder, and he conceded and gave it.

In one case he appeared to have achieved a complete cure. For ten years the woman had undergone convulsive fits with severe cramps and hysterical symptoms but no medical treatment had been of help. Franklin gave her a series of shock treatments and she reported, "the symptoms gradually decreased, till at length they entirely left me." Franklin had treated her for two weeks, then gave her a Leyden jar to take home and instructed her to electrify herself with it every day for three weeks. Two years later she was still in good health, and without any further record of complaint from her, it is safe to assume she is no longer disturbed by that ailment.

Franklin was very cautious about claiming advantages for his treatment. When treating persons with paralysis he found they showed encouraging signs of improvement at first, so that gradually a man could move his lame hand till he could take his hat off, but there was no improvement after the fifth day. "And how much the apparent, temporary advantage might arise from the exercise in the patient's journey . . . or from the spirits given by the hope of success," he would not pretend to say. He criticized some investigators who were "too premature in publishing their imaginations and expectations for real experiments." He was, however, ever ready to encourage worthy investigations and supported Ingenhousz in his attempt to persuade the doctors at the insane hospital at Bedlam, England, to try shock treatment on their patients. Franklin had written, "while we are solicitous about the health of the body, let us not forget there are diseases of the mind which concern us no less." One may wonder how much such ideas influenced the young Dr. Benjamin Rush, a Philadelphian and co-signer of the Declaration of Independence with Franklin, who was to write the first modern treatise on the diseases of the mind.

Franklin had a healthy skepticism about the practice of medicine in his day. It was deserved, for it was a physician's blade, not the British Army, that felled George Washington. On landing in France in 1776, Franklin fell ill, and a French physician gave him pills, which he took faithfully. "I continued to take the pills," he declared, "but finding my teeth loosening, and that I had lost three, I desisted the use of them." Later, when he was suffering from bladder stones, he told John Jay, "I am more afraid of the medicines than the malady." Had not *Poor Richard* said, "God heals and the doctor takes the fee?" Had not John Pringle told him that 92 out of 100 fevers cured themselves, 4 were cured by art, and 4 proved fatal. He had mentioned this to Benjamin Rush to whom he also said, "Quacks were the greatest liars in the world, except [for] their patients." He ascribed the success of quacks partly to patients, extolling the remedies they took from them, rather than confess their own ignorance and credulity.

In this same light he teased his good friend and doctor John Fothergill about his (Fothergill's) proposed retirement:

> When do you intend to live, *i.e.* to enjoy life? . . . To be hurried about perpetually from one sick chamber to another is not living. Do you please yourself with the fancy that you are doing good? You are mistaken. Half the lives you save are not worth saving, as being useless; and almost the other half ought not to be saved as being mischievous. Does your conscience never hint to you the impiety of being in constant warfare against the plans of providence? Disease was intended as the punishment of intemperance, sloth, and other

vices; and the example of that punishment was intended to promote and strengthen the opposite virtues. But here you step in officiously with your art, disappoint those wise intentions of nature, and make men safe in their excesses. Whereby you seem to me to be of just the same service to society as some favourite first minister, who out of the great benevolence of his heart should procure pardons for all criminals that applied to him. Only think of the consequences!

In his conversations with Rush, Franklin is recorded as believing the accounts of the plague in Turkey were exaggerated. There were plagues, indeed, he was told by Dr. Mackensie of Constantinople, like the plague of the doctors who were never paid for their attendance on patients that die unless it were with the plague, so they make most fatal diseases the plague. Like Rush, Thomas Jefferson recalled a story Franklin told him about doctors:

> When I was in London . . . there was a weekly club of physicians, of which Sir John Pringle was president, and I was invited by my friend Dr. Fothergill to attend when convenient. Their rule was to propose a thesis one week and discuss it the next. I happened there when the question to be considered was whether physicians had, on the whole, done most good or harm? The young members, particularly, having discussed it very learnedly and eloquently till the subject was exhausted, one of them observed to Sir John Pringle, that although it was not usual for the president to take part in a debate, yet they were desirous to know his opinion on the question. He said they must first tell him whether, under the appellation of physicians, they meant to include old women. If they did he thought they had done more good than harm, otherwise more harm than good.

It is surprising that Franklin and Pringle were such fast friends, considering their different temperaments. We know about this from none other than the famous biographer of Samuel Johnson, James Boswell, who dined with them in London. Boswell confided to his diary, ''Sir John, though a most worthy man, has a peculiar sour manner. Franklin is all jollity and pleasantry. I said to myself: Here is a prime contrast: acid and alkali.'' Pringle was an outstanding physician who first recognized the connection between the unsanitary disposal of human wastes and fevers such as typhoid. He also did the first quantitative investigation of antiseptics and included on his list of materials to be tested a local American product, rattlesnake root. It happened that Pringle was president of the Royal Society when King George interceded against Franklin's pointed lightning rods. When the King tried to pressure the Royal Society to suppress its report favoring the pointed rods, Pringle, though a Tory and a loyal subject, refused and lost both his position as president and his income as court physician. He is reputed to have told the King, "His Majesty can change the laws of the land at will, but he can neither revise nor alter even one of the laws of nature."

It was on the subject of the common cold that Franklin differed most dramatically from the medical ideas of his time. He referred to his ideas on colds as his heresy. In his words, the physicians were "on a wrong scent in supposing moist or cold air the causes of that disorder we call a cold." He believed that such things as stale air, overeating and excess drinking, lack of exercise, and bed clothes contaminated with perspired matter contributed to colds. He also recognized the contagious nature of colds. He told Rush, "I have long been satisfied . . . people catch cold from one another when shut up together in closed rooms . . . when sitting near and conversing so as to breathe in each other's transpiration." This was a century before Pasteur and the germ theory of disease.

Franklin was sold on fresh air, despite the fear and suspicion with which it was regarded by his contemporaries. He wrote the French scientist, Le Roy, "Our physicians have begun to discover that fresh air is good for people in . . . fevers. I hope in time they will find out that it does no harm to people in health." He complained, "What caution against air. Many London families go out once a day to take the air; three or four persons in a coach, one perhaps sick . . . with the glasses both up close, all breathing over and over again the same air, and rendered worse every minute. And this they call taking the air."

In that fateful year of 1776, Franklin and John Adams were on their way to Staten Island to confer with the British leader, Admiral Lord Howe, in a last attempt at preventing the war. On the trip, they stopped at an inn that was so crowded with soldiers that the two had to share a tiny room. "The window was open," Adams remembered, "and I, who was an invalid and afraid of the air at night, shut it close. 'Oh,' says Franklin, 'don't shut the window, we will be suffocated.' I answered I was afraid of the evening air. Dr. Franklin replied, 'The air within the chamber will soon be, and indeed is now, worse than that out doors. Come, open the window and come to bed, and I will convince you. I believe you are not acquainted with my theory of colds?' '' And with that Franklin threw up the window. Adams leaped into bed, and he related: ''The Doctor then began a harangue upon air and cold, and respiration and perspiration.'' This soon put Adams to sleep, and he believed that it had the same effect on Franklin, for the last words he heard were pronounced in a faraway drone as though Franklin were already losing conciousness.

Franklin told Adams that air was necessary for the free breathing and cooling of the body. He reasoned, ''if a free and copious perspiration is of use in diseases, that seems to be best obtained by light covering and fresh air continually changing.'' Franklin conducted an experiment on himself, measuring his weight loss due to perspiration, alternately naked and warmly clothed, hourly, for eight hours. Dr. Stark, a physician he engaged to assist him in this experiment, found that the perspiration nearly doubled during those hours when Franklin was naked.

Franklin advocated a cold air bath, which he referred to as his 'bracing or tonic bath.'' He thought a cold air bath to be less of a shock to the system than a cold water bath. ''I arise almost every morning and sit in my chamber without any clothes whatever, half an hour or an hour . . . reading or writing. If I return to bed afterwards . . . I make a supplement to my night's rest of one or two hours of the most pleasing sleep that can be imagined.''

Franklin preached the gospel of fresh air to all his friends. In writing to his sister, he was glad to hear of her good health and that she ''had learnt not to be afraid of her friend fresh air.'' Polly Stevenson had married a physician, Dr. Hewson, and Franklin was named godfather of their first child. Polly wrote to Franklin of his godson, ''he is fond of being in his birthday suit, and has not the least apprehension of catching cold in it; he is never troubled with airophobia, but always seems delighted with fresh air.'' In France, Franklin extolled the virtues of his bracing bath but he had few converts. Those who did try it caught cold and closed their windows, since, as one of them declared, it took a man of the Doctor's constitution to withstand such shock treatment. After the Revolution when Franklin returned home he built a new house where he could take his nude baths in the privacy of his garden. One day, it is told, he saw a friend's maid delivering a letter to his house and, forgetting that he was without his clothes, he came over to meet her. The girl was terrified. She ran home reporting that

Franklin had been murdered: "The Indians got possession of the farther end of the village in the night; the chief is in the poor Doctor's house, and as soon as he saw me he ran out, tomahawk in hand, to scalp me."

But Franklin did not substitute air baths for water baths. Dr. Rush commented upon Franklin's practice of taking hot baths. He claimed they "smoothed the descent of Dr. Franklin down the hill of life and helped to prolong it beyond 84 years." Franklin recommended a warm bath for cleaning and purifying the skin. Apparently it was not then a very common practice, for he attempted to convince others of its salutary nature based upon his own experience. When he had skin trouble he would sit in the hot water for two hours at a time and found that it brought him relief from the discomfort. In the latter part of his life he enjoyed the luxury of a warm bath every day in a curious bathing vessel he designed for himself. It was made of copper in the shape of a slipper. He sat in the heel with his legs under the vamp, and on the instep he had a support which held a book. A New England clergyman describing this tub remarked with Puritan disapproval, "and here he sits and enjoys himself." Noting that Franklin had just been chosen President of Philadelphia's Executive Council, the minister deridingly proposed as "a capital subject for an historical painting—the Doctor placed at the head of the Council Board in his bathing slipper." Even a tolerant 20th century man would have to admit it would have made an interesting portrait.

As is evident from his practice of frequent bathing Franklin put great emphasis on personal cleanliness. He was insistent on having clean clothes and a clean bed. After a pleasant visit with friends at Prestonfield, their estate in Scotland, he wrote his thanks in the form of a poem, the third verse reading:

> Chearfull meals, balmy rest,
> Beds that never buggs molest,
> Neatness and sweetness all around
> These at Prestonfield we found.

On one occasion his high standards caused him some discomfort. It was during his soldiering days on the way to the frontier at Gnadenhütte. On the second night from home, he wrote his wife, he lodged at a farmhouse where he was very comfortable with a feather-bed and warm blankets, in contrast to the night before at an inn. The woman at the inn was about to put very damp sheets on the bed, but Franklin stopped her and asked her to air them first. Half an hour later she said the bed was ready and the sheets well aired. Franklin got into bed, but jumped out immediately! The sheets were partly frozen and ''as cold as death.'' ''She had aired them indeed, but it was out on the hedge.'' He was forced to spend the night wrapped in his great coat and woolen trousers since everything else about the bed was shockingly dirty.

In yet another way, Franklin was far ahead of his time. This was on the subject of exercise: he was a staunch believer in the now unquestioned concept that regular exercise is necessary for a healthy body. He loved swimming, declaring it to be one of the most healthful and agreeable exercises in the world, and at the age of 80 he swam across the Seine River in France. He disagreed with a friend who thought himself too old to learn to swim. Franklin advised his friend to wade into calm water until breast deep, then ''throw an egg into the water, between you and the shore.'' The egg ''must lie in the water so deep that you cannot reach to take it up but by diving.'' The beginner never need panic, for whenever he wishes he may stand up with his head far out of the water. In plunging for the egg he will feel how the water buoys him up and opposes his effort to go to the bottom. Thus he will overcome his dread of sinking and drowning and soon enjoy the pleasure of swimming.

When he could not swim, Franklin told Adams: ''I walk every day a league in my chamber; I walk quick and for an hour . . . I make a point of religion of it.'' At the age of 82 when he was unable to take other exercise he lifted dumbbells. He held that the amount of exercise taken should be measured not in terms of time or distance but by the degree of warmth it produces in the body: ''There is more exercise in one mile's riding on horseback than five in a coach; and more in one mile's walking on foot than five on horseback; to which I may add, that there is more in walking one mile up and down stairs than five on a level floor.'' When one is pinched for time, he recommended the dumbbell. ''By the use of it,'' he continued, ''I have in forty swings quickened my pulse from 60 to 100 beats in a minute, counted by a second watch, and I suppose the warmth generally increases with the quickness of the pulse.'' Perhaps this scene of Franklin with his dumbbells taking his pulse might suggest itself to an enterprising artist as another likely subject for a historical painting.

Franklin didn't always practice what he preached, and he was his own worst critic concerning his laziness. He confessed to "a little nat-ural indolence" and in reference to a necessary business journey he wrote, "I am grown almost too lazy to undertake it." And in Europe he jokingly told a friend: "I love ease more than ever, and by daily using your horses I can be of service to you and them by preventing their growing too fat." There was no question but Franklin liked good living, which meant good eating. Yet he believed *Poor Richard's* proverbs, "Three good meals a day is bad living" and "Many dishes, many medicines," and was aware of his over-indulgence. He referred to himself as "a fat old fellow" and "Dr. Fatsides." Perhaps incor-rectly, he often blamed illnesses he suffered on his overeating. One illness he linked to having eaten "a hearty supper, much cheese, and drank a good deal of champagne." One wonders whether he didn't feel such a dinner was worth the payment. One big meal might be bad enough, but a big supper after a full dinner, Franklin averred, was sure to bring a restless night. He allowed, however, for differences in indi-vidual constitutions: "some rest well after these meals," he jested, "It costs them only a frightful dream and an apoplexy, after which they sleep till doomsday, [and] are found dead abed in the morning." Yet temptation was not to be overcome. He told James Madison that as a young man he was subject to fits of indigestion from indulgence at the table and he solved his problem by carrying a vial of oil of wormwood around with him as a remedy for overeating—and "went on sinning more freely than ever."

When he had his skin ailment, Dr. Pringle counseled abstaining from salt meats and cheese, "which advice I did not follow, often forgetting it," he confessed. This forgetfulness was inexcusable for *Poor Richard* had warned, "Cheeze and salt meat, should be sparingly eat." An indication of Franklin's epicurean appreciation is found in his acknowlegement that "many people are fond of accounts of old buildings and monuments, but for one, I confess that if I could find in any Italian travels a recipe for making Parmesan cheese, it would give me more satisfaction than a transcript of any inscription from any old stone whatever."

Like food, Franklin also enjoyed drinking, but he drank in moder-ation. He preferred wine, especially Madeira. Writing to Strahan, his printer colleague in London, he said, "You will say my advice 'smells of Madeira'. You are right. This foolish letter is mere chitchat be-tween ourselves over the second bottle." After having dined and drunk too freely he complained that it caused him pain in his great toe. In this case he may have been correct, since he had attacks of the gout, which is known to be aggravated by a rich diet.

In the area of nutrition, Franklin knew of the ability of lemon juice to prevent scurvy and he always took a supply of fresh fruit on his long ocean voyages. The use of citrus fruit as protection against scurvy was not generally known or practiced in his century. He had discovered it in a book written in 1625 by Samuel Purchas and stated regretfully, "This was printed 150 years ago, and yet it is not become a practice." Despite his advocacy, it was not until 1795 that the British navy ordered for its sailors a daily ration of lime juice, which was to cause them to be called "limeys." Before oxygen was discovered by his friend Joseph Priestley and combustion was explained by his associate Antoine Lavoisier, Franklin recognized that the food we eat is converted to heat in the body by a process he likened to yeast fermentation. He introduced kohlrabi, scotch cabbage, and chinese rhubarb into America and helped to popularize the cultivation of potatoes in France, where the peasants had shunned them, fearing that they would produce leprosy.

Franklin did not use tobacco; he never "snuffed, chewed, or smoked." He and Pringle had seen tremors in the hands of people who used excessive snuff, and Pringle was cured of a tremor by leaving off its use. Franklin's observations over thirty years in England and France indicated a great reduction in the use of tobacco. He saw no advantage to it, and though he had always been in the company of people who used it, no one had ever advised him to do so. All this being the case, he logically concluded that the use of tobacco would disappear in a few years. He regretted that the greatest part of the trade of the world was carried on for luxuries, most of which were injurious to health or society, such as tea, tobacco, rum, sugar, and Negro slaves. He added, "When I read the advertisements in our papers of imported goods for sale, I think of the speech of a philospher upon walking thro' a fair, 'How happy am I that I want none of these things.' "

The First Civilized American is the title of a book about Franklin. It is true that he seems to have founded many of the institutions which have become so important to later generations of his countrymen. One of his fondest and our most popular is the summer vacation. Franklin took off and traveled for a month or so every summer. "My constitution," he said, "and too great confinement to business during the winter seemed to require the air and exercise of a long journey once a year, which I have now practiced for more than twenty years past." He always returned invigorated from such trips, ready for more work and a flood of activities. It was his special safety valve.

While he was in France, Franklin served as the senior member of a Royal Commission of physicians and scientists to investigate mesmerism, or animal magnetism, the precursor of hypnotism. Named after its practitioner, Dr. Anton Mesmer of Vienna, mesmerism was a concoction of cosmology, magnetism, and quackery that for a few years became the rage of Paris. The story of Mesmer is a fantastic one of a deluded super-promoter and a gullible public; of seances and secret societies and mass hysteria. Mesmerism proclaimed that there was only one disease and one remedy, administered through the magnetic finger tips of the skillful practitioner, who is said to have made 100,000 pounds in six months. Franklin served on the commission with Lavoisier, Le Roy, and Guillotin, the latter being the surgeon who invented the guillotine. The government was not only worried about quackery and fraud, but also the fate of young women when entranced by the magnetic doctors. The commission studied the matter thoroughly, watched Mesmer's associate, Dr. Deslon, magnetize a tree in Franklin's garden, and tried some experiments of their own. They discredited mesmerism and credited Mesmer's results to the patient's nervous excitement and imagination. It was an excellent report, but it had the effect of delaying the development of hypnotism by a century. In addition to the public report, there was a secret report to the King on the fate of those young women. It concluded that women with their great susceptibility and vivid imagination were easy victims of immoral operators. These wise scientists were not unaware of the fundamental erotic nature of women. "Touch them in one point," they said, "and you touch them everywhere."

Living in a day when one had to depend on animal magnetism or the even greater dangers of reputable medicine, Franklin was fortunate in having generally good health, for which he was ever grateful. He wrote his wife from London, "I have been extremely hearty and well ever since my return from France; the complaints I had before I went on that tour being entirely dissipated and fresh strength and activity, the effects of exercise and change of air, have taken their place. I hope this will find you and Sally [Franklin's daughter] . . . as well as I am." As a generous gesture he included in his wish, "all we love or that love us" and with the further magnanimity born of healthful spirits he concluded, "and even those who don't."

He had his share of the medicine of his day and fortunately survived. He wrote his wife, "I am pretty well recovered of a slight illness . . . a pain and giddiness in my head. I have been cupp'd, blooded, physick'd and at last blister'd for it . . . but by these operations and very spare living, I am grown a little thin." When he developed painful infirmities in his old age he was philosophical: "One means of becoming content with one's situation is the comparing it with a worse. Thus, when I consider how many terrible diseases the human body is liable to, I comfort myself that only three incurable ones have fallen to my share, viz: the gout, the stone, and old age; and these have not yet deprived me of my natural cheerfulness, my delight in books, and enjoyment of social conversation."

Franklin had the gout, but, conversely, the gout had Franklin—a worthy adversary. He fenced with it, befriended it, ridiculed it, and himself as well. The gout, though very painful, was thought to have the beneficial effect of preventing more serious disabilities such as paralysis, dropsy and apoplexy; thus Franklin remarked, that the doctors were not decided whether the gout was "a disease or a remedy." He continued on this theme in a letter to a fellow sufferer: "If according to the custom here, I congratulate you on your having a severe fit of the gout, I cannot avoid mixing some condolence with my congratulation, for I too have lately had a visit or rather *visitation* from the same friend (or enemy) that confined me near a fortnight. And not withstanding the salutary effects people talk of to comfort us under our pain, I fancy we should . . . willingly hazard being without them rather have these means of procuring them. I may possibly be, as they tell me, greatly obliged to the gout; but the condition of this obligation is such that I cannot heartily say *I thank ye.*"

In France his infirmity frequently relieved Franklin, as the American ambassador, of his duty of making his formal appearance at the royal court of Versailles. He joked about the incongruity of a plenipotentiary "who can neither stand nor go." He told a correspondent, "Don't be proud of this long letter. A fit of the gout . . . has given me a little time to trifle." It was during such a two week siege which confined him to his bed that Franklin wrote his best-known bagatelle, "Dialogue Between the Gout and Mr. Franklin." Madame Brillon, whose husband also endured the gout, had written Franklin a fable in verse entitled, "The Sage and the Gout," which inspired him to respond with his prose version. In his bagatelle the gout is personified as "Madame Gout" who rebukes Franklin for his self-indulgence and lethargy. In Madam Brillon's version she had included, as well, his love for pretty mistresses, which he answered with tricky logic: "[In] your fable, Madam Gout seems to me to reason pretty well, except when she supposes that mistresses have helped to produce this painful malady. I, for one, believe exactly the opposite; and here is my argument. When I was young and enjoyed more of the favors of the sex than at present, I had no gout. Hence, if the ladies of Passy had shown more of that Christian charity that I have so often recommended to you in vain, I should not be suffering from the gout right now." She replied that she would love him in a spirit of Christian charity, but not his brand of Christian charity. In his Dialog, Franklin begins, saying: "Eh! O! Eh! What have I done to deserve these cruel sufferings?" The Gout replies: "Many things; you have eaten and drunk too freely, and too much indulged your legs in their indolence." Franklin: "Who is it that accuses me?" Gout: "It is I, the Gout." Franklin: "What! my enemy in person?" Gout: "No, not your enemy." Franklin: "I repeat, my enemy. You not only torment me to death, but ruin my good name. You reproach me as a glutton and a tippler."

This banter goes on, with the Gout accusing Franklin for leading a sedentary existence, not taking exercise, although he preaches it for others. Franklin tries to defend himself but he only exposes his failings. After a long lecture by Madam Gout in which she scolds him for sitting and playing chess for hours and for riding in his coach when he needs to walk to circulate his blood, Franklin tells her most disrespectfully, "Your reasoning grows very tiresome." The Gout responds, "I stand corrected. I will be silent and do my duty. Take this twinge, and that!" Franklin screams, "O! O-o-o! Talk on, I pray you!" The Gout, "No, no. I have a good number of twinges for you tonight, and more tomorrow." The Gout continues to reveal to Franklin his abuse of his body and at last he yields and says, "I am convinced now of the justness of *Poor Richard's* remark, 'Our debts and our sins are always greater than we think.'" The Gout answers, "It is true. You philosophers are sages in your maxims and fools in your conduct." When the Gout again condemns Franklin's use of his carriage, he asks what should he do with it? "Burn it," says the Gout, or use it to transport home the poor, tired peasants who have labored all

312 ◇ Peregrinations of an Agile Mind

day in the fields and deserve a rest. As for him, he can walk home. Again, Franklin is sassy and says, "How boring you are!" And again, the Gout returns to her duty, "It should not be forgotten," she says, "I am your physician. There! Take that!" Franklin reacts, "O-o-o-o! What a devil of a physician!" The Gout says she will leave him but with an assurance of visiting him again, insisting, "I am your real friend."

As Franklin grew older he was laid up and tortured not only by the gout but by the bladder stone as well. Still he could discuss his condition metaphorically, "though the upper part of the building appears yet tolerably firm, yet, being undermined by the stone and gout united, its fall cannot be far distant." Franklin recalled that in his youth he had often sung the "Old Man's Song." The chorus went:

> May I govern my passions with an absolute sway,
> Grow wiser and better as my strength wears away,
> Without gout or stone, by a gentle decay.

"But what signifies our wishing?" Franklin mused, "Things happen after all, as they will happen. I have sung that wishing song a thousand times when I was young, and now find at fourscore that the three contraries have befallen me—being subject to the gout and the stone, and not being yet master of all my passions. Like the proud girl in the country who wished and resolved not to marry a parson, nor a Presbyterian, nor an Irishman; and at length found herself married to an Irish Presbyterian parson."

PART FIVE

Four Score and More

22

FRANKLIN AND GOD

From a cross neighbor, and a sullen wife,
A pointless needle, and a broken knife,
From suretyship, and an empty purse,
A smokey chimney and a jolting horse;
From a dull razor, and an aching head,
From a bad conscience and a buggy bed;
A blow on the elbow and the knee,
From each of these, *Good Lord deliver me.*

POOR RICHARD SAUNDERS WAS A PRACTICAL AND resourceful fellow, in religion as in all other things. So was his creator. Franklin did not depend on faith and prayer to solve his problems. "Faith saves us in the next world, loses us in this one," he once remarked. He favored works rather than worship. "The scriptures assure me," he explained, "that the last day we shall not be examined [for] what we *thought,* but what we *did.*" His emphasis was on improving this world for himself and his fellow mortals. He looked upon good works not as charity but as payment of a debt. "I have received much kindness from men to whom I shall never have any opportunity of making the least return," he said, "and numberless mercies from God, who is infinitely above being benefited by our services. These kindnesses from men I can therefore only return on their fellow men, and [those] from God, by a readiness to help his other children."

Like Washington, Adams, Jefferson, and Paine, Franklin was religious but not doctrinaire. He was reared in an orthodox family in Puritan Boston but he soon found himself at odds with the theocracy of the preachers. His interest in books and ideas made him think and question, even in matters of faith. As long as he lived at home he dutifully attended church with his family, twice on Sunday, as well as frequent devotional meetings at home. But when he was apprenticed, he avoided public worship as much as he could to give himself more time for reading. His father, a devout Presbyterian, wanted Ben, as the last of his sons, to become a minister. But the expense of such an education made him change his plans for the boy. It was just as well, for the lad had trouble conforming to any pattern already cut out for him. He sometimes arrived at conclusions somewhat different from those expected, as he relates: "I was scarce 15, when, after doubting . . . several points, as I found them disputed in different books I read, I began to doubt of revelation itself. Some books against deism fell into my hands . . . It happened they wrought an effect on me quite contrary to what was intended by them; for the arguments of the deists, which were quoted to be refuted, appeared to be much stronger than the refutation. In short, I soon became a thorough deist."

His indiscreet disputations about religion along with his non-attendance at church soon got the boy in trouble. The good people of Boston began to point to him in horror, identifying him as an infidel and an atheist. Franklin was indignant when people equated deism with atheism because, he said, "I think they are diametrically opposite." When a preacher friend of his said of someone, "Mr B. was a deist, I had almost said an atheist," Franklin paraphrased him, "that is *chalk,* I had almost said *charcoal.*"

Despite his youthful rebellion, Franklin nevertheless joined the Presbyterian church when he settled in Philadelphia. He paid his regular assessments but seldom attended services for he was disgusted with the preacher whose sermons he found to be "dry, uninteresting and unedifying," without inculcating a single moral principal. Franklin believed that the sermons should have been conceived to make good citizens, not good Presbyterians, rather than the other way around. However when a young, eloquent Presbyterian preacher named Hemphill came from England to be assistant minister of the church, Franklin became his most ardent supporter. His sermons Franklin found to be "most excellent discourses" which stressed good works and were not dogmatic. The older preacher became very jealous of the younger man and formally charged him with heterodoxy. Franklin rose to the latter's defense writing pamphlets in his favor. There was a trial and, as expected, Hemphill was found guilty and ordered silent. However, he became an independent and continued to preach until it was discovered that his sermons were not original but were copied verbatim from sermons published in England. Many of his supporters then abandoned him, but Franklin stuck by him, saying, "I rather approved his giving us good sermons composed by others than bad ones of his own manufacture . . . the practice of our common preachers."

Eventually Franklin left the Presbyterian church. The dogmas of that persuasion "such as the eternal decrees of God, election, reprobation, etc.," he said, "appeared to me unintelligible, others doubtful . . ." He became a member of the Episcopal church in which he formally remained for the rest of his life, although in fact he was really non-sectarian and was generally recognized as such. When a board of trustees in town having one member from each sect on it needed a new member, Franklin was chosen, since he was an honest man of no sect at all and wouldn't unbalance it. He never forgot his Presbyterian upbringing and always felt free to joke about this denomination. He told the story of a member of Parliament who began one of his speeches saying he thanked God that he was born and bred a Presbyterian. This caused another member to observe, "that the gentleman must needs be of a most grateful disposition since he was thankful for such very small matters." He also told the story of a business manager of the High Church in Boston. This fellow had bought for speculation a cargo of Connecticut onions, which he happily believed he might sell again to great profit. But the price fell and they remained on his hands, unsold. He was heartily vexed with his bargain, expecially when he observed that they began to grow in the store he had filled with them. One day he showed them to a friend. "Here they are," said he, "and they are growing too! I damn them every day, but I think they are like the Presbyterians; the more I curse them, the more they grow."

In 1739 the Reverend George Whitefield came from England to stir America with his preaching. An itinerant preacher, he turned out multitudes of Philadelphians of all sects who were spellbound by his brilliant oratory. Franklin liked and admired the man. He supported him in his newspaper and gave him a place to stay when he came to town. Whitefield was collecting money by his sermons to build an orphanage in Georgia. Franklin approved of the project but thought it would be more practical for reasons of construction to build it in Philadelphia and bring the children to it. Whitefield firmly rejected this idea and Franklin refused to contribute. "I happened soon afterwards to attend one of his sermons, in the course of which I perceived he intended to finish with a collection, and I silently resolved he should get nothing from me. I had in my pocket a handful of copper money, three or four silver dollars, and five pistoles in gold. As he proceeded, I began to soften and concluded to give the coppers. Another stroke of his oratory made me ashamed of that and determined me to give the silver; and he finished so admirably that I emptied my pocket wholly into the collector's dish, gold and all.''

As a revivalist preacher, Whitefield prayed for Franklin's conversion, but he never had the satisfaction of believing that his prayers were heard. ''Ours was a mere civil friendship,'' Franklin explained, ''sincere on both sides, and lasting to his death.'' Franklin presents an incident which he said would show something of the terms on which they stood. When Whitefield came to Philadelphia and needed a place to stay, Franklin said, '' 'You know my house . . . You will be most heartily welcome.' He replied that if I had made that kind offer for Christ's sake, I should not miss of a reward. And I returned, 'Don't let me be mistaken; it was not for Christ's sake but for your sake.' One of our common acquaintance jocosely remarked that knowing it to be the custom of the saints when they received any favor to shift the burden of the obligation from off their own shoulders and place it in heaven, I had contrived to fix it on earth.''

Despite Whitefield's great popularity, or because of it, he lost favor with the clergy, who refused him their pulpits, and he was forced to preach in the fields. This was subject to uncertainties of the weather and was generally unsatisfactory, so Franklin led a drive to erect a building to be used as a meeting house. The proposal was met with enthusiasm and the building, 100 by 70 feet, was soon completed. Franklin was made a trustee and was no doubt responsible for the liberal dedication, that it would be ''for the use of any preacher of any religious persuasion who might desire to say something to the people of Philadelphia . . . so that even if the Mufti of Constantinople were to send a missionary to preach Mohammedanism to us, he would find a pulpit at his service.''

For a man of his time and place, Franklin must be considered unusually tolerant. ''A man must have a good deal of vanity who believes . . . that all the doctrines he holds are true and all he rejects are false,'' he wrote his parents, who were worried about his aberrant views. In relatively tolerant Pennsylvania every holder of public office had to take an oath that was violently anti-Catholic, referring to the invocation of the Virgin Mary or any saint, or the sacrifice of the Mass, as superstitious and idolatrous. After the Revolutionary War, when he was President of Pennsylvania, Franklin used all his influence in passing the Declaration of Rights insuring full religious freedom. In France, the papal nuncio consulted him frequently and followed his advice in appointing his friend, Father John Carroll of Maryland—who had nursed him when he was ill on their trip to Canada in 1776—to be the first Roman Catholic bishop of America. He wrote humorously about a New England clergyman's prayer against a French garrison during the French and Indian Wars: "Father Moody's prayers look tolerably modest. You have a fast and prayer day for that purpose; in which I compute five hundred thousand petitions were offered up to the same effect in New England, which, added to the petitions of every family morning and evening, multiplied by the number of days since January 25th, make forty-five millions of prayers; which set against the prayers of a few priests in the garrison to the Virgin Mary, give a vast balance in your favor."

When he proposed the marriage of his grandson, Temple, to Madam Brillon's daughter, he considered the fact that they were Catholic. "In every religion," he said, "beside the essential things there are others which are only forms and fashions, as a loaf of sugar may be wrapped in brown or white or blue paper, and tied with a string of flax or wool, red or yellow; but the sugar is always the essential thing. Now the essential principles of a good religion consist, it seems to me, of the following five articles, viz:

1. That there is one God who created the universe, and who governs it by His Providence.
2. That He ought to be worshipped and served.
3. That the best service to God is doing good to men.
4. That the soul of man is immortal, and,
5. That in a future life, if not a present one, vice will be punished and virtue rewarded.

Thus very simply, in these five sentences, Franklin summarized his credo, the result of a lifetime of searching, observing, and questioning. As to the differences in Protestant and Catholic beliefs that were so tremendously important to most people, Franklin told Madam Brillon, "These essential principles appear both in your religion and in

ours, the divergencies are only in the paper and the string . . ."
When she still rejected the marriage he spoke of the religious differences. "I am perfectly at ease concerning this subject. But since the
same arguments are not equally good for all people, I do not expect
that mine will be good for you . . ." He was tolerant of his friends
even when they differed with him for what he did not consider valid
reasons.

Franklin's impatience with denominational differences is illustrated by a story he liked to tell about a man who was applying for entrance to heaven on the grounds he was a Presbyterian. "What is
that?" St. Peter asked, and when told he answered, "We don't have
any here." The astonished man mentioned different sects only to be
rebuffed with the news that there were none of those persuasions in
heaven. Finally, the man saw his wife through the gate and claimed
that if she was there he should be too, for they were of the same
religion on earth. "Well," said St. Peter, "why didn't you say you
were a Christian, to begin with?" This story is apparently the basis for
one more liberal which he wrote in France and which became very
popular there.

> There was once an officer, a worthy man named Montresor, who
> was very ill. The priest of his parish, thinking him likely to die, ad-
> vised him to make his peace with God, that he might be received in
> Paradise. "I don't have much uneasiness on that subject," said
> Montresor, "for I had a vision last night which has perfectly tran-
> quillized my mind." "What vision have you had?" said the good
> priest. "I was," replied Montresor, "at the gates of Paradise with a
> crowd of people who wished to enter and St. Peter inquired of every
> one his religion. One answered, "I am a Roman Catholic."
> "Well," said St. Peter, "enter and take your place there among the
> Catholics." Another said he was of the Church of England.
> "Well," said the Saint, "enter and place yourself among the Angli-
> cans." A third said he was a Quaker. "Enter," said St. Peter, "and
> take your place among the Quakers." At length my turn having
> come, he asked me of what religion I was. "Alas!" said I, "poor
> Jacques Montresor has none." "It's a pity," said the saint. "I don't
> know where to put you, but enter nevertheless and place yourself
> where you can."

This was a large increase in tolerance, from acceptance of a Christian of any denomination into heaven to the acceptance of a man with

no religion. This liberality might be tolerated in France but not in America where in Pennsylvania, even after the Declaration of Rights, an officeholder had to swear his belief in the divine inspiration of the Old and New Testaments. Franklin took issue with this requirement, saying that if divine inspiration included "the detestable action of Jael, the wife of Heber the Kenite [who murdered Sisera. Judges 5:24], I should rather suppose it given by inspiration from another quarter." . . . But after his experiences in Boston as a youth Franklin was careful not to flaunt his religious opinions. "Talking against religion is unchaining the tiger; the beast let loose may worry his deliverer," declared *Poor Richard*. Franklin advised a friend who had expressed some unpopular notions in an article on religion to burn it immediately, saying, "He that spits against the wind spits in his own face." He further observed that "among us it is not necessary as among the Hottentots that a youth to be received into the company of men should prove his manhood by beating his mother." This wisdom saved him the bitter criticism that was later leveled at Paine and Jefferson for their unorthodox stances on religion.

Franklin once said "Orthodoxy is my doxy and heterodoxy is your doxy." He was joking, for just the opposite was true. He was no follower of conventional ideas, in religion or any other area. All his views were his own, Franklin originals. Let us examine some of them:

Piety. Franklin considered himself a religious man. He believed in God and his handiwork and had faith, based on reason. "I am much disposed to the world as I find it," he said. "I see so much wisdom in what I understand of its creation and government, that I suspect equal wisdom may be in what I do not understand. And thence have perhaps as much trust in God as the most pious Christian." As a scientist and an honest observer he could not deny the apparent weaknesses in the system, but he did his best to rationalize them. "If men are so wicked as we now see them with religion, what would they be if without it?" And like Job, he pondered a world where good people must suffer. "I sometimes wonder that all good men and women are not by Providence kept free from pain and disease. In the best of all possible worlds I should suppose it must be so; and I am piously inclined to believe that this world's not being made better was owing merely to the badness of the materials."

Prayer. Franklin was not a praying man. He was not opposed to prayer but he valued good works more highly. As *Poor Richard* said,

"Serving God is doing good to man, but praying is thought easier . . . and therefore most generally chosen." He favored "works of kindness, charity, mercy and public spirit; not holiday-keeping, sermon reading or hearing, performing church ceremonies, or making long prayers filled with flatteries and compliments—despised even by wise men and much less capable of pleasing the Deity." He declared "The worship of God is a duty, the hearing and reading of sermons may be useful; but if men rest in hearing and praying, as too many do, it is as if a tree should value itself in being watered and putting forth leaves, though it never produced any fruit."

William Temple Franklin told a story about his grandfather's youth that indicates something of Franklin's early attitude toward prayer. It was the custom of Franklin's devout father, Josiah, to say long graces before and after meals, a practice which seems to have proved tiresome to the younger element. One autumn day when the winter's provisions were being stored away, including a huge cask, Ben suggested to his father that if he would "say grace over the whole cask, once and for all, it would be a vast saving of time."

At the Constitutional Convention in 1789, the delegates appeared to be hopelessly deadlocked, and fearing that the chance of unifying the country under a constitution would be lost, Franklin made a motion that the Convention hereafter open its sessions with prayer. The small progress that had been made thus far, he argued, was proof of the imperfection of human understanding. "How has it happened, Sir,"—addressing Washington, who was presiding—"that we have not hitherto thought of humbly applying to the Father of lights to illuminate our understandings? . . . And if a sparrow cannot fall to the ground without His notice, is it probable that an empire can rise without His aid?" The delegates were surprised to hear this motion coming from Franklin, and he was surprised by their response. "The Convention," he jotted on the manuscript of his speech, "except three or four persons, thought prayers unnecessary."

Churches. While not a churchgoer himself, Franklin generously supported churches of all denominations. As a practical man, he felt that people needed religion and churches were therefore utilitarian, serving an important social purpose. He knew how sensitive people were about their church, saying, "Many have quarreled about religion that never practiced it." He offered some advice to a troubled minister whose congregation was badly split on the question of whether to divide itself and build another church. "Your tenderness of the Church's peace is truly laudable," Franklin told him, "but I think to build a new church in a growing place is not properly dividing but multiplying, and will really be the means of increasing the number of whose who worship God in that way. Many who cannot now be accommodated in the church go to other places or stay at home; and if we had another church, many who go to other places or stay at home would go to church. . . . I had for several years, nailed against the wall of my house, a pigeon-box that would hold six pair. And though they bred as fast as my neighbor's pigeons, I never had more than six pair, the old and strong driving out the young and weak, and obliging them to seek new habitations. At length I put up an additional box with apartments for entertaining twelve more pair, and it was soon filled with inhabitants by the overflowing of my first box and of others in the neighborhood. This I take to be a parallel case with the building a new church here."

Providence. By all odds, the English should have won the Revolutionary War. They had the guns, the ships, the money, and the men. But, despite many blunders on their side, the Americans won. This was for Franklin just more evidence of the "Hand of Providence more clearly in our favor." He believed in a divine Providence, which he said accounted for the good fortune of his life. In his "Advice to a Young Tradesman, written by an Old One," Franklin assured the young tradesman that the way to wealth was as plain as the way to market. "It depends chiefly on two words, industry and frugality . . . He that gets all he can honestly and saves all he gets . . . will certainly become rich—if that Being who governs the world . . . doth not in his wise Providence otherwise determine." Thus Providence was a useful concept for the supple-minded philosopher, as an explanation for unexpected good fortune, and as an escape-clause if things went awry.

Immortality. One of Franklin's religious tenets was the immortality of the soul and he employed an ingenious scientific argument to support this belief. Speaking of God's creation of the world, he marveled at the frugality and wisdom of God's works in saving labor.

An example was His system of continual self-propagation of plants and animals so that He wouldn't have to regularly troubled creating new ones. And in saving materials, Franklin cited the cyclic decay and reconstitution from its elements of such matter as wood, thus making it unnecessary for God to have to create new matter: "I say that when I see nothing annihilated and not even a drop of water wasted, I cannot suspect the annihilation of souls, or believe that He will suffer the daily waste of millions of minds . . . and put Himself to the continual trouble of making new ones. Thus finding myself to exit in the world I believe I shall, in some shape or other, always exist . . ." We might term this Franklin's law of the conservation of matter and souls."

He had another reason for believing in immortality, a reason more utilitarian though equally ingenious. Writing to Polly Hewson from Philadelphia, he told her about his life during his later years. He told her that during the long winter evenings he sometimes played cards. But never having completely shaken his Puritan background, he had to admit "a little compunction in reflecting that I spend time so idly. But another reflection comes to relieve me, whispering, 'You know that the soul is immortal; why then should you be such a niggard of a little time when you have a whole eternity before you?' So, being easily convinced, and like other reasonable creatures, satisfied with a small reason when it is in favor of doing what I have a mind to, I shuffle the cards again and begin another game."

Heaven and Hell. If he believed in immortality Franklin must have believed in heaven and hell. Yes he did, or at least he found it convenient to do so. He held King George III responsible for destroying one hundred thousand lives in the war; yet this criminal was apparently not suffering his just reward in this world. There had to be "a future state in which all that here appears to be wrong shall be set right, all that is crooked set straight." He defined heaven: "By heaven we understand a state of happiness, infinite in degree and eternal in duration." He had painted a Christian heaven for Madam Brillon and a pagan one for Madam Helvétius. For himself, he said of heaven he did not have the vanity to deserve it, the folly to expect it, or the ambition to desire it. He would put his trust in God, knowing that in this world he had been treated very well. He once got a bit closer to the worlds beyond, as he wrote from England to his wife. "In Cumberland I ascended a very high mountain where I had a prospect of a most beautiful country, of hills, fields, lakes, villas, etc., and at Whitehaven went down the coal mines till they told me I was eighty fathoms under the surface of the sea, which rolled over our heads; so that I have been nearer both the upper and lower regions than ever in my life before.''

Life and Death. As with many others before him, Franklin was fascinated with the mystery of life and death. He discoursed on the subject with the French physician Barbeu Dubourg, who had proposed experiments to recall to life people who appeared to be killed by lightning. Franklin agreed ''that the doctrines of life and death in general are yet but little understood,'' but he found precedents for hope. ''A toad buried in sand will live, it is said, till the sand becomes petrified, and then being enclosed in the stone, it may live for we know not how many ages.'' He had personally seen ordinary flies come back to life. They had been drowned in Madeira wine which had been shipped from Virginia to London. ''At the opening of one of the bottles . . . three drowned flies fell into the first glass that was filled. Having heard it remarked that drowned flies were capable of being revived by the rays of the sun, I proposed making the experiment upon these. . . . In less than three hours two of them began by degrees to recover life. They commenced by some convulsive motions of the thighs, and at length they raised themselves upon their legs, wiped their eyes with their forefeet, beat and brushed their wings with their hind feet, and soon after began to fly, finding themselves in Old England without knowing how they came thither. The third continued lifeless till sunset, when losing all hopes of him, he was thrown away.''

Always seeking practical applications of his experiments, Franklin wished it were possible ''to invent a method of embalming drowned persons in such a manner that they may be recalled to life at any period, however distant . . .'' Then, becoming personal, and reflecting on ''having a very ardent desire to see and observe the state of America a hundred years hence, he proclaimed, ''I should prefer to any ordinary death being immersed in a cask of Madeira wine with a few friends till that time to be recalled to life by the solar warmth of my dear country!''

Heresy. Franklin might have been a non-conformist but certainly not a heretic. His friend, Dr. Priestley, he referred to as an honest heretic. This was no distinction, he remarked, for ''all the heretics I have known have been virtuous men.'' They had to possess the virtue of fortitude or they would not express their heresy. Further, he noted on the subject of their virtues, "they cannot afford to be deficient in any of the other virtues, as that would give advantage to their many enemies; and they have not, like orthodox sinners, such a number of friends to excuse or justify them."

Evolution of Doctrine. Religions that hold fast to a rigid set of principles are sometimes forced into an untenable position, as Franklin observed in the case of the Quakers and their prohibition against war of any kind. They used various ridiculous subterfuges in order to assist in their own defense. An exceptional religious group in this regard were the Dunkers, a German Baptist sect which established itself in Pennsylvania in the 18th century. When the leader of the group complained that they were unjustly accused of abominable practices and principles, Franklin suggested that it might be well for them to publish the articles of their belief in order to put a stop to this treatment. The leader explained that this could not be done for the following reason: "When we were first drawn together as a society," he said, "it had pleased God to enlighten our minds so far as to see that some doctrines which we once esteemed truths were errors, and that others which we had esteemed errors were real truths. From time to time He has been pleased to afford us further light, and our principles have been improving and our errors diminishing. Now we are not sure that we are arrived at the end of this progression, and at the perfection of spiritual or theological knowledge. And we fear that if we should once print our confession of faith, we should feel ourselves as if bound and confined by it and perhaps be unwilling to receive further improvement, and our successors still more so, as conceiving what their elders and founders had done to be something sacred, never to be departed from." This modesty in a sect so delighted Franklin, he cited it as "perhaps a singular instance in the history of mankind, every other sect supposing itself in possession of all truth, and that those who differ are so far in the wrong." He made the analogy of a man traveling in foggy weather: "Those at some distance before him on the road he sees wrapped up in the fog, as well as those behind him, and also people in the fields on each side; but near him all appears clear, though in truth he is as much in the fog as any of them."

Sunday Laws. In 18th century America, Sunday laws were strictly enforced, particularly in New England. A Connecticut law of 1688 forbade the profanation of the Sabbath by playing or unnecessary travel. Such offense was penalized with a five shilling fine or sitting in the stocks for one hour. This law proved a handicap to President Washington during his tour of 1789. As can be imagined, Franklin did not enthusiastically endorse such a law. He wrote to a lawyer in Connecticut, "I should be glad to know what it is that distinguishes Connecticut religion from common religion . . ." Between August and September of 1761 Franklin had traveled in Europe and in his letter referred to his experiences there. "When I traveled in Flanders I thought of your excessively strict observation [observance] of Sunday; and that a man could hardly travel on that day among you upon his lawful occasions without hazard of punishment. While where I was, everyone traveled if he pleased or diverted himself any other way. And in the afternoon both high and low went to the play or the opera, where there was plenty of singing, fiddling, and dancing. I looked round for God's judgments but saw no signs of them. The cities were well built and full of inhabitants, the markets filled with plenty, the people well favored and well clothed; the fields well tilled; the cattle fat and strong; the fences, houses, and windows all in repair. And no *Old Tenor* [depreciated paper money such as existed in Connecticut] anywhere in the country. "All this evidence," Franklin concluded, "would almost make one suspect that the Deity is not so angry at that offense as a New England justice."

Sin. On this formidable subject, the doctor had a few thoughts. "Original sin," he alleged to be "as ridiculous as imputed righteousness." "Sin is not hurtful because it is forbidden," he opined, but "forbidden because it is hurtful." When Madam Brillon, in a gloomy mood, reflected, "There are so many sorrows and so few pleasures," Franklin replied in a characteristically cheerful tone. "Like you, I feel that there are many sorrows in this life. But it also appears to me that there are many more pleasures. This is why I love life. One must not blame providence inconsiderately. Reflect how many of our duties it has naturally made to be pleasures. And to several of them it has the further goodness to give the name sin, so that we might enjoy them the more."

Divinity of Jesus. When he was 84 years old and close to the end of his life, Franklin received a letter from the President of Yale College asking him about his religion and particularly for his opinion of Jesus of Nazareth. He was then very ill, yet he answered the letter with clarity and frankness, and a touch of brave levity considering that his death was at this time no joking matter. He summed up his religious beliefs in the same five statements he had enunciated for Madam Brillon. As to Jesus, he said, "I think his system of morals and his religion, as he left them to us, the best the world ever saw or is likely to see. But I apprehend it has received various corrupting changes and I have, with most of the present dissenters in England, some doubt as to his divinity. It is a question I do not dogmatize upon, having never studied it, and think it needless to busy myself with it now where I expect soon an opportunity of knowing the truth with less trouble." It was a judicious decision, for he died six weeks later.

He said he could see no harm, however, in Jesus' divinity being believed if that belief would have the good effect of making his doctrines more respected and observed. He added, "especially as I do not perceive that the Supreme takes it amiss, by distinguishing the unbelievers in his government of the world with any peculiar marks of his displeasure." Not wishing to unchain the tiger, Franklin requested that his letter be kept private. He explained, that he had let others enjoy their religious sentiments without criticism, even those that appeared to him unsupportable or absurd. There were a great variety of sects in Philadelphia and they all experienced his goodwill in assistance with money for building new places of worship. "As I have never opposed any of their doctrines," he concluded, "I hope to go out of the world in peace with them all."

Ordination. In 1784 while he was still in France, Franklin received an urgent request from two young clergymen in Maryland. It seemed that the Archbishop of Canterbury, mixing his religion with politics, had refused to ordain these clergymen as ministers of the Episcopal church unless they would first take the oath of allegiance to Great Britain. Properly incensed, and considering the ordination to be a mere technicality anyway, Franklin tried to be of assistance. He asked his friend the papal nuncio if he would ordain them but was assured, "the thing is impossible unless the gentlemen became Catholics." He therefore advised them what he thought might be their options. They could become Presbyterians, but if that did not suit them he suggested that they ordain themselves. He elaborated "If the British Islands were sunk in the sea (and the surface of the globe has suffered greater changes) you would probably take some such method as this. And, if they persist in denying you ordination it is the same thing. A hundred years hence, when people are more enlightened, it will be wondered at that men in America, qualified by their learning and piety to pray for and instruct their neighbors, should not be permitted to do it till they had made a voyage of six thousand miles out and home to ask leave of a cross old gentleman at Canterbury . . ." By their account, he thought, the Archbishop seemed to have as little regard for the souls of the people of Maryland as Attorney-General Seymour in King William's reign had for those of Virginia. And this reminder not surprisingly started him off recounting an anecdote.

"The Reverend Commissary Blair, who projected the college of that province [College of William and Mary, Williamsburg, Va., founded in 1693] and was in England to solicit benefactions and a charter, relates that the queen in the king's absence . . . ordered Seymour to draw up the charter, which was to be given with 2,000 pounds in money. He opposed the grant, saying that the nation was engaged in an expensive war, that the money was wanted for better purpose, and he did not see the least occasion for a College in Virginia. Blair represented to him that its intention was to educate and qualify young men to be ministers of the gospel, much wanted there, and begged Mr. Attorney would consider that the people of Virginia as well as the people of England had souls to be saved. "Souls!" said he, "damn your souls! Make tobacco!"

23

THE UNMELANCHOLY PHILOSOPHER

HERMAN MELVILLE REFERRED TO FRANKLIN AS A "household Plato."
But the sanguine Franklin does not conform to the stereotype of a philosopher. Perhaps that is because he was not a philosopher, at least not in the narrow, technical aspect of that discipline. He was called a philosopher because of his investigations in natural philosophy, the term then used for science. Early in his career he had tried his hand at metaphysical philosophy and found it wanting, when by its own logic he was able to prove that it is moral to be a horse thief.

That was in London, when at 19 he wrote a pamphlet entitled, "A Dissertation on Liberty and Necessity, Pleasure and Pain." As a journeyman printer he had printed "The Religion of Nature" by William Wollaston, an authority on moralistic thought, and had disagreed with some of the author's arguments, causing him to compose this refutation. According to Wollaston, every action that is done according to truth is good, and every action contrary to truth is evil. Employing this premise, Franklin pursues its logical conclusions:

1. To act according to truth is to use and esteem everything for what it is, etc. [This is Wollaston's postulate, which Franklin quotes.]

2. Thus if A steals a horse from B, and rides away upon him, he uses him not as he is in truth, *viz* the property of another, but as his own, which is contrary to truth, and therefore evil.

3. But, as this gentleman himself says . . . [quoting Wollaston], "In order to judge rightly what any thing is, it must be considered not only what it is in one respect, but also what it may be in any other respect."

4. So in this case it ought to be considered that A is naturally a covetous being, feeling an uneasiness in the want of B's horse, which produces an inclination for stealing him, stronger than his fear of punishment for so doing.

5. This is truth likewise, and A acts according to it when he steals the horse. Besides, if it is proved to be a truth that A has not power over his own actions, it will be indisputable that he acts according to truth, and impossible he should do otherwise.

But lest anyone believe that by this hocus pocus Franklin had convinced himself that horse stealing was good or that he condoned it, he continued:

I would not be understood by this to encourage or defend theft; 'tis only for the sake of the argument, and will certainly have no ill effect. The order and course of things will not be affected by reasoning of this kind; and 'tis . . . as much according to truth, for B to dislike and punish the theft of his horse, as it is for A to steal him.

Despite this disclaimer, Franklin reasoned that this and other controversial ideas in the work would injure his reputation and he destroyed most of the copies. Thus his first real philosophic venture became his last. He was personally dissatisfied with the arbitrary basis for philosophic argument and therefore turned to science which he found to be both sound and safe. If he did not become a philosopher it may be because he did not have the disposition for it.

Whenever possible, he saw the sunny side of things. When his sister Jane, whose life was full of tragedy, was melancholy in anticipation of further misfortune, he tried to reason with her: "It may not be amiss to allow ourselves beforehand the enjoyment of some expected pleasures, the expectation being often the greatest part of it, but it is not so well to afflict ourselves with apprehensions of misfortunes that may never arise." He had expressed his optimistic outlook in his newspaper. "I do not love to see the dark side of things; and besides I do not think such reflections on life altogether just. The world is a very good world, and if we behave ourselves well, we shall doubtless do very well in it.'' This statement was made to refute the sentiment expressed in a selection from an English clergyman's book which Franklin had published in the previous issue of the *Gazette*. The selection from this new book was entitled, ''Meditation on the Vanity and Brevity of Human Life,'' and it began:

> Unhappy we, children of the dust!
> Why were we born to see the sun?
> Why did our mothers bring us forth to
> Misery; and unkindly rejoice to
> Hear us cry?

The clergyman's point was that this world is insignificant, just a vale of tears; and that we must expect to suffer this unhappy existence to reach our reward in eternity. This dismal outlook was too much for the cheerful young printer; he had to respond. He did, in this way. He parodied the mournful lines of the clergyman, following each line with his own, comparing the clergyman's elegant expressions with his own irreverent counterparts. [Franklin's rejoinders are in italic.]

> All the few days we live are full of vanity;
> and choicest pleasures sprinkled with bitterness:
>
> *All the few cakes we have are puffed up with yeast;*
> *and the nicest gingerbread is spotted with ''flyshits''!*
>
> The time that's past is vanished like a dream;
> and that which is to come is not yet at all;
>
> *The cakes that we have eaten are no more to*
> *be seen; and those which are to come are not yet baked.*
>
> The present we are in stays but for a moment,
> and then flies away, and returns no more:
>
> *The present mouthful is chewed but a little while,*
> *and then is swallowed down, and comes up no more.*
>
> Already we are dead to the years we have lived;
> and shall never live them over again:
>
> *Already we have digested the cakes we have eaten,*
> *and shall never eat them over again.*
>
> But the longer we live, the shorter is our life;
> and in the end we become a little lump of clay.

And the more we eat, the less is the piece remaining;
and in the end the whole will become sir-reverence! [*a turd*]

O vain, and miserable world! How sadly true is all this story!

O vain and miserable cake-shop! etc.

And then he concluded: "Away with all such insignificant medita-
tions. I am for taking Solomon's advice, eating bread with joy, and
drinking wine with a merry heart. Let us rejoice and bless God, that
we are neither oysters, hogs, nor dray-horses. . . ."

Even though he was not a philosopher, Franklin "philosophized"
upon many subjects. Since he was an outstanding product of that century known as the Age of Reason, he firmly believed on action based
on reason. But sometimes, when frustrated by what seemed to him to
be people's irrational obstinacy, he wondered whether the world
wouldn't be better off if something more dependable, like instinct,
were substituted for reason. Such a thought occurred to him as he rode
from London to Dover by horse carriage to catch the boat to France.
He wrote to Mary Stevenson:

> All the way to Dover we were furnished with post-chaises, hung so
> as to lean forward, the top coming down over one's eyes like a
> hood, as if to prevent one's seeing the country; which being one of
> my great pleasures, I was engaged in perpetual disputes with the inn-
> keepers, hostlers, and postillions about getting the straps taken up a
> hole or two before and let down as much behind, they insisting that
> the chaise leaning forward was an ease to the horses and that the
> contrary would kill them. I suppose the chaise leaning forward looks
> to them like a willingness to go forward and that its hanging back
> shows a reluctance. They added other reasons that were no reasons
> at all, and made me, as upon a hundred other occasions, almost wish
> that mankind had never been endowed with a reasoning faculty . . .
> and that they had been furnished with a good sensible instinct in-
> stead . . .

About a decade later he expanded this same thought in a letter to
Madam Brillon following a point of disagreement between them:
"Human reason . . . must be a very uncertain thing," he said, "since
two sensible persons like you and me can draw diametrically opposed
conclusions from the same premises. I think reason is a blind guide.
True and sure instinct would be worth much more. All inferior animals
put together do not commit as many mistakes in the course of a year as

a single man within a month, even though this man claims to be guided by reason. This is why, as long as I was fortunate enough to have a wife, I adopted the habit of letting myself be guided by her opinion on difficult matters. For women, I believe, have a certain feel which is more reliable than our reasonings.''

This is only one of many apparent contradictions in Franklin's philosophy of life. He preached frugality but said he could never practice it. His virtue of humility he found even more difficult to attain. The work ethic was part of his heritage, reinforced regularly in his training. He believed in hard work and was never lazy, but all through his life he claimed to be seeking leisure while he readily accepted a heavy burden of public duties. He sometimes wondered what was the natural human condition—to strive and build by the sweat of the brow according to the Calvinistic doctrine of the Puritans, or to work just hard enough to survive and live simply off the land, as was the custom of the Indians. An answer to this fundamental question came to him from an unexpected source, a mysterious stranger from a far-off land.

"We had here some years since, a Transylvanian Tartar who had traveled much in the East and came hither merely to see the West, intending to go home through the Spanish West Indies, China, etc. He asked me one day what I thought might be the reason that so many . . . nations as the Tartars in Europe and Asia, the Indians in America, and the Negroes in Africa continued a wandering, careless life and refused to live in cities and cultivate the arts [trades] they saw practiced by the civilized parts of mankind? While I was considering what answer to make to him, he said in his broken English, 'God made man for Paradise. He make him for live lazy. Man make God angry. God turn him out of Paradise and bid workee. Man no love workee. He want to go to Paradise again. He want to live lazy. So all mankind,' the Tartar concluded, 'love lazy.' "

Franklin was intrigued with this hypothesis and postulated that this inherent love for the lazy life might actually be the source of man's ambition. He declared: "It seems certain that the hope of becoming at some time of life free from the necessity of care and labor, together with the fear of penury, are the main springs of most people's industry." More than thirty years later he returned to the same theme, this time with a quotation in Negro dialect, which resembles the Tartar's dialect: "Boccarorra (meaning the white men) make de black man workee, make de horse workee, make de ox workee, make eberyting workee; only de hog. He, de hog, no workee. He eat, he drink, he walk about, he go to sleep when he please, he libb like a gempleman."

This time Franklin came down strongly on the side of work. Advising Europeans who were considering moving to America, he assured them that America needed farmers, carpenters and shoemakers but not idle gentlemen who live on the labor of others. Such gentlemen he compared to the Negro's gentleman-hog. They are good for nothing till their death, when like the hog's carcass their estates are cut up. "In short," he said, "America is the land of labor and by no means what the English call Lubberland . . . where the streets are said to be paved with half-peck loaves, the houses tiled with pancakes, and where the fowls fly about ready-roasted, crying, Come eat me!"

He explained that in America the workman is honored, even the mechanic, because he is engaged in useful employment. "The people have a saying," he noted, "that God Almighty is himself a mechanic, the greatest in the universe; and He is respected and admired more for the variety, ingenuity, and utility of his handiworks, than for the antiquity of his family." Although most of Franklin's friends in Europe were members of the nobility, his stubbornly democratic nature combined with his practicality made him favor workmen over ladies and gentlemen, philosophers and artists. When a dancing society in Philadelphia excluded the mechanics, who were considered rough by the gentle people, Franklin countered that this rule would exclude "God Almighty, the greatest mechanic in the universe, who made all things, as the scripture testifies, by weight and measure."

Joke as he might, Franklin was a firm believer in the old-time virtues. After the Stamp Act was passed despite his efforts against it, he resigned himself to live with this tax. He told a friend that frugality and industry by Americans would go a great way toward indemnifying them for their losses. "Idleness and pride," he preached, "tax with a heavier hand than kings and parliaments. If we can get rid of the former, we may easily bear the latter." Self-reliance was another of those virtues that influenced Franklin in his own behavior. According to the Abbé de la Roche, he believed that "to be useful to others and to depend on them as little as possible is to approach the perfection of the all-powerful Being, who does good to everything and has need of nothing."

Unlike Thoreau at Walden Pond, Franklin did not associate self-reliance with solitude. "I have read abundance of fine things on the subject of solitude," he commented, "and I know 'tis a common boast in the mouths of those that appear to be thought wise, that they are never less alone than when alone. I acknowledge solitude an agreeable refreshment to a busy mind; but were these thinking people obliged to be always alone I am apt to think they would quickly find their very being insupportable to them. . . . One of the philosophers, I think it was Plato, used to say that he had rather be the veriest stupid block in nature than the possessor of all knowledge without some intelligent being to communicate it to."

Franklin recognized that the human being is a social animal and requires companionship to achieve happiness. That is why he joined social clubs. Happiness, of course, is one of those elusive conditions of man that philosophers are constantly attempting to comprehend. The pursuit of happiness was specified as an unalienable right of all persons in the Declaration of Independence, but how one was to achieve it was left for each individual to discover. Always ready with a fresh viewpoint, Franklin proposed that happiness could be discovered more readily in the mirror than in the major events of life, as he said: "Human felicity is produced not so much by great pieces of good fortune that seldom happen, as by little advantages that occur every day. Thus if you teach a poor young man to shave himself and keep his razor in order, you may contribute more to the happiness of his life than giving him a thousand guineas." Of course the negative factors would have to be eliminated. "And I find it of importance to the happiness of life, the being freed from vain terrors, especially of objects that we are every day exposed to." He cited the great fear people had in those days of fresh air, particularly damp, night air. The terror many people felt in going near the water for fear of falling in and drowning, he pointed out, could easily be overcome by people learning to swim.

However, when all was said that could be said on the subject, he decided that it was not events, large or small, that determine human happiness, but one's fundamental makeup, or to use his words, "internals" rather than "externals." Were there not "two sorts of people in the world, who with equal degrees of health and wealth and other comforts of life, become, the one happy, the other unhappy"? When he was in London he received the news of the death of Potts and Parsons, two former members of his club, the Junto. "Odd characters, both of them," was the way he remembered them. "Parsons was a wise man, that often acted foolishly; Potts a wit, that seldom acted wisely. If enough were the means to make a man happy, one [Parsons] had always the means of happiness, without ever enjoying the thing; the other [Potts] had always the thing, without ever possessing the means. Parsons, even in his prosperity, always fretting; Potts, in the midst of his poverty, ever laughing. It seems, then, that happiness in this life rather depends on internals than externals; and that besides the natural effects of wisdom and virtue, vice and folly, there is such a thing as a happy or an unhappy constitution."

Fortunately, as many testified, Franklin had a happy disposition. Herman Melville wrote of Franklin, that his mind was grave but never serious. Franklin was realistic but uncritical. He said of his personal servant, a black slave, "He has as few faults as most of them, and I see with only one eye and hear with only one ear." His normal outlook might be described as cautious optimism. Remarking about the war to Madam Brillon, he said, "in bad fortune I hope for good, and in good I fear bad. I play this game with almost the same equanimity as when you see me playing chess. You know I never give up a game before it is finished, always hoping to win . . . and when I have a good game I guard against presumption." In practical matters he was usually ready to compromise with an opponent. He told a fellow experimenter with whom he had a difference, "You see I am willing to meet you half way, a complaisance I have not met with in . . . any other hypothesis maker, and therefore may value myself a little upon it, especially as they say I have some ability in defending even the wrong side of a question, when I think fit to take it in hand."

He was always gracious, avoiding disagreement and trying to please. In fact, John Adams found fault with him in his dealings with the French officials, saying that he was too easy with them and never wanted to offend anyone. Franklin told Cabanis that bad humor was a vice, an uncleanliness of the soul, and politeness was a virtue, a kind of amiable benevolence, rather than the artificial etiquette expressed in prescribed gestures and formalities. Cabanis observed, "that which he esteemed was the politeness of the heart, the evidence of a habitual obligingness. He made of it a virtue. He thought that one is obliged to be cheerful, almost as one must pay his debts, and that only a higher interest may excuse a good man for offending another. . . . the most irreconcilable discords, the most violent hates, often stem, he said, 'from minor pricks such as those which released the winds enclosed

in Ulysses' leather bag. One may easily avoid many chagrins and misfortunes by a little attention to himself and consideration for others.
And even if an open rupture comes about, one is at fault if he does not
make the people with whom he lives as happy as he can.' "

No abstract philosopher, Franklin disseminated his ideas so that
they might be of benefit to others. In a reverse Dale Carnegie way, he
indicated by indirection, desirable social behavior in a piece he wrote
for the *Gazette* entitled, "Rules for Making Oneself a Disagreeable
Companion."

> Rules, by the observation of which, a man of wit and learning
> may nevertheless make himself a disagreeable companion. Your
> business is to *shine;* therefore you must by all means prevent the
> shining of others, for their brightness may make yours the less dis-
> tinguished. To this end,
>
> 1. If possible engross the whole discourse, and when other matter
> fails, talk much of yourself, your education, your knowledge, your
> circumstances, your successes in business, your victories in dis-
> putes, your own wise sayings and observations on particular oc-
> casions, etc., etc., etc.
>
> 2. If when you are out of breath, one of the company should seize
> the opportunity of saying something; watch his words, and, if pos-
> sible, find somewhat either in his sentiment or expression, immedi-
> ately to contradict and raise a dispute upon. Rather than fail, criti-
> cize even his grammar.
>
> 3. If another should be saying an indisputably good thing either
> give no attention to it or interrupt him; or draw away the attention
> of others; or, if you can guess what he would be at, be quick and say
> it before him; or, if he gets it said, and you perceive the company
> pleased with it, own it to be a good thing, and withal remark that it
> had been said by Bacon, Locke, Bayle, or some other eminent
> writer: thus you deprive him of the reputation he might have gained
> by it, and gain some yourself, as you hereby show your great read-
> ing memory.
>
> 4. When modest men have been thus treated by you a few times,
> they will choose ever after to be silent in your company; then you
> may shine on without fear of a rival; rallying them at the same time
> for their dullness, which will be to you a new fund of wit.

In a closing paragraph of the piece Franklin demonstrated his
touted ability for defending "even the wrong side of a question,"

when he showed that the obnoxious fellow can please twenty times as many people as the polite man: "Thus you will be sure to please yourself. The polite man aims at pleasing others, but you shall go beyond him even in that. A man can be present only in one company, but may at the same time be absent in twenty. He [the polite man] can please only where he is; you, wherever you are not."

Like all people, Franklin had his somber moments, when pessimism obscured his normal happy outlook. Such black moods might be traced to his grave concerns in the war and one was captured in a letter he wrote to Priestley in 1782. Speaking of the inanimate works of nature, he observed, "the more I discovered of the former, the more I admired them," and in respect to the animate forms, "the more I know of the latter, the more I am disgusted with them." He then expressed his disappointment with the human species. "Man, I find to be a sort of being very badly constructed, as they are generally more easily provoked than reconciled, more disposed to do mischief to each other than to make reparations, much more easily deceived than undeceived, and having more pride and even pleasure in killing than in begetting one another. For without a blush they assemble in great armies at noonday to destroy, and when they have killed as many as they can, they exaggerate the number to augment the fancied glory. But they creep into corners to cover themselves with the darkness of night when they mean to beget, as being ashamed of a virtuous action. A virtuous action it would be . . . if the species were really worth producing or preserving, but this I begin to doubt."

He was sure that Priestly, as a minister of the gospel, would have no such doubts about people for he was too busy saving their souls. But perhaps as he grew older he might look upon that as a hopeless project, and repent of having murdered so many harmless mice in his experiments with oxygen and wish instead, to save the world from further harm, he had used boys and girls instead. To support such a macabre notion and relieve the shock, Franklin had an anecdote to tell:

"A young angel of distinction being sent down to this world on some business for the first time, had an old courier-spirit assigned him as a guide. They arrived over the Seas of Martinico in the middle of the long day of obstinate fighting between the fleets of Rodney and DeGrasse." This was the great sea victory of the British over the French in 1782 in the West Indies, which news just received, probably accounted for Franklin's bitter mood. "When through the clouds of smoke," Franklin continued his story of the angel's travels, "he saw the fire of the guns, the decks covered with mangled limbs, and bodies dead or dying; the ships sinking, burning, or blown into the air; and the quantity of pain, misery, and destruction. The crews yet alive were thus with so much eagerness dealing round to one another; he turned angrily to his guide and said, 'You blundering blockhead . . . you undertook to conduct me to the earth, and you have brought me into Hell!' 'No, sir,' says the guide 'I have made no mistake, this is really the earth, and these are men. Devils never treat one another in this cruel manner; they have more sense, and more of what men vainly call humanity.' ''

In another letter to Priestley he compared man's progress in science to that in morality, and ended with the same mournful words. In it he correctly envisions much of what has been accomplished in science since his time, but not in "moral science." He said to Priestley, "The rapid progress true science now makes occasions my regretting sometimes that I was born too soon. It is impossible to imagine the height to which may be carried in a thousand years, the power of man over matter. We may perhaps learn to deprive large masses of their gravity and give them absolute levity for the sake of easy transport. Agriculture may diminsh its labor and double its produce. All diseases may by sure means be prevented or cured, not excepting even that of old age, and our lives lengthened even beyond the antediluvian standard. Oh that moral science were in as far a way of improvement, that men would cease to be wolves to one another, and that human beings would at length learn what they now improperly call humanity."

Moral science might be bankrupt but moral algebra was a going concern. Moral algebra was Franklin's scheme for making decisions on complex problems of judgment. He explained it to his nephew, Jonathan Williams, who asked him for advice on a business proposition. Franklin was unacquainted with the matter and responded as follows: "I do not know what to advise concerning Monsieur Monthieu's proposition. Follow your own judgment. If you doubt, set down all the reasons pro and con in opposite columns on a sheet of paper, and when you have considered them two or three days, perform an operation similar to that in some questions of algebra. Observe what reasons or motives in each column are equal in weight, one to one, one to two, two to three, or the like, and when you have struck out from both sides all the equalities, you will see in which column remains the balance."

Why go to all this trouble? Because, he explains, "it is for want of having all the motives for and against an important action present in or before the mind at the same time that people hesitate and change their determinations backwards and forwards, day after day, as different sets of reasons are collected or forgot. If they conclude and act upon the last set, it is perhaps not because those were the best, but because they happen to be present in the mind, and the better [ones] absent. This kind of moral algebra I have often practised in important and dubious concerns, and though it cannot be mathematically exact, I have found it extremely useful." And finally, saving his most persuasive argument for last, he confides to Jonathan, who was a young bachelor, "By the way, if you do not learn it, I apprehend you will never be married."

In all honesty, however, it must be reported that on another occasion he suggested to Jonathan a more traditional and less scientific basis for making his matrimonial selection. He wrote, "I think a connection with Mr. S. might be advantageous to you both in the way of business. Besides, he is rich and has handsome daughters."

24

AN AMERICAN AT HOME

IN 1785 AN OLD MAN LEFT EUROPE TO GO HOME to die in a floundering new nation. Some years before, on another journey from Europe to America, he had written, "I am going from the old world to the new and I fancy I feel like those who are leaving this world for the next; grief at the parting, fear of the passage, hope for the future . . ." Now, he was not thinking of the future. He expressed himself to David Hartly, who had signed the peace treaty for England: "We were long fellow laborers in the best of all works, the work of peace. I leave you still in the field, but having finished my day's task, I am going home *to go to bed*. Wish me a good night's rest . . ."

But he could not die, his country still needed him. As President of Pennsylvania his presence would lend stature and stability to the government of his own home state. As host to the Constitutional Convention he would help to unify the separate, sovereign states into a nation under law. And as the first great American he would write his autobiography to show millions of new Americans how it was possible in this country to rise from obscurity to become a successful businessman, scientist, and world-famous citizen.

Franklin left France with his two grandsons, his nephew, his friend LeVeillard, and the renowned sculptor Houdon. LeVeillard, the mayor of Passy, accompanied him as far as England and urged him to complete his memoirs (autobiography) on the voyage home. Houdon, who had already done a sculpture of Franklin, went with him to America to do a bust of Washington. The trip across the Channel was rough and Franklin was the only member of the party who did not get seasick. They spent four days in the English port of Southhampton before embarking for America. During this interval Franklin was happy to receive visits from friends, including Benjamin Vaughan, his English publisher, and Bishop Shipley with his wife and daughter Catherine. The latter was the talkative "Kitty" who had once entertained him on a memorable coach ride to London. Franklin's son William came from London and they arranged to legally convey William's lands in America to Temple for a sum of 48,000 French livres. This meeting between father and son was formal, there was no reconciliation. Franklin had recently written William, "I ought not to blame you for differing in sentiment with me in public affairs. We are men, all subject to errors. Our opinions are not in our power, they are formed and governed much by circumstances that are often as inexplicable as they are irresistible." Yet he could not forgive his son as he said, for "taking up arms against me in a cause wherin my good fame, fortune, and life were all at stake." He believed "there are natural duties which precede political ones and cannot be extinguished by them."

Loving the water, whether being on it or in it, Franklin took time during the interlude at Southhampton to bathe in St. Martin's saltwater hot baths. He reported, "I went at noon to bathe . . . and, floating on my back, fell asleep and slept near an hour by my watch, without sinking or turning! A thing I never did before and should hardly have thought possible. Water is the easiest bed that can be." Another first for Franklin! Jesus may have been the first to walk on water, but Benjamin was the first to sleep on it. And 200 years later another generation of Americans was to share his discovery of the comfort of a waterbed.

The voyage to America was a month and a half long. Franklin had promised LeVeillard and Vaughan to work on his memoirs but instead he plotted the Gulf Stream, took its temperature daily at different depths, and wrote three scientific papers. One was "On the Causes and Cure of Smoky Chimneys," another was a description of his "New Stove for Burning Pitcoal," which he had invented in 1771, and the third was entitled "Maritime Observations." Having grown up in a port city and having made eight trips across the ocean, he had given a lot of thought during his life to the efficient operation of ships, the comfort of the passengers, and the dangers to be avoided. He wrote of these at length, stating as his excuse, "the garrulity of an old man had got hold of me, and as I may never have another occasion of writing on this subject, I think I may as well now, once and for all, empty my nautical budget." He proposed water-tight compartments in ships to keep them from sinking; he designed a compartmented dish for serving soup so that "when the ship would make a sudden heel the soup would not, in a body, flow over one side and fall into the people's laps and scald them"; and he gave instructions for constructing swimming anchors to restrain ships where the water is too deep for bottom anchors. He discussed the Gulf Stream and its navigation and drew the first formal chart showing its course.

With regard for the passengers, he commented, "The worst thing in ordinary merchant ships is the cookery. They have no professed cook, and the worst hand as a seaman is appointed to that office, in which he is not only very ignorant but very dirty. The sailors have therefore a saying that 'God sends meat and the devil cooks [it].' Passengers . . . willing to believe heaven orders all things for the best, may suppose that . . . sea air and constant exercise, by the motion of the vessel, would give us extraordinary appetites, [and] bad cooks were kindly sent to prevent our eating too much." On the other hand, it might be considered that heaven "forseeing one should have bad cooks, good appetites were furnished to prevent our starving."

Franklin's landing in Philadelphia was signaled with cannon, bells, and a grand reception "by a crowd of people with huzzas." The affectionate welcoming crowd followed him to his door, and for the rest of the week he received visits of individuals and delegations greeting and acclaiming him. Leaders of all governmental bodies and parties came, followed by the provost and professors of the university, the officers of the militia, the Constitutional Society, the Freemasons, and the American Philosophical Society. It was as if his past life in Philadelphia were passing in review to do him honor. Not to be forgotten were the men of the Union Fire Company, of which only four of the original members were still alive. Franklin was delighted to meet with them and promised to bring his fire helmet and bucket to the next meeting. The printers saluted him on his 80th birthday and drank to his health.

In response to speeches of exuberant acclaim by aspiring orators, Franklin responded briefly and modestly. To the Constitutional Society he said, "My principal merit, if I may claim any in public affairs, is that of having been always ready and willing to receive and follow good advice."

They knew better, for he more than any other man in 1776 shaped the Constitution of Pennsylvania. It was he who proposed the plural executive with a council and a president, and a single legislature, the General Assembly. He strongly opposed the English system of two houses of parliament, making the analogy of a wagon hitched to a pair of steers at either end, and facing opposite directions, in order that it might thus be easier to descend a mountain. Another version of his metaphor, remembered by Thomas Paine, stated that Franklin likened a legislature with two houses to "putting one horse before a cart and the other behind it, and whipping them both. If the horses are of equal strength, the wheels of the cart, like the wheels of government, will stand still. And if the horses are strong enough, the cart will be torn to pieces."

In case this story would not carry the point, Franklin had concocted a fable that was sure to convince his listeners: "A snake with two heads and one body was going to a brook to drink and on her way was to pass through a hedge, a twig of which opposed her direct course. One head chose to go on the right side of the twig, the other on the left, so that time was spent in the contest and before the decision was completed the poor snake died of thirst." But good stories don't always produce results. The Legislature eventually did decide in favor of the single house, but the debates continued for two or three months, which led Franklin to look outside and remark: "Gentlemen, in the midst of our present anarchy life goes on just as before. Take care if our disputes continue, the people may come to realize they can easily do without our services."

When he left Europe, Franklin told his friends "I shall now be free of politics for the rest of my life." He was looking forward to a life without the care of duties and to the pleasure of pursuing his scientific interests again. But no sooner was he home than he was nominated for the Supreme Executive Council of Pennsylvania by the Anti-Constitutionalist party. The rival Constitutionalist Society could not allow the "father of the Pennsylvania Constitution" to be on the opposing ticket so they nominated him as well. The third party made up of the skilled mechanics, the Mechanical Society, laid claim to him as a printer and named him as their candidate. After this election, which Franklin won, the General Assembly with only one dissenting vote in 77 selected him to be President of Pennsylvania. Thus, the old workhorse who had been looking longingly at the pasture suddenly found himself again in harness. Why had he done it? He was not sure himself. To Madam Helvétius he wrote that he hoped to be of some further benefit to his people. "Otherwise," he added gallantly, "I shall wish I had accepted your friendly invitation to pass the rest of my days with you." To Thomas Paine he indicated he did not have the firmness to refuse the request of the different, opposing parties to try to reconcile them. He may have hit it more accurately when he suggested to Bishop Shipley that he was taken in by the overwhelming reception he received and succumbed to "some remains of ambition, from which I had imagined myself free." He said he hoped to be able to bear the fatigue for one year and then retire.

But it did not work out that way. A year later he wrote, I enjoy here everything I could wish for except repose, "and that I may soon expect, either by cessation of my office . . . or by ceasing to live." Yet, when his first annual term was up he ran for another, and did even better in the election than the first time. On April 15, 1787 he wrote LeVeillard, "Having served one year as President of Council, I had not resolution enough to refuse serving another, and was again chosen in November last, without a single dissenting voice." "By our laws," he observed, "one cannot serve more than three years, but I think I shall decline the third." A week later he was thinking differently, as he wrote Abbé Morellet, "Popular favor, not the most constant thing in the world, stands by me. My election to the presidency for the second year was unanimous. Will this disposition continue the same for the third?" He seemed now to be thinking of a third term. But it had its risks: "A man who holds high office so often finds himself exposed to the danger of disobliging someone in the fulfillment of his duty, that the resentment of those whom he has thus offended being greater than the gratitude of those whom he has served, it almost always happens that while he is violently attacked, he is feebly defended. You will not be surprised then, if you learn that I have not closed my political career with the same *eclat* with which it commenced."

By November he had made up his mind. He stood for election for a third term and his popularity held. He wrote his sister in Boston, "It was my intention to decline serving another year as President that I might be at liberty to take a trip to Boston in the spring, but I submit to the unanimous voice of my country which has again placed me in the chair. I have now been upwards of fifty years employed in public offices. When I informed your good friend Dr. Cooper that I was ordered to France, being then 70 years old, and observed that the public having, as-it-were, eaten my flesh, seemed now resolved to pick my bones, he replied that he approved their taste, for that the nearer the bone the sweeter the meat." Then Franklin confided to his sister why he seemed never to have had the resolve to say no. "I must own that it is no small pleasure to me . . . [that] I should be elected a third time by my fellow citizens without a dissenting vote but my own [out of modesty] to fill the most honorable post in their power to bestow. This universal and unbounded confidence of a whole people flatters my vanity much more than a peerage could do."

Franklin enjoyed the approbation of the public but he didn't fool himself in regard to it. Many years before, he had written to Katy Greene. "I must confess (but don't you be jealous) that many more people love me now than ever did before." He explained that he had been able to perform some services for the country and for the army, for which he received thanks and praise. And they "say they love me; they *say so,* as you used to do. And if I were to ask any favors of them, [they] would perhaps as readily refuse me. So that I find little real advantage in being beloved, but it pleases my humor."

"Popular favor," Franklin recognized, "is very precarious, being sometimes lost as well as gained by good actions," so he never felt secure for the future. When Congress showed its ingratitude by indefinitely holding up the money it owed him for his service in France, due to suggestions by the Lees and Adams that he had pocketed government money as ambassador, he wrote a friend, "I know something of the nature of such changeable assemblies and . . . what effect . . . one or two envious and malicious persons may have on the minds of members." When he was attacked in the newspapers, he observed, "I have long been accustomed to receive more blame and more praise than I have deserved. It is the lot of every public man. I take no notice. My friends defend me." But he did not leave it to chance for his friends to give him the best defense. In the case of the charges against him in Congress he gave one of the members a documented list of the services he had rendered his country in England and France, suggesting to his friend that these details would be very useful in case he wished to respond to the accusers.

He also knew that the popularity of a man in public life resulted as much from circumstances beyond his control as well as from his own satisfactory or unsatisfactory performance. He once observed during the war with the French that a long series of defeats had created such an appetite for good news that a small victory would be magnified into a great one, and "the man who procures us a bonfire and a holiday would be almost adored as a hero." In Franklin's position as President of Pennsylvania he was not in the storm of party politics but as a senior counselor giving advice and offering compromises when needed. This position allowed him to use his prestige and wisdom to best effect and to preserve his valued favor with the people. This experience helped him in playing a similar but more important role in the Constitutional Convention. He warned his countrymen about "the two passions which have a powerful influence in the affairs of men." He had reference to ambition and avarice, "the love of power" and "the love of money," which when combined might have the most violent effects. Fortunately at his age and station of life, he had neither and was thus able to earn the confidence of the conflicting parties, as reflected in his unanimous re-elections. "Wise and good men are the strength of a state," he had once remarked. Happily his fellows now found these qualities in him.

Franklin looked upon politics in much the same light as he looked upon science. One could theorize till the cows come home and it would be of no use. Experimentation was needed to supply the answer. He wrote Bishop Shipley, who had asked him how the government was functioning in the newly-liberated country: "We are, I think, in the right road of improvement, for we are making experiments. I do not oppose all that seems wrong, for the multitude are more effectually set right by experience than kept from going wrong by reasoning with them. And I think we are daily more and more enlightened." So convinced was he that the scientific method would be useful in the political sphere that he helped to found and became the first president of the Society for Political Enquiries, which paralleled the American Philosophical Society and was the first organization devoted to political science. He did not believe that "The arduous and complicated science of government" should solely be "left to the care of practical politicians or the speculations of individual theorists.'' America was not only a good place to perform new experiments in government; it itself was the greatest experiment in the new field of political science, and Franklin was confident of its success.

Long before he had any thought of political independence, Franklin believed that America would eventually become richer and more powerful than the mother country itself. During the darkest days of the revolution he nurtured that idea, as he prophesied rhapsodically to Washington: ''I must soon quit the scene, but you may live to see our country flourish, as it will amazingly and rapidly after the war is over. Like a field of young Indian corn which long fair weather and sunshine had enfeebled and discolored, and which in that weak state, by a thunder gust of violent wind, hail, and rain seemed to be threatened with absolute destruction: yet the storm being past, it recovers fresh verdure, shoots up with double vigor and delights the eye, not of its owner only but of every observing traveler.''

Happily, he was still on the scene to see his prophecy come true. He wrote his friend David Hartley not to believe the false accounts of distress and misery that the English papers were spreading about America in its early days of independence. ''You may believe me when I tell you,'' he emphasized, ''there is no truth in those accounts. I find all property in lands and houses augmented vastly in value [his own included] . . . The crops have been plentiful and yet the produce sells high, to the great profit of the farmer. At the same time, all imported goods sell at low rates . . . Working people have plenty of employment and high pay for their labor. These appear to me as certain signs of public prosperity.'' It followed, as he said, ''all among us may be happy who have happy dispositions, such being necessary to happiness even in Paradise.

As for his own prosperity, he wrote that after many years of foreign employment he was at last in his own niche. ''I live in a good house which I built 25 years ago . . . made still more convenient by an addition since my return. A dutiful and affectionate daughter with her husband and six children compose my family . . . My rents and incomes are amply sufficient for all my present occasions, and if no unexpected misfortunes happen . . . I shall leave a handsome estate to be divided among my relatives.''

What did one do for amusement in young America: ''We have assemblies, balls, and concerts.'' he told Polly Hewson, ''besides little parties at one another's houses, in which there is sometimes dancing and frequently good music. So that we jog on in life as pleasantly as you do in England.'' He did admit that London had one advantage over Philadelphia in having plays performed by good actors. But he maintained this was the only advantage. Being convinced, Polly came over with her family to settle in Philadelphia and become an American.

Franklin was happy to have Polly and her children as well as his own family about him. He was, as always, a family man. He wrote John Jay and Mrs. Jay, ''I am now in the bosom of my family, and find four new little prattlers, who cling about the knees of their grandpapa and afford me great pleasure.'' Of his older grandsons who had been with him in Europe, Benny Bache was now at the college in Philadelphia and Temple was a gentlemen farmer on the 600 acres of land on the Delaware river which he acquired from his father. ''He that raises a large family stands a broader mark for sorrow,'' Franklin quoted the poet, Watts, thinking no doubt of his estranged son in England, but as usual, coming back smiling, he added, ''he stands a broader work for pleasure too.'' A large family was natural for him, having had sixteen brothers and sisters. Now he and his sister, Jane, were the only ones left of that family.

When Franklin was twenty-one he wrote Jane, ''You know you were ever my peculiar favorite.'' She continued to be, and over the sixty-three years they corresponded he wrote more letters to her than to any one else. He had neglected her while he was in France, as he had Deborah when he was in England, but now that he was home again their correspondence flourished. She was more like him than she knew, and of the many Franklins she was the only one who can be compared with him, according to Carl VanDoren, her biographer and his. Though her life was fraught with tragedy and she was hounded with poverty, she was amazingly resilient and positive in her views. And despite her lack of education, she read what she could and was well informed on current affairs, especially as they pertained to her famous brother. When she was fifteen, he had written from Philadelphia that he had heard she was ''grown a celebrated beauty.'' Later, he said that he hoped his own daughter would become ''an ingenious, sensible, notable, and worthy woman like her aunt.'' When her daughter Abiah was born, he wrote, ''My compliments to Miss Abiah, and pray her to accept the enclosed piece of gold to cut her teeth; it may afterwards buy nuts for her to crack." And when Jane was forty-seven he said, "You are very good in not resenting some part of my letter of September 16 which I confess was a little rude; but you fat folks can't bear malice." This physical reference, she must have known, applied to himself as well.

Franklin helped Jane's son Benjamin Mecom, learn the printing business and in 1786 when her grandson, Josiah Flagg, appealed to Franklin for help in obtaining a clerkship in Philadelphia, he was well received and given employment. Franklin wrote to Jane about him, "Your grandson behaves very well and is constantly employed in writing for me . . . As to my reproving and advising him, which you desire, he has not hitherto appeared to need it, which is lucky as I am not fond of giving advice, having seldom seen it taken. An Italian poet in his account of a voyage to the moon tells us that *All things lost on earth are treasured there*. On which somebody observed, there must then be in the moon a great deal of *good advice*."

Jane was widowed early and had a hard time making ends meet. Franklin helped her from time to time and now wrote to Jonathan Williams in Boston, "How has my poor old sister gone through the winter? For I am afraid she is too cautious of acquainting me with all her difficulties, though I am always willing to relieve her when I am acquainted with them." In one letter he told her to stock up on firewood at his expense and in another he said he had sent her a barrel of flour and told her to be sure to buy whatever else she needed and charge it to him. Jane did not approve of Franklin's accepting the position of President of Pennsylvania, saying "I fear it will fatigue you too much." In reply, he gently chided her, "I do not wonder at your blaming me at accepting the government. We have all of us wisdom enough to judge what others ought to do, or not to do in the management of their affairs; and 'tis possible I might blame you as much if you were to accept the offer of a young husband." He suggested that both she and he should be less certain in their judgments of the other. And with a literary wink which must have amused and flattered her, he referred to his allusion of her taking a young husband, saying, "it teaches me not to be surprised at such an event should it really happen."

In the correspondence of Franklin and his sister there is a theme that recurs over the years. It has to do with soap. Soapmaking was a family craft and their elder brother John, a soapboiler by trade, had a reputation for making a fine soap, stamped with a crown for identification. Jane held the recipe and taught the art to several of the younger members of the family. When he was in France, Franklin had asked Jane to make some cakes as gifts for his French friends, since a good quality soap was a luxury anywhere in that century. He specified the green soap that was firm and hard, not white, soft, and crumbly. She made some excellent soap that was carried to France by John Adams. Back in Pennsylvania, now, he encouraged Jane to make some more soap for his friends in France. Jane wrote that she thought the trademark should be changed to thirteen states and she termed the crown soap then sold by competitors in America as "dirty stinking stuff," and, regarding the crown on it, it was "as contemptible as the British head that now wears one." This time there were problems with the soap. It was affected by the frost and tended to crumble into little pieces when handled. Franklin tried several experiments to re-melt it but they were not successful. He and Jane discussed the problem in many letters, and he was full of ideas on what to do. She responded, "There is a good deal of philosophy in the working of crown soap." He finally sent another batch to France, but this venture cannot be ranked among his major triumphs; and even his best friends in France, who received the crumbly cakes, were too polite to tell him.

Jane's spelling was better than that of Deborah Franklin or Katy Green but it was not good, and modest as she was, she apologized for it. Having acknowledged receipt of the soap she sent and thanked her for it, he brushed aside her apology on her spelling. He sent her his proposal for a new phonetic alphabet to simplify spelling and claimed that with the present alphabet that bad spelling was really the best.

> You need not be concerned in writing to me about your bad spelling, for in my opinion as our alphabet now stands, the bad spelling, or what is called so, is generally the best, as confoming to the sound of the letters and of the words. To give you an instance, a gentleman receiving a letter in which were these words, "not finding Brown at hom, I delivered your meseg to his yf." The gentleman finding it bad spelling and therefore not very intelligible, called his lady to help him read it. Between them they picked out the meaning of all but the yf, which they could not understand. The lady proposed calling her chambermaid, for Betty, says she, has the best knack at reading bad spelling of any one I know. Betty came and was surprized that neither sir nor madam could tell what yf was. "Why,"

says she, "yf spells wife, what else can it spell?" And indeed it is a much better as well as shorter methof of spelling wife than by doubleyou, i, ef, e, which in reality spells doubleyifey.

Franklin always had a keen interest in his family relationships. When he was in England he took the trouble to seek out members of the Franklin family who were still there. Franklin's mother was a Folger, born on the island of Nantucket, off the coast of Massachusetts. Franklin had been acquainted with two of the Folgers who were sea captains, one of them, Captain Timothy Folger, having given him information on the Gulf Stream. In writing to Jane he first referred to his grandnephew Jonathan Williams, Jr. and then asked about the relatives in Nantucket. "I am very much pleased to hear that you have had no misunderstanding with his good father. Indeed if there had been any such, I should have concluded that it was your fault, for I think our family were always subject to being a little miffy. By the way, is our relationship in Nantucket quite worn out? I have met with none from thence of late years . . . except Captain Timothy Folger. They are wonderfully shy. But I admire their honest plainness of speech. About a year ago I invited two of them to dine with me. Their answer was that they would—if they could not do better. I suppose they did better, for I never saw them afterward, and so had no opportunity of showing my miff, if I had one." This was written in 1789 when Franklin was one of the most honored men in the world. But as a plain man himself, he could not but admire the supreme independence and yankee spirit of these relatives. In his old age he was nostalgic about the land of his birth. He wrote the Reverand Lathrop, Jane's neighbor, that he was afraid he would never be able to visit Boston again. "But I enjoy the company and conversation of its inhabitants when . . .[they] visit me . . . the Boston manner, turn of phase, even tone of voice, and accent in pronunciation, all please and seem to refresh and revive me."

Franklin's amusing "story of the poker," which he related in French dialect after the Stamp Act, had become very popular and was reprinted in newspapers, receiving embellishment by some of the editors. Jane saw such a version and was shocked at the profanity in it. When the Frenchman on the bridge with the red hot poker asks the Englishman for permission to thrust it into his backside, the Englishman retorts "D—— your soul," a phrase used more than once in the anecdote. Jane implored Franklin to assure her that his original piece did not contain such language. He sent her a copy and said, "As you observe, there was no swearing in the story of the poker when I told it." He indicated that the person who dressed it up in its new fashion was like the one who told about the dispute between Queen Anne and the Archbishop of Canterbury. The dispute pertained to an appointment to an opening for bishop which the Queen wanted to bestow on a person the Archbishop thought unworthy. The teller of the tale "made both the Queen and the Archbishop swear three or four thumping oaths in every sentence of the discussion, and the Archbishop at last gained his point. One present at this tale, being surprised said, 'But did the Queen and the Archbishop swear so at one another?' 'Oh, no, no,' says the relator, 'that is only *my way* of telling the story.' "

The second year he was home Franklin found a new activity to occupy his time and interest—building. Not one to keep his money idle, and with rents high he started his own building boom. "I had begun to build two good houses next to the street instead of three old ones which I pulled down," he told Jane. There was some delay due to a boundary dispute, but since the workmen and materials were ready, he ordered an addition to the house he was living in, saying it had become too small for the growing family. Within the year the three houses were finished and he was ready to begin two others. In the new addition to his house was a dining room 30.5 x 16 feet which would seat twenty-four persons and had a fireplace faced with marble slabs over which was a mirror 59.5 x 43 inches he imported from France. "Over this room is my library, of the same dimensions . . . and lined with books to the ceiling," he wrote. Each book was numbered in his system and had its place on the shelf so he could find it easily. "I hardly know how to justify building a library at an age that will so soon oblige me to quit it," he mused, "but we are apt to forget that we are grown old, and building is an amusement." He told his French banker, whom he instructed to sell his French stocks to provide money for the building enterprise, "Building is an old man's amusement. The advantage is for his posterity."

As if building, being President of Pennsylvania, and being President of the Society for Political Enquiries were not enough to keep him occupied, Franklin now became president of the first anti-slavery society in the United States. Opposition to slavery had begun early in America by the Quakers. As Franklin's personal information showed,

George Keith of Philadelphia wrote a paper about the year 1693 giving a strict charge to Quakers, "that they should set their negroes at liberty after some reasonable time of service." Franklin recalled that in 1728 or 1729 and again in 1736 he had printed books for Quakers against keeping negroes in slavery. Now they asked him to head up their organization to eliminate slavery and prepare freed slaves to live in freedom. In his time he had owned slaves and sold them, but he personally did not like slaves as servants, and in 1751 he wrote that slave labor was not economically competitive with free labor. In 1758 he had proposed a school in Philadelphia to teach trades to ex-slaves so that they could be self-sufficient. As president of the anti-slavery society he appealed for funds and wrote propaganda, lending his name to this cause. Just a month before he died he produced one of his best hoaxes, "On the Slave Trade," which satirically depicted Algerian pirates enslaving Christians just as American Christians enslaved blacks. It was his last literary effort and it proved that age and illness had not dulled his scintillating wit.

Still one more matter, a very important one, was to focus Franklin's attention on public affairs during his "waning" years. This was the Constitutional Convention, which met at Philadelphia during four months of 1787. Since the Declaration of Independence the separate states had been operating as separate nations, joined only by their voluntary association under the Articles of Confederation. The Congress under the Confederation did not have the power to levy taxes to pay its bills and each state, being sovereign, printed money and imposed duties on goods from other states as well as those from foreign countries. This and other problems made for an unsatisfactory situation urgently calling for a remedy, and all of the states except Rhode Island sent delegates, fifty-five in all, to Philadelphia to draw up a better constitution. Less provincial than most of the delegates, Franklin thought of himself first as an American, then as a Pennsylvanian. He had represented some of the states as their agent in England and all of them as their Ambassador in France. Therefore, while as President of the host state he welcomed the delegates, as a long and enthusiastic servant of America he welcomed their purpose.

The convention was scheduled to begin on May 14 and Washington arrived on the 13th and dined with Franklin the next day. It wasn't until May 25, however, that there was a quorum of seven states present and the convention formally opened in Independence Hall.

During the interval, the delegates who had arrived came over and dined with Franklin in his new dining room. He opened a cask of porter sent to him by a London brewer, which the men agreed unanimously "was the best porter they had ever tasted." He referred to the delegates, several of whom were old friends from the Continental Congress, as "what the French call *une assemblée des notables,*" and said this was the most august and respectable assembly he was ever in in his life. He wrote Jefferson in France, "The delegates . . . are men of character for prudence and ability, so that I hope good from their meeting. Indeed if it does not do good it must do harm, as it will show that we have not wisdom enough to govern ourselves and will strengthen the opinion . . . that popular governments cannot long support themselves." This was a concern that Abraham Lincoln under other circumstances, was to echo again at Gettysburg.

As the Second Continental Congress in 1775 Franklin had been the oldest man present; now in 1787 he again had that distinction, being twenty years older than the next oldest. He and Washington, who was elected President of the Convention, were the two most prestigious men of the group, and were treated with great respect. Although his role, as in the state government, was more that of statesman than of partisan, Franklin was nevertheless absorbed in the activities that took place. Benjamin Rush noted on June 2, "Dr. Franklin exhibits daily a spectacle of transcendent benevolence by attending the convention punctually and even taking part in its business and deliberations." This performance was actually very difficult for Franklin because of the pain he was suffering from the bladder stone. During his later years he had to be carried about Philadelphia in a sedan chair and he quipped that he should have brought a balloon with him from France to provide less painful locomotion.

Though Franklin received personal respect, the Convention belonged to the younger men who paid little attention to most of his proposals. These proposals included his preference for a one-house legislature, his motion to make the position of president non-salaried, and his call for beginning the daily meetings with prayers. But his talent for finding a compromise for difficult problems of diplomacy, in cooling hot tempers, and his conviviality and humor in his relations with the other members made him a vital element in the success of the enterprise. When members clashed angrily over a point of major difference, Franklin reminded the opponents, "We are sent here to consult, not to contend with each other. . . . positiveness and warmth . . . tend to create and augment discord and division . . . where harmony and union are extremely necessary.'' The members responded to his plea and picked up their debates ''with great coolness and temper.'' When angers flared up again Franklin proposed prayers for each session, declaring ''that 'except the Lord build the house they labor in vain to build it.' I firmly believe this; and I also believe that without His concurring aid we shall succeed in this political building no better than the builders of Babel.'' While prayers were not voted, the suggestion of them nevertheless produced the desired, soothing effect. When the deliberations turned to the subject of the payment of members of the Congress it was felt that they should be well paid in order to get the best men. Liberal compensation was specified but Franklin disliked the word ''liberal'' as being too easily subject to abuses, which would tend to grow of themselves when once begun. The words ''gratuitous provision'' he related, had been originally used for the support to be received by the Apostles, but out of that had developed the establishment of the entire papal system. The method for appointing federal judges elicited from one member the proposal that they be appointed by the President. Another member disagreed, thinking selection by the legislature would be preferable since the other method put too much power in the hands of one man. Franklin observed that only two methods had been mentioned. He hoped other methods would be suggested by the members, it being a point of great moment. Why not consider, for example, the method he understood was practiced in Scotland. According to Madison, he then ''in a brief and entertaining manner related a Scotch mode,'' in which the judges were selected by the lawyers, who always selected the ablest of the profession, ''in order to get rid of him and share his practice among themselves.'' Franklin's stories added a touch of levity that relieved tensions and lightened the mood of the sessions. The delegate from Georgia wrote of Franklin, ''He does not shine much in public council—he is no speaker, nor does he seem to let politics engage his attention. He is, however, a most extraordinary man, and tells a story in a style more engaging than anything I ever heard.'' He was also impressed by Franklin's alert mental faculties: ''He is 82 and possesses an activity of mind equal to a youth of 25 years of age.''

The most severe test of the Convention was the dispute over representation of the large and the small states in Congress. The large states demanded representation based upon number of people whereas the small states fearing to be overwhelmed by that system vociferously called for equal representation regardless of size. Franklin favored representation based on population, feeling that congressmen should represent people, not geographical or political units. He recognized that representation based on population was objected to "from an apprehension that the greater states would then swallow up the smaller." However, he argued "I do not at present see what advantage the greater states could propose to themselves by swallowing the smaller, and therefore do not apprehend they would attempt it." When the union of Scotland and England was proposed, the Scotch patriots, he noted, were full of fears that unless they had an equal number of representatives in Parliament they would be ruined by the superiority of the English. "And yet to this day I do not recollect that anything has been done in the Parliament of Great Britain to the prejudice of Scotland. The same problem of the small versus the large states had come up in the Second Continental Congress and referring then to this fear by the Scots, he commented that the Duke of Argyle was most violently opposed to the union and predicted that "as the whale had swallowed Jonah, so Scotland would be swallowed up by England. However, when Lord Bute [of Scotland] came into the government," Franklin continued, "he soon brought into its administration so many of his countrymen, that it was found . . . that Jonah swallowed the whale." According to Jefferson, the story "produced a general laugh and restored good humor, and the article of difficulty was passed."

In this convention the article of difficulty was not so easily disposed of. Franklin, as a member of a special committee to resolve the matter, stated the problem in its simplest terms: "The diversity of opinions turns on two points. If a proportional representation takes place, the small states contend their liberties will be in danger. If an equality of votes is to be put in its place, the large states say their money will be in danger." Then, he appealed for a compromise: "When a broad table is to be made and the edges of planks do not fit, the artist takes a little from both and makes a good joint. In a like manner here both sides must part with some of their demands in order that they may join in some accommodating proposition." He made a compromise motion which was adopted by the committee and reported to the Convention. It provided that in one branch (House) representation be proportioned on population, and it would originate all money bills, and in the second branch (Senate) each state would have an equal vote. Madison commented "Dr. Franklin did not mean to go into a justification of the report, but as it had been asked what would be the use of restraining the second branch from meddling with money bills, he could not but remark that it was always of importance that the people should know who had disposed of their money and how it had been disposed of. It was a maxim [actually of Franklin's own creation] 'that those who can feel can best judge.' "

The compromise motion was subject to long debate but finally passed by a vote of five states to four. This was called "The Great Compromise" of the constitution and was Franklin's great contribution to it. The Connecticut delegates played an important part in getting the compromise adopted and it has sometimes been called the "Connecticut Compromise." The historian Max Farrand, however, thinks that it is incorrect to exclude any delegation or individual from credit in the general concession. But, it is probable that without this compromise, authored by Franklin, the convention might well have broken up without producing any document.

After the daily sessions, Franklin occasionally had dinner and socialized with the delegates at the Indian Queen. This was a Philadelphia tavern, kept in elegant style, with many spacious halls and numerous small apartments where a number of the Convention delegates lodged. This description of the Indian Queen was given by Manasseh Cutler, a Massachusetts clergyman who visited Philadelphia and stayed there for a few days during the Convention. He sought out the delegates, visited the State House, and the museum, writing his impressions of all he saw. Most of all, however, he wanted to meet Franklin: "There was no curiosity in Philadelphia which I felt so anxious to see as this great man, who has been the wonder of Europe as well as the glory of America." He thought he was going to be introduced into the presence of a European monarch, but instead saw "a fat, trunched old man in plain Quaker dress, bald pate, and short white locks, sitting without his hat under a tree." When he was introduced to Cutler, Franklin rose from his chair, expressed his joy to see him and welcomed him to the city. "His voice was low, but his countenance was open, frank, and pleasing," Cutler recorded in his diary. Tea was served under the tree by Franklin's daughter, who had three of her children about her. The children, Cutler noticed, did not respond to their mother but appeared "to be excessively fond of their grandpapa."

Since Cutler was a botanist and a member of the American Philosophical Society, Franklin talked to him about scientific things and showed him a two-headed snake which was preserved in a bottle of alcohol. He told Cutler his fable of the two headed snake and then mentioned that the snake reminded him of "a humorous matter" that had come up that day in the Convention. He seemed to have forgotten that everything that was said in the Convention was to be kept a profound secret, but one of the other guests who was a delegate reminded him, and Cutler was disappointed for this stopped him, and as Cutler lamented, "deprived me of the story he was going to tell." It is a disappointment that is shared by posterity. After dark, Franklin took the guests to his study which was lined with books. Cutler presumed that this was by far the largest and best private library in America. It was. Franklin showed Cutler the long, artificial arm and hand he invented for taking down and putting up books on the high shelves which were out of his reach. (This device was adopted and used in all grocery stores for reaching cans and packages prior to the advent of the low-shelved, self-service markets.) Cutler was impressed with the glass machine Franklin showed him for exhibiting the circulation of the blood in the arteries and veins, and a rolling press he had invented for copying letters. Cutler was even more impressed with Franklin's "great armed chair with rockers, and a large fan placed over it, with which he fans himself, keeps off the flies, etc., while he sits reading, with only a small motion of his foot." Cutler saw also many other curiosities of Franklin's invention which, while noteworthy, could hardly be compared with the air-cooled, bug-repelled, foot-energized, dandy rocker.

While the other men were engaged in talking politics Franklin gave his whole attention to Cutler who expressed his pleasure: "I was highly delighted with the extensive knowledge he appeared to have of every subject, the brightness of his memory, and clearness and vivacity of all his mental faculties, notwithstanding his age. His manners are perfectly easy," Cutler observed, "and everything about him seems to diffuse an unrestrained freedom and happiness. He has an incessant vein of humor, accompanied with an uncommon vivacity, which seems as natural and involuntary as his breathing."

In addition to the hotly-contested issues of the control of money and power, there was an underlying issue in the Convention that was even more basic to the future government of the United States. This was whether the new country was to be a democracy or an aristocracy, and in 1787 it was not at all clear that the former would win out. Elbridge Gerry, delegate from Massachusetts, said that democracy was "the worst of all political evils" and he feared power in the hands of the people. The great landholders in Virginia and New York were staunch advocates of an aristocratic government and were fearful of their economic security if the landless multitudes were to come into control. Gouverneur Morris of New York eloquently argued for making the second branch of the legislature an aristocracy, "to be composed of men of great and established property . . . chosen for life." Such an aristocratic body, he insisted, was necessary "to keep down the turbulency of democracy." Even their esteemed leader in the Convention, George Washington, was an aristocrat so aristocratic, according to an anecdote, that even his intimate friends were not allowed to be familiar with him. When Gouverneur Morris scoffed at this, saying that he could be as familiar with Washington as with any of his other friends, Alexander Hamilton, himself an ardent proponent of aristocracy, challenged Morris to a bet. "If you will," said Hamilton, "at the next reception evening, gently slap him on the shoulder and say, 'My dear General, how happy I am to see you look so well!' " The challenge was accepted and at the reception Morris entered, bowed, shook hands with Washington, and laid his left hand on Washington's shoulder while making the friendly greeting agreed upon. With this, "Washington withdrew his hand, stepped suddenly back, fixed his eye on Morris for several minutes with an angry frown, until the latter retreated abashed, and sought refuge in the crowd."

One can verify the substance of this story, if not the details, in the stiff, formal style of Franklin's letters to Washington, whom he addressed as "Your Excellency." In contrast, Franklin was not only approachable and affable, he was staunchly democratic in spirit. At this time Franklin was himself a large landholder, but on this basic issue he spoke his conviction, not his special interest. Cautious of too strong an executive for fear of slipping back into a monarchy, Franklin proposed only a single term of office for the executive. Other members replied it would be degrading to the executive to be made ineligible for a second term. Franklin responded, "In free governments the rulers are the servants and the people their superiors and sovereigns." To allow the executive to return among the people would therefore not be degrading him but promoting him. He referred to the Congress in the same democratic vein: "They are of the people, and return again to mix with the people, having no more durable pre-eminence than the different grains of sand in an hourglass. Such an assembly cannot easily become dangerous to liberty."

A more delicate issue for the Convention was to decide who should have the right to vote. Many of the delegates held that only those who owned property, freeholders, should be eligible to vote but Franklin vigorously contested this position. He was afraid such restriction of suffrage would "depress the virtue and public spirit of our common people." These qualities, which they greatly displayed during the war, was a principal contribution to its success. American sailors taken prisoner by the British refused all inducements to defect, even when threatened with chains, because they were "free and equal to any of your fellow citizens." Conversely, the British seamen who had lost their voting privilege, Franklin indicated, readily defected to the American side. Later, in a defense of the Pennsylvania constitution, Franklin tackled this question of property being given extra privilege in the government. "Is it supposed," he wrote, "that wisdom is the necessary concomitant of riches?" And if there are twenty times as many men who have lands of less than a thousand pounds value as those who do, does it follow that "one man worth a thousand pounds must have as much wisdom as twenty who have only 999?" Franklin asked a fundamental and radical question, "Why is property to be represented at all?" Supposing one of the Indian nations should agree to become part of the civil society, he argued. Each individual would have little more property than his gun and blanket. Then, he made a bold statement on the subject of private property, far ahead of its time. "Private property therefore is a creature of society and is subject to all the calls of that society . . . even to its last farthing." The contributions of private property should not be considered as conferring a benefit on the public, entitling the contributors to distinctions of honor and power, but rather as the return of an obligation previously received, or the payment of a just debt. "I am sorry to see the signs . . ." he said, "of a disposition among some of our people to commence an aristocracy by giving the rich a predominance in government."

When property qualifications for holding office were proposed in the Convention, Pinkney of South Carolina, who made the proposal, said he did not want "an undue aristocratic influence," but he "thought it essential that the members of the legislature, the executive, and the judges should be possessed of competent property to make them independent and respectable." Franklin arose in opposition. According to Madison's notes, "Dr. Franklin expressed his dislike of everything that tended to debase the spirit of the common people. If honesty were often the companion of wealth, and if poverty was exposed to peculiar temptation, it was not less true that the possession of property increased the desire of more property. Some of the greatest rogues he ever was acquainted with, were the richest rogues." In Franklin's view, wealth was not to be represented in government because the safety of property was ultimately of less importance to society than other considerations: "The personal securities of life and liberty, these remain the same in every member of the society, and the poorest continues to have an equal claim to them with the most opulent."

The delegates worked from the end of May till late in September to forge a constitution for the United States of America. The document was a series of compromises accommodating so many different points of view that no one was completely pleased with it. But the hardworking members of the Convention had at last produced a document which was now ready for signing. Some members had already announced they would not sign it, others were uncertain whether they would or not. It was a critical moment. Franklin arose with a speech he had written. The exertion of standing and speaking being too great for him, he asked James Wilson of the Pennsylvania delegation to read it for him.

> Mr. President, I confess there are several parts of this constitution which I do not at present approve, but I am not sure I will never approve them. For, having lived long, I have experienced many instances of being obliged by better information or fuller consideration to change opinions, even on important subjects, which I once thought right but found to be otherwise. It is therefore that the older I grow, the more apt I am to doubt my own judgment and to pay more respect to the judgment of others. Most men indeed, as well as most sects in religion, think themselves in possession of all truth. . . . Steele, a Protestant. . . . tells the Pope that the only dif-

ference between our churches . . . is that the Church of Rome is infallible and the Church of England is never in the wrong. But though
many private persons think almost as highly of their own infallibility
as that of their sect, few express it so naturally as a certain French
lady, who in a dispute with her sister, said, "I don't know how it
happens, sister, but I meet with nobody but myself that's always in
the right. (*Il n'y a que moi qui a toujours raison*).

In the *Records of the Federal Constitution,* Madison did not include the audience reaction, but it is certain this story produced a general round of laughter and perhaps some remarks about "that old rascal Franklin and his stories." One of the members wrote to Jefferson
telling about the last days of the Convention and repeated Franklin's
story about the "French girl." Franklin then drove home his point:

> In these sentiments, Sir, I agree to this Constitution with all its
> faults, if they are such; because I think a general government neces-
> sary for us, and there is no form of government but what may be a
> blessing to the people if well administered . . . and can only end in
> despotism . . . when the people shall become so corrupted as to
> need despotic government, being incapable of any other. I doubt
> too, whether any other convention we can obtain may be able to
> make a better Constitution. For when you assemble a number of men
> to have the advantage of their joint wisdom, you inevitably assemble
> with those men all their prejudices, their passions, their errors of
> opinion, their local interests, and their selfish views. From such an
> assembly can a perfect production be expected? It therefore as-
> tonishes me, Sir, to find this system approaching so near to perfec-
> tion as it does. . . . Thus I consent, Sir, to this Constitution because
> I expect no better, and because I am not sure that it is not the
> best. . . .
>
> On the whole, Sir I cannot help expressing a wish that every
> member of the Convention who may still have objections to it
> would, with me, on this occasion doubt a little of his own infalli-
> bility, and to make manifest our unanimity, put his name to this in-
> strument.

His speech completed, Franklin then made the motion that the
Constitution be signed by the members of the Convention. The speech
had a solidifying effect. It settled the doubts of the sincere but troubled
delegates, as to how they could accept a document to which they had
so many objections. Of the twelve states represented, all voted "aye,"
except South Carolina, which was "divided". James McHenry of

Maryland, who confessed he opposed many parts of the Constitution, made notes to explain why he had signed it. Almost quoting Franklin, he said: "I distrust my own judgment, especially as it is opposite to the opinion of a majority of gentlemen whose abilities and patriotism are of the first cast; and as I have had frequent occasions to be convinced that I have not always judged right." Referring to Franklin's "persuasive" speech, he observed that it contained the reasons Franklin supported the Constitution even though he disapproved some of it, which "guarded the Doctor's fame." He was thus doing likewise, and guarding his own reputation.

Franklin's speech was considered the literary triumph of the Convention and members asked for copies, which they circulated widely in their further struggle to get the Constitution ratified by the states. Nathaniel Gorham of Massachusetts requested a copy for publication, praising the sentiments and alluding especially to the story of the French lady. The prestige of Franklin and Washington and their support of the Constitution greatly aided in its eventual acceptance by the states, where suspicions run high. Appraising Franklin's contribution to the Constitution, Van Doren comments, "The Constitution was not his document. But without the weight of his prestige and the influence of his temper there might have been no document at all." Madison recorded, "in the Convention Dr. Franklin seldom spoke," but when he did, "he would make short extemporaneous speeches with great pertinency and effect." Madison's records preserved a memorable anecdote of the historic signing of the Constitution: "The members then proceeded to sign the instrument. While the last members were signing it, Dr. Franklin, looking towards the President's chair at the back of which a rising sun happened to be painted, observed to a few members near him that painters had found it difficult to distinguish in their art a rising from a setting sun. 'I have,' said he, 'often and often in the course of the session, and the vicissitudes of my hopes and fears as to its issue, looked at that behind the President without being able to tell whether it was rising or setting. But now at length I have the happiness to know that it is a rising and not a setting sun.' "

25

WITHOUT VANITY

"OUR GRAND MACHINE HAS AT LENGTH BEGUN TO WORK," Franklin declared exultantly in May, 1789. He was speaking of the government of the United States of America under its new constitution, which had been ratified by all but one of the 13 states and was now in operation. Rhode Island, the least, was last, finally ratifying in 1790. Writing to LeRoy in France, Franklin sent the good news: "Our new Constitution is now established and has an appearance that promises permanency . . ." Then, with his natural caution, he added, "but in this world nothing can be said to be certain, except death and taxes." The latter was to become a famous maxim, those using it seldom knowing its source. But optimism always won out in Franklin's outlook and he said of the new government, "I pray God to bless and guide its operations. If any form of government is capable of making a nation happy, ours I think bids fair now for producing that effect."

Realistically, he did not expect the new government to start up smoothly and run without opposition. To Dupont de Nemours, he ventured, "we must not expect that a new government may be formed as a game of chess may be played, by a skillful hand without a fault. The players of the game are so many, their ideas so different, their prejudices so strong . . . [that] the wisest must agree to some unreasonable things that reasonable ones of more consequence may be obtained; and thus chance has its share in many of the determinations, so that the play is more like *tric-trac* with a box of dice.'' The dice must have been in our favor for later he proudly announced, ''We have had one session of Congress under our new Constitution, which was conducted with, I think, a greater degree of temper, prudence, and unanimity than could well have been expected, and our future prospects seem very favorable.''

Franklin was staunchly democratic and feared that centralized authority in an executive might lead to a monarchy. According to James McHenry of Maryland, at the closing of the Constitutional Convention, ''A lady [Mrs. Powell of Philadelphia] asked Dr. Franklin, 'Well Doctor, what have we got, a republic or a monarchy?' 'A republic,' replied the Doctor, 'if you can keep it!' '' But there was the rub. ''Much depends on the people to be governed,'' he asserted. ''We have been guarding against an evil that old states are most liable to, *excess of power* in the rulers; but our present danger seems to be *defect of obedience* in the subjects.'' He may have been thinking of Shay's Rebellion in Massachusetts and similar popular uprisings in Connecticut. But he was more troubled by the scurrilous attacks on public figures in the newspapers and elsewhere, which occurred in the absence of any laws on libel and slander to afford protection to individuals unjustly assaulted. ''Only a virtuous people are capable of freedom,'' he maintained. ''As nations become corrupt and vicious they have more need of masters.''

It was one thing, however, for him to find flaws in the government that needed correcting, quite another when the criticism came from abroad. When LeVeillard commented that there was too much apathy among the American people, Franklin rushed to their defense: ''Never was any measure so thoroughly discussed as our proposed new Constitution.'' he protested. ''Many objections were made to it in the public papers, and answers to those objections. Much party heat there was, and some violent, personal abuse,'' he admitted. But he assured his friend that ''our affairs mend daily and are getting into good order very fast.'' As to the two houses of the legislature, he agreed with LeVeillard. ''I am of your opinion that one alone would be better, but my dear friend, nothing in human affairs . . . is perfect, and perhaps that is the case with our opinions.''

He had an audacious suggestion for his European friends. Let Europe follow in America's footsteps ''by forming a federal union and one grand republic of all its different states and kingdoms, by means of a like convention." He was encouraged by the news he had heard from abroad. There was a fire spreading over Europe, a fire of liberty. "I hope the fire of liberty . . . will act upon the inestimable rights of man as common fire does upon gold—purify without destroying them." The French Declaration of the Rights of Man, to which Franklin was apparently alluding, had just been adopted, one month prior to the proposal of our own Bill of Rights as the first ten amendments to the Constitution. His hope and fear for the rights of man in Europe was initiated by the early events of the French Revolution.

Franklin lived only to hear the overture to the French Revolution and part of the first act of that tragic drama. He missed the bloody scenes that were to follow and would have deeply grieved him. In February of 1788 he joked with Le Veillard about his friend's not having written, when always before he had been a faithful correspondent. "I therefore rather suspect," wrote Franklin, "you may probably have written something too freely concerning public affairs and . . . may be . . . lodged in the Bastille." He had then no inkling that the fast-moving events would soon bring this dear friend's life to an end on the guillotine. Neither could he imagine that the Bastille, the dread symbol of tyranny, would in a few months be stormed by the people of Paris.

When that news reached him, he wrote again to Le Veillard expressing his concern over the violence but looking forward to better times. "I am much concerned to hear the broils in your country but hope they will lead to its advantage. When this fermentation is over and the troubling parts subsided, the wine will be fine and good and cheer the hearts of those that drink it." Le Veillard wrote exuberantly of "the beautiful moment we are living. . . . The nation has shaken the yoke of priests, nobles and king, she is the absolute mistress of her fate." Franklin heard, however, a more restrained note from his chemist friend, Lavoisier: "But the moderates who have remained cool-headed in the general effervescence believe that circumstances have carried us too far, that it is a pity to be compelled to arm the people, to arm all the citizens." It is a pity, too, that Lavoisier, this giant of science, who produced so much for mankind and could have produced much more, would soon end his days on the guillotine.

Happily oblivious of such forthcoming events, Franklin wrote to another scientist in France, LeRoy, in the same jocular manner he had earlier used with LeVeillard: "It is now more than a year since I have heard from my dear friend LeRoy. What can be the reason? Are you still living? Or has the mob of Paris mistaken the head of a monopolizer of knowledge for a monopolizer of corn, and paraded it about the streets upon a pole?" Then, seriously, he said that a great part of the news from Paris had been very afflicting and he hoped it might end well and happy. It was not, however, a good time for science. "The voice of philosophy, I apprehend, can hardly be heard among those tumults." He observed to Vaughn in England, "The revolution in France is truly surprising. I sincerely wish it may end in establishing a good constitution for that country."

It did indeed, a constitution establishing a legislature with one house, thanks to Franklin's influence through his friends and his writings. Subsequent turmoil, however, was to lead to that constitution being overturned and one with two houses being substituted. Merciful death was to spare Franklin that news as well. In December, 1789 he made his last comment on French problems to his fellow peacemaker, David Hartley. "The convulsions in France are attended with some disagreeable circumstances, but if by the struggle," he suggested, "she obtains and secures for the nation its future liberty and a good constitution, a few year's enjoyment of those blessings will amply repair all the damages their acquisition may have occasioned." Then, in a burst of triumphant rhetoric, he stated prayerfully a universal wish. "God grant that not only the love of liberty but a thorough knowledge of the rights of man may pervade all the nations of the earth, so that a philosopher may set his foot anywhere on its surface and say, 'this is my country.' "

As both Franklin and Hartley knew, universal liberty alone was not sufficient for the kind of world this philosopher envisioned—there had also to be universal peace. Apart from the inhumanity of war, he thought it to be impractical. Whatever advantage one nation would obtain from another, whether for territory or commerce "it would be much cheaper to purchase such advantage with ready money than to pay the expense of acquiring it by war." He described an army as "a devouring monster." that had to be recruited and maintained with all the contingent expenses and the outrageous charges of the numerous contractors demanding exorbitant prices for their supplies. "It seems to me," he suggested, "that if statesmen had a little more arithmetic . . . wars would be much less frequent. I am confident that Canada might have been purchased from France for a tenth part of the money England spent in the conquest of it. And if, instead of fighting with us for the power of taxing us, she had kept us in good humor by allowing us to dispose of our own money, and now and then giving us a little of hers by way of donation to colleges or hospitals . . . she might have easily drawn from us much more by occasional voluntary grants and contributions. Sensible people will give a bucket or two of water to a dry pump that they may afterwards get from it all they have occasion for.'' England's ministry, he maintained, lacked common sense and so they spent one hundred millions and lost all they fought for.

When will people, who "call themselves reasonable creatures, have reason and sense enough to settle their disputes without cutting throats? What vast additions to the conveniences and comforts of living might mankind have acquired if the money spent in wars had been employed in works of public utility''—what an extension of agriculture, rivers rendered navigable, what bridges, aqueducts, new roads— instead of bringing misery into thousands of families and destroying the lives of so many thousands of working people, who might have performed the useful labor. Ever-cheerful, Franklin said, "Thank God the world is growing wiser and wiser; and, as by degrees, men are convinced of the folly of wars of religion, for dominion, or for commerce, they will be happier and happier.'' He wrote to Ferdinand Grand, his French banker, "Long may the peace of Europe continue! . . . I think your minister, who is so expert in composing quarrels and preventing wars, the great blessing of this age. The devil must send us three or four heroes before he can get as much slaughter of mankind done as that one man has prevented.''

It should not be assumed that all of Franklin's attention was concentrated on such solemn subjects as liberty and war. In this same letter to Grand, he mentioned that he was glad to hear of the marriage of Mademoiselle Brillon and stated "everything that may contribute to the happiness of that beloved family gives me pleasure.'' He was astonished to hear that Cardinal Rohan of Strasbourg was charged with the theft of a diamond necklace and he couldn't help putting on his Poor Richard mask and rattling off a series of proverbs that might apply: "Prodigality begets necessity; Without economy no revenue is sufficient; and "It is hard for an empty sack to stand upright.''

To Abbé de la Roche he wrote, "Your project of transporting rather than drowning the good lady's [Madam Helvétius] eighteen cats is very humane. The kind treatment they experience from their present mistress may possibly cause an unwillingness to hazard the change of situation.'' But, if they happened to be of the Angora breed, they might wish to escape to America, for his grandson had brought over two and they were caressed and adored here. The cats' friends therefore should advise them that rather than risk the persecution of the abbés, they would do well ''to submit voluntarily either to transport or castration.''

Franklin apologized for the oversight of his fellow delegate in the Constitutional Convention, Gouverneur Morris, in his apparent discourtesy in failing to call on LeVeillard when he arrived in Paris. He wrote LeVeillard, ''I am sorry my friend Morris failed in the attention he ought to have shown you, but I hope you will excuse it when you consider that an American transported from the tranquil villages of his country and set down in the turbulence of such a great city as Paris, must necessarily be for some days half out of his senses.'' This was the same city that dazzled American farm boys in World War I.

Madam Lavoisier sent Franklin a portrait of himself which she had painted. He told her that those who had seen the portrait praised it in every respect, but what particularly endears it to me,'' he added, mustering up his old charm, ''is the hand that drew it.'' He reflected back to the Revolutionary War and recalled, ''Our English enemies, when they were in possession of this city and my house, made a prisoner of my portrait and carried it off with them, leaving that of its companion, my wife, by itself a kind of widow. You have replaced the husband, and the lady seems to smile as well pleased.''

Turning to another subject, he says, ''I like much young Monsieur Dupont.'' This was the son of his friend Dupont de Nemours, who with his brother had come to America to start a business making ammunition and explosives. They had learned how to make gunpowder from Lavoisier, whom Franklin had encouraged to experiment in this field on behalf of the American war effort. The business they started developed into the huge corporate empire of E. I. Dupont de Nemours, the largest chemical company in the world. Franklin says of young Dupont: ''He appears a very sensible and valuable man, and I think his father will have a great deal of satisfaction in him.'' Before closing his letter to Madam Lavoisier he reminisces on the nine years of happiness he enjoyed with his fine friends in Paris. Now he has the attention of a loving family, the comfort of his own home, and more public honors, he continues, than he can possibly merit—"yet all do not make me forget Paris . . . and now, even in my sleep, I find that the scenes of all my pleasant dreams are laid in that city or in its neighborhood."

Paris might be all right for dreams but when he was wide awake Franklin's thoughts were very much in America. For one thing, he didn't like the choice of the bald eagle for the emblem of the United States: "I wish the bald eagle had not been chosen as the representative of our country; he is a bird of bad moral character; he does not get his living honestly. You may have seen him perched on some dead tree where, too lazy to fish for himself, he watches the labor of the fishing hawk; and when that diligent bird has at length taken a fish and is bearing it to his nest for the support of his mate and young ones, the bald eagle pursues him and takes it from him. . . . Like those men who live by sharping and robbing he is generally poor and often very lousy. Besides, he is a rank coward; the little king-bird, not bigger than a sparrow, attacks him boldly and drives him out of the district." He would have preferred a turkey, as being a much more respectable bird and a true, original native of America. One of Franklin's ideas was to imprint Poor *Richard* type adages on copper coins in order to impress their moral messages on the people's minds. It might have been an excellent teaching method, but Congress preferred instead to leave wise sayings to the makers of almanacs and fortune cookies.

Noah Webster, the dictionary maker, sent Franklin a copy of his book on the English language which he had dedicated to him. In his reply Franklin took the opportunity to express some of his own ideas on the subject. He thought that a nation with a language which is easy to learn and use by its citizens and foreigners has considerable advantage.

"It enables its authors to inculcate and spread through other nations such sentiments and opinions on important points as are most conducive to its interests, or which may contribute to its reputation by promoting the common interests of mankind." He cited Voltaire's treatise on *Toleration* as having so sudden an effect on the bigotry of Europe "as almost entirely disarm it." Bookselling and commerce in a country, he pointed out, were also aided by the knowledge of its language. He noted that Latin had been replaced by French as the most nearly universal language, with English following in second place. "If therefore we would have the benefit of seeing our language more generally known among mankind,'' he told Webster, ''we should endeavor to remove all the difficulties, however small, that discourage learning it.'' Some of these difficulties could be blamed on modern printers. It formerly had been standard to capitalize all nouns as in German. This was desirable, Franklin maintained, since English had many nouns and verbs spelled the same way, which could be readily differentiated by capitalization of the nouns. Modern printers, however, were doing away with this capitalization for the flimsy reason, that they wanted to give the line of type a more even appearance.

It was the same thing with the letter ''s.'' ''Another fancy,'' he complained, ''has induced some printers to use the short round 's' instead of the long one, which formerly served well to distinguish a word readily by its varied appearance.'' He admitted that ''omitting this prominent letter makes the line appear more even,'' but he argued that it ''renders it less immediately legible.'' He alleged, by way of comparison, that ''paring all men's noses might smooth and level their faces but would render their physiognomies less distinguishable.''

Another modern trend that disturbed him as a language purist was the formation of new verbs from nouns. ''During my late absence in France,'' he said, ''I find that several new words have been introduced.'' From the noun ''notice'' a new verb ''noticed'' was produced. Also ''advocate'' led to ''advocated,'' and ''progress'' to ''progressed,'' which he thought to be ''the most awkward and abominable of the three.'' Franklin suggested to Webster, ''If you should happen to be of my opinion with respect to these innovations, you will use your authority in reprobating them.'' If Webster *advocated* such action it is unlikely it *progressed* very far, for little effect can be *noticed* in present usage.

Franklin had another black mark for the printers, or was it gray? His letter continued, ''Add to all these improvements backwards, another modern fancy, that gray printing is more beautiful than black; hence the English new books are printed in so dim a character as to be read with difficulty by old eyes. . . . Lord Chesterfield pleasantly remarked this difference to Faulkener, the printer of the Dublin *Journal,* who was vainly making encomiums on his own paper, as the most complete of any in the world. 'But, Mr. Faulkener,' said my Lord, 'don't you think it might be still farther improved by using paper and ink not quite so near of a color?'' As a printer himself, nothing annoyed Franklin more than illegible printing. He once wrote to his niece, "I thank you for the Boston newspapers, though I see nothing so clearly in them as that your printers do indeed want new letters. They perfectly blind me in endeavoring to read them. If you should ever have any secrets that you wish to be kept, get them printed in those papers."

Unexpectedly, he received three letters from Polly telling about her children, how Tom, genius-like, struck out new paths and changed the names of the letters, calling "U" *bell* and "P" *bottle,* and "how Eliza began to grow jolly, that is fat and handsome resembling Aunt Rooke, whom I used to call *my lovely.*" These letters were unexpected because they were over ten years old, having lain undelivered in Philadelphia because of the disturbance of the war. He said they "just now broke out upon me like words that had been, as somebody says, congealed in northern air." He thanked Bishop Shipley for a book he had given him. He thought the book was well written and should do well, "though the reading time of most people is of late so taken up with newspapers and little periodical pamphlets that few nowadays venture to attempt reading a quarto volume." Comparing his century with that before, he said, "We have more readers now but not of such large books."

He loved books and when a new town in Massachusetts had named itself Franklin in his honor and asked him for a bell for the church, he sent the people instead a small parish library, advising them to accept "books instead of a bell, sense being preferable to sound." Franklin always preferred the useful over the purely aesthetic, as he wrote to a friend in England: "I am glad to hear that Mr. Fitzmaurice is married and has an amiable lady and children. It is a better plan than he once proposed, of getting Mrs. Wright to make him a waxwork wife to sit at the head of his table."

In another instance of his utilitarian approach, Franklin proposed a useful way to dispose of a letter which he sent to his niece in Boston. She wanted him to send her a copy of an old letter he had written to her but he couldn't do it because the copies he always made of each letter he wrote were lost when his house was captured and occupied during the war. Speaking of the letter, he said, "I too should have been glad to have seen that again among others I had written to you. But you inform me they were eaten by the mice. Poor little innocent creatures, I am sorry they had no better food. But since they like my letters, here is another treat for them."

In letters Franklin received from LeVeillard and Vaughan, they continued to press him to work on his autobiography, as they had done earlier when they saw him off for America. In April, 1788, he wrote LeVeillard that his three years of service as President of Pennsylvania would expire in October and, he said "I had the project of retiring then to my grandson's estate in New Jersey, where I might be free from the interruption of visits, in order to complete the work for your satisfaction. For in this city my time is so cut to pieces by friends and strangers that I have sometimes envied the prisoners in the Bastille."

Franklin had never given his autobiography a high priority, and other activities consumed his time. Now, having considered "the little remnant of life I have left," he promised LeVeillard, "I have come to the resolution to proceed in that work tomorrow and continue it daily till finished." If his health permitted, that would be the next summer. He had written the first part during his happy three-week visit with the Shipleys in 1771. After the revolution, in 1784 at Passy, he had written a few pages more at the insistence of his French friends. In June, 1788, he wrote again to LeVeillard who had asked him if he had been taking part in the political activities necessary for gaining adoption of the Constitution. He replied that his health would not permit it, besides he was determined not to engage any more in public affairs after the expiration of his presidentship, even if required. But he knew his countrymen would be too reasonable to require it. "You are not so considerate," he accused LeVeillard, "you are a hard taskmaster. You insist on his writing his life, already a long work, and at the same time would have him continually employed in augmenting the subject, while the time shortens in which the work is to be executed." October found him as promised, "diligently employed in writing the history of my life." He was then up to 1756, the year he was sent to England. In encouraging him to continue his memoirs his friends had persuaded him that his life would serve as model to instruct young people. Thus, to shorten the work, he was now omitting all incidents that might not benefit the young reader. Since June he had doubled its size but there was much more ahead if it were to be finished. As he read over what he had written he discovered he liked it: "If a writer can judge properly his own work, I fancy . . . the book will be found entertaining, interesting, and useful; more so than I expected when I began it."

In November he began to have doubts about what he had written. Would it be proper for publication, at least during his lifetime? Perhaps some material should be deleted? He asked his friends for their candid advice. During the next year his health got progressively worse and he carried his account only two years further. By September, 1789, he began to doubt whether he would ever finish it. In November, he wrote Vaughan a long letter. Vaughan had asked for criticism of his writing. Franklin identified its fault then recommended methods for correcting it. "You see I give my counsel rather bluntly, without attempting to soften my manner of finding fault by any apology, which would give some people great offense." "But," he added, "in the present situation of affairs between us, when I am soliciting the advantage of your criticisms on a work of mine, it is perhaps my interest that you should be a little offended in order to produce a greater degree of wholesome severity."

He sent copies of the manuscript made for him by his grandson Benny Bache to Vaughan and LeVeillard for their criticism. After that he wrote only seven pages more, his failing health and the hopelessness of finishing the work making it unrealistic for him to proceed further. The autobiography ends with the year 1758 when Franklin was 52 years old. His friends, later readers, and historians, alike, share the disappointment of not having in these memoirs his reflections on the great revolution, his life in France, and the events of the Constitutional Convention. This part of his life, however, was itself history; the incidents of his early years, which would certainly have died with him, are fortunately revealed for all to read.

Franklin's autobiography begins as a letter to his son giving his excuse for writing it. "Dear Son, I have ever had a pleasure in obtaining any little anecdotes of my ancestors." He thought that similarly William might be interested in knowing about his father's life, many of the particulars of which he was as yet unacquainted. There were also some other incentives for undertaking this work. Having emerged from poverty and obscurity and raised himself to a state of affluence and position of reputation in the world, his life might be a guide to others who find themselves in like circumstances. Since one cannot live his life over again, the next best thing is calling back to mind the past events in it. He allowed himself to yield to the inclination so natural to old men of talking of themselves and their own actions. But this way no one would be obliged to listen. They would be free to read him or not. "And lastly," he admitted, "I might as well confess it as the denial of it would be believed by nobody, I shall . . . gratify my own vanity." He had never heard the introductory words, "Without vanity I may say," but some vain thing immediately followed. "Most people," he averred, "dislike vanity in others whatever share they have of it themselves, but I give it fair quarter wherever I meet with it, being persuaded that is often productive of good to the possessor and to others who are within his sphere of action. And therefore, in many cases it would not be altogether absurd if a man were to thank God for his vanity among the other comforts of life."

Having given his reasons for writing, Franklin plunged into the narration of his adventures in the world and his philosophical comments on them, hesitating only long enough to apologize for his discursive style: "By my rambling digressions I perceive myself to be grown old. I used to write more methodically. But one does not dress for private company as for a public ball." After all, when he began the autobiography it was intended only for the amusement and information of his son and friends. But it was read by millions who shared his own appraisal of it as entertaining, interesting, and useful. At least for a century it was, excepting the Bible, the American best-seller. It was translated into many languages, published in hundreds of editions, was read by more people in the world and had greater influence than any other book in the English language. It portrayed, as Vaughan indicated, not only the life of a man but "the detail of the manners and situation of a rising people." It inspired endless numbers of those who had not yet risen, like Thomas Mellon, a farmer of western Pennsylvania. After reading the autobiography in 1827 he left the farm and founded his banking firm in Pittsburgh, which his son Andrew later took over. Orion Clemens was another American attempting to rise. A printer, he followed Franklin as a model, calling his shop the "Ben Franklin Book and Job Office." He was no success but his brother Sam, who worked in the shop, did well as a writer under the name Mark Twain. As a humorist, Twain enjoyed twitting his brother's hero. Referring to the autobiography, he said: "The subject of this memoir was of a vicious disposition and early prostituted his talents to the invention of maxims and aphorisms calculated to inflict suffering upon the rising generation of all subsequent ages. . . . He was always telling how he entered Philadelphia for the first time, with nothing in the world but two shillings in his pocket and four rolls of bread under his arm. But really, when you come to examine it critically, it was nothing. Anybody could have done it."

Twain's comic vendetta was not really directed against Franklin, whom he respected, but against those insufferable fathers who "had read Franklin's pernicious biography" and believed that by making their boys live according to Poor *Richard's* mottoes they would transform them into Franklins: "Benjamin Franklin did a great many notable things for his country and made her young name to be honored in many lands as the mother of such a son." It was not his purpose, Twain said, to ignore or cover up what Franklin did. "I merely desired to do away with somewhat of the prevalent calamitous idea among heads of families that Franklin acquired his great genius by working for nothing, studying by moonlight, and getting up in the night instead of waiting till morning like a Christian; and that his program, rigidly inflicted, will make a Franklin of every father's fool."

According to Professor Russel B. Nye, in the autobiography Franklin answers three questions, "Who am I, how did I come to be, and why am I a human being as I am." One does not wish to quarrel, but it is doubtful that he answers these questions. That is, if we can depend upon Poor Richard for 1736.

> Walking and meeting one not long ago,
> I asked who 'twas, he said, he did not know.
> I said, I know thee; so said he, I you;
> But he that knows himself I never knew.

Whether Franklin really knew himself or not is a moot question, but he certainly told a great story. His personal history was something new to literature; it was, as characterized by Van Doren, the first masterpiece of autobiography by a self-made man. "Here were the homeliest memoirs that had ever been written, in the plainest language."

26

LET THE EXPERIMENT BE MADE

THE AUTOBIOGRAPHY WAS THE HARVEST OF FRANKLIN'S productive old age. He wrote to his friend George Whatley about his advancing age: "You are now 78 and I am 82; you tread fast upon my heels. But though you have more strength and spirit, you cannot come up with me till I stop, which must now be soon. For I am grown so old as to have buried most of the friends of my youth, and I now often hear persons whom I knew when [they were] children, called Old Mr. such-a-one, to distinguish them from their sons, now men grown and in business. So that by living twelve years beyond David's period, I seem to have intruded myself into the company of posterity when I ought to have been abed and asleep." And then expressing the sentiment that Browning would put to rhyme in his "Rabbi Ben Ezra," Franklin continued, "Yet, had I gone at 70, it would have cut off twelve of the most active years of my life, employed, too, in matters of the greatest importance."

In his old age Franklin was not only a producer, he was a philosopher of old age itself; his philosophy being best described as "ignore it, overcome it, enjoy it." When he was 50 he had already started his campaign to "ignore it." A niece in Boston had written humorously of one of her family who at 81, doddering and blind, became foolishly romantic like a young swain following the death of his wife. Franklin replied, "Old age, we see, is subject to love and follies as well as youth. All old people have been young and . . . they laughed as we do at the amours of age . . . I see you begin to laugh already at my ranking myself among the young! But you, my girl, when you arrive at 50, will think no more of being old than does your affectionate uncle." By the age of seventy-four he was determined to "overcome it." "I do not find that I grow any older," he told a friend, "being arrived at seventy, and considering that by traveling further in the same road I should probably be led to the grave, I stopped short, turned about, and walked back again; which having done these four years, you may now call me sixty-six. Advise those old friends of ours to follow my example. Keep up your spirits and that will keep up your bodies; you will no more stoop under the weight of age than if you had swallowed a handspike."

"Enjoy it? Yes! True, old age is accompanied by infirmities, but if one has the proper attitude one may find enjoyment none-the-less, according to our philosopher of gerontology at eighty-one years. "You give me joy in telling me that you are 'on the pinnacle of content,' " he told an old companion. "Without it no situation can be happy; with it, any." How is contentment to be achieved? "One means of becoming content with one's situation is comparing it with worse. Thus when I consider how many terrible diseases the human body is liable to, I comfort myself that only three incurable ones have fallen to my share, viz. the gout, the stone, and old age." He was comforted also that these had not yet deprived him of his natural cheerfulness, delight in books, and enjoyment of social conversation. To a visitor he said, "I think happiness does not consist so much in particular pieces of good fortune that perhaps accidentally fall to a man's lot, as to be able in his old age to do these little things which, was he unable to perform himself, would be done by others with a sparing hand."

Even before he became old himself; Franklin had a sympathetic feeling for old people and their troubles. When his sister Jane was having a little problem with their older sister, he wrote Jane, "As *having their own way* is one of the greatest comforts of life to old people, I think their friends should endeavor to accommodate them in that, as well as in anything else. When they have long lived in a house it becomes natural to them: they are almost as closely connected with it as the tortoise with his shell: they die if you tear them out of it. Old folks and old trees, if you remove them, 'tis ten to one that you kill them. So let our good old sister be no more importuned on that head.

We are growing old fast ourselves and shall expect the same kind of indulgences. If we give them, we shall have a right to receive them in our turn."

As a gregarious person with a wide range of interests, Franklin formed many bonds of friendship with people in the three countries in which he had resided. One of the hardest blows of old age was the loss of many of those friendships through death. To his brewer friend, Jordan, he wrote, "Your letter reminds me of many happy days we have passed together and the dear friends with whom we passed them, some of whom, alas, have left us." As he philosophized upon it elsewhere, he concluded, "Losing our friends thus, one by one, is the tax we pay for long living, and it is indeed a heavy one." Taken all altogether, however, the debits with the credits, Franklin was an exemplary senior citizen who enjoyed to the fullest the extra portion of life that was alloted to him. When he was a mere youngster in his middle seventies, Madam Helvétius said to him, "I like to believe that you are happy." He replied, "I become more so every day. . . . First poor, then rich, I have always been content with what I have, without thinking of what I have not. But since I have begun to age, since my passions have diminished, I feel a well-being of mind and heart that I never knew before and which is impossible to know at the age of these young people." He was pointing to Cabanis and another young man, Volney, who reported the incident. "At that age," Franklin went on, using droll imagery, "the spirit is exterior; at mine, it is interior; it looks out the window at the stir of those who pass by without taking part in their disputes."

When Franklin was approaching his 83rd birthday, his niece asked him about his condition. "You kindly inquire about my health," he responded, "I have not of late much reason to boast of it. People who live a long life and drink to the bottom of the cup must expect to meet some of the dregs . . . And those not withstanding, I enjoy many comfortable intervals in which I forget all my ills and amuse myself in reading or writing, or in conversation with friends, joking, laughing, and telling merry stories, as when you first knew me, a young man about 50." His illness kept him confined to his bed for most of his last two years, and if all the comfortable intervals he mentions were added together, they would not amount to two months, an eyewitness reported. His doctor stated that Franklin retained "the fullest and clearest possession of his uncommon mental abilities and not unfrequently indulged himself in those *jeux d'esprit* and entertaining anecdotes which were the delight of all who heard them.''

Of his three maladies, the stone was the most constant and painful. In his uncomplaining way he told LeVeillard in 1787 that although it felt like it had grown heavier it did not bother him ''except in standing, walking, or making water.'' He took care of himself as best he could. Twice a week he sat in a hot bath, Benjamin Rush reported, and as if to convince unbelievers and himself as well, Rush added in parentheses, ''for hours.'' This was his shoe-shaped, copper tub equipped with a book holder so he wouldn't spend the hours idly. The French naturalist Buffon, who suffered from the same disorder, asked him what he was doing to treat himself. He replied that he had tried all the regular prescriptions for diminishing the stone without good effect. ''But observing temperance in eating, avoiding wine and cider, and daily using the dumbbell, which exercises the upper part of the body without much moving the parts in contact with the stone, I think has prevented its increase.'' To reduce the frequent urgency to make water and relieve the pain of it, he took at bedtime blackberry jelly, an amount the size of a pigeon's egg. He sent the recipe to Buffon, saying that other kinds of jelly would probably be as useful since he believed the value of the jelly to be in the boiled sugar.

Unfortunately the stone got worse and the pain with it, forcing his doctor to prescribe opium as the only way to relieve the pain. On visiting him, Madison was worried that the opium would undermine his constitution. Franklin indicated that he was aware of that but he had no other remedy. According to Madison, ''he thought the best terms he could make with his complaint was to give up a part of his remaining life for the greater ease of the rest.'' It was true; he had made a bargain and had to pay the price. He told LeVeillard that the opium afforded him some ease from the constant and grievous pain but it took away his appetite and so impeded his digestion that he became totally emaciated, ''and little remains of me,'' he said, ''but a skeleton covered with a skin.'' Perhaps there was a trace of consolation in this drastic weight reduction. He had previously observed to Jane, ''Faith, hope, and charity have been called the three steps of Jacob's ladder, reaching from earth to heaven. . . . Faith is then the ground floor, hope is up one pair of stairs . . . the best room in the house [in the garret] is charity. For my part, I wish the house were turned upside down; 'tis so difficult, when one is fat, to get up stairs.''

Fortunately, Franklin had no trouble in reading or hearing, but such was not the case with his friend Alexander Small. He wrote Small, "the deafness you complain of gives me concern . . . it must diminish considerably your pleasure in conversation." If moderate, the problem might be remedied easily "by putting your thumb and fingers behind your ear, pressing it outwards, and enlarging it, as it were, with the hollow of your hand." This was no old wives' tale, it actually worked, as Franklin demonstrated: "By an exact experiment I found that I could hear the tick of a watch at forty-five feet distance by this means, which was barely audible at twenty feet without it. The experiment was made at midnight when the house was still."

Despite pain and suffering he could find time to experiment, to joke, and to laugh. But his time was short. The inexorable cycle of life and death was closing for Franklin. How would he face the inevitable? In his zest for living would he shun death, or would he welcome it as a relief to his misery? The answer is, neither. He looked forward to death and what followed with inquisitive anticipation. He was curious to discover what it would be like, to explore it, to learn what it was made of. He was not religious enough to accept the standard version of the hereafter occupied by angels with harps and devils with pitchforks, but he was too religious to believe that man's destiny was oblivion in a dark, endless void. This was the age of reason, where ideas were accepted not by axiom or by authority: they were put to the test! Benjamin Franklin was ready! Let the experiment be made!

Franklin's preparation for death can be traced in the letters of his last years. In February, 1786, when he was 80, he wrote Bishop Shipley that in his easy circumstances, surrounded as he was by family and friends, he had many reasons to like living. "But the course of nature," he went on, "must soon put a period to my present mode of existence. This I shall submit to with less regret, as having seen during a long life a good deal of this world, I feel a growing curiosity to be acquainted with some other." In February, 1787, reminiscing with Alexander Small about his English friends who had departed "to join the majority in the world of spirits," he commented, "Every one of them now knows more than all of us they have left behind. It is to me a comfortable reflection that since we must live forever in a future state, there is a sufficient stock of amusement in reserve for us to be found in constantly learning something new to eternity, the present quantity of human ignorance infinitely exceeding that of human knowledge." In his letter of May 18, 1787, to Thomas Jordan in London, he marveled at the wonderful discoveries made by the astronomer, Herschel. "Let us hope, my friend," he added, "that when free from these bodily embarrassments we may roam together through some of the systems he has explored, conducted by some of our old companions already acquainted with them. Hawkesworth [a writer] will enliven our progress with his cheerful, sensible conversation and Stanley [a musician] accompany the music of the spheres." By May, 1788, however, he was regretful that he would have to give up his earthly residence. "I have sometimes almost wished it had been my destiny to be born two or three centuries hence," he told a Boston minister. "For invention and improvement are prolific and beget more of their kind. . . . Many of great importance now unthought of will, before that period, be produced; and then I might not only enjoy their advantages, but have my curiosity gratified in knowing what they are to be." Then with a gesture of awkwardness, he said, "I see a little absurdity in what I have just written, but it is to a friend, who will wink and let it pass."

The same month he wrote his sister, "Death, however, is sure to come to us all and mine cannot be far off . . . but that may be to me no misfortune." "I look upon death," he wrote to George Whatley in England, "to be as necessary to our constitution as sleep. We shall rise refreshed in the morning." Death, however, was to come first to his dear friend Bishop Shipley, who had defended him and the American cause in England to the peril of his own position. In April, 1789, he sent his condolences to Kitty Shipley. "Your reflections on the constant calmness and composure attending his death are very sensible," he told her. "Such instances seem to show that the good sometimes enjoy, in dying, a foretaste of the happy state that they are about to enter."

In September, 1789, he wrote to George Washington, who had been inaugurated President on April 29. It was to say congratulations and farewell. He noted the growing strength of the new government under Washington's administration and, turning to his own condition, he remarked, "For my own personal ease I should have died two years ago, but though those years have been spent in excruciating pain, I am pleased that I have lived them since they have brought me to see our present situation. I am now finishing my 84th [year] and probably with it my career in this life, but in whatever state of existence I am placed hereafter, if I retain any memory of what has passed here I shall with it retain the esteem, respect, and affection with which I have long been, my dear friend, yours most sincerely, . . . [Benjamin Franklin.]

Franklin had known Washington since 1755 when the latter was just 23 and was serving as aide to General Braddock. Since that time their paths had crossed numerous times in the great affairs that led to the founding of a nation. They were never close friends but they had a profound respect for each other. After the Constitutional Convention, Franklin wrote to LeVeillard, "General Washington is the man that all our eyes are fixed on for President, and what little influence I may have is devoted to him."

President Washington now replied to Franklin's letter in words that composed a eulogy. He first expressed his deep sympathy for Franklin in his suffering, regretting that there was nothing he or a grateful people could do to help. Then in his dignified, eloquent style, he wrote, "If to be venerated for benevolence, if to be admired for talents, if to be esteemed for patriotism, if to be beloved for philanthropy, can gratify the human mind, you must have the pleasing consolation to know that you have not lived in vain. And I flatter myself that it will not be ranked among the least occurrences of your life to be assured that so long as I retain my memory you will be recollected with respect, veneration, and affection by your sincere friend, . . . [George Washington]" If Franklin noticed that Washington had copied his sincere closing for his own letter, it probably didn't bother him.

In March, back from France to serve in Washington's cabinet, Jefferson stopped at Philadelphia to visit Franklin. The old man was happy to see his young colleague and eager to hear the news of his friends in France. Jefferson mentioned that he heard Franklin had been preparing the history of his life. "I cannot say much of that," said Franklin, "but I will give you a sample of what I will leave." Jefferson replied that he would read it and return it. "No, keep it," Franklin said, and repeated it when Jefferson seemed unsure of whether he should. On March 9 Franklin wrote to Ezra Stiles, President of Yale College. In reply to Stiles' question on his opinion of the divinity of Jesus, Franklin didn't think it worth his speculation now when he would soon know the truth with less trouble. With regard to Stiles' request for a portrait of him to be placed in the same room as Governor Yale's, he didn't think any he had were adequate and offered to pay the expense to have one painted. He warned Stiles, however, that the artist "must not delay setting about it or I may slip through his fingers."

Franklin's last letter was April 8. Jefferson had written on March 31 for information on the boundary between the U.S. and Canada in Maine. Franklin apologized for not having replied sooner but a severe fit of his malady prevented him from attending to any kind of business. He sent Jefferson details of the affair and the map tracing the boundary that he and the other peace commissioners had used. "I am perfectly clear in the remembrance," he assured Jefferson.

Franklin died on April 17, 1790, at the age of 84. The immediate cause of death was empyema, an infection of the lung cavity. According to Benjamin Rush, Franklin's daughter told him that she hoped he would recover and live many years longer. He calmly replied: "I hope not." And on being advised to change his position in bed so that he might breathe easy, he said, "A dying man can do nothing easy." It was his last philosophic observation. He told his doctor the same thing that he told his sister when she lamented on his suffering. His present afflictions, he said, were but a trifle when compared to the long life of health and ease he had enjoyed. "And it is right that we should meet with something to wean us from this world and make us willing, when called, to leave it. Otherwise the parting would indeed be grievous."

Franklin left this world with no complaints and few regrets. His family was well provided for. His country was in good hands, with Washington as President and Jefferson as Secretary of State and the government functioning under a good constitution. America was a great landbased country and if it should take a fall it would recover, he was certain, like Antaeus, the giant wrestler of Greek mythology who gained renewed strength every time he touched the earth. As for himself, he had lived a full, productive life. He had composed himself well and, as *Poor Richard* said, "He that can compose himself is wiser than he than composes books." He may have made mistakes, but as he wrote near the end of his life, "whether I have been doing good or mischief is for time to discover. I only know that I intended well and I hope all will end well."

Franklin's will begins, "Benjamin Franklin of Philadelphia, printer, late Minister Plenipotentiary from the United States of America to the Court of France, now President of the State of Pennsylvania . . ." He was first just Benjamin Franklin, printer—the fancy titles took second place. He gave his estranged son only his lands in Nova Scotia and excused the debts William owed him; saying "the part he acted against me in the late war . . . will account for my leaving him no more of an estate he endeavored to deprive me of." The bulk of his estate was left to his daughter and her husband. Two of the gifts, however, had reserve clauses. The picture of the King of France set with 408 diamonds was given to Sarah with the request "that she would not form any of those diamonds into ornaments . . . and thereby introduce or countenance the expensive, vain, and useless fashion of wearing jewels in this country." All his lands near the Ohio and the lots near the center of Philadelphia were willed to his son-in-law with the proviso that he would immediately set free his black man Bob. To his sister he gave a house in Boston and a pension of 60 pounds a year. Temple was given his right to land in Georgia plus debt forgiveness on the farm in New Jersey. Benny was given all his types and printing materials. "My fine crab-tree walking-stick with a gold head curiously wrought in the form of the cap of liberty, I give to my friend and the friend of mankind, General Washington." He added, "If it were a scepter, he has merited it and would become it."

Two unusual provisions of Franklin's will were conceived to make a little money go a long way in doing good, a project worthy of the creator of Father Abraham. The first was a scheme for turning the debts owed him into charity. He bequeathed all the unpaid sums due him through the years, which were listed in his great folio ledger E, to the Pennsylvania Hospital in the hope that the deadbeats would thereby be inspired or shamed into paying up. It was a noble experiment, but it failed. After seven years the discouraged managers of the hospital gave up and returned the ledger to the executors. The second scheme had more chance of success but it would take a long time. That, however, would be no trouble to him now. He would take a small sum and make it grow into a large amount of money for use in public projects, and help worthy young people while it was growing. To accomplish this goal he willed a thousand pounds each to the cities of Philadelphia and Boston, to be lent out at interest to virtuous young tradesman who were, as he had once been, in need of assistance in getting started in business. As soon as the money was paid back it would be lent out again, always keeping it working. He calculated that in 100 years at 5 percent interest the total amount accumulated, if not interrupted, would be 130,000 pounds in each city. Of this 100,000 pounds might then be used for the benefit of each city, putting the remainder back to work in the same way for a second hundred years, when there would be 4,061,000 thousand pounds and the project would be terminated. The growth would be due to the amazing power of compound interest, as he had shown years before in his paper on the growth of populations.

In the first centennial period the Boston fund had $391,000 and the Philadelphia fund in 1907 had $172,350. In Philadelphia $133,000 was transferred to the prestigious scientific institution, The Franklin Institute, and in Boston the money helped build the Franklin Union, a technical training school for young men. The remaining monies were returned to the fund and at the end of the second hundred years, in 1991, the total for both cities is expected to amount to around $5,000,000. That falls short of the amount Franklin computed as possible if the money were never allowed to be dead; nevertheless this tidy sum must be regarded as a generous return for the patient investor.

"Life, like a dramatic piece," Franklin once wrote, "should not only be conducted with regularity but . . . should finish handsomely. Being now in the last act, I begin to cast about for something fit to end with. Or, if my life should be more properly compared to an epigram, as some of its lines are barely tolerable, I am very desirous of concluding on a bright point." What was this bright point? Was it his unusual will, the absorbing autobiography, or perhaps his closing speech to the Constitutional Convention? Being Ben Franklin, he was not likely to have chosen any of these notable documents. It would have been more like him to shuffle through his old papers and pull out a worn sheet with an epitaph he had written for himself when he was 22—just for the fun of it.

The Body of
B. Franklin Printer,
Like the Cover of an old Book
Its Contents torn out
And stripped of its Lettering & Gilding
Lies here, Food for Worms.
But the Work shall not be lost;
For it will, as he believed, appear once more,
In a new and more elegant edition
Revised and corrected
By the Author.

ACKNOWLEDGEMENTS

In the preparation of this book I wish to acknowledge the kindness of Patricia Rambeau for helping me to get the manuscript typed. I want also to thank my wife, Gertrude H. Block, who not only gave me editorial assistance, helpful criticism, and smiling encouragement, but cooked the meals, cut the grass, and paid the bills, along with many other chores, so that I could devote myself to writing without interruption.

I wish to acknowledge the translation from the French of the Letter from Franklin to the Abbé Morellet from *Franklin's Wit and Folly, the Bagatelles,* edited by Richard E. Amacher (copyright, 1953, by the Trustees of Rutgers College, New Jersey. Reprinted by permission of the Rutgers University Press) also selections from *Mon Cher Papa: Franklin and the Ladies of Paris,* by Claude-Anne Lopez, published by the Yale University Press, New Haven, Connecticut, and used by permission.

AUTHOR'S EXPLANATION OF CHANGES

The reader may have observed that Franklin's writing style changed markedly during the seventy-year span of his career, eventually becoming much like what we recognize as modern English. This was due in part to the change in Franklin himself, as he outgrew his provincial beginnings and became a man of the world. It was also due to changes in the writing style of all educated persons during the 18th century. By the end of that century writing in general had become more similar to that of the 20th century.

The gradual change in writing style of the 18th century may not be so evident in my book, however, since whenever I considered it desirable for easier reading I have made minor changes in usage, modernizing the spelling, capitalization, and punctuation, and replacing or defining obsolete words. To obtain brevity and avoid the awkwardness of the old-fashioned style, I have often paraphrased; but in order to be faithful to Franklin I have retained as fully as possible Franklin's own words and phrases in the portions not in direct quotation. In the quoted passages, when parentheses are used, the comments enclosed are Franklin's own; when brackets are used the comments are the author's.

Fig. I.

Fig. 2.

D'après le dessin original envoyé par Franklin.

Illustrations for Franklin's bagatelle on drinking wine, sketched by his grandson (see page 214).

BIBLIOGRAPHY

The Works of John Adams. 10 Vol. A Life of the Author, Notes, and Illustrations by His Grandson Charles Francis Adams. Boston, 1850–1856.

Aldridge, Alfred, O. *Franklin and His French Contemporaries.* New York, 1957.

Aldridge, Alfred, O. *Benjamin Franklin, Philosopher & Man.* Philadelphia, 1965.

American Academy of Arts and Sciences. *The New England Courant. A Selection of Certain Issues Containing Writings of Benjamin Franklin or Published by Him During His Brother's Imprisonment. Introduction by Perry Miller.* Boston, 1956.

Amacher, Richard E. *Benjamin Franklin.* New York, 1962.

Amacher, Richard E. *Franklin's Wit & Folly. The Bagatelles.* New Brunswick, N.J., 1953.

Bell, Whitfield, J. *Benjamin Franklin and the Practice of Medicine.* The Bull. of the Cleveland Medical Library, 9, (3), 51–62 (July, 1962)

The American Museum, or Repository of Ancient and Modern Fugitive Pieces, etc., Prose and Poetical. Vol. 4. Mathew Carey, Ed. Philadelphia, 1788.

Cohen, I. Bernard. *Benjamin Franklin's Experiments. A New Edition of Franklin's Experiments and Observations on Electricity. Edited, With a Critical and Historical Introduction.* Cambridge, Mass., 1941.

Cohen, I. Bernard. *Benjamin Franklin. His Contributions to the American Tradition.* Indianapolis, 1953.

Cohen, I. Bernard. *Franklin and Newton, An Inquiry into Speculative New-*

tonian Experimental Science and Franklin's Work on Electricity as an Example Thereof. Philadelphia, 1956.

Crane, Verner W. (ed.). *Benjamin Franklin's Letters to the Press 1758–1775.* Chapel Hill, N.C., 1950.

Currey, Cecil B. *Road to Revolution. Benjamin Franklin in England, 1765–1775.* Garden City, N.Y., 1968.

Farrand, Max (ed.). *The Records of the Federal Convention of 1787.* 3 Vols. New Haven, Conn., 1911.

Fäy, Bernard. *Franklin. The Apostle of Modern Times.* Boston, 1929.

Fisher, S. G. *The True Benjamin Franklin.* Philadelphia, 1899.

Ford, Paul L. *The Many-Sided Franklin.* New York, 1915.

The Complete Works of Benjamin Franklin including his private as well as his official and scientific correspondence, and numerous letters and documents now for the first time printed with many others not included in any former collection, also the unmutilated and correct version of his autobiography. Compil. and ed. by John Bigelow. 10 Vol. New York, 1887–1889.

The Writings of Benjamin Franklin. Collected and edited with a Life and Introduction. by Albert Henry Smyth. 10 Vol. New York, 1905–1907.

The Papers of Benjamin Franklin. Vol. 1–18 to date (Presently to year 1772. Projected to go to over 40 volumes.) Leonard W. Labaree, Ed. Vol. 1–14. William B. Wilcox, Ed. Vol. 15–18., New Haven, 1959–1974.

The Autobiography of Benjamin Franklin. Leonard W. Labaree (ed.). New Haven, 1964.

The Franklin Institute. *Meet Dr. Franklin.* Philadelphia, 1943.

Granger, B. I. *Benjamin Franklin. An American Man of Letters.* Ithaca, New York, 1964.

Indian Treaties Printed by Benjamin Franklin 1736–1762. Reproductions in Facsimile, with an Introduction by Carl Van Doren and Historical and Bibliographic Notes by Julian P. Boyd. Philadelphia, 1938.

Franklin, Benjamin. *The Complete Poor Richard Almanacs. Reproduced in Facsimile with an Introduction by Whitfield J. Bell, Jr. 2 Vol.* Barre, Mass., 1970.

The Writings of Thomas Jefferson. 20 Vol. Andrew A. Lipscomb, Ed. Washington, 1903.

Jeffries, John. *Diary.* Edited by B. Joy Jeffries. Magazine of American History, 13, 66–88 (1885).

Jorgenson, C. E. and Mott, F. L. *Benjamin Franklin. Representative Selections with Introduction, Bibliography and Notes.* New York, 1962.

Leeds, Titan. *American Almanac for 1734.* Philadelphia. (In American Philosophical Society Library).

Leeds, Titan. *American Almanac for 1735.* Philadelphia. (In American Philosophical Society Library).

Lopez, Claude-Anne. *Mon Cher Papa. Franklin and the Ladies of Paris.* New Haven, 1966.

McMaster, J. B. *Benjamin Franklin as a Man of Letters.* Boston, 1887.

Monaghan, Frank. *John Jay, Defender of Liberty.* New York, 1935.

Morellet, Abbe. *Memoires.* 2nd ed., Vol. 1, Paris, 1822.

Oswald, John C. *Benjamin Franklin Printer.* Garden City, N.Y., 1917.

Pennsylvania Gazette. 1728–1815. Microfilm. Pennsylvania Historical Society. Philadelphia, 1962.

Pepper, William. *The Medical Side of Benjamin Franklin.* Philadelphia, 1911.

Richardson, L. N. *A History of Early American Magazines, 1741–1789.* New York, 1931.

Roelker, William Greene (ed.). *Benjamin Franklin and Catherine Ray Greene: Their Correspondence 1755–1790.* Philadelphia, 1949.

Rosenbach, A. S. W. *The All-Embracing Dr. Franklin.* Philadelphia, 1932.

Letters of Benjamin Rush. 2 Vol. L. H. Butterfield, Ed. Princeton, 1951.

"Excerpts from the Papers of Dr. Benjamin Rush," *Pennsylvania Magazine of History and Biography, 29,* pp. 15–30 (Jan., 1905).

Benjamin Franklin and the American Character. Charles L. Sanford, Ed. Boston, 1955.

Sedgwick, Theodore, Jr. *The Life of William Livingston.* New York, 1833.

Sellers, Charles C. *Benjamin Franklin in Portraiture.* New Haven, 1962.

Smyth, Albert H. *"Life of Benjamin Franklin"* in Vol. X of *The Writings of Benjamin Franklin.* New York, 1905–1907.

Stifler, J. M. (ed.). *"My Dear Girl." The Correspondence of Benjamin Franklin with Polly Stevenson, Georgiana and Catherine Shipley.* New York, 1927.

Jonathan Swift—Bickerstaff Papers and Pamphlets on the Church. Herbert Davis, Ed. Oxford, 1940.

Twain, Mark. *The Late Benjamin Franklin* in "Sketches New and Old." New York, 1875.

Van Doren, Carl. *Benjamin Franklin.* New York, 1938.

Van Doren, Carl (ed.). *Benjamin Franklin's Autobiographical Writings.* New York, 1945.

Van Doren, Carl. *Letters and Papers of Benjamin Franklin and Richard Jackson, 1753–1785.* Philadelphia, 1947.

Van Doren, Carl. *The Great Rehearsal. The Story of the Making and Ratifying of the Constitution of the United States.* New York, 1948.

Van Doren, Carl. *The Letters of Benjamin Franklin & Jane Mecom.* Princeton, 1950.

Weems, Mason L. *The Life of Benjamin Franklin; with many Choice Anecdotes and Admirable Sayings of this Great Man.* Baltimore, 1815.

INDEX

A Kempis, Thomas, 271
Aaron, 29
Abolition, foundation, 182
Abortion, 41
Abraham, 29, 386; "Father Abraham's Speech," 51, 53
Academy of Sciences, French, 215
Adam, 29, 159, 160, 162, 163, 169, 170, 171, 173, 190, 197, 207-210, 217, 248, 271, 303, 314, 336
Adams, John, viii, 2, 6, 13, 16, 22, 346, 357; Abigail, 13, 262
Addertongue, Alice, 97-100
Addison, 27, 115
"Advice to a Young Tradesman Written by an Old One," 322
Aesop, 198
Africans, 333
Aftercast, Margaret, 105
Afterwit, Anthony, 93-96
Age of Reason, 332
Albany Plan of Union, 148
Albertus Magnus, 116
Aldridge, Alfred Owen, ix, 22, 238, 243, 270

Ambition and avarice, 347
American Almanac, 44, 77
American Magazine, 44
American Philosophical Society, vii, 131, 343, 347, 359
American Weekly Mercury, 40
Amherst, General, 145, 246, 248
Anchors, swimming, 343
Andrews, St., (V.), 297
Anne, Queen, 353
Anspach, Prince of, 188
Anteus, 385
Antiseptics, 302
Apoplexy, 310
Apostles, 356
Argyle, Duke of, 357
Aristocracy, in government, 360
Aristotle, 195
Arm extension for reaching books, 359
Armacher, Richard E., ix
Armies, wastefulness in maintaining, 365
Armonica, 5, 212
"Art of Procuring Pleasant Dreams," 256

Articles of Confederation, 354
Aspasia, 91
Astrology, 45, 49, 61, 68, 69, 73, 115
Astronomy, 383; astronomical calculations, 45
Autobiography, Franklin, 41, 341, 342, 374

Baal, false prophets of, 78-80
Babel, tower of, 356
Bache, Benny, 273, 349, 375
Bacon, 337
Bailly, 206
Baker, Polly, Speech of, 179-182
Bald eagle, 371
Balloon, hot air, 292; manned, 217
Balzac, Honore de, 177
Baptists, German, 325
Barwell, Miss, 233, 240
Baskerville, John, 192
Bastille, 367, 374
Baths, 342; cold air, 304; hot water, 305
Bayard, Secretary of State, 258
Bedlam, Hospital, 301
Belcher, Governor, 85
"Ben Franklin Book and Job Office", 376
Bentham, Jeremy, 167, 235
Bergen, Edgar, 71
Bernard, Mademoiselle, 37
Bethlehem, Pennsylvania, 136, 138
Bible, 29, 44, 85, 86, 191, 376
Bickerstaff, Isaac, 169, 170
Bickerstaff Papers, 60, 73
Bigelow, John, 258
Bill of Rights, 367
Billiard, Mr., 97
Biological warfare, 145
Birken, William, 77
Blackbeard, 26
Blackberry jelly, against stones, 381
Bladder stone, 355
Blair, Reverend Commissary, 328
Blas, Gil, 249
Bleeding, 63

Blistering, 310
Blooding, 310
Blount, Dorothea, 240
Blunt, Miss, 233
Bob, slave, 386
Bonaparte, Napoleon, 14
Bookish, Mr., 97
Booth, Captain, 84
Bostock, Mr. Nathaniel, 42
Boston Independent Chronicle, 188
Boswell, James, 235, 302
Botany Bay, 185
Bouquet, Colonel, 246
Bourbon, Duchess of, 167
Braddock, General, 134, 135, 289, 384
Bradford, William, 32, 41, 43, 44, 76, 77, 110; Andrew, 40, 42
"Breakfast in Bed," 47
Brillon de Jouy, 2, 3-8, 12, 20, 207, 209, 210, 272, 273, 293, 310, 311, 318, 323, 326, 327, 332, 336, 369
Browning, Robert, 378
Brownrigg, William, 292
Buckrum, Peter, 117
Buffon, 381
Building, Franklin's interest in, 353
Bunyan, John, 114
Burke, Edmund, 235
The Busy Body Papers, 41, 42, 88
Bute, Lord, 357

Cabanis, 14-17, 20, 22, 197, 210, 212, 248, 336, 380
Cabbage, scotch, 308
Calvinism, 333
Cana, miracle at, 213
Canada, boundary with, 385
Canassatego, 144
Canterbury, Archbishop of, 327, 353, 328
Cantharides, Spanish fly, 294
Cards, playing, 38, 323
Careful, Martha and Molly, 41
Careless, Mrs., 96, 97
Carlisle, conference at, 139, 146
Carlyle, Thomas, 120

Carmichael, William, 216
Carnegie, Dale, 337
Carroll, Father John, 318
Casanova, 23
"A Case of Conscience," 92
The Case of the Missing Horse, 92
Caslon, 192
Casuism, 92, 93
Catheter, urinary, 298
Catholicism, 49, 78, 318
Cato, 111
"Causes and Cures of Smoky Chimneys," 342
Censor Morum, 115
Charles I, 190
Charles, J. A. C., 292, 293
Charles, Prince, 234
Charles' Law, of the expansion of gases, 212
Charting, by Franklin, 343
Chaumont, 208; Bobie, 209-211; Monsieur, 243
Chess, 125, 150, 311
Chesterfield, Lord, 372
Christ Church, Philadelphia, 285
Churches, Franklin on, 321
Cincinnati, the Society of the, 29
Circulation, glass machine for exhibiting, 359
Citrus fruit, against scurvy, 308
Civil War, 183
Clare, Lord, 154
Clemens, Samuel, Orion, 376
Clerk, of Assembly, Franklin as, 130
Clinton, Governor, 128
Clio, 91
Cloud seeding, 291
Cochineal dye, 294
Cohen, Bernard, ix
Cold, common, 303
Collins, 30, 34, 35
Collinson, 286, 290
Combustion, 308
Common Prayer, Book of, 23, 67, 87
Commonplace Book, 93
Compromise, Great, 358; Connecticut, 358

Condorcet, 12
Confederation, Articles of, 148
Confessions, Rousseau's, 208
Congress, 144, 159, 160, 162, 174, 218, 346, 366; Continental, 148, 355
Conspirator, 283
Constitution, 365, 366, 367, 374
Constitution Convention, 321, 341, 347, 354, 356, 357, 360, 361, 366, 370, 375; Society, 344
Constitutionalist Party, Anti-Constitutionalist Party, 344
Cookery, sea, 343
Cooper, Dr., 346
Copley Gold Medal, 286
Cornelius Agrippa, 116
Cornwallis, 10
Cosmology, 309
"Counterfeit spider," 283
Courant, New England, 101, 103-105, 107
Crane, Verner W., ix
Craven Street Gazette, 239, 241
Creek Indians, 145
Cretico, 111
Croker, Josey, 224
Crownhim, Mr., 97
Crumerus, Dr., 187
Cupping, medical, 310
Cutler, Manasseh, 358, 359
Cycle, Natural of decay and reconstitution, 323

Daphnis, 91
Dashwood, Sir Francis, 23 (see Lord Despencer)
David, 85, 378
Daylight Saving Time, 296
D'Azyr, Vicq, 297
Deane, Silas, 158, 163, 168, 169, 181, 209
Death, Life and, 324
De Chaumont, 16
Declaration of Independence, vii, 160, 301, 335, 354

Declaration of Rights of Man, French, 367

D'Hardancourt, Madame, 5

Deism, 315

De la Freté, Mme, 15, 16

De la Roche, Abbe, 14, 15, 17, 19, 20, 207, 212, 248, 369

De Grasse, 338

De Passy, Mme., 208

De Schaumbergh, Count de, 187, 188

De Tonnerre, Marquis, 208

Descartes, 195

Deslon, Dr., 309

The Devil of a Drummer, 88

"Dialogue Between Dr. Franklin and the Gout," 11, 310

Diderot, 12

Digges, Thomas, 172

"Of the Diseases of the Year," 50

"Dissertation on Liberty and Necessity, Pleasure and Pain," 329

Doctrine, evolution of, 325

Dogood, Widow Silence, Dogood Papers, Essays to Do Good, 28, 29, 39, 41, 88, 98, 101-118, 177; son William, 103

Dolphin, 37; colors, 281

Domien, Father, 285

Drinking, 103, 108

Dropsy, 310

Drummer of Tedsworth, 88

Dry belly ache, dry gripes, 299, 300

Dubourg, Dr. Barbeu, 266, 324

Ducking, 82

Dudley, Paul, 181

Dumbbells, for exercise, 306, 381

Dunkers, 325

Dupont de Nemours, 365; E. I., Co., 370; son, 370

Duquesne, Fort, 134

Dutch in New York, 50

Duties, state, 354

Eddystone Lighthouse, 267

Efficiency expert, 137

Electrical jack, 284

Electricity, light, 200-296 *passim,* 143, 312; experiment, 131

"An Elegy upon the Much Lamented Death of Mrs. Mehitebell Kitel, Wife of Mr. John Kitel of Salem," 108

"The Elysian Fields," 19

Emphyema, 385

England, Queen of, 189

Euclid, 293

Eurydice, 20

Evaporation, 56; of rivers and lakes, 294

"Every Man his own Doctor, or the Poor Planter's Physician," 297

Executive, single term of office for, 360

Exercise, Franklin idea of, 306, 311

Eyeglasses, bifocal, 282

Faber, 117

Falkenstein, Count, 167

Farrand, Max, 358

Fatsides, Dr., 307

Faulkener, 372

Federal Gazette, 182

Fermentation, yeast, 308

Fielding, 95

Finck, 210

Finikin, Mr., 97

Fireplace, Pennsylvania, 298, 299

"First Civilized American," 308

Fitzgerald, Lt., 189

Fitzherbert, 173, 174

Fitzmaurice, Mr., 373

Flagg, Josiah, 350

Flying fish, 37, 281

Folger family (Franklin's mother's), Capt. Timothy Folger, 352

Fothergill, Dr. John, 301, 302

Foucald, 211

Foucault, Madam, 208

Fox, Charles, 235

France, King of, 309, 386

France, Queen of, 205, 236

Franklin: Boyhood family, 272

Benny, 386
Debby, 22, 32, 120, 150, 222, 225, 262, 265, 309, 323, 333, 349, 351
Francis, 220, 299
grandchildren, 262, 341
Jane Mecom, sister, 230, 330, 349, 350, 352, 353, 379, 380, 386
James, 27, 28, 30, 34
John, brother, 298, 350
Josiah, father, 44, 315, 321
nephew, 341
niece, 266, 378, 380
Sally, cousin, 231
Sarah, 168, 220, 223, 239, 243, 269, 309, 348, 349, 358, 385, 386
Temple, grandson, 3, 15, 231, 257, 258, 272, 318, 321, 342, 349, 386
William, son, 131, 220, 221, 231, 235, 273, 342, 349, 375, 385
Franklin, Benjamin, in Portraiture, 244
The All-Embracing Franklin, 219
Franklin Institute, 387
Franklin Union, 387
Frederick the Great, 165, 186, 187
Freemasons, 131, 343
French and Indian wars, 134, 318
Fresh air, Franklin idea of, 303, 304; popular fears, 335
Frontenac, 134
Frugality, 50
Funeral Elegy, New England, 108-110
Furnace, invention of, 131

Gage, General, 174
Galileo, 294
Gay, 98
General Magazine, 44
Gentleman's Magazine, 179, 181
George, III, 148, 323
George, St., 132
Georgia, delegate from, 356; governor of, 273
Germ theory of disease, 303
Gerrish, Capt., 188, 189
Gerry, Elbridge, 360

Gettysburg, 355
Gibbon, Edward, 166, 167
Glasses, bifocal, 219, 298
Gnadenhütten, Pennsylvania, 136, 137
Godfrey, 44
Golden fish, 282, 283
Gorham, Nathaniel, 364
Gout, 10, 11, 308, 310-312, 379
Granada, Archbishop of, 294
Grand, Ferdinand, 369
Granger, Bruce I., ix
Greene, William, 229; Katy, 238, 247, 346, 351
Grenadiers March, 89
Greutzins, 90
Gulf Stream, 282, 342, 343, 352
Gulf Weed, 281
Guillotin, 309
Guillotine, 309, 367
Gulliver's Travels, 73

Haldimand, Col., 188
Haly, 69
Hambden, 190
Hames, Lord, 191
Hamilton, Alexander, 267, 360
Hancock, John, 161
Happiness, Pursuit of, 335
Hartley, David, 172, 173, 341, 348, 368
Harvard College, 103, 104, 109, 192
Hawkesworth, Dr., 232, 233, 383; Lady, 240
Hearing, 299
Heat production in body, 308
Heaven and hell, views on, 323
Heber the Kenite, 320
Heberdus, Dr. William, 298
Hell Fire Club, 23
Helvetius, Anne-Catherine de Ligniville, 12, 13, 14, 16-18, 210, 212, 248, 323, 345, 369, 380
Hemphill, 315, 316
Henroost, Ichabod, 28
Hercules, 172

Heresy, 324
Heron feeding, 281
Herschel, 383
Hessians, 187
Hewson, William, 237, 304; Mrs., 323, 348, 349 (see Polly Stevenson)
Hill, James, 85
Hillsborough, Lord, 155
Historicus, pen name, 182, 183
History of the Decline and Fall of the Roman Empire (Gibbon), 166
History of Man, 192
Hobbists, 88
Hohendorf, Baron, 187, 188
Hopson, Admiral, 42
Hortensia, 91
Hospital project, 126, 127
Hot air rising, 282
Hottentots, 320
Houdetot, Countess, 208, 218
Houdini, 34
Houdon, 341, 342
House of Representatives, 182; popular representation in, 357
Howe, Lord, 162, Admiral, 303; General Sir William, 167
Hudibras, 75
Hudson Bay, 70
Humility, 125, 333
Hutton, Lord, 240
Hyde, Mr., 100
Hypnotism, early, 309
Hysteria, mass, 309

Ibrahim, Sidi Mehemet, 177, 182, 183
Immortality, 322
Independence Hall, 354
Indian Queen, 358
Indians, 128, 134-146, 182, 333, 361; Indian corn, 348
Inflation, in Colonial America, 122
Ingenhousz, 297, 299, 301
Inquisition, 294
Insects, study of, 294
Instinct, 332
Izard, Ralph, 168-170

Jackson, Richard, 246, 247; James, 182, 183
Jael, 320
Jason, 248
Jay, John, viii, 171, 173, 174, 215, 216; and Mrs., 349; Mrs., 215, 216, 301
Jeckyll, 100
Jefferies, John, 217
Jefferson, Thomas, vii, viii, 27, 159, 160, 163, 171, 176, 181, 217, 218, 248, 257, 263, 302, 314, 320, 355, 363, 384, 385
Jenner, Edward, 299
Jerman, John, 44, 77-80
Jesus, 326, 327, 342, 384
Job, 320
Johnson, Samuel, 302
Jonah, 357
Jones, John Paul, 57, 190
Jones, Tom, 95
Jordan, brewer, 380
Jordan, Thomas, 382
Joseph, 29
Joseph, Emperor, III, 167
Journal, Dublin, 372
Judges, Book of, 320
Junto, 122, 124, 125-127, 131, 222, 259, 335
Jupin, Mme., 6, 9

Kant, Immanuel, 287
Keimer, Samuel, 32, 33, 35, 38, 40, 41, 42, 43, 110, 111
Keith, George, 354
Kelsey, 43
Kerry, County of, 87
Kindness, repayment of, 315
Kinnersley, Ebenezer, 184
Kite propulsion, 280, 281
Kohlrabi, 301
Koran, 183

La Fayette, Marquis de, 165, 201; Madam, 202; Virginia, 201

La Fontaine, 198
La Rouchefoucald, 48
Langmuir, Dr. Irving, 291
Lathrop, Reverend, 352
Lavoisier, 308, 309, 367; Mme., 370
Laureano, 228
Laurens, 174
Lawrence, D. H., 51
Laziness, 333
Lead poisoning, 299, 300
Lees, 346; William, 168, 169; Richard Henry, 168
Le Despenser, 155, 186
Leeds, Titan, 44, 46, 61, 66, 73-80, 115; Arthur, 163, 164, 168, 169
Lemon juice, prevention of scurvy, 308
Lending, 127, 128; library, first, 125, 126
Leonidas, 187
Le Roy, 303, 309, 365, 367, 368; Madam, 208, 211, 243, 293
Le Vaillant (see Le Veillard)
Le Veillard, 6, 10, 34, 208, 211, 245, 257, 258, 342, 345, 366, 368, 370, 374, 375, 381, 384
Lighthouse Tragedy, 26, 102
Lincoln, Abraham, 49, 355
Leprosy, French superstition that potatoes cause, 308
Life and Death, 324
Light, 294; nature of, 282
Lighting, 285; street, 294, 303
Lightning, 324; lightning rod, 285, 286
Lime juice, against scurvy, 308
Limeys, 308
Lith, 250, 251
Locke, John, 337
Logan, James, 129
Lopez, Claude-Anne, viii, 193, 210
Lot, 29
Loudon, Lord, 135, 149, 150
Louis XVI, 22
Louisburg, garrison at, 129
"Luxuries that are injurious to health and society," 308

Mackensie, Dr., 302
Madeira wine, 128, 307, 324
Madison, James, 248, 307, 356, 358, 362, 364, 381
Magnetism, animal, 309
Mandeville, Bernard, 37
"March of the Insurgents," 7
Maria Theresa, 297
Maritime Observations, 342
Martin's account, 182
Martinico, Seas of, 338
Mary, maid, 96, 97
Mary, Virgin, 29, 79
Masonic Lodge of the Nine Sisters, 214
Mass, 318
Mass hysteria, 309
Massachusetts assembly, 138; Governor, 158
Mathers, 103; Cotton, Increase, 28; Cotton, 38, 39, 179, 299
McCarthy, Charlie, 71
McHenry, James, 363, 366
Mechanic, God as, 334
Mechanical Society, 345
Mecom, Benjamin, 350; see also Franklin, Sarah
Medical Society of London, 297
Medmenham Monks, 23
Meditation on the Vanity and Brevity of Human Life, 331
Mellon, Thomas, Andrew, 376
Melville, Herman, 336
Memory, 42, 43
Mental illness, 301
Mercury, 42, 98, 110
Mesmer, Dr. Anton, 217, 309
Mesmerism, 309
Methuselah, 256
Mickle, Samuel, 120, 121
Middleton, Captain, 70
Mirror, Happiness in, 335
Mohammedanism, 317
Monaghan, Frank, 173, 174
Mon Cher Papa, viii, 193, 210
Money, bills in Congress, 357, 358
Monomolecular films, 291

Montaigne, 48
Montgolfier brothers, 292, 293
Monthieu, Monsieur, 339
Montresor, Jacques, 319
Moody, Father, 318
Moore, 198
Moral science and algebra, 339
Moravians, 136, 138; Indian, 146
Morellet, Abbe, 14, 15, 18, 19, 20, 22, 143, 212, 213, 248, 345
Morris, Gouverneur, 360, 370
Morris, Robert, 175
Moses, 29, 136, 163
Mournful, Fanny, 28
Mufti of Constantinople, 317
Muley Ishmael (King George), 190

"A Narrative of the Late Massacres in Lancaster County," 145
Negroes, 274, 308, 333, 334, 336
Nero, 190
Nervous excitement in mesmerism, 309
New England Courant, 27, 28, 30
New England Militia, 188
New Stove for Burning Pitcoal, 342
New Testament, 320
Newton, Isaac, Sir, 37, 69, 195, 285, 294, 295
Niagara Falls, 134; Indians near, 143
Noah, 29, 213; and vine, 123
Nobel Prize, 291
Notre Dame D'Auteuil, 15, 18, 21
Nouns, Capitalization of, 372; verbs from, 372
Nye, Professor Russel B., 377

O'Folivey, Dermond, 86
Oil on Water, experiment, 290, 291, 292
Old Man's Song, 312
Old Tenor, 326
Old Testament, 320
Old age, 379
Oneida, 139

Opium, 381
Order, virtue of, 124
Ordination, 327
Osborne, Charles, 33, 34
Oswald, 173, 174
Overeating, 307
Oxford University, 297
Oxygen, discovery of, 308
Oyster lawsuit, 47

Paine, Thomas, 201, 314, 320, 344, 345
Pamela, 95
Pantagruelian Prognostication, 49
Panza, Sancho, 32
"Parable against Persecution," 191
Paradise, 5, 17, 20, 333
Paralysis, 300, 310
Parliament of Paris, 2
Parmesan cheese, 307
Parsons, 335, 336
Partridge, Elizabeth Hubbard, 73, 77, 78, 247
Paul, the Apostle, 214, 228
Paxton Boys, 145, 146
Peale, Charles Willson, 243, 244
Pegasus, 44
Penn, William, 129, 139, 145; Sons, 131
Pennsylvania Assembly General, 345
Pennsylvania Gazette, 41-43, 46, 75, 76, 80, 81, 100, 177, 179, 184, 199, 270, 298, 337
Pennsylvania, Governor of, 35, 36, 131-133
Pennsylvania Hospital, 386
Pennsylvania, President of, 341, 345, 347, 350, 353, 374
Pennsylvania, Supreme Executive Council, 344
Perspiration, use in cure of disease, 304
Pessimism, 338
"Petition of the Left Hand," 274, 275
Pharaoh, 136, 163
Philadelphia Academy, 230

Philadelphia, Constitution of, 344
Philadelphia, Executive Council, 305
Philadelphia Gazette, vii
Philoclerus, 91
Philosophical and Political History, 181
Philosophy, natural, 329; metaphysical, 329
Physick, 310
Piety, 320
Piles, fiddler, 81
Pilgrim's Progress, 95, 114
Pilot fish, 37
Pinckney, 362
Plain Truth, 128
Planets, 295
Plato, 328, 335
Pleiades, 115, 116
Pliny, 290
Plow deep, don't dig more than, 118
Plum pudding, 292
Police, reform of Philadelphia, 83
Polignac, Countess, 205
Politeness, 336
Pollution, air, 298
Pontack's
Poor Robin's Almanack, 44, 60
Poor Richard's Almanack, 23, 44-71, 123, 199, 204, 222, 263, 297, 301, 307, 311, 320, 369, 371, 377, 385
Poor Will's Almanac, 77
Portugal, Conquest of, 165
Postmaster General of Colonies, Deputy, vii, 23, 131; First, 217
Potato cultivation in France, 308
Potts, 335, 336
Poupon, cat, 17, 20
Powell, Mrs., 366
Prayer, 320; suggestion about, 355, 356
Predictions for the Year 1708, 73
Preitnal, Joseph, 110
Presbyterians, 315, 316, 319
Prestonfield, Scottish estate, 305
Presty, 137
Price, Dr. Richard, 195
Priestly, Dr., 195, 308, 324, 338, 339

Pringle, Dr. John, 236, 298, 301, 302, 308
Prometheus, 287
Propagation, self, of plants and animals, 322
Property, in government, 361
Proprietors, 128, 131, 136, 147
Protestantism, 319
Providence, Franklin on, 140, 322
Psalms, 18, 33, 71
Pulse after exercise, 306
Purchas, Samuel, 308
Puritans, 28, 31, 40, 129, 314, 323, 333, 416

Quackery, 309
Quakers, 31, 32, 37, 38, 121, 125, 128-132, 146, 183, 204, 325, 353, 354
Queens College, 155
Quixote, Don, 132

"Rabbi Ben Ezra," 378
Rabelais, 49, 50, 154
Rachel, 29
Ralph, James, 33, 34, 36, 37
Ray, Catherine (Greene), 226, 228-230
Rattlesnake, 297; root, 302
Raynal, Abbe, 176, 181, 182
Read, Deborah, 220, 221, 226, 227 (see Deborah Franklin)
Rebecca, 29
Records of the Federal Constitution, 363
Religion of Nature, 329
Repayment, Franklin on, 127, 128
Representation in Congress, size of states, 356, 357
Revolution, French, 367
Revolutionary War, 57, 200, 264, 322, 370; runaway inflation in, 288, 318
Rhubarb, Chinese, 308
Richard, Bonhomme, 57
Richardson, Samuel, 95

Ridley, Matthew, 171, 174
Rights, Declaration of, 318, 320
Rocker, with attachments designed by Franklin, 359
Rodney, 338
Roelker, William G., ix
Rogers, Will, viii
Rohan, Cardinal of, 369
Rolling press for copying letters, 359
Rome, Church of, 79, 80
Rooke, Aunt, 373
Roosevelt, Theodore, 243
Rosenbach, A. S. W., 219, 258
Rousseau, 142, 145; Jean Jacques, 204, 208
Royal Academy of Brussels, essay to, 194
Royal Commission of physicians and scientists to investigate mesmerism, 309
Royal Medical Society, Paris, 297
Royal Society, 70, 286, 288; English, 303
"Rules by which a Great Empire may be Reduced to a Small One," 185
"Rules for Making Oneself a Disagreeable Companion," 337
Rum as Injurious, 308
Rum, Jamaica, 299
Rush, Benjamin, viii, 163, 170, 301, 302, 355, 385
Rutledge, 162

Sabbath, 325, 326
Sage and the Gout, 11, 311
Saratoga, 7
Sargent family, 271
Saul, 88
Saunders, Richard and Bridget, 221; See Poor Richard's Almanack
Savage, noble, 142
"School for Lovers," 232
Scot, 116
Scotosh, 143, 144
Scots traveler, 89
Scotus, Duns, 19

Scurvy, citrus fruit against, 308
Seances, 309
Secret societies, 309
Self-reliance, 334
Sellers, Charles C., 244
Senate, 358
Seneca, 54
Seneca Indians, 188
Seymour, Attorney General, 328
Shandy, Tristram, 246
Sharks, 37
Shaw, George Bernard, 243
Shawnee, 136
Shay's Rebellion, 361
Shipley family, 253, 254, 342, 345, 347, 373, 374, 382, 383; Anna Maria, 252, 254, 256; Betsy, 253; Catherine, "Kitty", 252, 256, 342, 345, 383; Emily, 253; General Rufane, 254; Georgiana, 253, 254; Mungo, squirrel, 254, 255
Shirley, General, 132, 133, 135
Shock treatments, electrical, 300, 301
Shoreham, 84
Shortface, Caelia, 41
Silkworm, 294
Sin, 326
Single, Celia, 95-97
Sisera, 320
Six Nations, Delaware, Shawnee, Miami, Wyandot, 138, 141
Slavery, 133, 182, 308, 336, 354; anti-slavery society, Franklin as President of, 353; preparation of slaves to live in freedom, 354
"Slave Trade" on the, 354
Small, Alexander, 382
Smallpox, 299
Smollet, 249
Smyth, Albert H., 257
Snake, 2 headed, 359
Snuff, 308
Soap making, 350, 351
Social animal, human being as, 335
Social Bliss Considered, 181
Society for the Abolition of Slavery, 274

Society for Political Enquiries, 347, 353

Socrates, 19, 32, 57, 221

Soissons, Congress of, 42

Solitude, 335

Solomon, 332

Solon, 215

Some Account of the Success of Enoculation for the Small-Pox, 299

Somer, 71

Sophocles, 215

Souls, 328, 338; recycling of, 323

Soup dish, compartmented, 343

Spectator, 21, 27, 72, 73, 115

Spinozists, 88

Stamp Act, 153, 154, 155, 221, 334, 352

Stanhope, 42

Stanley, 383

Steele, 86, 115, 362

Stevens, Henry, 257, 258

Stevenson, Margaret, 3, 231, 232, 234, 239; Mary (Polly), 233-237, 293, 304, 332, 373; Eliza and Tom, 373

Stifler, J. M., ix, 235

Stiles, Ezra, 384

Stocks, 326

Stones, bladder, 310, 312, 379, 381

Stormont, Lord, 166

Stove, 218, 282

Strachey, 173, 174

Strahan, 159, 225, 248, 249, 250, 307; daughter, 243

Sturgis, 83

Sugar, as injurious, 308

Sugar Islands, British, 165

Sunday laws, 325, 326

Susquehannah, Indians, 142

Swift, Jonathan, 60, 73, 190; Dean, 77

Swimming, 127, 306, 335; fins, 280

Talkative, Tabitha, 28

Tannent, John, 297

Tartars, 41, 84, 333

Tasker, Colonel, 289, 290

Tatler, 169, 286

Tax, property, 131

Tea, as injurious, 308

Teach, Captain Edward, 26

Ten Commandments, 4

Thermopyle, 187

Thomas, St., 19

Thompson, John, 263

Thoreau, 141, 334

Tichell, Anne, 243

Timothy, 214

Titles of Honor, 29

Tobacco, 328; Franklin's non-use, 308

Toleration, on, 371

Torragh, Barony of, 87

Transylvania, 333

Tremors and tobacco, 308

Trenton, Battle of, 187

True Prognostications, 49

Truth, and good and evil, 329; Indian idea of, 142

Tuesday club, 270

Turgot, 14, 18, 22, 201

Turkey, guests in, 112, 113; plague in, 302

Turkeys, 371

Twain, Mark, viii, 51, 376, 377

Tweedledum, 97

Typhoid fever, 302

Typography, 370

Ulysses, 337

Union Fire Company, 343

Uprisings, in states, 366

Vacation, summer, Franklin's idea, 308, 309

Van Doren, Carl, 23, 194, 243, 248, 349, 364, 377

Vaughan, Benjamin, 342, 368, 374, 375

Vegetarianism, 31, 33

Venus, 219

Vergennes, 171, 172, 174, 175, 214

Versailles, Royal Court, 214, 310

Virgil, 192

Virgin Mary, 318
Volney, 380
Voltaire, 12, 214, 215, 371
Von Steuben, Baron, 165, 201

Walden Pond, 141, 334
Walpole, Horace, 191, 235
Washington, George, vii, 29, 150, 159, 160, 165, 170, 230, 250, 251, 277, 301, 314, 321, 326, 344, 348, 355, 360, 364, 383, 384, 385, 386
Waste disposal, connected with disease, 302
Water, popular fear of, 335
Waterbeds, 342
Water-tight ship compartments, 343
Watts, 109, 349
The Way to Wealth, 51, 204
Webbe, John, 43
Webster, 371, 372
Weather prediction, 281
Weems, "Parson," 159, 218
Weiser, Conrad, 144
Whale, Biblical, 357
Whaleman, 84
Whatley, George, 378

Whirlwind, 289, 290
Whiston, 69
Whitefield, Rev. George, 316, 317
Whitehead, Mr., 186
William and Mary College, 141, 328
William the Conqueror, 86, 328
Williams, Jonathan, 168, 169, 339, 340, 350, 352
Wilson, James, 362
Winthrop, Governor, 181
Witch of Endor, 88
Witch Trials, 177, 179
Witches, detection of, 114
Wollaston, William, 329
Women's rights, 97
Wormwood, 307
Wright, Mrs., 373
Wyandot nation, 143, 144. See also Sir Nations

Yale College, viii, 326, 384
Yankees, New England, 50
Yeast fermentation, 308
York, Sir Jos., 190
Yorktown, 10